‘Protection’ in European Union Asylum Law

International Refugee Law Series

VOLUME 18

The titles published in this series are listed at *brill.com/irls*

‘Protection’ in European Union Asylum Law

International and European Law Requirements for Assessing Available Protection as a Criterion for Refugee and Subsidiary Status

By

Julian M. Lehmann

BRILL
NIJHOFF

LEIDEN | BOSTON

The Library of Congress Cataloging-in-Publication Data is available online at http://catalog.loc.gov
LC record available at http://lccn.loc.gov/2020029406

Typeface for the Latin, Greek, and Cyrillic scripts: "Brill". See and download: brill.com/brill-typeface.

ISSN 2213-3836
ISBN 978-90-04-43024-2 (hardback)
ISBN 978-90-04-43039-6 (e-book)

This book is printed on acid-free paper and produced in a sustainable manner.

Contents

Acknowledgments

This book is based on a doctoral research project supervised at the Faculty of Law of Dresden University, Germany. The thesis was submitted for examination in February 2017, examined by October 2018 and defended on 20 November 2018. While the manuscript has been substantially revised and includes several new legal developments, it does not systematically incorporate subsequent law from the various jurisprudences of focus in the research. Thus, the law in this book remains current as of December 2016.

There have been many individuals who have accompanied me for the research and to whom I remain grateful. At the University of Dresden, I wish to express my gratitude to my supervisor, Thilo Rensmann, who instilled confidence in me to embark on the journey of PhD research, and to Dominik Steiger for the comments that were very helpful in the revision of the manuscript. For that revision, I am also grateful to the anonymous peer reviewer at Brill. At the University of Michigan, where I spent four months as a Grotius Research Fellow, Jim Hathaway set me on the right track with his unparalleled enthusiasm for refugee law and offered the best research environment a visiting scholar could wish for. Gregor Noll, then at the University of Lund, welcomed me as a visiting scholar to the productive quietude of that University. The *Evangelisches Studienwerk Villigst* funded research with a stipend and has been as flexible and unbureaucratic as a funder could possibly be. My colleagues at the GPPi in Berlin, in particular Katrin Kinzelbach, made sure I did not lose sight of the murkier grounds of policy and politics as a result of my legal academic endeavours. Dermot Cudmore assisted with the editing of the footnotes.

On numerous occasions, I have been privileged to be able to present pieces of work and receive or exchange feedback with dedicated scholars and practitioners, including David James Cantor, Eleni Karageorgiou, Emanuela Parisciani, Jens Vested-Hansen, Jessica Schultz, Jürgen Bast, Marten den Heijer, Matthew Scott, Nora Markard, Samo Bardutzky, Tino Hruschka, Thomas Gammeltoft-Hansen and Violetta Moreno-Lax.

Finally, I am indebted to my loved ones: Elli, Marlene, Immo, Jonas, Tine, Lila, and also Michael.

Treaties and EU Legislation

International Treaties

Constitution of the International Refugee Organization, as Annexed to UN General Assembly (adopted 15 December 1946) 18 UNTS 3.

Convention Against Torture and Other Cruel, Inhuman or Degrading Treatment or Punishment (adopted 10 December 1984, entered into force June 1987) 1465 UNTS 85.

Convention Concerning the Status of Refugees Coming from Germany (adopted 10 February 1938) CXCII 4461 LNTS 59.

Convention Determining the State Responsible for Examining Applications for Asylum Lodged in One of the Member States of the European Communities (adopted 19 August 1997) 254 OJ 1.

Convention for the Protection of Human Rights and Fundamental Freedoms (adopted 4 November 1950, entered into force 3 Septmeber 1953) 5 CETS 4.

Convention on the Elimination of All Forms of Discrimination against Women (adopted 18 December 1979, entered into force 3 Septmeber 1981) 1249 UNTS 13.

Convention on the Rights of the Child (adopted 20 November 1989, entered into force 2 September 1990) 1577 UNTS 3.

Convention Relating to the Status of Refugees (adopted 28 July 1951, entered into force 22 April 1954) 189 UNTS 137.

International Convention on the Elimination of All Forms of Racial Discrimination (adopted 21 December 1965, entered into force 4 Janurary 1969) 660 UNTS 195.

International Covenant on Civil and Political Rights (adopted 16 December 1966, entered into force 23 March 1976) 999 UNTS 171.

International Covenant on Economic, Social and Cultural Rights (adopted 16 December 1966, entered into force 3 January 1976) 993 UNTS 3.

Optional Protocol to the International Covenant on Civil and Political Rights (adopted 16 December 1966, entered into force 223 March 1976) 999 UNTS 171.

Optional Protocol to the International Covenant on Economic, Social and Cultural Rights (adopted 10 December 2006, entered into force 5 May 2013), A/RES/63/117, 2922 UNTS.

Protocol to Prevent, Suppress and Punish Trafficking in Persons, Especially Women and Children, Supplementing the United Nations Convention Against Transnational Organized Crime (adopted 15 November 2000, entered into force 29 September 2003) 2237 UNTS 319.

Statute of the International Court of Justice (signed 18 April 1946) 33 USTS 993.

Statute of the Office of the United Nations High Commissioner for Refugees (signed 14 December 1950) A/RES/428 (V).

Universal Declaration of Human Rights (adopted 10 December 1948) A/RES/217 A(III).

Vienna Convention on the Law of Treaties (adopted 23 May 1969, entered into force 27 January 1980) 115 UNTS 331.

EU Legislation

Charter of Fundamental Rights of the European Union [2000] OJ C364/1.

Consolidated Version of the Treaty on the Functioning of the EU [2010] OJ C83/47.

Council Directive 2003/86/EC of 22 September 2003 on the right to family reunification [2003] OJ L251.

Council Directive 2003/9/EC of 27 January 2003 on laying down minimum standards for the reception of asylum seekers [2003] OJ L31/18.

Council Directive 2004/83/EC of 29 April 2004 on minimum standards for the qualification and status of third country nationals or stateless persons as refugees or as persons who otherwise need international protection and the content of the protection granted [2004] OJ L304/12.

Council Directive 2011/95/EU of 13 December 2011 on standards for the qualification of third-country nationals or stateless persons as beneficiaries of international protection, for a uniform status for refugees or for persons eligible for subsidiary protection, and for the content of the protection granted (recast) [2011] OJ L33/9.

Council Directive 2013/32/EU of 26 June 2013 on common procedures for granting and withdrawing international protection (recast) [2013] OJ L180/60.

Council Regulation (EC) 604/2013 of 26 June 2013 establishing the criteria and mechanisms for determining the Member State responsible for examining an application for international protection lodged in one of the Member States by a third-country national or a stateless person [2013] OJ L180.

Treaty of Amsterdam Amending the Treaty on European Union, the Treaties Establishing the European Communities and Related Acts [1997] OJ C340.

National Laws and Regulations

Germany

Gesetz zur Umsetzung aufenthalts- und asylrechtlicher Richtlinien der Europäischen Union, 19 August 2007, BGBl I, 1970.
Gesetz zur Umsetzung der Richtlinie 2011/95/EU, 28 August 2013, BGBl I 2013, 3474.
Asylgesetz, 2 September 2008, BGBl I, 1798, as amended by Article 6 of the Act of 31 July 2016, BGBl I, 1939.

Netherlands

Vreemdelingencirculaire 2000 (C) of 13 August 2015.
Vreemdelingencirculaire 2000 (C) of 1 December 2017.
Voorschrift Vreemdelingen 2000, as of 1 July 2016.

France

Code de l'entrée et du séjour des étrangers et du droit d'asile, consolidated version as of 3 July 2016, Légifrance.
Loi No 2015–925 du 29 juillet 2015 relative à la réforme du droit d'asile, Légifrance.

United Kingdom

The Refugee or Person in Need of International Protection (Qualification) Regulations 2006.

Sweden

Lag om ändring i utlänningslagen (2005:716), 31 March 2006, SFS 2005:1239 (Act amending the Aliens Act), riksdagen.se.
Lag om ändring i utlänningslagen (2005:716), 1 January 2010, SFS 2009:1542 (Act amending the Aliens Act), riksdagen.se.
Lag om ändring i utlänningslagen (2005:716), 1 January 2015, SFS 2014:1400 (Act amending the Aliens Act), riksdagen.se.

Cases

International Criminal Court

Decision on an Amicus Curiae application and on the 'Requête tendant à obtenir présentations des témoins DRC-D02-P-03509, DRC-D02-P-0236, DRC-D02-P-0228 aux autorités néerlandaises aux fins d'asile' (articles 68 and 93(7) of the Statute), ICC Trial Chamber II, June 2011, ICC-01/04-01/07-3003-tENG, <https://www.icc-cpi.int/pages/record.aspx?uri=1093334> accessed 1 July 2019.

Permanent Court of Justice and International Court of Justice

Lotus [1927] PCIJ Rep 10 (series A).
Mavrommatis Palestine Concessions Greece v U.K. [1924] PCIJ Rep 2.
Reparations for Injuries Suffered in the Service of the United Nations (Advisory Opinion) [1949] ICJ Rep 179.
Interpretation of the Agreement of 25 March 1951 between the WHO and Egypt (Advisory Opinion) [1980] ICJ Rep 73.

European Court of Justice and Court of Justice of the European Union[1]

Joined Cases C-175/08, C-176/08, C-178/08 and C-179/98 *Aydin Salahadin Abdulla, Kamil Hasan, Ahmed Adem, Hamrin Mosa Rashi and Dler Jamal v Bundesrepublik Deutschland* [2010] ECR I-01493.
Joined Cases C-175/08, C-176/08, C-178/08 and C-179/98 Aydin Salahadin Abdulla, Kamil Hasan, Ahmed Adem, Hamrin Mosa Rashi and Dler Jamal v Bundesrepublik Deutschland [2010] ECR I-01493, Opinion of AG Mazák.
Joined Cases C-57/09 and C-101/09 *Bundesrepublik Deutschland v B and D* [2010] ECR I-10979.
Joined Cases C-57/09 and C-101/09 *Bundesrepublik Deutschland v B and D* [2010] ECR I-10979, Opinion of AG Mengozzi.

1 All cases as of 2013 are referred to by their European Case Law Indentifier (ECLI) and the digital rather than the printed reports, given a change in the court's reporting.

C-285/12 *Aboubacar Diakité v Commissaire général aux réfugiés et aux apatrides* [2013] ECR 2014-00000.

Joined Cases C-71/11 and C-99/11 *Bundesrepublik Deutschland v Y and Z* [2012] digital reports.

C-472/13 *Andrew Lawrence Shepherd v Bundesrepublik Deutschland,* ECLI:EU:C:2015:117 [2015] digital reports.

Joined Cases C-71/11 and C-99/11 *Bundesrepublik Deutschland v Y and Z* [2012] digital reports, Opinion of AG Bot.

C-562/13 *Centre public d'action sociale d'Ottignies-Louvain-la-Neuve v Moussa Abdida,* ECLI:EU:C:2014:2453 [2014] digital reports.

C-112/00 *Eugen Schmidberger, Internationale Transporte und Planzüge v Austria* [2003] ECR I-5659.

C-477/11 *Gennaro Currà and Others v Bundesrepublik Deutschland,* ECLI:EU:C:2012:292 [2012] digital reports.

C-481/13 *Bundesrepublik Deutschland v Qurbani,* ECLI:EU:C:2014:2101 [2014] digital reports.

Joined Cases C-21/72 to C-24/72 *International Fruit Company NV v Produktshap voor Groenten en Fruit* C-21/72 to C-24/72 [1972] ECR I-1219.

C-245/11 *K v Bundesasylamt,* ECLI:EU:C:2012:685 [2012] digital reports.

Joined Cases C-443/14 and C-444/14 *Kreis Warendorf v Ibrahim Alo and Amira Osso v Region Hannover,* ECLI:EU:C:2016:127 [2016] digital reports.

C-353/16 *MP v Secretary of State for the Home Department,* ECLI:EU:C:2018:276 [2018] digital reports.

C-465/07 *Meki Elgafaji and Noor Elgafaji v Staatsecretaris van Justitie* [2009] ECR I-921.

C-542/13 *Mohamed M'Bodj v Belgian State,* ECLI:EU:C:2014:2452 [2014] digital reports.

C-542/13 *Mohamed M'Bodj v Belgian State,* ECLI:EU:C:2014:2113 [2014] digital reports, Opinion of AG Bot.

Joined Cases C-411/10; C-411/10 *N.S. v Secretary of State for the Home Department and M. E. and Others v Refugee Applications Commissioner and Minister for Justice, Equality and Law Reform* [2011] ECR I-13905.

C-31/09 *Nawras Bolbol v Bevándorlási és Állampolgársági Hivatal* [2010] ECR I-05539.

C-31/09 *Nawras Bolbol v Bevándorlási és Állampolgársági Hivatal,* Opinion of AG Mazák [2010] ECR I-05539.

C-208/17 *NF v European Council* ECLI:EU:C:2018:705 [2017] digital reports.

Opinion 2/13 on the accession of the European Union to the Convention for the Protection of Human Rights and Fundamental Freedoms ECLI:EU:C:2014:2454 [2014] digital reports, para 189.

C-695/15 PPU *Shiraz Baig Mirza v Bevándorlási és Állampolgársági Hivatal* ECLI:EU:C:2016:188 [2016] digital reports.
C-533/08 *TNT Express Nederland BV v AXA Versicherung AG* [2010] ECR I-04107.
C-26/62 *Van Gend en Loos v Nederlandse Administratie der Belastingen* [1963] ECR 1–12.
Joined Cases C-402/05 P and C-415/05 P *Yassin Abdullah Kadi Al Barakaat International Foundation v Council of the European Union and and Commission of the European Communities* [2008] ECR II-03649.

European Commission on Human Rights

European Commission of Human Rights, 10 December 1986, no 12461/6 (Lebanon)
European Commission of Human Rights, 13 October 1993, no 21250/90 (Togo).
European Commission of Human Rights, 11 March 1994, no 23551/94 (Turkey).

European Court of Human Rights[2]

AA and others v Sweden App no 14499/09 (ECtHR, 28 June 2012).
Abu Qatada 8139/09 ECHR 2012 817.
Ahmed v Austria ECHR 1996-VI 2206.
Ahorugeze v Sweden ECHR 2011 1829.
Al Nashiri v Poland [2011] ECHR 1829.
Al-Skeini and Others v United Kingdom ECHR 2011-IV 99.
Audad v Bulgaria App no 46390/10 (ECtHR, 11 October 2011).
Bosphorus Hava Yolları Turizm ve Ticaret Anonim Şirketi v Ireland ECHR 2005-VI 107.
Budina v Russia App no 45603/05 (ECtHR, 16 June 2009).
Case relating to certain aspects of the laws on the use of languages in education in Belgium v Belgium (1968) Series A no 5.
Catan and Others v the Republic of Moldova and Russia ECHR 2012-V 309.
Chahal v United Kingdom ECHR 1996-V, 54.
Collins and Akaziebie v Sweden App no 23944/05 (ECtHR, 8 March 2007).
Čonka v Belgium ECHR 2002-I 47.

2 All reported cases refer to the Reports of Judgments and Decisions (ECHR). Unreported cases are referred to with application number and (App no) date of judgment.

DNM v Sweden App no 28379/11 (ECtHR, 27 June 2013).
D v United Kingdom ECHR 1997-III 792.
Gebremedhin v France ECHR 2007-II 79.
HLR v France ECHR 1997-III 745.
Hilal v United Kingdom ECHR 2001-II 293.
Hirsi Jamaa and Other v Italy ECHR 2012 97.
Ilașcu and Others v Moldova and Russia ECHR 2004-VII 1.
M and Others v Bulgaria App no 41416/08 (ECtHR, 26 July 2011).
MSS v Belgium and Greece ECHR 2011-I 121.
MYH and Others v Sweden App No 50859/10 (ECHR, 27 June 2013).
Makaratzis v Greece ECHR 2004-X 195.
Müller and Others v Switzerland App no 10737/84 (1991) Series A no 133.
N v Sweden App no 23505/09 (ECtHR, 20 July 2010).
N v United Kingdom ECHR 2008-III 227.
NMY and Others v Sweden App no 72686/10 (ECtHR, 27 June 2013).
Niedzwiecki v Germany App no 58453/00 (ECtHR, 25 October 2005).
Öneryıldız v Turkey ECHR 2004-XII 79.
Opuz v Turkey ECHR 2009-III 107.
Osman v United Kingdom ECHR 1998-VIII 101.
Özgür Gündem v Turkey ECHR 2000-III 1
SA v Sweden App no 66523/10 (ECtHR, 27 June 2013).
SHH v United Kingdom App no 60367/10 (ECtHR, 29 January 2013).
Saadi v United Kingdom ECHR 2008-I 31.
Salah Sheekh v the Netherlands App no 1948/04 (ECtHR, 11 January 2007).
Soering v United Kingdom (1989) Series A no 161.
Sufi and Elmi v United Kingdom App nos 8319/07, 11449/07 (ECtHR, 28 November 2011).
Tarakhel v Switzerland ECHR 2014-VI, 195.
TI v United Kingdom ECHR 2000-III 435.
Timishev v Russia ECHR 2005-XII 169.
Tyrer v UK (1978) Series A no 26.
Vilvarajah and Others v United Kingdom (1991) Series A no 215.
Z and T v United Kingdom 2006-III 315.

Inter-American Court of Human Rights

The Effect of Reservations on the Entry into Force of the American Convention (Arts 74 and 75) Advisory Opinion OC-2/82 IACHR Series A no. 2 (1982).

UN Committee Against Torture

Sathurusinghe Jagath Dewage v Australia Communication no 387/2009, 14 November 2013, CAT/C/51/D/387/2009.
SSS v Canada Communication no 245/2004, 16 November 2005, CAT/C/35/D/245/2004.
GRB v Sweden Communication no 83/1997, 2 June 1997, CAT/C/20/D/83/1997.
Halil Haydin v Sweden Communication no 101/1997, 16 December 1998, CAT/C/21/D/101/1997.
Ismail Alan v Switzerland Communication no 21/1995, 31 January 1995, CAT/C/16/D/21/1995,
BSS v Canada Communication no 183/2001, 12 May 2004, CAT/C/32/D/183/2001.
Orhan Ayas v Sweden Communication no 97/1997, 12 November 1997, CAT/C/21/D/097/1997.
SNAW et al v Switzerland Communication no 231/2003, 25 November 2005, CAT/C/35/D/231/2003.
SV v Canada Communication no 49/1996, 15 May 1996, CAT/C/26/D/49/1996.

Human Rights Committee

ARJ v Australia Communication no 692/1996, 28 July 1997, CCPR/C/60/D/692/1996.
Mehrez Ben Abde Hamida v Canada Communication no 1544/2007, 11 May 2010, CCPR/C/98/D/1544/2007.
Naveed Akram Choudhary v Canada Communication no 1898/2009, 17 December 2013, CCPR/C/109/D/1898/2009.
X v Sweden Communication no 1833/2008, 17 January 2012, CCPR/C/103/D/1833/2008.

Cases before Domestic Courts

Australia

Dranichnikov v Minister for Immigration and Multicultural Affairs [2003] HCA 26.
Minister for Immigration and Multicultural Affairs v Khawar [2002] HCA 14.
NAGV and NAGW of 2002 v Minister for Immigration and Multicultural and Indigenous Affairs [2005] HCA 6.
Rajaratnam v Minister for Immigration and Multicultural Affairs [2000] FCA 1111.

Canada

Attorney General v Ward [1993] 2 SCR 689.
Zalzali v Canada [1991] 3 FC 605.
Canada (*Minister* of *Employment* and *Immigration*) *v Mayers* [1993] 1 FC 154.

Denmark[3]

Flygtningenævnet afg/2010/17.
Flygtningenævnet afgh/2010/46.
Flygtningenævnet afgh/2010/78.
Flygtningenævnet afgh/2011/15.
Flygtningenævnet afgh/2011/37.
Flygtningenævnet afgh/2011/52.
Flygtningenævnet afgh/2011/52.
Flygtningenævnet afgh/2012/18.
Flygtningenævnet Arme/2013/3.
Flygtningenævnet Iran/2012/20.
Flygtningenævnet Se-Mo/2004/20.
Flygtningenævnet Syri/2011/17.

France[4]

D CRR 18 May 2007, no 589676.
MBN CNDA 18 October 2012, no 12013647 C.
M et Mme M CNDA 6 February 2012, no 09002796 et no 09002797 C.
MH CNDA 9 April 2010, no 09013398 C+.
MJ CNDA, 28 October 2010, no 09015404 C+.
MK CNDA 8 July 2010, no 09016217 C.
ML CNDA 30 March 2011, no 10013804 R.
MS CNDA 24 July 2012, no 11017592 C.
MS CNDA 30 November 2010, no 09001370, R.
M CRR 1 March 2007, no 566183.
M CRR 25 May 2007, no 589662.
Mlle A CNDA 3 April 2008, no 584799.
Mlle A CNDA 18 December 2007, no 596205.
Mlle B CRR, 14 March 2006, no 558577.

---

3 All decisions are retrieved from the digital reports at Flygtningenævnet, <http://www.fln.dk/da/Praksis.aspx> accessed 20 October 2016.

4 All decisions are retrieved from the annual digital case compilations of the CNDA, <http://www.cnda.fr/Ressources-juridiques-et-geopolitiques/Recueils-de-jurisprudence> accessed 20 October 2016.

Mlle D CNDA 8 April 2011, no 10013535 C+.
Mlle D CRR,2 November 2007, no 535997.
Mlle E CNDA 23 October 2009, no 642112/09000931.
Mlle G CNDA 23 December 2009, no 640410/08020867.
Mlle O CNDA 3 April 2012, no 11020945 C.
Mlle O CNDA 26 October 2009, no 08008209/627707.
Mlle O CNDA 29 July 2011, no 10020534 C+.
Mlle O CNDA 3 April 2012, no 11020945 C.
Mlle R CRR 29 September 2006, no 533070.
Mlle R CNDA 29 September 2009, no 616251/07019306.
Mlle S CRR 15 mars 2007, no 585846.
Mlle S CRR 5 November 2007, no 557030.
Mlle V CNDA 6 September 2011, no 10023173 R.
Mlle Y CRR 30 November 2006, no 535001.
Mlle Y CNDA 4 September 2009, no 645353/09004158, D.
Mme B CNDA 23 February 2011, no 10012782 C+.
Mme B CNDA 5 December 2008, no 620881.
Mme M CRR 19 July 2006, no 526541.
S CRR 28 June 2005, no 519680.
T CRR 16 February 2007, no 573815.
T CRR 14 April 2006, no 481175.

Germany[5]

BVerfG, 19 July 1989, 2 BvR 502/86 – BVerfGE 80, 315.
BVerwG, 17 May 1983, 9 C 36.83 – BVerwGE 67, 184.
BVerwG, 2 August 1983, 9 C 600.81 – juris.
BVerwG, 22 April 1986, 9 C 31885 – 74 BVerwGE 160, 163.
BVerwG 4 June 1991, 1C 42.88 – BVerwGE 88, 254
BVerwG, 14 December 1993, C 45.92 – juris.
BVerwG, 18 January 1994, 9 C 48.92 – BVerwGE 95, 42
BVerwG, 5 July 1994, 9 C 194 – InfAuslR 1995, 24, 27.
BVerwG, 8 December 1998, 9 C 17.98 – BVerwGE 108, 84.
BVerwG, 16 January 2001, 9 C 16.00 – BVerwGE 112, 345.
BVerwG, 1 February 2007, 1 C 24.06 – NVwZ 2007, 590.
BVerwG, 29 August 2008, 10 C 11.07 – BVerwGE 131.
BVerwG, 5 September 2009, 10 C 21.08 – juris.
OVG Mecklenburg-Vorpommern, 16 May 2007 – 3 L 54/03.

5 All administrative court decisions are retrieved from juris.de or asyl.net.

OVG Nordrhein-Westfalen, 12 July 2005 – 11A 2307/03.A.
OVG Nordrhein-Westfalen, 20 July 2015 – 13 A 1531/15.A.
OVG Saaraland, 11 May 2005 – 1 Q 16/05.
OVG Saarland, 29 September 2006 – 3 R 6/06.
OVG Schleswig, 3 November 2005 – 1 LB 211/01.
OVG Schleswig-Holstein, 13 November 2005 – 1 LB 211/01 UA.
OVG Schleswig-Holstein, 29 April 2009 – 1 LB 11/05.
OVG Thüringen, 28 February 2008 – 2 KO 899/03.
OVG Thüringen, 28 November 2013 – 2 KO 185/09.
VG Aachen, 15 October 2004 – 9 K 1480/03.A (Kosovo).
VG Aachen, 14 December 2004 – 9 K 3309/04.A.
VG Aachen, 20 April 2005 – 9 L 224/05.
VG Aachen, 10 June 2005 – 9 K 4171/04.A.
VG Aachen, 11 October 2006 – 6 K 4487/04.A.
VG Aachen, 23 October 2006 – 6 K 2348/05.A.
VG Ansbach, 25 January 2005 – AN 19 04.32135.
VG Ansbach, 2 February 2005 – AN 15 K 04.31820.
VG Ansbach, 24 July 2007 – AN 4 K 06.31070.
VG Arnsberg, 7 January 2010 – 6 K 197/09.A.
VG Bayreuth, 13 July 2015 – B 3 K 14.30344.
VG Berlin, 30 January 2009 – 37 X 193.05.
VG Braunschweig, 24 June 2008 – 7 A 172/06.
VG Braunschweig, 12 August 2015 – 5 A 123/13.
VG Cottbus, 27 October 2006 – 5 K 718/02.A
VG Darmstadt, 11 May 2000 – 3 E 30481/98.A.
VG Dresden, 08 August 2016 – 7 K 915/16.A.
VG Düsseldorf, 23 November 2005 – 7 K 3570/02.A.
VG Frankfurt a M, 21 January 2004 – 1 E 2518/03.A.
VG Frankfurt a M, 28 September 2006 – 2 E 1235/05.A
VG Frankfurt a M, 10 December 2014 – 8 K 4089/14.F.A.
VG Freiburg, 5 February 2001 – A 2 K 10475/00.
VG Freiburg, 26 April 2007 – A 1 K 11083/04.
VG Gera, 25 November 2004 – 4 K 20215/01.GE.
VG Gießen, 9 June 2005 – 2 E 1383/04.A.
VG Göttingen, 28 January 2002 – 3 A 3027/02.
VG Göttingen, 1 April 2010 – 4 A 43/09.
VG Hannover, 18 February 2015 – 1 A 109/13.
VG Hamburg, 19 February 2015 – 8 A 1470/13.
VG Karlsruhe, 3 March 2005 – A 4 K 10294/02.
VG Karlsruhe, 23 June 2005 – A 2 K 11324/04.

VG Kassel, 06 May 2004 – 7 E 674/02.A.
VG Köln, 15 September 2015 – 14 K 4683/14.A.
VG Lüneburg, 10 May 2005 – 3 A 118/04 (Turkey).
VG Magdeburg, 16 December 2011 – 5 A 59/11 MD.
VG Meiningen, 2 March 2010 – 2 K 20133/08 Me.
VG Minden, 23 October 2000 – 3 K 2602/97.A
VG Minden, 18 August 2008 – 7 K 790/08.A.
VG München, 17 July 2019 – M 11 S 19.50722, M 11 S 19.50759.
VG München, 22 April 2016 – M 16 K 14.30987.
VG Osnabrück, 21 March 2000 – 5 A 16/99.
VG Regensburg, 25 November 2004 – RN 8 K 04.30383.
VG Sigmaringen, 27 June 2000 – A 3 K 1209/98.
VG Sigmaringen, 9 October 2010 – A 2 K 10792/05.
VG Stuttgart, 17 January 2005 – A 10 K 10587/04.
VG Stuttgart, 29 January 2007 – A 4 K 1877/06.
VG Stuttgart, 8 September 2008 – A 10 K 13/07.
VG Trier, 27 April 1999 – 4 K 1157/98.TR.
VG Wiesbaden, 27 January 2000 – 5 E 31472/98.A (2).
VG Wiesbaden, 14 March 2011 – 3 K 1465/09.WI.A.
VG Würzburg, 9 March 2015 – W 1 K 13.30030.
VGH Bayern, 31 August 2007 – 11 B 02.31724.

Greece

Decision 05/133782 of 17 May 2016 (Asylum Appeals Committees of Greece (Presidential Decree 114/2010)), on file with the author.

Ireland

Msengi v Minister for Justice, Equality and Law Reform [2006] IEHC 241.

Netherlands[6]

Raad van State, 18 August 1978, Ars Aequi Libri No 30.
Raad van State, 21 June 1979 No 8.
Raad van State, 19 July 2002 in 200202206/1.
Raad van State, 28 April 2003, 200300547/1.
Raad van State, 29 July 2010, 201000726/1/V3.
Raad van State, 9 March 2011, 201006822/1/V2.
Raad van State, 27 February 2012, 201110164/1/V2.

6 All decisions are retrieved from Rechtspraak, <https://uitspraken.rechtspraak.nl/>.

Raad van State, 6 August 2013, 201205299/1/V1.
Raad van State, 12 November 2013, 201303197/2/V3 and 201303198/2/V3.
Rechtbank 's-Gravenhage, 6 March 1997, AWB 96/7941.
Rechtbank 's-Gravenhage, 13 September 1999, AWB 99/4335.
Rechtbank 's-Gravenhage, 10 June 2003, AWB 01/50117 BEPTDN.
Rechtbank 's-Gravenhage, 10 July 2003, AWB 02/23734 and 01/68315.
Rechtbank 's-Gravenhage, 25 July 2003, AWB 03/37082 and 03/37080.
Rechtbank 's-Gravenhage, 21 November 2003, AWB 01/69346.
Rechtbank 's Gravenhage, 25 November 2003, AWB 02/25468 and 02/25473.
Rechtbank 's-Gravenhage, 9 December 2003, AWB 01/66695 and 01/66700.
Raad van State, 20 January 2004, JV 2004/98.
Rechtbank 's-Gravenhage, 30 December 2005, AWB 04/54263 and 04/54264.
Rechtbank 's-Gravenhage, 19 April 2006, AWB 05/27593.
Rechtbank 's-Gravenhage, 11 October 2007, AWB 06/29887.
Rechtbank 's-Gravenhage, 11 November 2009, AWB 09/13455.
Rechtbank 's-Gravenhage, 15 January 2010, AWB 09/47171 and AWB 09/47169.
Rechtbank 's-Gravenhage, 25 March 2010, 09/11135 and 09/14677.
Rechtbank 's-Gravenhage, 8 October 2010, AWB 10/32872 and 10/32868.
Rechtbank 's-Gravenhage, 11 June 2012, 12/16751, 12/16750 and 12/16817.
Rechtbank 's-Gravenhage, 9 October 2012, AWB 11/32480.
Rechtbank Den Haag, 11 November 2013, AWB 12/2596 en 12/2599.
Rechtbank Den Haag, 7 August 2014, AWB 14/16874.
Rechtbank Den Haag, 28 April 2015, AWB 15/7048 & 15/7047.

New Zealand

Refugee Appeal No 71427/99 [2000] NZAR 545.
Refugee Appeal No 71684/99 [2000] INLR 165.
Daniel Martin Butler v Attorney General and Refugee Status Appeals Authority [1999] NZAR 205.
AC (Egypt) [2011] NZIPT 800015.

Sweden

Migrationsöverdomstolen 21 November 2008, MIG 2008:3, UM1042-08.
Migrationsöverdomstolen 14 January 2009, MIG 2009:4, UM4118-07.
Migrationsöverdomstolen 11 May 2010, MIG 2010:10, UM6397-09.
Migrationsöverdomstolen 24 February 2011, MIG 2011:4, UM10061-09.
Migrationsöverdomstolen 21 April 2011, MIG 2011:8, UM7851-10.
Migrationsdostolen 16 May 2011, UM 27323-10, EDAL.
Migrationsöverdomstolen 03 September 2011, MIG 2011:6, UM3363-10.

Migrationsöverdomstolen 02 November 2011, MIG 2013:2, UM2953-12.
Migrationsöverdomstolen 11 February 2013, MIG 2013:2, UM2953-12.

United Kingdom

AB (Protection, criminal gangs, internal relocation) Jamaica CG [2007] UKAIT 00018 (IAT).
Adan and Aitseguer [2000] UKHL 67 (House of Lords).
AE and FE [2003] EWCA Civ 1032 (Court of Appeal (England and Wales)).
AH (Sudan) [2007] UKHL 49 (House of Lords).
AJH (Minority group, Swahili speakers) Somalia CG [2003] UKIAT 00094 (IAT).
AK (Article 15(c)) Afghanistan CG [2012] UKUT 163 (IAC).
AM and AM (Armed conflict, risk categories) Somalia CG [2008] UKAIT 00091 (IAT).
AM and BM (trafficked women) Albania CG [2010] UKUT 80 (IAC).
AMM and others (conflict; humanitarian crisis; returnees; FGM) Somalia CG [2011] UKUT 445 (IAC).
AT and Others (Article 15c; risk categories) (CG) [2014] UKUT 318 (IAC).
Bagdanavicius and another [2004] 1 WLR 1207 (House of Lords).
Banomova [2001] EWCA Civ 807 (Court of Appeal (England and Wales)).
DJ (Bantu, not generally at risk) Somalia CG [2005] UKIAT 00089 (IAT).
DM (Majority Clan Entities Can Protect) Somalia [2005] UKAIT 00150 (IAT).
Dyli [2002] INLR 372 (IAT).
EH (blood feuds) Albania CG [2012] UKUT 00348 (IAC).
ES (Ashkaelians, mixed Ashkaelian ethnicity) Serbia and Montenegro (Kosovo) CG [2006] UKAIT 00071 (IAT).
FD (Kosovo – Roma) Serbia and Montenegro CG [2004] UKIAT 00214 (IAT).
Gardi [2002] 1 WLR 2755.
GH (Former Kaz, Country Conditions, Effect) Iraq CG [2004] UKIAT 00248 (IAT).
Harakal [2001] EWCA Civ 884 (Court of Appeal (England and Wales)).
Horvath [2000] UKHL 37 (House of Lords).
Hussein v SSHD [2005] CSIH 45 (Scottish Court of Session).
Islam and Another, Ex Parte Shah [1999] UKHL 20 (House of Lords).
Januzi [2006] [2006] UKHL 5 (House of Lords).
JK (Serbia) [2007] EWCA Civ 1321 (Court of Appeal (England and Wales)).
KD (Nigeria) v Refugee Appeals Tribunal & others [2013] IEHC 481 (High Court of Ireland).
Kacaj [2001] UKIAT 0018 (IAT).
Karanakaran [2000] EWCA Civ (Court of Appeal (England and Wales)).

Kinuthia [2002] INLR 133 (Court of Appeal (England and Wales)).
KX (Mixed marriages, Roma, Albanian, *Januzi* applied) Serbia and Montenegro (Kosovo) CG [2006] UKIAT 00072 (IAT).
LT v The Minister for Justice & Ors [2014] IEHC 290 (High Court of Ireland).
McPherson [2001] EWCA Civ 1955 (Court of Appeal (England and Wales)).
MD (Women) Ivory Coast CG [2010] UKUT 215 (IAC).
MN [2012] ScotCS CSIH 63 (Scottish Court of Session).
NM and Others (Lone women, Ashraf) Somalia CG [2005] UKIAT 00076 (IAT).
R v Secretary of State for the Home Department, Immigration Appeals Tribunal, ex parte Robinson [1997] INLR 182 (Court of Appeal (England and Wales)).
R v Immigration Appeal Tribunal, ex parte Jonah [1985] Imm AR 7 (IAT).
R v Secretary of State for the Home Department, ex parte Yunelki [1990] Imm AR 278 (Court of Appeal (England and Wales)).
RD (Sufficiency of Protection, IFA Roma) Poland [2002] UKIAT 00983 (IAT).
RK (India) [2012] CSOH 194 (Scottish Court of Session).
SA (political activist – internal relocation) Pakistan [2011] UKUT 30 (IAC).
SF (Sufficiency of protection, KAA, Michigan Guidelines) Iraq CG [2002] UKIAT 07376.
SI (mixed Serb/Roma parentage) Kosovo CG [2009] UKAIT 00011 (IAT).
SK (Roma in Kosovo – update) Serbia and Montenegro [2005] UKIAT 0023 (IAT).
SR (Iraqi Arab Christian, relocation to KRG) Iraq CG [2009] UKAIT 00038 (IAT).
ST (child asylum seekers) Sri Lanka [2013] UKUT 00292 (IAC).
VM (FGM risks Mungiki Kikuyu/Gikuyu) Kenya CG [2008] UKAIT 00049.
W (lesbians – *HJ* and *HT* applied) Jamaica CG [2011] UKUT 251 (IAC).
YS and HA (Midgan, not generally at risk) Somalia CG [2005] UKIAT 00088 (IAT).

Abbreviations

1951 Convention	1951 Convention Relating to the Status of Refugees
1967 Protocol	1967 Protocol Relating to the Status of Refugees
AIT	Asylum and Immigration Tribunal
AN	Author's Note
BGBl	*Bundesgesetzblatt*
BVerfG	*Bundesverfassungsgericht*, German Federal Constitutional Court
BVerwG	*Bundesverwaltungsgericht*, German Federal Administrative Court
CAT	Committee Against Torture
CEAS	Common European Asylum System
CEDAW	Convention on the Elimination of Discrimination against Women
CESCR	Committee on Economic, Social and Cultural Rights
CFR	Charter of Fundamental Rights of the European Union
CJEU	Court of Justice of the European Union
CNDA	*Cour nationale du droit d'asile* (French National Asylum Law Court)
COI	Country of Origin Information
CRC	Convention on the Rights of the Child
CRR	*Commission de Recours des Refugiés*, French Refugee Appeals Commission)
EC	European Communities
ECHR	European Convention on Human Rights
ECJ	European Court of Justice
ECOSOC	Economic and Social Council of the United Nations
ECRE	European Council on Refugees and Exiles
ECtHR	European Court of Human Rights
ELENA	European Legal Network on Asylum
EU	European Union
EUCFR	European Union Charter of Fundamental Rights
EURODAC	European Dactyloscopy (database for fingerprints of applicants for international protection)
EXCOM	Executive Committee of the UNHCR
FRONTEX	European Border and Coast Guard/*Frontières Extérieures*
HRC	Human Rights Committee (of the ICCPR)
IAT	Immigration Appeals Tribunal (UK)
IAC	Upper Tribunal (Immigration and Asylum Chamber) (UK)
ICC	International Criminal Court
ICCPR	International Covenant on Civil and Political Rights

ICERD	International Covenant on the Elimination of All Forms of Racial Discrimination
ICESCR	International Covenant on Economic, Social and Cultural Rights
ICJ	International Court of Justice
ICRC	International Committee of the Red Cross
ICTY	International Criminal Tribunal for the Former Yugoslavia
IDP	Internally Displaced Person
IFA	Internal Flight Alternative
ILC	International Law Commission
IPA	Internal Protection Alternative
IRO	International Refugee Organization
LGBTI	Lesbian, Gay, Bisexual, Transsexual, Intersex
MIG	*Migrationsöverdomstolen* (Swedish High Court of Migration)
MINUSCO	United Nations Mission to the Democratic Republic of Congo
NGO	Non-governmental Organization
OCHA	Office for the Coordination of Humanitarian Affairs
OVG	*Oberverwaltungsgericht* (German High Administrative Court)
QD	Qualification Directive
TEU	Treaty of the European Union
TFEU	Treaty on the Functioning of the European Union
UDHR	Universal Declaration of Human Rights
UK	United Kingdom of Great Britain and Northern Ireland
UKAIT	United Kingdom Asylum and Immigration Tribunal
UKHL	United Kingdom House of Lords
UN	United Nations
UNC	United Nations Charter
UNCAT	Convention against Torture and Other Cruel, Inhuman or Degrading Treatment or Punishment
UNHCR	United Nations High Commissioner for Refugees
UNHCR Handbook	UNHCR Handbook on Procedures and Criteria for Determining Refugee Status under the 1951 Convention and the 1967 Protocol relating to the Status of Refugees
UNMIK	United Nations Mission in Kosovo
UNRRA	United Nations Relief and Rehabilitation Administration
UNRWA	United Nations Relief and Works Agency
UNTS	United Nations Treaty Series
VCLT	Vienna Convention on the Law of Treaties
VG	*Verwaltungsgericht* (German Administrative Court)

CHAPTER 1

Introduction: Why Researching the Uses of the Term 'Protection' in EU Asylum Law?

1.1 Research Puzzle – When Is There 'Protection' in the Home – or Another Country of an Asylum Seeker?

Around the world, people are fleeing harm from violence, conflict and persecution. In its annual statistical compilation on the world refugee population, the United Nations High Commissioner for Refugees (UNHCR) makes out a 'longer-term rising trend in the number of people needing safety'.[1] In the European Union (EU), this trend was particularly apparent with the arrival of Syrians, who contributed to the high increase in asylum applications in the mid-2010s, rising from some 335,000 in 2014 to 1.3 million in 2015, and 1.2 million in 2016.[2] In the past years, Syrians were also among the largest group of newly and displaced people worldwide, alongside and among others, Congolese, South Sudanese, Somalis and Eritreans.[3]

From the geographic perspective of the EU, the location of source countries means that people who flee harm have usually crossed other, non-EU countries before arriving in EU member states. This is because few regular and airborne pathways to flight exist and displaced people choose routes and destinations based on factors such as proximity/feasibility, 'cultural and ethnic similarities' and patterns of movement of other people who have fled in similar circumstances.[4] Besides, displaced people may first seek refuge within their home countries if circumstances permit. The number of Internally Displaced Persons (IDP) is considerably and consistently higher than those of refugees. In contrast to IDPs, a refugee, under the definition of the 1951 Convention relating to the Status of Refugees, is *outside of his or her country of nationality,*

1 UNHCR, 'Global Trends – Forced Migration in 2018' (2019) <www.unhcr.org/5d08d7ee7.pdf> accessed 20 June 2019, 4.

2 Eurostat, 'Asylum and First Time Asylum Applicants – data (rounded)', <https://ec.europa.eu/eurostat/databrowser/view/tps00189/default/table?lang=en> accessed 3 January 2019.

3 UNHCR, 'Global Trends – forced Migration in 2017' (2018) <www.unhcr.org/5b27be547.pdf> accessed 20 June 2019.

4 Seraina Rüegger and Heidrun Bohnet, 'The Ethnicity of Refugees (ER): A New Dataset for Understanding Flight Patterns' (2018) 35 Conflict Management and Peace Science, 65, 82.

 | DOI:10.1163/9789004430396_002

has a 'well-founded fear of being persecuted for reasons of race, religion, nationality, membership of a particular social group or political opinion' and is, 'owing to such fear, unwilling to avail himself of the protection of' his country of nationality.[5]

The geographic characteristics of flight patterns coincide with predominant concepts in refugee law. This includes, in particular, the influential notion of 'surrogacy',[6] according to which refugee status is a 'surrogate' for lacking 'protection' at home. The notion of surrogacy has been used to describe when refugees may not be in need of international protection given there is 'national' or 'domestic' protection available. This is also reflected in EU asylum law, that is, the EU's acquis of minimum standards for refugees and individuals who have fled human rights harm, but do not qualify for refugee status (so called 'subsidiary' status, for this distinction and the definition of EU law, see Section 1.3 and 1.4.2 below).[7] First, the notion of surrogacy is relevant when enquiring whether there is, in the home country, protection against harm inflicted by non-state actors, such as criminal networks, political or religious extremists, or insurgent non-state armed groups (Articles 6–7 of the EU Qualification Directive,[8] the Directive which contains minimum standards on eligibility criteria for refugee and subsidiary status and the treatment of those receiving status).[9] According

5 Convention Relating to the Status of Refugees (adopted 28 July 1951, entered into force 22 April 1954) 189 UNTS 137 Art 1A(2). Note the somewhat different requirement for stateless persons who need to be outside their habitual country of residence, have a well-founded fear of being persecuted on account of one of the same five grounds, and who are, owing to such fear, unwilling to return to that country of habitual residence.

6 As far as the author can ascertain, the term was coined by James C. Hathaway, *The Law of Refugee Status* (Butterworths Canada, 1991) 5, referring to refugee law as 'a system for the surrogate or substitute protection of human rights'. This has been taken up by the leading Canadian case of *Attorney General v Ward* [1993] 2 SCR 689, 58, referring to 'international protection as a "surrogate" approachable upon failure of local protection'.

7 In the legal language of several EU states, 'asylum' is often used to mean only refugee status, rather than applying to individuals who do not qualify for refugee status but who cannot be returned because of the risk of other serious harm – so-called subsidiary protection (eg, Article 78(2) TFEU). For practical reasons, however, this book refers to 'asylum law' as the law regulating the procedural and material eligibility for both refugee status and subsidiary protection status, as do other scholarly works, eg, Kai Hailbronner and Daniel Thym (eds), *EU Immigration and Asylum Law – A Commentary* (2nd edn, C.H.Beck 2016).

8 Council Directive 2011/95/EU of the European Parliament and of the Council of 13 December 2011 on standards for the qualification of third-country nationals or stateless persons as beneficiaries of international protection, for a uniform status for refugees or for persons eligible for subsidiary protection, and for the content of the protection granted (recast) [2011] OJ L33/9.

9 An example for relevant claims is those of Lesbians, Gays, Bisexuals, Transgender and Intersexuals (LGBTI), when there are frequent physical assaults by private individuals and

to EU law, not just states, but also actors other than states that control substantial parts of the territory can provide 'protection' against harm.[10] An example are international organisations when they yield quasi-governmental functions such as providing safety and delivering services.[11]

Second, the surrogacy notion is relevant in enquiring whether there is an alternative area to flee to, the so called 'Internal Protection Alternative' (Article 8 of the Directive). The Internal Protection Alternative (IPA) is of practical relevance in all cases in which harm is potentially localised. Here, too, the pertinent cases are those in which harm would be inflicted by non-state actors, or in which there is generalised violence caused by conflict in one part of the territory, but not or to a lesser degree in another.[12]

Third, the underlying rationale of the surrogacy notion is increasingly extended beyond its normal scope, to countries of (potential) asylum rather than the home country of those who flee. The EU Procedures Directive,[13] regulating the minimum standards for asylum procedures in EU member states, foresees that member states may reject asylum applications if an applicant has already found protection in a 'first country of asylum' or a 'safe third country' (Articles 35 and 38 of the Directive respectively). Beyond the EU, this practice has found expression as 'protection elsewhere' in the 2016 New York Declaration

---

groups rather than official criminalisation of conduct. For example, Human Rights Watch in its World Report 2018 on Pakistan deplored that despite a Supreme Court Order on better police protection of transgender people, 'violent attacks on transgender and intersex women in Khyber Pakhtunkhwa province surged in 2016, with unknown assailants frequently targeting those involved in activism.' Human Rights Watch, 'World Report 2018' (2018), <www.hrw.org/sites/default/files/world_report_download/201801world_report_web.pdf> accessed 3 January 2019.

10 Article 6(c) Qualification Directive.

11 UNMIK for a long time assumed quasi-governmental responsibilities, including basic civilian administrative functions, establishment of police forces and maintenance of public order; see UN Security Council Resolution SC/RES/1244 (1999).

12 For example, in Nigeria, the country's Middle Belt is affected by conflict between pastoralists (by majority of Muslim faith) and farmers (by majority of Christian faith), while the north-eastern part of the territory was and partly still is affected by violence of the Jihadist terrorist group Boko Haram. See eg, International Crisis Group, 'Herders against Farmers: Nigeria's Expanding Deadly Conflict, Africa Report No 252' (September 2017) <www.crisisgroup.org/africa/west-africa/nigeria/252-herders-against-farmers-nigerias-expanding-deadly-conflict> accessed 1 July 2019 and IRIN, 'Boko Haram: Nigeria winning the battle but losing the war?' (May 2017) <www.refworld.org/docid/591316d94.html> accessed 3 January 2019.

13 Directive 2013/32/EU of the European Parliament and the Council of 26 June 2013 on common procedures for granting and withdrawing international protection (recast) [2013] OJ L180/60.

for Refugees and Migrants, an authoritative document on the protection of refugees and migrants adopted by all United Nations (UN) member states:

> We will ensure that refugee admission policies or arrangements are in line with our obligations under international law. [...] At the same time, we recognize that the ability of refugees to lodge asylum claims in the country of their choice may be regulated, subject to the safeguard that they will have access to, and enjoyment of, *protection elsewhere*.[14]

Several academic authors have been critical of the notion of surrogacy for some time, arguing that it is ambiguous and may unduly change the perspective on the inclusion criteria of refugee status when assessing whether an individual faces a well-founded fear of being persecuted by non-state actors (thus, the first of the three issues mentioned),[15] that it is wrongly elevated to the status of a normative principle rather than a descriptive concept pointing to core features of refugeehood,[16] or that it has conceptual limitations.[17] While this book will revisit and take position on this criticism, the notion of surrogacy will for now be used in pure descriptive rather than normative terms, so as to demonstrate commonalities of different aspects of asylum law that all raise a similar question worthy of academic exploration: when is *protection strong enough so as to reject an application for asylum?* It is a question that is also hotly debated in the reform of the EU's asylum system, as the next section will show.

14 UN General Assembly, 'New York Declaration for Refugees and Migrants', 2 October 2016, A/RES/71/1. para 70 (emphasis added). The term has also been used previously by the UNHCR and academic commentary. See, eg, UNHCR, 'The Concept of 'Protection Elsewhere' (1995) 7 International Journal of Refugee Law 1; James C. Hathaway and others, 'The Michigan Guidelines on Protection Elsewhere, adopted January 3, 2007' (2006) 28 Michigan Journal of International Law 207.

15 Guy S. Goodwin-Gil and Jane McAdam, *The Refugee in International Law* (Oxford University Press 2007) 9-11; Susan Kneebone, 'Refugees as Objects of Surrogate Protection: Shifting Identities' in Susan Kneebone and others (eds), *Conflicting Identities: Refugee Protection and the Role of Law* (Routledge 2014).

16 Jessica Schultz, *The Internal Protection Alternative in Refugee Law: Treaty Basis and Scope of Application Under the 1951 Convention Relating to the Status of Refugees and its 1967 Protocol* (Brill 2018) 134. On this criticism, see also below, Section 2.3.4.

17 David Cantor argues that the notion of surrogate protection 'sits uneasily with the established understanding that the State receiving or hosting a refuges does not – by virtue of Articles 3 to 34 of the Refugee Convention – automatically acquire rights and assume obligations vis-à-vis the person that are the prerogative of the State of nationality.' David James Cantor, 'Defining Refugees: Persecution, Surrogacy and the Human Rights Paradigm' in David James Cantor (ed), *Human Rights and the Refugee Definition – Comparative Legal Practice and Theory* (Brill 2016) 364.

1.2 The Research Puzzle in Emerging Practice and Reform Debates of EU Asylum Law

Beyond the many pressing humanitarian challenges caused by the influx of Syrians, the increase in asylum applications in the EU has led to significant political pressure on member states and EU institutions, visible, among others, in the adoption of a plethora of policy documents, legislative reform and financial measures. In particular, the EU Commission has adopted in early 2015 a 'European Agenda on Migration',[18] a policy planning instrument that lays out emergency measures to address the inflow of asylum seekers, as well as medium- and longer-term policy tenets. These have remained unchanged since. The EU seeks to cooperate with third countries to address irregular migration upstream, by fighting migrant smuggling and addressing root causes; to improve return systems and border management; to establish labour migration channels and, finally and most contentiously, to improve implementation of and to reform the Common European Asylum System (CEAS), that is, the EU's set of legal acts on all issues relating to asylum.[19]

In the discussions on the current state and the future reform of the CEAS, a reoccurring theme is whether particular applicants are genuinely in need of asylum in EU states given they have already found or might potentially find 'protection' closer to their home countries. For example, in October 2018, the Austrian government, then holding the presidency of the EU Council, jointly with the Danish government, presented a vision paper for a better asylum system centered around the idea of 'safe havens' to which people can flee as an alternative to EU countries.

> A sustainable European asylum policy will […] need to distinguish between refugees who have already found a safe haven close to home, and those who absolutely need to move further afield in order to be safe. The European Union and its Member States should therefore strive towards a

18 European Commission, 'A European Agenda on Migration' (May 2015) <https://ec.europa.eu/anti-trafficking/sites/antitrafficking/files/communication_on_the_european_agenda_on_migration_en.pdf> accessed 3 January 2019. For an overview of EU measures, see the state of play of the EU Agenda for Migration, European Commission, European Agenda on Migration – Factsheets <https://ec.europa.eu/home-affairs/what-we-do/policies/european-agenda-migration/background-information_en> accessed 3 January 2019.

19 The CEAS is referred to as the set of legal standards on the responsibility of Member States to decide on asylum applications, the procedures for admissibility and merits of asylum applications, the substantive eligibility criteria for asylum, the treatment of those eligible and the treatment of those not eligible.

> shared understanding that an application for asylum in Europe will only be accepted, if the country of arrival is indeed the 'nearest safe haven'. In other words, the person must be a refugee *and* have either 1) faced persecution in a neighbouring country or 2) had no realistic possibility to claim *effective protection* (emphasis added) in a country located between the EU and the country of origin.[20]

These reform considerations build on political practice since 2016, in particular the landmark political precedent of the so-called 'EU-Turkey Statement' of 18 March 2016.[21] Relying on the EU Procedures Perspective, the statement foresees, among others, that migrants arriving into the Greek Islands after 20 March 2016 from Turkey will be returned. According to the statement, 'Migrants not applying for asylum or whose application has been found unfounded or inadmissible in accordance with the [...] [Procedures Directive] will be returned to Turkey'.[22] In response, Greek authorities as well as the European Border and Coast Guard (EBCG/FRONTEX) have returned individuals to Turkey, although the exact number of asylum seekers returned on admissibility grounds, in accordance with the Procedures Directive, remains unclear.[23]

Since the adoption of the EU-Turkey Statement, there has been debate not only how to use it as a blueprint for other countries,[24] but also on the reform of the Procedures Directive. One of the contentious issues is the requirements for safe countries, in particular the list of criteria for safety and other basic

20 The Austrian Federal Ministry of Interior, the Danish Ministry of Immigration and Integration, 'Vision for a Better Protection System in a Globalized World' (2018) <http://uim.dk/filer/nyheder-2018/vision-for-a-better-protection-system-in-a-globalized-world.pdf> accessed 3 January 2019.

21 European Council, 'EU Turkey Statement of 18th March 2016' (March 2016) <www.consilium.europa.eu/en/press/press-releases/2016/03/18/eu-turkey-statement/#> accessed 3 January 2019.

22 Ibid para 1.

23 The statistics provided by the EU Commission do not differentiate between asylum seekers and those that did not lodge an asylum application. For the overall number of returns, see EU Commission, 'Operational Implementation of the EU-Turkey Statement' (March 2016) <https://ec.europa.eu/home-affairs/sites/homeaffairs/files/what-we-do/policies/european-agenda-migration/press-material/docs/state_of_play_-_eu-turkey_en.pdf> accessed 3 January 2019.

24 Reuters, 'Merkel: We need migrant deals with African states like EU-Turkey pact' (September 2016) <www.reuters.com/article/us-europe-migrants-germany/merkel-we-need-migrant-deals-with-egypt-tunisia-like-eu-turkey-pact-idUSKCN11W1FR> accessed 3 January 2019.

requirement for essential self-reliance and access to basic services.[25] A 2017 joint non-paper of France and Germany, for instance, proposes to adjust substantially these criteria, limiting them to a core of non-return obligations in respect of those whose physical safety is at risk.[26]

The reform discussions on the CEAS as well as the practice under the EU-Turkey Statement bring us back to the question when protection in another location is 'strong enough' so as to reject an asylum application. Or, more fundamentally, is there a common core to the multiple uses of the term protection, a term that is at the core of the cited EU laws, as well as of the primary international instrument on refugees, the 1951 Convention Relating to the Status of Refugees (1951 Convention)? If yes, is it just safety, as the above-cited paper suggests? Is protection provided only by states? And is protection different for different legal status of people fleeing? Before laying out the research questions in detail, a brief look of the various (legal) uses of the term is in order.

1.3 The Multiple Uses of the Term 'Protection' in Asylum Law and Policy

'Protection' is a term that is so frequently used in asylum law and policy that it is hard to see how the term retains distinct, analytical value. At first glance, 'protection' is the totality of activities safeguarding the rights and well-being of those forcibly displaced. In the language of international organisations, it comprises 'all activities aimed at obtaining full respect for the rights of the individual'.[27] The UNHCR Executive Committee and the UN General Assembly emphasised that refugee protection includes activities by states and by the UNHCR, inter alia '[...] the promotion and facilitation of [...] the admission,

25 See Article 44 in Council of the EU, Proposal for a Regulation of the European Parliament and of the Council stablishing a common procedure for international protection in the Union and repealing Directive 2013/32/EU (First reading), 14098/17, 15 November 2017.

26 France – Germany Note, 'A Crisis-Resistant Common European Asylum System (CEAS)' (February 2017) <www.statewatch.org/news/2017/feb/eu-refugees-france-germany-note-feb-17.pdf> accessed 3 January 2019.

27 International Committee of the Red Cross, 'Workshop on Protection for Human Rights and Humanitarian Organizations: Doing Something About It and Doing It Well' (1999) 5. See also Inter-Agency Standing Committee, 'Handbook for the Protection of Internally Displaced Persons', (2010) 5 <http://www.unhcr.org/4c2355229.pdf> accessed 20 October 2016; Anne Evans Barnes, 'Realizing Protection Space for Iraqi Refugees: UNHCR in Syria, Jordan and Lebanon' (2009) UNHCR New Issues in Refugee Research Paper 167, 8, <www.unhcr.org/4981d3ab2.pdf> accessed 20 October 2016.

reception and treatment of refugees in accordance with internationally agreed standards and the ensuring of durable, protection-oriented solutions'.[28] For Guy Goodwin-Gil, refugee protection is an 'unrestricted human rights competence' to assist refugees, in order to achieve their rights, security and welfare, with a view to resolving their situation by providing solutions.[29]

In legal instruments, however, 'protection' is more than an umbrella term for activities, but first and foremost refers to legal safeguards, by way of vesting individuals with legal status. The preamble of the 1951 Convention makes clear that protection of refugees is one of the objects of the treaty, which is in large part about the status of refugees in their countries of asylum.[30] In EU asylum law, the term 'protection' first refers to the legal status of two groups of people: 'international protection' means both refugee status in accordance with the 1951 Convention, and 'subsidiary' status,[31] a distinction that will be further explained and discussed in the next paragraphs as well as in Section 1.4.2 below. This wording of 'international protection' is also reflected in the Global Compact on Refugees, an authoritative soft-law instrument intended to promote greater collaboration by all stakeholders on refugees, adopted by the UN General Assembly in December 2018.[32]

The term protection, then, is also an integral term in the *refugee definition* and the definition of a beneficiary of 'subsidiary' status in both EU law and in the 1951 Convention. As stated above, refugees are individuals who are outside their country of nationality, have a well-founded fear of being persecuted on account of race, religion, nationality, political opinion, or membership of a particular social group, and are unable or, because of their well-founded fear of being persecuted, unwilling to *avail themselves of the 'protection' of their country of nationality*.[33] This definition is the same in the Qualification Directive as

28 UNHCR EXCOM, No 89 (LI) – 2000, UN General Assembly, Resolution 63/148, 27 January 2009, A/RES/63/148, para 14; Resolution 64/127, 27 January 2010, UN Doc A/RES/64/127 para 19; *Resolution 65/194*, 28 February 2011 UN Doc A/RES/65/194 para 20.

29 Guy S. Goodwin-Gil, 'The Language of Protection' (1989) 1 International Journal of Refugee *Law* 6.

30 According to para 3 of the Convention's preamble, '… it is desirable to revise and consolidate previous international agreements relating to the status of refugees and to extend the scope of and protection accorded by such instruments by means of a new agreement.'

31 Directive 2011/95/EU of the European Parliament and of the Council of 13 December 2011 on standards for the qualification of third-country nationals or stateless persons as beneficiaries of international protection, for a uniform status for refugees or for persons eligible for subsidiary protection, and for the content of the protection granted (recast) OJ L337/9, Article 2a),e),f), in connection with recital 24 of the preamble.

32 United Nations High Commissioner for Refugees, 'Report of the UNHCR Part 2, Global Compact on Refugees', UN Doc A/73/12 (2018).

33 Article 2d) Qualification Directive.

it is in the 1951 Convention[34] in connection with the 1967 Protocol relating to the Status of Refugees, which removed the Convention's limitation to events that occurred in Europe in connection with the Second World War.[35]

Beyond the refugee definition, EU law also uses the term for the definition of a beneficiary of subsidiary status – an individual outside his country of nationality or stateless person facing a real risk of serious (human rights related) harm[36] and is unable, or owing to the risk of harm, *unwilling to avail himself of the protection* of his country of nationality or habitual residence.[37]

Given its prominent place in the refugee definition as well as in the definition of subsidiary status, the analysis of available protection is relevant at multiple stages of the *determination* of status. These have been named already: protection against harm from non-state actors, the IPA, first countries of asylum and safe third countries. Beyond this, the analysis of available protection is relevant for the *cessation* of refugee status – which most commonly is relevant when circumstances in the home countries change. According to Article 11(1)a) of the Qualification Directive, a 'third-country national or a stateless person shall cease to be a refugee if he or she [...] has voluntarily re-availed himself or herself of the protection of the country of nationality'. This again mirrors the wording of the 1951 Convention.[38] Because cessation of status is to a large extent the flipside of status determination and recognition,[39] this book will focus on the criteria for recognition of status rather than cessation.

In sum, protection is a term central to asylum law and policy, with this book focusing on a *selection of legal contexts of the term in the determination of status*, with a view to relate them to each other and enquire what substantive legal standard is to be used for each of them. Meanwhile, the answer to this puzzle may be a matter of different legal obligations of different bodies of law at play. This hypothesis is outlined in the next section.

---

34 Article 1A(2) 1951 Convention.

35 Protocol relating to the Status of Refugees (New York, 31 January 1967), United nations Treaty Series vol 606, p 267.

36 See Section 1.4.2 below.

37 Article 2(d); (e) Qualification Directive.

38 According to Article 1C(1);(3);(5) of the 1951 Convention, the Convention ceases to apply to a person who has 'voluntarily re-availed himself of the protection of the country of his nationality'; who has acquired a new nationality and 'enjoys the protection of the country of his new nationality'; or who can no longer, because of a change of circumstances on his original claim for refugee status, 'continue to refuse to avail himself of the protection of his country of nationality.'

39 On this issue, see also the reference to the CJEU judgment in Abdullah, Section 3.3.1.1

1.4 The Research Puzzle and the Interplay of Refugee and Human Rights Law in EU Law

In enquiring into different legal meanings and standards around the term 'protection', this book will also scrutinise an overarching issue on the interplay of different bodies of law, namely of international refugee and human rights law in the law of the EU. The hypothesis is that obligations of different bodies of law may contain different, and potentially conflicting, obligations on the overall research puzzle. However, why can we say that there is, *prima facie*, an interplay or even convergence of different bodies of law in the first place? This is because EU norms relevant for this research (Articles 6–8 of the Qualification Directive and Articles 35 and 38 of the Procedures Directive) apply to both refugee and subsidiary status, which partly originate in international law obligations. The criteria for refugee status, which have been laid out in Section 1.1, originate in the international law obligations of the 1951 Convention. In contrast, subsidiary status, although it has no international law counterpart as direct as the 1951 Convention, is partly based on international human rights law.[40] What this means for the primacy of relevant international law over EU secondary law is explored in the following sections.

1.4.1 *The Primacy of the 1951 Convention for Secondary EU Law*

Although the EU is not and cannot be party to the 1951 Convention,[41] the Convention clearly takes precedence over the relevant EU secondary law, as manifested in both primary and secondary EU law.[42] In primary law, according to Article 78(1) of the Treaty of the Functioning of the EU (TFEU), the common policy on asylum and subsidiary protection 'must be in accordance with the Geneva Convention of 28 July 1951 and the Protocol of 31 January 1967 relating

---

40 For the emergence of the regime, see Jane McAdam, *Complementary Protection in International Refugee Law* (Oxford University Press 2007). For an analysis of the scope of obligations as well as the overlap and differences between obligations from these bodies of law, see below, Chapter 2–2.2.

41 Kay Hailbronner and Daniel Thym, 'Legal Framework for EU Asylum Policy' in Hailbronner and Thym (eds), *EU Immigration and Asylum Law – A Commentary* (Ch 1 n 7) 1046, pointing to Article 39(2) of the Convention.

42 On this, see also Anja Klug, 'Regional Developments – Europe' in Andreas Zimmermann, Jonas Dörschner, Felix Machts (eds.), *The 1951 Convention and its 1967 Protocol – A Commentary* (Oxford University Press 2011), 127, 135–136; Hailbronner, Thym 'Legal Framework for EU Asylum Policy' in Hailbronner and Thym, *EU Immigration and Asylum Law – A Commentary* (Ch 1 n 7) 1029; 1046.

to the status of refugees [...]'. Article 351 TFEU also gives precedence to the rights and obligations arising from agreements concluded before 1 January 1958 or, for newly acceding member states, from agreements concluded before the date of their accession. All new EU states were parties to the 1951 Convention prior to their accession to the EU. What is more, the primacy of the 1951 Convention is apparent from the Treaty of Amsterdam, which shifted legislative competence on these matters to the EU in 1999.[43] The Treaty provided that the criteria for determining the member state responsible for an asylum application; the minimum standards for the reception of asylum seekers; and the minimum standards on the qualification for refugee status and for asylum procedures must be 'in accordance with the Geneva Convention of 28 July 1951 and the Protocol of 31 January 1967 relating to the status of refugees and other relevant treaties'.[44]

In respect of secondary law, all relevant secondary EU instruments[45] leave 1951 Convention obligations intact as the 'governing international treaty on asylum law'.[46] The Directive reiterates conclusions by the European Council that the EU standards are 'based on the full and inclusive application of the Geneva Convention',[47] meaning the Convention as amended by the 1967

43 Treaty of Amsterdam Amending the Treaty on European Union, the Treaties Establishing the European Communities and Related Acts [1997] OJ C340, Article 73k.

44 Treaty of Amsterdam Amending the Treaty on European Union, the Treaties Establishing the European Communities and Related Acts (ibid) Article 73k. See Pieter Boeles and others, *European Migration Law* (Intersentia 2009) 317. Indeed, even before legislative competence shifted to the EU, the European Council confirmed that the first joint EU position on the refugee definition made clear that the CEAS sought a 'harmonized application' of Article 1A(2) of the 1951 Convention; Joint Position of 4 March 1996 defined by the Council on the basis of Article K.3 of the Treaty on European Union on the harmonised application of the definition of the term 'refugee' in Article 1 of the Geneva Convention of 28 July 1951 relating to the status of refugees, [1996] OJ L63/2.

45 Council Directive 2003/9/EC of 27 January 2003 on laying down minimum standards for the reception of asylum seekers [2003] OJ L31/18. Directive 2011/95/EU (Recast Qualification Directive); Directive 2013/32/EU (Procedures Directive); Council Regulation (EC) 604/2013 of 26 June 2013 establishing the criteria and mechanisms for determining the Member State responsible for examining an application for international protection lodged in one of the Member States by a third-country national or a stateless person [2013] OJ L180 (Dublin Regulation).

46 Hugo Storey, 'EU Refugee Qualification Directive: a Brave New World?' (2008) 20 International Journal of Refugee Law 1, 7.

47 Council of the European Union, 'Presidency Conclusions, Tampere European Council', 15–16 October 1999.

Protocol.[48] Furthermore, the Directive's refugee definition is that of the 1951 Convention; Article 2(c) of the Directive transposes Article 1A(2) of the 1951 Convention[49] and Recital 24 makes clear that the Directive seeks to 'introduce common criteria for recognising applicants for asylum as refugees within the meaning of Article 1 of the Geneva Convention'. Finally, the Directive also refers to the 1951 Convention's concepts of 'being persecuted',[50] cessation,[51] and exclusion[52] and provides that all rights granted to refugees 'shall be without prejudice to the rights laid down in the Geneva Convention'.[53] Indeed, as made clear by the preamble of the Qualification Directive and reiterated by the CJEU, 'the provisions of the [Qualification] Directive [...] were adopted to *guide* the competent authorities of the member states *in the application of* [*the 1951 Convention*] *on the basis of common concepts and criteria*'.[54] Thus, the CJEU has, in rulings on the interpretation of the Qualification Directive, repeatedly stated that secondary law must be interpreted 'in a manner consistent with the 1951 [...] Convention'.[55]

48 Article 2(c) Qualification Directive. For reasons of simplicity, the book will, like EU asylum law, mean 'the 1951 Convention as amended by the 1967 Protocol' when speaking of the '1951 Convention' in the EU law context.

49 The definition is taken verbatim from the 1951 Convention, with the exception of excluding EU citizens. '"Refugee" means a third-country national who, owing to a well-founded fear of being persecuted for reasons of race, religion, nationality, political opinion or membership of a particular social group, is outside the country of nationality and is unable or, owing to such fear, is unwilling to avail himself or herself of the protection of that country, or a stateless person, who, being outside of the country of former habitual residence for the same reasons as mentioned above, is unable or, owing to such fear, unwilling to return to it [...].'

50 Article 9 Qualification Directive, 'Acts of persecution within the meaning of article 1 A of the Geneva Convention [...].'

51 Article 11 Qualification Directive.

52 Article 12(1)(a) Qualification Directive '[...] he or she falls within the scope of Article 1 D of the Geneva Convention'.

53 Article 20(1) Qualification Directive.

54 Cases C-175/08, C-176/08, C-178/08 and C-179/98 *Aydin Salahadin Abdulla, Kamil Hasan, Ahmed Adem, Hamrin Mosa Rashi and Dler Jamal v Bundesrepublik Deutschland* [2010] ECR I-01493 para 37 (emphasis added). See Recital 23 (and 33) of the QD, 'Standards for the definition and content of refugee status should be laid down to guide the competent national bodies of Member States in the application of the Geneva Convention.'

55 ibid paras 53-54; Case C-31/09 *Nawras Bolbol v Bevándorlási és Állampolgársági Hivatal* [2010] ECR I-05539 para 38; Joined Cases C-57/09 and C-101/09 *Bundesrepublik Deutschland v B and D* [2010] ECR I-10979 para 78; *Bundesrepublik Deutschland v Y and Z*, judgment of 5 September 2012, C-71/11, C-99/11, digital reports, para 48; *Minister voor Immigratie en Asiel v X and Y and Z v Minister voor Immigratie en Asiel* C-199/12 to C-201/12, digital reports, para 40; Joined Cases C-443/14 and C-444/14 *Kreis Warendorf v Ibrahim Alo and Amira Osso v Region Hannover*, ECLI:EU:C:2016:127 [2016] digital reports, para 28.

In sum, the 1951 Convention is the primary legal benchmark for EU asylum law – EU asylum law seeks to guide member states in the application of the Convention. The next section will show to what extent the same is true for other international law obligations.

1.4.2 *The Application of Other International Legal Obligations in EU Asylum Law*

Beyond the 1951 Convention, other international law obligations are also relevant to EU asylum law. According to Article 78(1), TFEU, the common policy on asylum, subsidiary protection and temporary protection must be not only in accordance with the 1951 Convention, but also with 'other relevant treaties'. For the purpose of EU asylum law, other relevant treaties include, in particular, other treaties of human rights law. First, this is because the 1951 Convention, the supreme international treaty on refugees, refers to human rights in its preamble and is to be interpreted with reference also to human rights law.[56] Second, this is because the preamble of the TEU confirms member states' attachment to respect for human rights; and given that there is an overlap in material scope between EU asylum law and human rights treaties. Finally, it is apparent in the definition of 'acts of persecution'[57] and in the eligibility criteria of subsidiary status. Eligible for such subsidiary protection are persons who would, if returned to their country of origin, face a real risk of suffering serious harm and are, owing to such risk, unwilling to avail themselves of the protection of that country.[58] Serious harm includes the death penalty or execution; torture, inhuman or degrading treatment or punishment in the country of origin; or a serious or individual threat to life by reason of indiscriminate violence in situations of international or internal armed conflict.[59] The Directive thereby codifies at the EU level long-standing law and practice of the member states,[60]

56 Ralf Alleweldt, 'Preamble 1951 Convention' in Zimmermann; Dörscher; Machts (eds), *The 1951 Convention Relating to the Status of Refugees and its 1967 Protocol: A Commentary* (n 42) 233.

57 Article 9 Qualification Directive.

58 Article 2(f) in conjunction with Article 15 Qualification Directive.

59 Article 15 Qualification Directive.

60 Jane McAdam, 'The European Union Qualification Directive: The Creation of a Subsidiary Protection Regime' (2005) 17 International Journal of Refugee Law 461 – also listing in note 2 various calls by international organisations to regulate the situation of persons not falling under the refugee definition. Eg, Committee of Minsters of the Council of Europe, Recommendation 1088 (1988) on the right to territorial asylum, advising '[examination of] the possibility of preparing a European convention, including the establishment of a consultative body, dealing with people falling outside

as well as obligations under international human rights law. According to Recital 34 of the Qualification Directive,

> It is necessary to introduce common criteria on the basis of which applicants for international protection are to be recognised as eligible for subsidiary protection. Those criteria *should be drawn from international obligations under human rights instruments* and practices existing in Member States.[61]

The most important human rights treaty for EU asylum law is the European Convention on Human Rights (ECHR). Article 6(3), TEU confers upon fundamental rights guaranteed by the ECHR the status of 'general principles of the Union's law'.[62] What is more, the Charter of Fundamental Rights of the European Union (CFR),[63] which is itself on an equal footing with primary law and applies to EU institutions, bodies and member states when they are implementing EU law,[64] stipulates a 'correspondence rule'[65] for EU fundamental rights protection: according to Article 52(3) of the Charter, the rights of the Charter correspond to the rights contained in the ECHR and shall not go below the ECHR standard.[66] Secondary law on matters of asylum also contains references to the ECHR. The Qualification Directive links the definition of 'acts of persecution' in Article 9(1) to non-derogable rights under the ECHR, and the scope of serious harm, in Article 15(b), refers to 'torture or inhuman and degrading treatment or punishment'. According to the CJEU in *Elgafaji*, that Article 'corresponds, in essence, to Article 3 of the

the scope of the Geneva Convention, but requiring protection, and on whose fate the Council of Europe, under the term "de facto refugees", has been proposing concrete measures for many years.'

61 Emphasis added.

62 This codifies established practice by the ECJ according to which 'fundamental rights form an integral part of the general principles of law the observance of which the Court ensures. For that purpose, the Court draws inspiration from the constitutional traditions common to the Member States and from the guidelines supplied by international treaties for the protection of human rights on which the Member States have collaborated or to which they are signatories. The ECHR has special significance in that respect.' Case C-112/00 Eugen Schmidberger, *Internationale Transporte und Planzüge v Austria* [2003] ECR I-5659.

63 Charter of Fundamental Rights of the European Union [2000] OJ C364/1.

64 Article 51 CFR.

65 Steve Peers, *The EU Charter of Fundamental Rights: A Commentary* (Hart Publishing 2013).

66 See also Hailbronner and Thym, 'Legal Framework for EU Asylum Policy' in Hailbronner and Thym, *EU Immigration and Asylum Law – A Commentary* (Ch 1 n 7) 1045.

ECHR'.[67] Interpretation of secondary law provisions that do not correspond to the ECHR 'must [...] be carried out independently, although with due regard for fundamental rights as they are guaranteed under the ECHR'.[68]

Although Article 6(3) TEU explicitly mentions only the ECHR, EU law must also accord with other *international* human rights treaties, the most important being the International Covenant on Civil and Political Rights (ICCPR);[69] the International Covenant on Economic, Social and Cultural Rights (ICESCR);[70] the Convention against Torture (UNCAT);[71] and the Convention on the Rights of the Child (CRC).[72] This is for three reasons.

First, the ECHR is conceived in such a way as to create concordance with international human rights law. Even before the entry of force of the ICCPR, for instance, the Committee of Ministers of the Council of Europe entrusted an expert committee with identifying differences between the ECHR and the Covenant. The report of the committee paved the way for Protocols Nos 4 and 7 to the ECHR, which removed many of the differences.[73] The European Court of Human Rights (ECtHR) has also referred to provisions of both the ICCPR and the ICESCR as 'relevant rules and principles of international law applicable between the Contracting Parties' in order to interpret provisions of the ECHR.[74]

Second, both the Qualification Directive and the Procedures Directive also explicitly refer to a legal concept in other human rights treaties, in particular that of the 'best interest of the child' from the CRC,[75] and human rights related forms of harm in the eligibility criteria for refugee and subsidiary status.[76]

---

67 Case C-465/07 *Meki Elgafaji and Noor Elgafaji v Staatsecretaris van Justitie* [2009] ECR I-921. For the overlap between Article 15(b) and the ECHR obligations under Article 3, see Section 1.2.5.

68 Ibid.

69 International Covenant on Civil and Political Rights (adopted 16 December 1966, entered into force 23 March 1976) 171 UNTS.

70 International Covenant on Economic, Social and Cultural Rights (adopted 16 December 1966, entered into force 3 January 1976) 993 UNTS 3.

71 Convention Against Torture and Other Cruel, Inhuman or Degrading Treatment or Punishment (adopted 10 December 1984, entered into force June 1987) 1465 UNTS 85.

72 Convention on the Rights of the Child (adopted 20 November 1989, entered into force 2 September 1990) 1577 UNTS 3.

73 William A Schabas, *The European Convention on Human Rights – A Commentary* (Oxford University Press 2015) 18–19.

74 Generally, eg, *Bosphorus Hava Yolları Turizm ve Ticaret Anonim Şirketi v Ireland* ECHR 2005-VI 107, para 150. In respect of the ICCPR, eg, *Müller and Others v Switzerland* App no 10737/84 (1991) Series A no 133, para 27; in respect of the ICESCR, eg, *Catan and Others v the Republic of Moldova and Russia* ECHR 2012-V 309, para 138.

75 Recital 18 of the preamble of the QD, and Recital 9 of the Procedures Directive.

76 Articles 10 and 15 of the Qualification Directive.

Finally, beyond the necessity to apply international human rights law by virtue of Article 78(1), TFEU and references in primary law, international human rights law creates binding commitments on EU member states by virtue of their ratification of these treaties.[77]

In sum, international law obligations take precedence over EU secondary law, so that it is plausible that different bodies of law interact and potentially differ. The next section will explain why such potential differences are worthy of exploration, given the EU's special position in the international regime on refugee protection.

1.4.3 *EU Asylum Law as Part of an International Legal Regime*

It has become apparent that refugee and human rights law, *prima facie*, interact in EU law. Meanwhile, what makes such interplay worthy of academic exploration in the context of different meanings of 'protection' is, in addition to potential conflict of norms, also the relevance of the EU to the international refugee regime. This will be discussed below.

EU asylum law is part of a global legal regime of refugee and human rights protection,[78] in which there is – much like in other areas of international law – no universal arbitrator or enforcer. According to Article 38 of the 1951 Convention and Article IV of the 1967 Protocol, state parties shall refer to the International Court of Justice (ICJ) disputes relating to the interpretation or the application of the 1951 Convention that they cannot solve by other means. However, no state has ever done so, so that those states applying the 1951 Convention have been left with general rules on treaty interpretation and a plethora of *opinio juris* from different jurisdictions. It has thus been for domestic courts to adjudicate material disagreements over the meaning of the 1951 Convention and to achieve, as far as possible, universal meaning, when the Convention frequently leaves a 'large scope of interpretation'.[79] Given the problem of indeterminacy of language, law is created by 'semantic struggles'[80] by courts and jurists within and across

77 All EU member states have ratified UNCAT, the ICCPR, the ICESCR and the CRC.

78 In the broadest sense, regimes are cooperative institutions constituted by principles, norms, rules and procedures, that in specific fields of policy address conflicts between States, Harald Müller, *Die Chancen der Kooperation: Regime in den internationalen Beziehungen* (Wissenschaftliche Buchgesellschaft 1993) 26. Legal regimes are such cooperative institutions only to the extent that they constitute sources and supervising entities of sources of law.

79 Ibid 12.

80 Ingo Ventzke, *How Interpretation Makes International Law* (Oxford University Press 2012) 57.

jurisdictions,[81] prompting one commentator to speak of a cross-border 'community of courts'.[82] On the basis of common interpretative means and rules – literal, systematic, teleological and historical – actors engage in judicial conversation aimed at forging universal meanings, demarcating particular legal obligations from others, signaling the observance of international law or strengthening their own standpoint.[83] Eventually, these semantic struggles are part of the community of practice that is relevant to compliance with and evolution of the law. In their account of the creation and persistence of international legal obligations, Brunnée and Toope argue that the ongoing practice of law builds, upholds or destroys norms:

> For law to exist and to endure, a community of practice needs to maintain or expand underlying shared understandings [...], and to embed those understandings in a legal practice that assures day-to-day application in concrete settings of the criteria of legality.[84]

As a matter of law, EU law is an *opinio juris* for non-EU countries.[85] In the concurrent application of international human rights law and refugee law, the EU stands out as a particularly important player in a global community of practice.[86] No other group of states has created binding supranational rules on asylum as sophisticated as those of the EU. Absent jurisprudence on the 1951 Convention by the International Court of Justice (ICJ), the Court of Justice of the European Union (CJEU) is the only supranational court that interprets – if only indirectly – the 1951 Convention and its relationship to human rights law. In practice, the court has accepted jurisdiction to interpret the 1951 Convention when a provision of secondary EU law makes clear that it is specifying a provision of the 1951 Convention. While in *Qurbani* the court denied jurisdiction to interpret Article 31 of the 1951 Convention, even though Article 14 of the

81 Anne-Marie Slaughter, 'A Typology of Transjudicial Communication' (1994) 29 University of Richmond Law Review 99.

82 Anne-Marie Slaughter, *A New World Order* (Princeton University Press 2004) 68.

83 In respect of the latter, see Marco Bronckers, 'The Relationship of the EC Courts with other International Tribunals: Non-Committal, Respectful or Submissive?' (2007) 44 Common Market Law Review 601, in an analysis of EC courts' engagement with international law.

84 Jutta Brunnée and Stephen J Toope, *Legitimacy and Legality in International Law* (Cambridge University Press 2010) 352.

85 Hailbronner and Thym, *EU Immigration and Asylum law – A Commentary* (Ch 1 n 7) 12.

86 Klug refers to the EU as the 'most important [...] regional body shaping European Asylum law and policy'. Anja Klug, 'Regional Developments – Europe' in Zimmermann; Dörschner, Machts *The 1951 Convention and its 1967 Protocol – A Commentary* (Ch 1 n 42) 127.

Qualification Directive mentions the Convention,[87] it has accepted jurisdiction to interpret the 1951 Convention in respect of Article 9 (acts of persecution);[88] Article 11 (cessation of refugee status);[89] and Article 12 (exclusion from refugee status)[90] of the Qualification Directive.[91]

Indeed, recent scholarship suggests that EU asylum law is influential beyond the borders of the EU. Guided by theories of norm diffusion, scholarship has identified two domestic drivers of why this may happen – new challenges and uncertainty on the one hand, and the social pressure to conform to transnational professional standards on the other.[92] Case studies based on this theory suggested that EU asylum law is emulated in Switzerland, Israel, Australia and Canada, and partly in jurisdictions on the African continent.[93] Yet, there

87 Case C-481/13 *Bundesrepublik Deutschland v Qurbani,* ECLI:EU:C:2014:2101 [2014] digital reports, para 23, with reference to the doctrine of functional succession and Case C 533/08 *TNT Express Nederland BV v AXA Versicherung AG* [2010] ECR I-04107: 'It is only where and in so far as the European Union has assumed the powers previously exercised by the Member States in the field to which an international convention not concluded by the European Union applies and, therefore, the provisions of the convention have the effect of binding the European Union that the Court has jurisdiction to interpret such a convention. In the present case, although several pieces of EU legislation have been adopted in the field to which the Geneva Convention applies as part of the implementation of a Common European Asylum System, it is undisputed that the Member States have retained certain powers falling within that field, in particular relating to the subject-matter covered by Article 31 of that convention. Therefore, the Court does not have jurisdiction to interpret directly Article 31, or any other article, of that convention.'

88 *Case C-472/13 Andrew Lawrence Shepherd v Bundesrepublik Deutschland,* ECLI:EU:C:2015:117 [2015] digital reports.

89 *Aydin Salahadin Abdulla, Kamil Hasan, Ahmed Adem, Hamrin Mosa Rashi and Dler Jamal v Bundesrepublik Deutschland* (Ch 1 n 54).

90 *Nawras Bolbol v Bevándorlási és Állampolgársági Hivatal* (Ch 1 n 55).

91 In *Alo and Osso,* on Article 33 of the Qualification Directive (freedom of movement), the CJEU made recourse to the 1951 Convention although Article 33 of the Directive does not mention the 1951 Convention. However, the CJEU did not have to interpret the standard of the 1951 Convention obligation, but instead had to decide whether the Qualification Directive confers the rights of the Convention on beneficiaries of subsidiary protection. *Kreis Warendorf v Ibrahim Alo and Amira Osso v Region Hannover* (Ch 1 n 55).

92 Hélène Lambert, Jane McAdam and Maryellen Fullerton (eds), *The Global Reach of European Refugee Law* (Cambridge University Press 2013) 7.

93 Ibid. An earlier analysis made out a policy influence on Japan, see Emiko Nakasaka, 'Too Different to be Relevant?: Considering the Global Influence of EU Asylum Laws and Policy with Respect to Japan' in Wetzel J (ed), *The EU as a "Global Player" in Human Rights?* (Routledge 2011). A more recent analysis looks at the transjudicial dialogue on complementary protection, Naomi Hart, 'Complementary Protection and Transjudicial Dialogue: Global Best Practice or Race to the Bottom?' (2016) 28 International Journal of Refugee Law 2. See also Hailbronner and Thym, 'Legal Framework for EU Asylum Policy' in Hailbronner and Thym, *EU Immigration and Asylum Law – A Commentary* (Ch 1 n 7),

appear to be mixed opinions about the contribution of EU asylum law on the evolution of refugee law internationally.[94] In particular, academic commentators have studied an increasing influence of human rights law, assuring both evolution of refugee law but also marginalising it.[95]

The potentially prominent role of the EU in maintaining and developing international refugee law begs the question as to how 'detached' from the 1951 Convention EU asylum law can be. This question cannot be conclusively answered by looking at single provisions of the Asylum Procedures Directive and the Qualification Directive, as this book will do. Answering it will require a comprehensive comparison of points of differences between EU asylum law and the law and practice in other, non-EU jurisdictions. However, this book, through analysis of the interplay between different bodies of international law and EU law in respect of available 'protection' intends to contribute to one particular aspect of that interplay in asylum law.

Indeed, the wider debate on the relationship between EU fundamental rights protection and international law goes far beyond asylum law,[96]

---

pointing out that national courts continue to play an important role given their specialization in refugee law', 1048.

94 From a regime perspective, however, there is more caution or even fear of an erosion of the 1951 Convention regime; see, for example, Cantor, 'Defining Refugees: Persecution, Surrogacy and the Human Rights Paradigm' (Ch 1 n 17); Violetta Moreno-Lax, 'Of Autonomy, Autarky, Purposiveness and Fragmentation: The Relationship between EU Asylum Law and International Humanitarian Law' in David James Cantor and Jean-François Durieux (eds), *Refuge from Inhumanity? War Refugees and International Humanitarian Law* (Brill 2014); Roland Bank, 'The Potential and Limitations of the Court of Justice of the European Union in Shaping International Refugee Law' (2015) 27 Int Journal of Refugee Law 213.

95 Many scholars argue that the influence of human rights law assures the evolution of refugee law, eg, Hugo Storey, 'What Constitutes Persecution? Towards a Working Definition' (2014) 26 International Journal of Refugee Law 272. Yet, there is also an argument that refugee law is becoming superfluous *vis à vis* human rights law; in respect of refugee rights, see Vincent Chetail, 'Are Refugee Rights Human Rights? An Unorthodox Questioning of the Relations between Refugee Law and Human Rights Law' in R. Rubio Marin (ed), *Migration and Human Rights* (Oxford University Press 2011); Jean-François Durieux, 'The Vanishing Refugee: how EU Asylum Law Blurs the Specificity of Refugee Protection' in Hélène Lambert, Jane McAdam, and Maryellen Fullerton (eds), *The Global Reach of European Refugee Law* (Cambridge University Press 2013); Laurens Lavrysen, 'European Asylum Law and the ECHR: An Uneasy Coexistence' (2012) 4 Goettingen Journal of International Law 197.

96 It has heatedly been debated in the context of the CJEU's *Kadi* ruling – Joined Cases C-402/05 P and C-415/05 P *Yassin Abdullah Kadi Al Barakaat International Foundation v Council of the European Union and Commission of the European Communities* [2008] ECR II-03649. For criticism, see, eg, Federico Casolari, 'Giving Indirect Effect to International Law Within the EU Legal Order: The Doctrine of Consistent Interpretation' in Enzo

although one of the aspects of that debate, the EU's accession to the ECHR[97] is related to asylum law, given that the CJEU is visibly worried about differences between its own rulings and those of the European Court of Human Rights (ECtHR) in respect of returns under the Dublin Regulation.[98] What is at stake is in this context is not only the distribution of judicial review among member states, EU courts and the ECtHR, but also the engagement with, and development of, international law as an important part of the international rule of law.

In respect of EU asylum law and international refugee law, meanwhile, the stakes are high too. The EU not only has to be accountable to the 1951 Convention, but as a group of states with common minimum standards, it is also among the most important legal actors influencing the Convention's future.

To conclude, EU asylum law is situated in a multilayer system of norms – norms of international refugee and human rights law apply in parallel, making it plausible to assume that they complement each other or diverge on the research puzzle. This interaction is particularly worthy of academic exploration given the EU's special position in the international regime on asylum.

1.5 Research Questions and Structure of the Book

To reiterate, the term 'protection' is at the heart of several features of EU asylum law: practice and reform considerations that make the need for 'international protection' contingent on lack of protection in another state than the state of nationality and parts of the eligibility criteria that relate to a risk of harm to lacking protection in the country of origin. These issues are also connected by the notion of 'surrogacy'.

Cannizzaro, Paolo Palchetti and Ramses A. Wessel (eds), *International law as law of the European Union* (Martinus Nijhoff Publishers 2012) 397.

97 See, eg, Louise Halleskov Storgaard, 'EU Law Autonomy Versus European Fundamental Rights Protection – On Opinion 2/13 on EU Accession to the ECHR' (2015) 15 Human Rights Law Review 485; Mattias Wendel, 'Der EMRK-Beitritt als Unionsrechtsverstoß: Zur völkerrechtlichen Öffnung der EU und ihren Grenzen' (2015) 13 *Die Neue Juristische Wochenshrift* 921. For a list of criticism, see Daniel Halberstam, ''It's the Autonomy, Stupid!' A Modest Defense of Opinion 2/13 on EU Accession to the ECHR, and the Way Forward' (2015) 16 German Law Journal 105.

98 *Opinion 2/13 on the accession of the European Union to the Convention for the Protection of Human Rights and Fundamental Freedoms* ECLI:EU:C:2014:2454 [2014] digital reports, para 189.

Scholarship has examined single issues in the analysis of available 'protection' for some time, in particular in respect of the international law requirements of the 1951 Convention. Thus, there has been debate not only about the meaning of the term 'protection' in Article 1A(2); the requirements of Article 1A(2) in cases of harm by non-state actors,[99] and beyond,[100] but also on the legality and requirements of the IPA,[101] the international law safeguards on 'protection elsewhere',[102] and, in the EU context, the question whether non-state

99 Eg, Elizabeth Adijin-Tettey, 'Failure of State Protection within the Context of the Convention Refugee Regime with Particular Reference to Gender-Related Persecution' (1997) 3 Journal of International Legal Studies 53; Deborah Anker, Lauren Gilbert, and Nancy Kelly, 'Women Whose Government are Unable or Unwilling to Provide Reasonable Protection From Domestic Violence May Qualify as Refugee Under United States Asylum Law' (1997) 11 Georgetown Immigration Law Journal, 709; Walter Kälin, 'Non-state Agents of Persecution and the Inability of the State to Protect' (2000) 15 Georgetown Immigration Law Journal 415; Jennifer Moore, 'From Nation State to Failed State: International Protection from Human Rights Abuses by Non-State Agents' (1999) 31 Columbia Human Rights Law Review 81; Catherine Phuong, 'Persecution by Non-state Agents: Comparative Judicial Interpretations of the 1951 Refugee Convention' (2002) 4 European Journal Migration and Law 521; Daniel Wilsher, 'Non-State Actors and the Definition of a Refugee in the United Kingdom: Protection, Accountability or Culpability?' (2003) 15 International Journal of Refugee Law 68; Penelope Mathew, James C Hathaway and Michelle Foster, 'The Role of State Protection in Refugee Analysis' (2003) 15 International Journal of Refugee Law 444; Helen Lambert, 'The Conceptualisation of "Persecution" by the House of Lords: Horvath v. Secretary of State for the Home Department' (2001) 13 International Journal of Refugee Law 16.

100 In respect of protection against harm, see the Chapter 'State Protection' in James C. Hathaway and Michelle Foster, *The Law of Refugee Status* (2nd edn, Cambridge University Press 2014).

101 Jonah Eaton, 'The Internal Protection Alternative Under European Union Law: Examining the Recast Qualification Directive' (2012) 24 International Journal of Refugee Law 765; Bríd Ní Ghráinne, 'The Internal Protection Alternative Inquiry and Human Rights Considerations – Irrelevant or Indispensable?' (2015) 27 International Journal of Refugee Law 29; James C Hathaway and Michelle Foster, 'Internal Protection/Relocation/Flight Alternative as an Aspect of Refugee Status Determination' in Erika Feller and others (eds), *Refugee Protection in International Law* (Cambridge University Press 2003) as well as the IPA Chapter in *The Law of Refugee Status* (ibid); Jessica Schultz and Terje Einarsen, 'The Right to Refugee Status and the Internal Protection Alternative: What does the Law Say?' in David J Cantor (ed), *Human Rights and the Refugee Definition – Comparative Legal Practice and Theory* (Brill 2016); Penelope Mathew, 'The Shifting Boundaries and Content of Protection: The Internal Protection Alternative Revisited' in Satvinder Juss (ed), *The Ashgate Research Companion to Migration Law, Theory and Policy* (Ashgate 2013).

102 Eg, Hemme Battjes, *European Asylum Law and International Law* (Martinus Nijhoff 2006); Stephen H. Legomsky, 'Secondary Refugee Movements and the Return of Asylum Seekers to Third Countries: The Meaning of Effective Protection' (2003) 15 International Journal of Refugee Law 567, 620; Violetta Moreno-Lax, 'The Legality of the "Safe Third Country" Notion Contested: Insights from the Law of Treaties' in Guy S Goodwin-Gill and Philippe

actors can be actors of the protection.[103] However, there is to date no overarching study that demonstrates whether and how these issues are connected, and allows pinpointing systematic incoherence and instances of norm conflict in the EU context.[104]

Against this background, this book seeks to systematise the different legal concepts of 'protection' in EU asylum law, as contained in the Qualification Directive and the Procedures Directive, that is protection against harm (Arts. 6–7, Qualification Directive), the Internal Protection Alternative (Article 9, Qualification Directive) and protection in third countries (Articles 35, 38 Procedures Directive). The book carves out the normative differences and similarities in these concepts, enquires how obligations of international human rights law and refugee law interplay in the respective legal provisions and, where relevant, questions their compliance with international law. Ultimately, and against the background of a plethora of different uses of the term 'protection',[105] this work seeks to contribute to greater clarity on the use of one of the most central terms of asylum law.

The book seeks to answer the following research questions:

Research Question 1: How does EU law, in line with international law, circumscribe protection in countries of origin, in EU countries of asylum and in countries of asylum outside the EU (third countries)?

1.1. (How) do human rights affect the scope of international protection in the EU Qualification Directive and the relevance of 'protection' in the 1951 Convention's refugee definition?

1.2. How do the legal requirements for the concepts of 'protection' in the country of origin (protection against harm, Internal Protection Alternative)

Weckel (eds), *Migration & Refugee Protection in the 21st Century: Legal Aspects* (Martinus Nijhoff 2015), 687.

103 Maria O'Suillivan, 'Acting the Part: Can Non-State Entities Provide Protection Under International Refugee Law?' (2012) 24 International Journal of Refugee Law 85.

104 The most comprehensive overarching reflections are Cantor, 'Defining Refugees: Persecution, Surrogacy and the Human Rights Paradigm' (Ch 1 n 17) and Dallal Stevens, 'What Do We Mean by Protection?' (2013) 20 International Journal on Minority and Group Rights 233. In respect of single issues, the IPA comprehensively has been assessed by Schultz, *The Internal Protection Alternative in Refugee Law* (Ch 1 n 16). For commentary on relevant instruments of EU asylum law, a comprehensive resource is Kay Hailbronner, Daniel Thym, *EU Immigration and Asylum Law – A Commentary* (Ch 1 n 7).

105 Stevens (ibid, at 259) posited that 'Notwithstanding the undoubted centrality of "protection" to the refugee condition, its meaning remains somewhat elusive. This is due, on the one hand, to an inability to determine the fundamental obligation at the core of protection, and, on the other, to the range of actors involved in delivering protection.'

compare legally to those in asylum countries (international protection and 'protection elsewhere') and do these requirements differ for refugee status and subsidiary protection status?

Research Question 2: In light of the interplay of human rights law and refugee law in these three contexts, does EU law succeed in harmonising international law compliant standards?

2.1. What role do human rights play in gauging the availability of 'protection' in the country of origin or elsewhere?
2.2. Which actors are legally capable of providing protection in the country of origin and in third countries?
2.3. Does the Qualification Directive succeed in harmonising international law-compliant 'actor of protection', IPA and 'protection elsewhere' (safe third country and first country of asylum) concepts?
2.4. How do the common standards for refugees and beneficiaries of subsidiary protection in Article 7 and Article 8 of the Qualification Directive influence international law compliance?

To answer these questions, the book will address one concept of 'protection' after the other. Given the notion of surrogacy links 'international protection' to lacking national, or 'domestic' protection, Chapter 2 addresses international protection. Chapter 3 analyses protection against harm, while Chapter 4 is concerned with the Internal Protection Alternative. Finally, Chapter 5 addresses the EU Procedures Directive's rules on protection in third counties, that is, non-EU states. The remainder of the introduction will lay out the research style.

1.6 Research Style

The following section briefly lays out the research style, that is, the type of approach underlying the research questions. Harry Arthurs has differentiated between several legal research styles that fittingly illustrate the very basic strands of legal research, even though their boundaries can at times be blurry: doctrinal methodology as opposed to interdisciplinary methodology on the one hand, and 'applied' research styles as opposed to 'pure' research styles on the other.[106] The book adopts a doctrinal, applied approach; it is 'in the law'

---

106 Social Sciences and Humanities Research Council of Canada, Law and Learning/Le droit et le savoir: Report of the Consultative Group on Research and Education in Law (Ottawa: The Council, 1983), cited in Paul Chynoweth, 'Legal Research' in Andrew Knight

rather than about the law as a 'social entity.'[107] Doctrinal approaches are concerned with, among others, issues of consistency of legal norms, hierarchies of norms and compliance.

Dogmatic approaches use a set of legal interpretation rules and principles which, however, vary in respect of different bodies of law relevant in this book. In particular, the principles of EU law interpretation vary from that of international law, the interpretation of which is governed by the treaty interpretation rules of the Vienna Convention on the Laws of Treaties (VCLT).[108] Given there are no express interpretation rules and principles in EU law, and given EU law is autonomous from the legal orders of the member states, the Court of Justice of the EU has relied not on the VCLT but on general interpretation principles consensual in member states. These include in particular grammatical, systematic, teleological and historic methods of interpretation,[109] with the court having a tendency to favour grammatical and teleological methods.[110] The discussion of these methods of interpretation is streamlined, where relevant, into Chapters 2–5. The same is true for the methods of interpretation of international law which, in contrast to EU law, is guided by the VCLT.

Within the doctrinal approach of this book, the starting point in the analysis will always be the respective legal norm(s) of EU secondary law. Given that EU asylum law has to be in accordance with international law, norms of international law are, to the extent possible, woven into the analysis of EU law, rather than exploring international law standards in a standalone fashion.

At several points, the book makes recourse to jurisprudence from within and outside the EU for comparative legal analysis. In particular, domestic legal acts as well as jurisprudence of selected EU member states are included either

---

and Les Ruddock (eds), *Advanced Research Methods in the Built Environment* (Wiley-Blackwell 2008) 29.

107 Ibid 30.

108 Vienna Convention on the Law of Treaties (adopted 23 May 1969, entry into force 27 January 1980) 115 UNTS 331, Articles 31-33.

109 The methods were articulated originally for the Gernan Civil Law system by Friedrich Carl von Savigny, *System des heutigen Römischen Rechts* (vol 1, Berlin 1840) 213. The CJEU approach was laid out for EU law generally in *Merck v Hauptzollamt Hamburg-Jonas*, Case C-292/82 [1983] ECR-3781 para 12. For the interpretation of EU law, see, eg, Gunnar Beck, *The Legal Reasoning of the Court of Justice of the EU* (Hart Publishing 2012).

110 Hannes Rösler, 'Interpretation of EU Law', in Jürgen Basedow, Klaus Hopt, Reinhard Zimmermann (eds), *The Max Planck Encyclopedia of European Private Law* (Oxford University Press 2012) 979.

as examples of subsequent practice, serving to identify a predominant interpretation of a legal rule, or as a *prima facie* indication of whether or not EU law has successfully harmonised legal standards that conform with international law. It is beyond the scope of this research, however, to include a detailed analysis of the respective jurisdictions' national asylum systems as anchored in their respective national constitutional norms.

While subsequent practice is not an interpretative tool for EU (asylum) law, it does play a role in the interpretation of 1951 Convention. For the Convention, subsequent practice is to be taken into account in addition to the context, as part of the general rule of treaty interpretation of Article 31, Vienna Convention on the Laws of Treaties, binding all EU member states. According to the International Law Commission's Draft Articles on Subsequent Agreements and Practice, subsequent practice contribute 'in their interaction with other means of interpretation, to the clarification of the meaning of a treaty', which 'may result in narrowing, widening, or otherwise determining the range of possible interpretations'.[111] However, caution is appropriate in considering subsequent practice for the 1951 Convention and human rights treaties generally, given states owe their obligations to individuals as well as to the international community,[112] and shall not restrict the scope of their obligations.[113]

Although the book does not aim to test the influence of independent variables on the outcome of asylum decisions, the selection of countries aims at diversity in respect of potentially relevant factors affecting jurisprudence on the determination of refugee status generally. This concerns the legal system, the opt-in and transposition of the first Qualification Directive from 2004, as well as the opt-in of the current recast Qualification Directive. These factors are not empirically tested, but rather serve to avoid selection bias. The factors are weighted against the accessibility of case law and linguistic accessibility. In particular, Central, Eastern and Southern European jurisprudence is hardly accessible in searchable databases. In the result, case law from Denmark, France, Germany, the Netherlands and Sweden is included in the analysis.

111 International Law Commission, Subsequent agreements and subsequent practice in relation to the interpretation of treaties, Text of the draft conclusions provisionally adopted by the Drafting Committee on first reading, 6 June 2016, A/CN.4/L.874.

112 For human rights as *erga omnes* obligations, see Christian J. Tams, *Enforcing Obligations Erga Omnes in International Law* (Cambridge University Press 2010) 119–121, 132–133.

113 See James C. Hathaway, *The Rights of Refugees under International Law* (Oxford University Press 2005) 68-74.

TABLE 1 Country-selection – diversity

	Legal system	Opt-in 2004 qualification directive	Transposition of articles 6–7, 9 of 2004 qualification directive	Opt-in recast qualification directive
Germany	German civil law	Yes	Yes	Yes
United Kingdom	Common law	Yes	Yes	No
Netherlands	Civil law/ common law/ independence	Yes	Yes	Yes
Sweden	Scandinavian civil law	Yes	Yes	Yes
France	French civil law	Yes	Yes	Yes
Denmark	Scandinavian civil law	No	N/A (opt-out)	No

Depending on the available case law databases, searches included all judicial decisions after the initial status determination by the respective domestic status determination authority (eg, Germany) or only the final instance (eg, Sweden).

CHAPTER 2

International Protection vs. 'Domestic' Protection

2.1 Introduction

This chapter explores the origins of the notion of 'surrogacy', according to which international protection is linked to lacking protection in the home country. First, it enquires about the content of international protection, EU jargon for the entitlements for refugees and beneficiaries of subsidiary protection.[1] Second, the chapter will relate this EU law understanding of international protection to the entitlements under international law, and discuss whether and how international protection relates to 'domestic' protection.

The chapter will argue that the Qualification Directive's entitlements for refugee and subsidiary status ('international protection') reflect the influence of international human rights law. The influence of human rights law is also mirrored in the 1951 Convention: In particular, it has facilitated a human rights-informed concept of 'surrogate' international protection, needed when domestic protection is lacking. This understanding has implications for the meaning of the term 'protection' in the Convention's refugee definition, which has shifted to no longer function as an inclusion criterion independent of, and additional to the requirement of a 'well-founded fear of being persecuted'.

Chapters 1 lays the groundwork for Chapters 2, 3 and 4, which will discuss how the protection should and should not be construed in various contexts of status determination.

2.2 The Meaning of 'International Protection'

2.2.1 *The Content of Refugee and Subsidiary Statuses under the EU Qualification Directive*

Individuals who fulfil the eligibility criteria for refugee or subsidiary status[2] receive 'international protection' in EU member states. So as to later contrast

1 According to Article 1 Qualification Directive, the purpose of the Directive is to 'lay down standards for the qualification of third-country nationals or stateless persons as beneficiaries of international protection, for a uniform status for refugees or for persons eligible for subsidiary protection, and for the content of the protection granted'.

2 See above, 1.3. For the particular aspects of eligibility criteria relating to protection, see Chapters 3 and 4.

 DOI:10.1163/9789004430396_003

international protection with domestic protection, the following sections explore how EU asylum law circumscribes international protection and in particular how entitlements for refugees and beneficiaries of subsidiary protection under EU asylum law overlap with obligations under refugee and human rights law. Rather than mapping out gaps or norm conflicts arising from the practical application of these entitlements, this section addresses the black letter commitments under the Qualification Directive and respective international instruments, so as to demonstrate the extent to which extent 'international protection' is informed by obligations of international law.

The Qualification Directive is concerned both with the eligibility criteria for refugee and subsidiary status, and with the content of those statuses (international protection). The Qualification Directive's chapter VII on the 'Content of International Protection' lays out a catalogue of minimum entitlements following from recognition of status.[3] These apply to status holders across the board, albeit there are special obligations for member states on the representation, care and well-being of unaccompanied minors, and special regard is due, after individual evaluation, to the specific situation of vulnerable persons.[4]

On the most basic level, entitlements concern the legality of residence or legal protection in a more narrow sense: refugees and beneficiaries of subsidiary protection shall not be returned (non-refoulement) unless in case of danger to the security of the respective member state or after conviction of a particular serious crime, and if international law so allows.[5] This is closely connected to an entitlement to a residence permit, to be granted as soon as possible after recognition of status,[6] the granting of travel documents,[7] as well as information on the rights and obligations of their status.[8]

A second set of entitlements concerns maintaining family unity and the entitlements of family members not qualifying for international protection.[9]

---

3 On the content of international protection, see Hemme Battjes, 'Content of International Protection' in Hailbronner, Thym, *EU Immigration and asylum Law: A Commentary* (Ch n 7) 1248–1280.

4 Article 20(3)–(4). Special regard due to the 'specific situation of vulnerable persons such as minors, unaccompanied minors, disabled people, elderly people, pregnant women, single parents with minor children, victims of human trafficking, persons with mental disorders and persons who have been subjected to torture, rape or other serious forms of psychological, physical or sexual violence.'

5 Article 21 Qualification Directive.

6 Article 24 Qualification Directive.

7 Article 25 Qualification Directive.

8 Article 22 Qualification Directive.

9 Article 23 Qualification Directive.

A third set of entitlements revolves around socio-economic integration and self-reliance. In particular, the Qualification Directive warrants access to procedures for recognition of professional qualifications, access to employment and self-employment, vocational training and retraining on a par with nationals, freedom of movement within the member states, on a par with other third-country nationals legally staying, and access to integration facilities.[10]

A fourth set of entitlement is about social protection and access to basic services, including access to education, health care, social welfare, accommodation on a par with other third-country nationals, and non-discrimination in respect of laws on 'access to social security systems relating to employed or self-employed'.[11] Finally, a stand-alone entitlement is assistance with voluntary repatriation.[12]

In sum, 'international protection' is a set of entitlements in particular on the legality of residence, socio-economic integration/self-reliance and access to basic services, which are granted to both refugees and beneficiaries of subsidiary protection. To what extent do these entitlements overlap with those granted to refugees under the 1951 Convention?

2.2.2 *The Qualification Directive's Content of 'International Protection' in Comparison with the 1951 Convention*

The content of international protection under Chapter VII of the Qualification Directive is, according to Article 20(1), Qualification Directive, 'without prejudice to the rights laid down in the [...] [1951] Convention'. Examining how the rights conferred by Chapter VII Qualification Directive compare to those under the 1951 Convention will help to gauge the international law influence on the notion of 'international protection'. While from the international law perspective the Directive does not need to include norms that grant contracting parties a wider margin of consideration,[13] it would seem to require congruence

---

10 Articles 26(1)-(3); 28; 33; 34 Qualification Directive.

11 Articles 27; 29; 30; 26(4) Qualification Directive.

12 Article 35 Qualification Directive.

13 The Convention does include entitlements that are clearly less strongly worded than others. For example, Article 28(2) requires: 'The Contracting States *shall issue* to refugees lawfully staying in their territory travel documents for the purpose of travel outside their territory, unless compelling reasons of national security or public order otherwise require, and the provisions of the Schedule to this Convention shall apply with respect to such documents. The Contracting States *may issue* such a travel document to any other refugee in their territory; they *shall in particular give sympathetic consideration* to the issue of such a travel document to refugees in their territory who are unable to obtain a travel document from the country of their lawful residence' (emphasis added).

with all mandatory norms of the Convention which are not imposed by other EU secondary law, given the Directive contains minimum standards of member states.

The norms of the 1951 Convention can be structured into three areas: the eligibility criteria for refugee status (Article 1), the substantive rights attached to refugee status (Articles 2–34), and the effectiveness of the Convention (Articles 35–43). The overlap between the eligibility criteria of the Qualification Directive and the wording of the refugee definition in Article 1A(2) have already been mentioned and are most prominently acknowledged in EU asylum law.[14] Particular aspects of that overlap will be examined in detail in Chapters 3 and 4. However, there is also overlap in respect of the substantive rights under the Convention. That overlap can be demonstrated by looking at the substantive areas of Articles 2–34 in conjunction with what has been called the Convention's 'structure of entitlement'.[15] The 1951 Convention's catalogue of rights and obligations depends on and grows with the level of attachment with the asylum state. While the Convention includes some obligations in respect of those refugees who are merely under a state party's jurisdiction,[16] other obligations require physical presence, lawful presence, lawful stay or durable residence by the refugee.[17] The meaning of these concepts is, according to James Hathaway, 'defined by practical circumstances rather than by any official decision or status',[18] because of the declaratory nature of recognition of refugee status.[19] For the Qualification Directive's concept of 'international protection', all of these obligations are relevant, given that the concept circumscribes the substantive rights of all those falling within the eligibility criteria for refugee status and subsidiary protection. In particular, the 1951 Convention contains obligations on non-discrimination (Article 3); freedom of religion (Article 4); freedom of association (Article 15); freedom of movement (Article 26) and provision of travel documents (Article 28); access

14 Article 78(1), TFEU, Recital 3 and Article 21 Qualification Directive.

15 Hathaway, *The Rights of Refugees under International Law* (Ch 1 n 113) 154.

16 For a discussion of jurisdiction in the more contested contexts of refugee law, see, eg, Thomas Gammeltoft-Hansen, *Access to Asylum – International Refugee Law and the Globalisation of Migration Control* (Cambridge University Press 2011); Seunghwan Kim, 'Non-Refoulement and Extraterritorial Jurisdiction: State Sovereignty and Migration Controls at Sea in the European Context' (2007) 30 Leiden Journal of International Law 1. Beyond the refugee law context, see Marko Milanovic, *Extraterritorial Application of Human Rights Treaties: Law, Principles and Policy* (Oxford University Press 2013).

17 Hathaway, *The Rights of Refugees under International Law* (Ch 1 n 113).

18 Ibid 198.

19 See below, 5.3.1.

to courts (Article 16); exemption from exceptional measures against fellow nationals of the refugee (Article 8); artistic rights, movable and immovable property (Articles 13–14); employment (Articles 17–19); access to rationing systems, housing, public education, public relief and assistance, labour legislation and social security (Articles 20–24); as well as facilitation of naturalisation (Article 34).

Although the Convention generally seeks to establish for refugees a treatment 'as favourable as possible', its minimum standard is that of non-discrimination with other 'aliens generally in the same circumstances'[20] or 'the most favourable treatment accorded to nationals of a foreign country, in the same circumstances'.[21] However, the highest standard of treatment, 'as favourable as that accorded to their nationals', does extend to a number of particularly sensitive areas, including freedom of religion; access to a rationing system, public relief and social security; employment; and elementary education.

Chapter VII of the Qualification Directive corresponds to multiple 1951 Convention provisions, such as on travel documents, employment, and access to health, education and welfare. Some provisions appear to vary in respect of the standard of entitlement or the level of attachment required. For instance, while in respect of access to accommodation, the 1951 Convention requires contracting parties to '[…] accord to refugees lawfully staying in their territory treatment as favourable as possible and, in any event, not less favourable than that accorded to aliens generally in the same circumstances',[22] the Directive only foresees treatment on a par with third country nationals.[23] What is more, the 1951 Convention demands contracting parties to accord to refugees a number of entitlements, such as non-refoulement and freedom of movement, once they are either *within the jurisdiction* or *lawfully in the territory*,[24] thus even

20 Eg, Article 18.

21 Eg, Article 15 of the 1951 Convention.

22 On the meaning of the notion 'in the same circumstances', see Article 6 of the Convention, according to which '[…] the term "in the same circumstances" implies that any requirements (including requirements as to length and conditions of sojourn or residence) which the particular individual would have to fulfil for the enjoyment of the right in question, if he were not a refugee, must be fulfilled by him, with the exception of requirements which by their nature a refugee is incapable of fulfilling.'

23 Article 32 Qualification Directive. On this point see the comments of the UN High Commissioner for Refugees, *UNHCR Annotated Comments on the EC Council Directive 2004/83/EC of 29 April 2004* <https://www.unhcr.org/43661eee2.pdf> accessed 1 July 2019.

24 Article 26 of the 1951 Convention.

before a formal recognition of status. In contrast, the Chapter VII Qualification Directive generally speaks of 'beneficiaries of international protection' or clarifies that entitlements are to be granted *after* recognition of status,[25] so that the Convention's parallel applicability is an important backup to entitlements under the Qualification Directive. Finally, the Directive does omit some entitlements from the 1951 Convention, most importantly Article 34 on naturalisation.

While the Directive does not have equivalent rules for all of Articles 2–34 of the Convention, Chapter VII also goes beyond the 1951 Convention in multiple ways. First, it contains rules that find no corresponding provision in the 1951 Convention. On employment, the Convention requires a minimum of three years of residence before restrictive measures are not applied. In contrast, the Directive provides for full access to employment.[26] The Directive also exceeds the Convention in respect of rules for family unity. While Recommendation B of the Final Act of the Conference of Plenipotentiaries advised contracting parties to take measures for the protection of the refugee's family, in particular in cases of separated families, the issue does not appear in the Convention.[27] Similarly, the Directive prescribes access to the full education system for minors, rather than merely to the elementary school system, as required by Article 22 of the Convention. Finally, the Directive warrants access to the health system and integration facilities and contains standards of treatment for unaccompanied minors, neither of which are mentioned in the Convention.

The second way in which the Directive exceed the 1951 Convention is by applying to EU asylum law's different legal statuses. With some exceptions, entitlements are the same for refugees and beneficiaries of subsidiary protection.[28] As the CJEU pointed out in *Alo and Osso*, except where the Qualification Directive includes an express provision that refugees and beneficiaries of subsidiary protection status should not be subject to the same rules under Chapter VII of the Directive, those rules (which by the majority stem from the 1951 Convention) apply to both groups.[29] Thus, the Qualification Directive differentiates

25 Eg, Article 22 Qualification Directive. A notable exception is the norm of non-refoulement in Article 21, where no such requirement is written into the provision and member states are required to '[…] respect the principle of non-refoulement in accordance with their international obligations.'

26 Articles 17 of the Convention and Article 26 of the Directive respectively.

27 In respect of refugees, Council Directive 2003/86/EC of 22 September 2003 on the right to family reunification [2003] OJ L251.

28 Article 20(2) Qualification Directive.

29 *Kreis Warendorf v Ibrahim Alo and Amira Osso v Region Hannover* (Ch 1 n 55) paras 22–37.

between the two statuses only in respect of residence permits,[30] travel documents,[31] and allows member states, by way of derogation, to 'limit social assistance granted to beneficiaries of subsidiary protection status to core benefits'.[32] However, the other entitlements in all substantive areas mentioned above are identical. Indeed, the 2011 Qualification Directive has further approached the content of statuses. Thus, the 2004 Qualification Directive,[33] arising from the first phase of lawmaking on the Common European Asylum System (CEAS), and still applicable in some member states, contains additional differences in treatment in relation to benefits of family members of beneficiaries of subsidiary protection, the provision of travel documents, and access to employment.[34] In other words, the common concept of 'international protection' in the Qualification Directive has approximated the content of both statuses.[35] According to the preamble,

> [...] with the exception of derogations which are necessary and objectively justified, beneficiaries of subsidiary protection status should be granted the same rights and benefits as those enjoyed by refugees under this Directive, and should be subject to the same conditions of eligibility.[36]

In brief, the Qualification Directive is clearly modelled after 1951 Convention obligations. However, it also omits refugee entitlements under the Conventions while going beyond others, in particular by conferring rights on individuals who do not come within the ambit *ratione personae* of the Convention. As the next section will demonstrate, these differences can partly be explained by other international law obligations beyond the 1951 Convention, notably of human rights law.

30 Article 24 Qualification Directive.

31 Article 25 Qualification Directive specifies that the residency permit for a refugee must be valid for at least three years and be renewable, while beneficiaries of subsidiary protection receive a permit valid for at least one year, and in case of renewal at least two years.

32 Article 29 Qualification Directive.

33 Council Directive 2004/83/EC of 29 April 2004 on minimum standards for the qualification and status of third country nationals or stateless persons as refugees or as persons who otherwise need international protection and the content of the protection granted [2004] OJ L304/12.

34 Articles 23, 25 and 26 Qualification Directive.

35 On this issue, see also Jürgen Bast, 'Vom subsidiären Schutz zum europäischen Flüchtlingsbegriff' (2018) 14 Zeitschrift für Ausländerrecht und Ausländerpolitik 41.

36 Recital 39.

2.2.3 *Comparing the Qualification Directive's Content of International Protection to International Human Rights Law and the EU Charter of Fundamental Rights*

The omission of single entitlements under the 1951 Convention and the extension of many to beneficiaries of international protection raises the question how other bodies of law complement the Directive's Chapter VII. These are, in particular, obligations of international human rights law[37] and the EU Charter of Fundamental Rights, which is to be respected for its legal value as primary EU law.[38] Before looking at how this plays out for particular norms of Chapter VII of the Directive, this section elaborate on the general scope and nature of obligations under human rights laws.

Generally, obligations of international human rights law have a different scope than those of both the Directive and the 1951 Convention. First, there is only one level of attachment relevant to the applicability of human rights treaties, and there is no eligibility definition: Most treaties apply to *all individuals within the territory and subject to the jurisdiction* of a state party, rather than being tied to particular circumstances of residence or stay. While the ICCPR, for instance, in limited cases circumscribes rights of entry to or residence in a state party,[39] as a general rule it applies without discrimination between nationals and non-nationals. According to the HRC's guidance on Article 2(1) of the ICCPR:

> [...] the enjoyment of Covenant rights is not limited to citizens of States Parties but must also be available to *all individuals, regardless of nationality or statelessness, such as asylum seekers, refugees, migrant workers and other persons, who may find themselves in the territory or subject to the jurisdiction of the State Party.*[40]

37 For a rationale on the applicability of human rights law, see above, Section 1.4.2.

38 According to Article 6(1) TEU, the Charter 'shall have the same legal value as the Treaties'. In addition, according to Article 67 TFEU – the general provision on the Area of Freedom, Security and Justice, which includes asylum policies – the Union shall 'respect fundamental rights'. The Charter is hence the yardstick for secondary law, which is also recognised by, inter alia, the Qualification Directive and the Procedures Directive – both provide for respect for fundamental rights and observance of the principles of the Charter (Recitals 10 and 60 of the Qualification Directive and Procedures Directive respectively).

39 Human Rights Committee, 'CCPR General Comment No 15: The Position of Aliens Under the Covenant', UN Doc HRI/GEN/1/Rev.1, 18 (1994) para 5.

40 Human Rights Committee, 'General Comment No 31: The Nature of the General Legal Obligation Imposed on State Parties to the Covenant' CCPR/Rev.1/Add. 13 para 8.

Given that other human rights treaties are also couched in the language of the ICCPR, this principle of jurisdiction, irrespective of nationality, applies to other human rights treaties too.[41] What is more, the applicability to *everyone* under the jurisdiction of a state party means that international human rights treaties have far greater scope *ratione personae* than the 1951 Convention. Similarly, while the EU Charter of Fundamental Rights applies only when EU institutions, bodies and member states apply EU law, the Charter's rights clearly apply to 'everyone' rather than a subset of persons defined by eligibility criteria.

Second, international human rights treaties circumscribe a triadic framework of obligations to *respect, protect* and *fulfil* the substantive rights, which often provide for a higher standard than the 1951 Convention. States' obligations under human rights treaties are above all obligations of *respect*, thus imposing a *negative obligation* to refrain from any act that infringes on a human right.[42] Such negative obligations apply immediately for both civil and political, and economic, social and cultural rights.[43] In particular, the CESCR has stated in relation to a number of Covenant provisions that immigration status is not a permissible ground of differential treatment.[44] Human rights treaties also include *positive obligations*, comprising measures to prevent, punish or redress harm or maltreatment relevant to the treaty. The obligation to respect

41 Eg, Article 2(1) CAT; Article 2(1) CRC. The ICESCR contains no jurisdiction clause comparable to the ICCPR, but at least the territorial dimension of jurisdiction is, in contrast to the extraterritorial dimension, uncontested, given the omission of such a clause.

42 Human Rights Committee, 'General Comment No 31' (Ch 2 n 40) para 6.

43 The ESC Committee has stressed since the 1990s that all provisions of the Convention entailed minimum core obligations that were not subject to progressive realisation but had to be immediately realised, see Committee on Economic Social and Cultural Rights, General Comment No 3 – 'The nature of States parties obligations (Art 2, para 1)'. UN Doc. E/1991/23 (1990) para 10.

44 Committee on Economic Social and Cultural Rights, 'General Comment No 14, The right to the highest attainable standard of health (article 12 of the International Covenant on Economic, Social and Cultural Rights)', UN Doc E/C.12/2000/4 para 34: 'In particular, States are under the obligation to *respect* the right to health by, *inter alia*, refraining from denying or limiting equal access for all persons, including prisoners or detainees, minorities, asylum seekers and illegal immigrants, to preventive, curative and palliative health services; abstaining from enforcing discriminatory practices as a State policy; and abstaining from imposing discriminatory practices relating to women's health status and needs'; Committee on Economic Social and Cultural Rights, 'General Comment No 20: Non-discrimination in economic, social and cultural rights (art 2, para 2)', UN Doc E/C.12/GC/20 (2009), para 30; Committee on Economic Social and Cultural Rights, 'General Comment No 3: The nature of States parties' obligations (ibid), which mentions education.

thereby circumscribes state liability, by act or by omission, for the acts of non-state actors. According to the HRC:

> [...] the positive obligations on States Parties to ensure Covenant rights will only be fully discharged if individuals are protected by the State, not just against violations of Covenant rights by its agents, but also against acts committed by private persons or entities that would impair the enjoyment of Covenant rights in so far as they are amenable to application between private persons or entities. There may be circumstances in which a failure to ensure Covenant rights as required by article 2 would give rise to violations by States Parties of those rights, as a result of States Parties' permitting or *failing to take appropriate measures or to exercise due diligence to prevent, punish, investigate or redress the harm* caused by such acts by private persons or entities.[45]

What do the positive obligations entail? A primary positive obligation, mentioned by some ICCPR provisions, is to protect a substantive right by creating relevant laws.[46] Legislative measures have be commensurate with the threats of harm to a Covenant provision by a non-state actor.[47] By analogy, the CEDAW Committee recommended the design of criminal law in a way that '[...] [acts] with due diligence to prevent and provide redress for crimes that disproportionately or solely affect women'.[48] The ECtHR has been a particular driving force of positive obligations.[49] The court's jurisprudence has specified positive obligations in respect of the ECHR's provisions in concrete case settings in relation to the rights to life; to freedom from torture, inhuman and degrading treatment or punishment; to freedom of association; to family life; and to privacy.[50]

The triadic framework of international human rights law complements the 1951 Convention's Articles 2–34, given that it pertains to substantive minimum standards of human rights law rather than comprising mere rules on how to treat refugees as compared to nationals, as in the majority of Articles 2–34 of the Convention. Thus, human rights also contribute to a change in the content

45 Human Rights Committee, 'General Comment No 31' (Ch 2 n 40) para 8.

46 Some provisions explicitly mention positive obligations, eg, the ICCPR Articles 6, 17, 26.

47 Manfred Nowak, *UN Covenant on Civil and Political Rights: CCPR Comentary* (2nd edn, Engel 2005) 123.

48 Committee on the Elimination of Discrimination against Women, *General recommendation on women's access to justice,* CEDAW/C/GC/33 (2015) para 47.

49 For further discussion of the scope of positive obligations, see Chapter 3, Section 3.3.

50 David J Harris et al, *Law of the European Convention on Human Rights* (Oxford University Press 2009) 19–20.

of international protection under the Convention, which at the outset is, as David Cantor points out, 'a set of rules directed mainly towards clarifying how the refugee [...] must be treated by host State'.[51]

As the scope of human rights for refugees has been explored elsewhere,[52] suffice is to highlight areas in which complementarity is particularly relevant: This includes, first, the 1951 Convention obligations on religion (Article 4) and the right of association (Article 15), for which the ICCPR circumscribes substantive standards. Besides, the non-discrimination clause of the 1951 Convention prescribes equal treatment *among refugees* while human rights treaties prohibit discrimination based on nationality,[53] with few exceptions.[54] Thus, the ECtHR interpreted the ECHR's non-discrimination clause as a bar to different treatment with regard to child benefits for parents with different categories of residence permits.[55]

What is more, human rights law contains civil and political rights that the Convention is silent about, but which have been at the forefront of evolutionary interpretation, including the right to life; freedom from torture, inhuman or degrading treatment; freedom from arbitrary arrest or detention; freedom of speech; or the right to private and family life. The last-mentioned provides a powerful example of additional obligations under human rights law. The HRC has interpreted Article 23 of the ICCPR to include a positive obligation for 'appropriate measures [...] to ensure the unity or reunification of families, particularly when their members are separated for political, economic or similar reasons'.[56] What is more, according to case law of the ECtHR and the CJEU, the

51 David J. Cantor, 'Defining Refugees: Persecution, Surrogacy and the Human Rights Paradigm' (Ch 1 n 17) 370.

52 Cathryn Costello, *Human Rights of Migrants and Refugees in European Law* (Oxford University Press 2016); Hathaway, *The Rights of Refugees under International Law* (Ch 1 n 113).

53 Eg, Article 2(1) ICCPR; Article 2(2) ICESCR; Article 2(1) CRC.

54 Article 2(3) ICESCR allows developing countries to make a distinction between nationals and non-nationals in guaranteeing economic rights.

55 *Niedzwiecki v Germany* App no 58453/00 (ECtHR, 25 October 2005) para 33, 'The Court is not called upon to decide generally to what extent it is justified to make distinctions, in the field of social benefits, between holders of different categories of residence permits. Rather it has to limit itself to the question whether the German law on child benefits as applied in the present case violated the applicant's rights under the Convention. [...] the Court does not discern sufficient reasons justifying the different treatment with regard to child benefits of aliens who were in possession of a stable residence permit on one hand and those who were not, on the other. It follows that there has been a violation of Article 14 in conjunction with Article 8 of the Convention.'

56 Human Rights Committee, *General Comment No 19: The Family (Article 23)*, Compilation of General Comments and General Recommendations Adopted by Human Rights Treaty Bodies, HRI/GEN/1/Rev. 1 (1990) para 5.

ECHR and CFR rights to respect for family and private life (Articles 8 and 7 respectively) may, in certain cases, give rise to an obligation to issue a residence permit to a family member of an alien or an obligation of non-return to another member state.[57] As such, however, the human rights obligations exceed the family unity provision of the Qualification Directive, which only apply for those individuals who hold either refugee or subsidiary protection status.

The norms of human rights law help to explain some of the higher standards in the Qualification Directive than those arising from the 1951 Convention. In respect of economic and social rights, both human rights law and the 1951 Convention appear to have influenced the standards of the Qualification Directive. The ICESCR obligations on access to education (Article 13) exceed those of the Convention. In particular, the Covenant demands access to the full education system, albeit with different forms of progressive realisation for non-primary education, while prohibiting discrimination against non-nationals in guaranteeing the right to education.[58] Likewise, Article 14, CFR, which mirrors the obligations under Article 2, First Protocol of the ECHR,[59] guarantees equal access to education. Thus, the ECtHR has rejected the proposition that access to education could be denied on the basis of immigration status but also made clear that the right to education does not give any entitlements to the issuing of a residence permit.[60]

Similarly to access to education, human rights obligations on access to health care exceed the 1951 Convention. Article 12, ICESCR contains the right to the highest attainable standard of health. According to the Covenant's authoritative monitoring body, the Committee on Economic, Social and Cultural Rights, respecting the right to health warrants state parties to refrain from limiting equal access to 'preventive, palliative and curative health services' for asylum seekers.[61] This would *a fortiori* apply to those individuals whose legal

57 In respect of the ECHR, see Daniel Thym, 'Respect for Private and Family Life under Article 8 ECHR in Immigration Cases: A Human Right to Regularize Illegal Stay?' (2008) 57 The International and Comparative Law Quarterly 87. In respect of the CJEU, C-245/11 *K v Bundesasylamt,* ECLI:EU:C:2012:685 [2012] digital reports. For a discussion on differences between human rights law and the 1951 Convention in respect of family life, see also Alice Edwards, 'Human Rights, Refugees, and the Right "To Enjoy" Asylum' (2005) 17 International Journal of Refugee Law 293.

58 Social Commitee on Economic, and Cultural Rights, *General Comment No 13: The right to education (article 13),* E/C.12/1999/10 (1999) para 34.

59 For the additional personal scope for EU nationals, see Peers, *The EU Charter of Fundamental Rights: A Commentary* (Ch 1 n 65) 14.31.

60 *Timishev v Russia* ECHR 2005-XII 169.

61 Committee on Economic Social and Cultural Rights, 'General Comment No 14, The right to the highest attainable standard of health' (Ch 2 n 44) para 34.

status has been recognised, such as refugees and beneficiaries of subsidiary protection.

On the Qualification Directive's employment norms, however, human rights law is not the source of higher standards. Although Article 6, ICESCR guarantees 'the right of everyone to the opportunity to gain his living by work which he freely chooses or accepts', the core of the provision has in practice been interpreted restrictively and the CESCR has generally been reluctant to brand differential treatment in respect of residence status as a discrimination under the Covenant.[62] Similarly, Article 15, CFR does not enshrine a free-standing right to be granted an authorisation to seek employment, given that Article 15(3), CFR confers rights on third-country nationals who are '*authorised* to work in the territories of the Member States'.[63]

What explains higher standards in Chapter VII, Qualification Directive? To a certain extent, the approximation of rules appears to follow a needs-based rationale. The Commission proposal for the 2004 Qualification Directive had foreseen few differences between the rules on the content of status because of 'the fact that the needs of all persons in need of international protection are broadly similar',[64] a view shared by UNHCR.[65] Based on this needs-based rationale, there were also legal considerations of non-discrimination at play. When the EU Commission presented the proposal for a recast Qualification Directive, it pleaded for a further approximation of status, arguing with non-discrimination and children's rights:

> It is [...] necessary to remove any limitations of the rights of beneficiaries of subsidiary protection which can no longer be considered as necessary and objectively justified. Such an approximation of rights is *necessary to ensure full respect of the principle of non-discrimination*, as interpreted in recent case law of the ECtHR, *and of the UN Convention on the Rights of*

62 Hathaway, *The Rights of Refugees under International Law* (Ch 1 n 113) 740.

63 Emphasis added.

64 Commission of the European Union, 'Proposal for a Council Directive on minimum standards for the qualification and status of third country nationals and stateless persons as refugees or as persons who otherwise need international protection' COM/2001/510 final, 4 (Qualification Directive Proposal 2001).

65 UN High Commissioner for Refugees, 'UNHCR's Observations on the European Commission's Proposal for a Council Directive on Minimum Standards for the Qualification and Status of Third Country Nationals and Stateless Persons as Refugees or as Persons Who Otherwise Need International Protection (COM(2001) 510' final) <https://www.refworld.org/docid/3c6a69254.html> accessed 1 July 2019.

> *the Child*. It responds moreover to the call of the Hague Programme for the creation of a uniform status of protection.[66]

However, differences can also be linked to policy considerations. In the legislative process leading to the adoption of the 2004 Qualification Directive, the Commission explained that differences between the two statuses were needed in order to recognise the 'primacy of the Geneva Convention and the fact that the regime of subsidiary protection starts from the premise that the need for such protection is temporary in nature'.[67] In the negotiation of the Directive, the Council introduced differences between the statuses in respect of the politically sensitive issue of access to welfare. Where governments were in favour of approximating status, it was in order to limit the number of appeals by beneficiaries of subsidiary protection intended.[68]

Above all, however, it is the goal to limit secondary movement between member states that explains approximation of status. The approximation of rules on the content of status had been an explicit aim since the beginnings of the CEAS, with the Tampere Conclusions of the Council providing that, 'in the longer term, Community rules should lead to a common asylum procedure and a uniform status for those who are granted asylum'.[69] The 2004 and Recast

66 Commission of the European Communities, 'Proposal for a Directive of the European Parliament and of the Council on minimum standards for the qualification and status of third country nationals or stateless persons as beneficiaries of international protection and the content of the protection granted' COM/2009/0551 final, 8, emphasis added (Qualification Directive Proposal 2009).

67 Commission of the European Union, '2001 Qualification Directive Proposal' (Ch 1 n 64).

68 Jane McAdam, 'The European Union Qualification Directive: The Creation of a Subsidiary Protection Regime' (2005) 17 International Journal of Refugee Law 461, 498. More recently, in *Bundesrepublik Deutschland v B and D*, the CJEU has put forward similar consideration, arguing that the Qualification Directive's exclusion clause seeks to keep the different sources of status distinct so as to retain the credibility of the international legal regime. Asked to clarify whether EU states could grant protection to individuals excluded from international protection, it stated that the Qualification Directive 'is based on the principle that host Member States may, in accordance with their national law, grant national protection [...]'. However, any other kind of protection outside the scope of the Directive 'must not [...] be confused with refugee status [...]' (para 190). Member states need to make a clear distinction between international protection under the Directive and any other form of protection, because, as Advocate General Mengozzi pointed out in his Opinion, they would otherwise jeopardise the 'credibility of the international system for protecting refugees' Joined Cases C-57/09 and C-101/09 *Bundesrepublik Deutschland v B and D* [2010] ECR I-10979, Opinion of AG Mengozzi, para 105.

69 Originally, the Council intended to approximate only the rules for the recognition and content of refugee status between countries and later achieve a 'uniform status' for

Qualification Directives note that, 'The approximation of rules on the recognition and content of refugee and subsidiary protection status should help to limit the secondary movements of applicants for asylum between Member States, where such movement is purely caused by differences in legal frameworks.'[70]

In sum, while the content of 'international protection' under Chapter VII, Qualification Directive is not entirely congruent with international law obligations (the Directive partly exceeds these obligations given policy considerations on secondary movement), it reflects human rights norms and entitlements under the 1951 Convention. International protection under EU asylum law, thus, *is enfranchisement with 1951 Convention rights and human rights in parallel.* How does this understanding compare to the international law understanding of international protection?

2.2.4 *Human Rights-Informed 'International Protection' and the Rights of Refugees under the 1951 Convention*

Although the Statute of the UNHCR does refer to 'international protection' as the agency's function,[71] the term is not used by the 1951 Convention as an equivalent for Articles 2–34 of the Convention.[72] However, there are ample indications that the Convention is intended to vest refugees with individual entitlements under both the Convention and human rights law, from the text of the Convention in light of its context. The Convention's preamble considers the principle in the UDHR and UN Charter 'that human beings shall enjoy fundamental rights and freedoms without discrimination' and that 'the United Nations has, on various occasions, manifested its profound concern for refugees and endeavoured to assure refugees the widest possible exercise of these fundamental rights and freedoms.' That the Convention attempts to achieve the widest possible scope of entitlements for refugees is also apparent from

refugees and beneficiaries of international protection. See Council of the European Union, *Presidency Conclusions, Tampere European Council, 15–16 October 1999* paras 14–14.

70 Recital 7 and 13 of the 2004 and Recast Qualification Directives respectively.

71 Chapter 1(1), Statute of the Office of the United Nations High Commissioner for Refugees, 14 December 1950, A/RES/428 (V) (UNHCR Statute).

72 The Convention does, however, refer to 'protection' in multiple contexts – on the refugee definition, see below, Section 2.4. Beyond this, the Convention refers to 'protection accorded by international agreements', in the preamble. The drafters expressed their desire to 'revise and consolidate' previous agreements protecting refugees and noted that the UNHCR is charged with responsibility for existing treaties with that purpose. Furthermore, in Article 15 the Convention uses protection synonyms for the standards of treatment in respect of a specific refugee right.

Article 5, according to which, 'Nothing in this Convention shall be deemed to impair any rights and benefits granted by a Contracting State to refugees apart from this Convention.' Finally, this aim of the Convention is reflected in its 'structure of entitlement',[73] which consists in a carefully calibrated continuum that reserves non-discrimination with nationals only to a sub-set of rights. Likewise, the drafting history shows that delegates to the Conference of Plenipotentiaries did use rights-based language. For instance, the delegates made clear that 'rights and obligations of a citizen of a given country' comprised both economic and social, and political rights.[74] There was also frequent mention that the Convention was intended to guarantee 'minimum rights and guarantees' for refugees.[75] In particular, delegates referred to rights in matters of non-discrimination.[76]

73 Hathaway, *The Rights of Refugees under International Law* (Ch 1 n 113) 154.

74 UN Conference of Plenipotentiaries on the Status of Refugees and Stateless Persons, *Summary Record of the Twenty-third Meeting, 26 November 1951*, A/CONF.2/SR.23, Mr Warren (USA) in response to a question from Baron van Boetzelaer (Netherlands).

75 UN Conference of Plenipotentiaries on the Status of Refugees and Stateless Persons, 'Conference of Plenipotentiaries on the Status of Refugees and Stateless Persons: Summary Record of the Nineteenth Meeting', UN Doc A/CONF.2/SR.19, statement by Mr Hoare (United Kingdom); UN Conference of Plenipotentiaries on the Status of Refugees and Stateless Persons, 'Compte rendu analytique de la vingtième séance', UN Doc A/CONF.2/SR.20 (1951), statement by Mr Hermet (Belgium). See also Ad Hoc Committee on Statelessness and Related Problems, 'Fist Session: Summary Record of the Seventh Meeting', statement by Mr Perozo of Venezuela '[…] [The Convention] would be no less important than the conventions which the United Nations had already adopted or hoped to adopt in the near future, such as those of genocide, prostitution, displaced persons and freedom of the press and information or the Declaration of Human Rights. The convention on refugees was intended to codify in a single document all the existing international instruments on the subject. It would proclaim the rights of refugees and grant them the privileges and facilities resulting from the recognition of their rights'; UN Conference of Plenipotentiaries on the Status of Refugees and Stateless Persons, 'Compte rendu analytique de la deuxième séance', UN Doc A/CONF.2/SR.2, statements by Mr von Truzschler (Federal Republic of Germany) and Mr. Shaw (Australia); UN Conference of Plenipotentiaries on the Status of Refugees and Stateless Persons, 'Summary Record of the Thirtieth Meeting', UN Doc A/CONF.2/SR.30 (1951), statement by Msgr. Comte (The Holy See).

76 UN Conference of Plenipotentiaries on the Status of Refugees and Stateless Persons, 'Conférence de plénipotentiaires sur le statut des réfugiés et des apatrides: Compte rendu analytique de la sixième séance' UN Doc A/CONF.2/SR.6; discussion on non-discrimination or on the right to form trade unions as codified in the UDHR, UN Ad Hoc Committee on Refugees and Stateless Persons, 'First Session: Summary Record of the Twenty-Fourth Meeting', UN Doc E/AC.32/SR.24 (1951); 'Summary Record, of the Tenth Meeting', UN Doc E/AC.32/SR.10 (1950).

That the Convention does not cross refer more to human rights may also be explained by the state of evolution of international law at the time. Indeed, the structure of the international legal order at the time of drafting of the 1951 Convention was still an inter-state order in which individuals had little place. Entitlements of foreigners stemmed primarily from the (historic) branch of international law regulating state responsibility for injuries to aliens.[77] As Chetail points out, a contested issue within that branch of law was the adequate substantive standard of treatment to be accorded to aliens. In particular, it was contested whether customary law only regulated the comparative treatment of nationals and aliens, or whether there was, as Western states contended, a minimum international standard shared by all countries that should not be transgressed, irrespective of how badly a state treated its own nationals.[78] Litigation between states formed a set of guarantees as part of such an international minimum standard, including in respect of physical integrity and life, arbitrary detention, fair trial and ownership of property.[79] States were enforcing such standards by exercising diplomatic protection, thereby asserting their *own (state) right to ensure respect for international law* in respect of their nationals.[80]

International law on state responsibility for injuries to aliens and the guarantees of international minimum standards reflected the state of the law at the time of the 1951 Convention's drafting. In its infancy, however, was a major legal development that would gradually replace applicable law on state responsibility for injuries to aliens: the development of (international) human rights law. The Universal Declaration of Human Rights (UDHR) had been adopted by the UN General Assembly in 1948,[81] and although not binding, it authoritatively listed a broad array of standards recommended by UN member states that 'pledged themselves to achieve […] the promotion of universal respect for and observance of human rights and fundamental freedoms'[82] in the UN Charter.[83]

77 Vincent Chetail, 'The Human Rights of Migrants in General International Law: From Minimum Standards to Fundamental Rights' (2014) 28 Georgetown Immigration Law Journal 225.

78 Ibid.

79 Ibid. Also Annemarieke Vermeer, 'Diplomatic Protection as a Source of Human Rights Law' in Dinah Shelton (ed), *The Oxford Handbook of International Human Rights Law* (Oxford University Press 2013).

80 *Mavrommatis Palestine Concessions Greece v UK* [1924] PCIJ Rep 2.

81 Universal Declaration of Human Rights, UN Doc A/RES/217A (III) of 10 December 1948.

82 Preamble of the UDHR.

83 According to Article 1(3) of the UN Charter, it is a principle of the organisation, 'To achieve international cooperation in solving international problems of an economic, social, cultural, or humanitarian character, and in promoting and encouraging respect for human

Regionally, in 1950 the ECHR marked the first time that states agreed by treaty to guarantee the rights of all individuals within their jurisdiction. The ECHR makes direct reference to the UDHR and states that the parties were 'resolved, [...] to take the first steps for the collective enforcement of certain of the rights stated in the Universal Declaration'.

The substantive minimum standards of human rights have been influenced by the international law on injuries to aliens, but have also largely replaced that law, both and in particular as a source of rights, but also in respect of remedies.[84]

Since the evolution of human rights law, a human rights-informed use of the term 'international protection' is also apparent in the UNHCR Executive Committee (EXCOM) conclusions. These are relevant for the interpretation of the 1951 Convention because they can be regarded as context and as subsequent practice of the Convention, in accordance with Article 31(2)–(3) VCLT.[85]

---

rights and for fundamental freedoms for all without distinction as to race, sex, language, or religion.' See also Paul Weis, *The Refugees Convention, 1951: The Travaux Préparatoires Analysed with a Commentary by Dr. Paul Weis* (Cambridge University Press 1995). Online version made available by UNHCR at <http://www.unhcr.org/4ca34be29.html>. According to the author, 'the Convention is based on humanitarian ideals embellished in the concept of human rights. Indeed, the preamble to the Convention Relating to the Status of Refugees affirms the principle enunciated in the Charter of the United Nations that human beings shall enjoy fundamental rights and freedoms without discrimination.'

84 For instance, state parties to the ICCPR, ICERD (International Covenant on the Elimination of All Forms of Racial Discrimination) or UNCAT may bring to the attention of another party that they consider this other party is not respecting its obligations under the treaty, both in relation to their own nationals or any other national. They may also recognise the competence of the relevant treaty-based monitoring body to receive and consider communications to such effect, Article 41 ICCPR; Article 11 ICERD; Article 21 UNCAT. In the words of the International Law Commission (ILC) in its 2006 Draft Articles on Diplomatic Protection, 'the customary international law rules on diplomatic protection and the rules governing the protection of human rights are complementary. The present draft articles are therefore not intended to exclude or to trump the rights of States [...] to protect the individual under either customary international law or a multilateral or bilateral human rights treaty or other treaty. They are also not intended to interfere with the rights of natural and legal persons or other entities, involved in the protection of human rights, to resort under international law to actions or procedures other than diplomatic protection to secure redress for injury suffered as a result of an internationally wrongful act.' International Law Commission, 'Draft articles on the responsibility of international organizations, with commentaries, Adopted by the International Law Commission at its sixty-third session', UN Doc A/66/10 (2011) II Yearbook of the International Law Commission, Part Two, para 4.

85 The VCLT provides, in Article 31(2)(a), that the context comprises agreements made in connection with the conclusion of the treaty, as well as instruments made in connection with the conclusion of the treaty and accepted by the parties as related to the treaty.

While the Committee's earlier conclusions refer to international protection only in respect of the functions of the UNHCR,[86] the Committee since the 1980s used the term 'international protection' also in connection with refugee rights under international law, by reaffirming '[…] the importance of the basic principles of international protection and in particular the principle of non-refoulement […]'[87] and human rights obligations.[88] More recently, the Committee referred to *international protection needs* as an equivalent for needs of both refugees and forcibly displaced people in similar situations.[89]

The changed language on 'international protection' coincides with an increased importance of human rights law as a source of entitlements for those forcibly displaced, even beyond the 1951 Convention. Indeed, as past research has demonstrated, the substantive standards of human rights law often exceed those of the 1951 Convention, the Convention being characterised by a specific structure of entitlement dependent on the level of attachment with the state of refuge, and mostly concerned with the relative standard of treatment as between refugees and nationals, with obligations under the Convention framed as state obligations rather than as refugee *rights*.[90] These limitations may hamper the effectiveness of 1951 Convention provisions that have no equivalent in human rights law – such as non-penalisation of refugees for unlawfully entering the territory, a provision which, as Vincent Chetail points out, is often interpreted in a way that does not prohibit detention of undocumented asylum seekers.[91] The same commentator argued that evolving interpretations of human rights law could expand the scope of human rights so as to cater for distinctive needs of refugees, for instance, the right to identity papers, which could be derived from the principle of recognition as a person before the law as well as the principle of equality before the law.[92] Given that human rights law creates minimum standards whereas the Convention only provides for a comparative frame between nationals and refugees, human

86 Eg, EXCOM Conclusion no 14 (XXX) – 1979.

87 EXCOM Conclusion no 25 (XXXIII) – 1982.

88 EXCOM Conclusion no 93 (LIII) – 2002; no 95 (LIV) – 2003; no 100 (LV) – 2004, emphasising that states' obligations towards refugees stemmed from the 1951 Convention and international human rights law, and that these two branches of law were complementary.

89 EXCOM Conclusion no 103 (LVI) – 2005.

90 Chetail, 'Are Refugee Rights Human Rights? An Unorthodox Questioning of the Relations between Refugee Law and Human Rights Law' (Ch 1 n 95). See also Colin Harvey, 'Time for Reform? Refugees, Asylum-seekers, and Protection Under International Human Rights Law' 34 (2015) Refugee Survey Quarterly 1.

91 Chetail, 'Are Refugee Rights Human Rights?' (Ch 1 n 95) 67–68.

92 Ibid 67.

rights law provides the normative base for domestic legislation, making human rights law and refugee law indissociable.[93] Indeed, it has even been stated that the 1951 Convention only 'retains some symbolic relevance'.[94] In contrast, Hathaway asserts that unlike human rights law, the Convention is couched in specific terms that respond directly to the 'particular disabilities that derive from involuntary migration'.[95] The Convention retains distinct value, as it contains standards that have no equivalent in human rights law, standards that may be harder to construe under human rights law under an evolutionary interpretation, in particular, more powerful standards in respect of access to the labour market (Articles 17–18), welfare (Article 23) and naturalisation (Article 34). In addition, there are also more general impediments to the effectiveness of human rights treaties for refugees, including the possibility of derogation (albeit with strict requirements)[96] and the nature of obligations under the ICESCR, which is subject to available resources and progressive realisation.[97] Even where the economic rights obligations of the 1951 Convention are generally lower, they are immediate and independent of states' resources.[98] Conclusively, the question on the distinct value of human rights law in respect of refugee law can only be answered by looking beyond the substantive standards of treatment to the eligibility criteria of status, as set out in Chapters 3–6 below. For now, suffice to say that the

---

93 Ibid.

94 Ibid.

95 Ibid 110.

96 Ibid 121. The ICCPR and the Human Rights Committee, interpreting the Covenant, have imposed high hurdles for such derogation. First, an emergency must threaten the life of the nation, which is a state of affairs that goes beyond mere 'disturbances'. Second, derogation pursuant to such emergency must be exceptional and temporary. Third, and arguably most importantly, there are strict conditions as to the actual measures of derogation. The HRC has stated that use of limitation clauses, where they exist, is 'generally sufficient during [an emergency] and no derogation from the provisions [having a limitation clause, AN] … would be justified by the exigencies of the situation.' Any derogation must thus be strictly necessary in the circumstances. There can be no derogation where the derogation threatens a breach of an absolute right. This makes for the Committee belief that every ICCPR provision has a non-derogable core. Human Rights Committee, 'General Comment No 29: States of Emergency (article 4)', UN Doc CCPR/C/21/Rev.1/Add.11 (2001) para 3.

97 The ICESCR not only contains a general clause on subjective realisation in Article 2(1) but also a clause on differential treatment between nationals and non-nationals where resources are scarce. Article 2(3) of the ICESCR provides that, 'Developing countries, with due regard to human rights and their national economy, may determine to what extent they would guarantee the economic rights recognized in the present Covenant to non-nationals.'

98 Hathaway, *The Rights of Refugees under International Law* (Ch 1 n 113) 122.

human rights-informed understanding of 'international protection' in EU law also resonates with the modern interpretation of refugee entitlements under international law. Yet, how does this understanding of protection relate to the eligibility criteria of EU asylum law? This question will be addressed in the following two sections.

2.3 International Protection as a 'Surrogate' of 'Domestic' Protection

2.3.1 *'Surrogacy' and the Eligibility Criteria of the Qualification Directive*

So far, it has become clear that international protection under EU asylum law and the 1951 Convention is a rights-based concept. Within the natural meaning of the language, 'international protection' implies that it relates to another, non-international, form of protection. Yet, what is the meaning of this 'other' concept of protection? The following sections will explore how EU asylum law and international law mark out international protection as 'surrogate' protection.

While EU asylum law does not use the term of 'surrogacy', the notion clearly underlies the CEAS. The main objective of the Qualification Directive is, in addition to ensuring minimum standards, the 'identification of persons genuinely in need of international protection'.[99] When the European Commission in 2011 tabled its proposal for the Qualification Directive laying out common criteria for refugee status and subsidiary protection, it sought to establish an 'international protection regime'[100] subsidiary to the protection regime of the country of origin. According to the Commission, international protection under EU asylum law is 'the protection applied for by third-country nationals or stateless persons, or given to them by member states, *instead of protection previously provided by an individual's country of origin or habitual residence*'.[101] Even more clearly, the Commission stated in its proposal on Chapter II of the recast Qualification Directive:

> The second set of rules focuses on the general nature of international protection, identifying the many common characteristics of its two constitutive elements, refugee status and subsidiary protection status. [...] Its *guiding principle is that international protection of any sort is a type of*

99 Recital 12, Qualification Directive (emphasis added).

100 Commission of the European Union, *Qualification Directive Proposal 2009* (Ch 2 n 66).

101 Ibid Article 2(a), emphasis added, also Article 2(e) of the Directive 2004/83/EC (Qualification Directive).

> *surrogate protection to be provided in lieu of national protection only when the realistic possibility of obtaining protection from an applicant's country of origin is absent.*[102]

Finally, in his opinion on the CJEU case of *Aboubacar Diakité*, Advocate General Mengozzi stated that 'subsidiary protection is a form of "*surrogate protection*" granted [...] where there is *no realistic possibility of the applicant gaining protection in his or her country of origin*'.[103] Seen this way, the notion of 'surrogacy' leads to the eligibility criteria of refugee status, in particular how the lack of protection is relevant for these eligibility criteria.

In the text of the Qualification Directive, the lack of protection prominently occurs in the eligibility criteria of both refugees and persons eligible for subsidiary protection, who, respectively, have a well-founded fear of being persecuted or face a real risk of suffering serious harm and are, owing to such risk, '*unwilling to avail himself or herself of the protection of that country*'.[104] The phrase is borrowed from Article 1A(2) of the 1951 Convention, according to which a refugee is a person who, 'owing to a well-founded fear of being persecuted for reasons of race, religion, nationality, political opinion or membership of a particular social group, is outside the country of nationality and is unable or, owing to such fear, is unwilling to avail himself or herself of the protection of that country', a clause discussed in detail in the following section below. While the Qualification Directive does not specify this notion as explicitly as it specifies other parts of the 1951 Convention's refugee definition (in particular 'acts of persecution' under Article 9), it does contain further standards on the assessment of status that relate to protection. Both Articles 6(c) in conjunction with 7(2) and Article 8 of the Qualification Directive are guided by the rationale that individuals are not deemed in need of international protection if they can find protection in the home state against acts of persecution or serious harm.[105] What is more, the Qualification Directive incorporates provisions of the 1951 Convention whereby refugee status ceases if an applicant 'has voluntarily re-availed himself or herself of the protection of the country of nationality', has voluntarily re-acquired nationality after having lost nationality,

102 Commission of the European Union, *Qualification Directive Proposal 2009* (Ch 2 n 66) para 5(b).

103 Case 285/12 *Aboubacar Diakité v Commissaire général aux réfugiés et aux apatrides* [2013] ECR 2014-00000.

104 Article 2(d)–(f), Qualification Directive.

105 See Chapter 3 for protection against persecution or serious harm and Chapter 4 for the internal protection alternative.

or 'has acquired a new nationality, and enjoys the protection of the country of his or her new nationality.'[106]

2.3.2 *'Surrogacy', 'Protection' and the Text of the 1951 Convention*

This section explores how the refugee eligibility criteria of the 1951 Convention have been interpreted to reflect the notion of 'surrogacy'. The term, which does not appear in the Convention, was first used by Hathaway, who described refugee law as a 'system for the surrogate or substitute protection of human rights'.[107] It has been influential in the interpretation of Article 1A(2) of the Convention, as will be demonstrated below.

The starting point of interpretation of the Convention is its text.[108] As laid out earlier, that Convention provision defines a refugee as a person who is outside the country of nationality owing to a well-founded fear of being persecuted for reasons of race, religion, nationality, political opinion or membership of a particular social group, and *is unable or, owing to such fear, unwilling to avail himself or herself of the protection of that country*.[109] This sentence is mirrored by other parts of Article 1A(2) that give the country of nationality precedence over refugee status, notably for people with multiple nationalities.[110] According to the UNHCR Handbook on Procedures and Criteria for Determining Refugee Status (UNHCR Handbook), '[...] [whenever] the protection of the country of nationality is available, and there is no ground based on well-founded fear for refusing it, the person concerned is not in need of international protection

106 Article 11 b)-c).

107 Hathaway, *The Law of Refugee Status* (Ch 1 n 6) 5.

108 Following the general rule of interpretation in Article 31, VCLT, 'a treaty shall be interpreted in good faith in accordance with the ordinary meaning to be given to the terms of the treaty in their context and in the light of its object and purpose'. According to the International Law Commission's commentary on the codification of the rule, its application is a 'single combined operation'; see International Law Commission, Draft Articles on the Law of Treaties with Commentaries (1966) II Yearbook of the International Law Commission.

109 The Convention uses the same wording in its rules on cessation in Article 1C; refugee status ceases for those who enjoy the protection of another country by virtue of a new nationality (Article 1C(3)) or for those who can no longer refuse to avail themselves of the protection of their country of nationality because the circumstances that have led to recognition of status have ceased to exist (Article 1C(5)).

110 'In the case of a person who has more than one nationality, the term "the country of his nationality" shall mean each of the countries of which he is a national, and a person shall not be deemed to be lacking the protection of the country of his nationality if, without any valid reason based on well-founded fear, he has not availed himself of the protection of one of the countries of which he is a national.'

and is not a refugee'.[111] Opinions by the UNHCR are authoritative given that the UNHCR is vested with a supervisory function over refugee law under its statute[112] and corollary provisions in the 1951 Convention and 1967 Protocol.[113]

The precedence of 'protection' by the country of nationality over protection of a refugee by a Contracting Party to the Convention has led courts to argue that Article 1 embodies an 'underlying rationale' of the Convention to provide 'surrogate' protection.[114] In particular, as stated in the leading Canadian case of *Ward*, on the possibility of the Convention to accommodate harm by non-state actors –

> The international community was meant to be a forum of second resort for the persecuted, *a "surrogate", approachable upon failure of local protection*. The rationale upon which international refugee law rests is not simply the need to give shelter to those persecuted by the state, but, more widely, to provide refuge to those whose home state cannot or does not afford them protection from persecution.[115]

This interpretation has also been influential in other common law jurisdictions, in particular the United Kingdom, Australia and New Zealand.[116] In the UK case of *Horvath*, likewise revolving around harm by non-state actors, it was noted that –

> It is no part of the international scheme that people should qualify as refugees merely because private persons in their home state seek to interfere with their rights and freedoms. If there is a sufficiency of protection available to them in that state, then there should be no obligation on another state to afford a surrogate protection.[117]

---

111 UN High Commissioner for Refugees, 'Handbook on Procedures and Criteria for Determining Refugee Status under the 1951 Convention and the 1967 Protocol relating to the Status of Refugees', reissued 2011 <www.unhcr.org/3d58e13b4.pdf> acessed 20 October 2016, para 100 (UNHCR Handbook on Refugee Status Determination). Note that the Convention does not include in the refugee definition those individuals who hold the nationality of a country in respect of which they do not have a well-founded fear of being persecuted (Article 1A(2)).

112 Paragraph 8 of the UNHCR Statute (Ch 2 n 71).

113 Articles 35–36 of the 1951 Convention, Article II of the 1967 Protocol.

114 *Canada v Ward* [1993] 2 SCR 689, 96.

115 Ibid 45, per Justice La Forest.

116 This has been traced by Susan Kneebone, 'Refugees as Objects of Surrogate Protection: Shifting Identities' in Kneebone et al, *Conflicting Identities: Refugee Protection and the Role of Law* (Ch 1 n 15) 110.

117 *Horvath v Secretary of State for The Home Department* [2000] UKHL 37, per Lord Clyde.

Both these and other decisions are grounded on the premise that the term 'protection' in Article 1A(2) of the Convention refers to effective safeguarding of rights in the country of nationality, which also appears to be the majority opinion in academic debate.[118]

Meanwhile, the text of the Convention is inconclusive on this interpretation. It is clear from the text that the fear of being persecuted must relate to the country of nationality, because the lack of protection that incorporates this notion also relates to the country of nationality. However, the text is inconclusive as to what the Convention means by 'protection' of the country of nationality. The various other uses of the term in the Convention, which are relevant context according to Article 31, VCLT, do not assist in the interpretation. They either mirror the wording of Article 1A(2) (in particular the provision on cessation in Article 1C(1)), or refer to the special case of 'protection' of the UN Relief and Works Agency as a ground for exclusion (Article 1D). Article 14 and the Convention's preamble generically refer to the protection of specific entitlements under the Convention and the Convention as a whole[119] by Contracting Parties, rather than the country of nationality. Finally, paragraph 16 of the schedule to the Convention, which is also relevant context to the text of Article 1A(2),[120] speaks of 'protection of the diplomatic or consular authorities' of the country that has issued a refugee's travel document.

In light of the ambiguity of the text, there has been some debate on the term in the past, with some authors arguing that 'protection' historically referred to,[121] or continues to refer to, diplomatic or consular protection.[122] However,

---

118 Goodwin Gil and McAdam, *The Refugee in International Law* (Ch 1, n 15) 10; Zimmermann, Claudia Mahler, 'Article 1A, para. 2' in Zimmermann; Dörscher; Machts, *The 1951 Convention and its 1967 Protocol – A Commentary* (Ch 1 n 42) 444 state that any other meaning would 'find itself at odds with the ordinary meaning of Art. 1A, para. 2' and would even be against the Convention's object and purpose. However, they also concede that a different interpretation is achieved when looking at the Convention's drafting history.

119 See Article 14 as well as the preamble of the Convention, noting that 'the United Nations High Commissioner for Refugees is charged with the task of supervising international conventions providing for the protection of refugees.'

120 According to Article 31(2) of the VCLT, a treaty's provisions, preamble and annexes form part of the context for the purpose.

121 Goodwin-Gil and McAdam, *The Refugee in International Law* (Ch 1 n 15) 10, stating that 'Historically, the references to protection in article 1 were seen primarily as references to diplomatic and consular protection, rather than to the effectiveness of a State and its system of government to ensure rights at home.'

122 Antonio Fortin, 'The Meaning of "Protection" in the Refugee Definition' (2000) 12 International Journal of Refugee Law 548; Kneebone, 'Refugees as Objects of Surrogate Protection: Shifting Identities' (Ch 1 n 15). On this debate, see also: Eeva Nykänen, *Fragmented State Power and Forced Migration – Study on Non-State Actors in Refugee Law* (University of Turku 2012).

the meaning of the term in Article 1A(2) may have also evolved over time. This was argued in the UK case of *Januzi:*

> The other approach, relied upon by the appellants, is to focus on the words "is unable [...] to avail himself of the protection of that country." There is some reason to suppose that when the Convention was originally drafted the protection intended in this provision was that furnished in another country by diplomatic or consular authorities [...] Since the temporal provision in article 1A(2) was removed in 1967 it has not been so interpreted and it may be said that ongoing interpretation of the Convention as a living instrument and adaptation to modern conditions have brought about a shift in meaning.[123]

Yet, what has brought about a shift in meaning? Susan Kneebone suggested that it was a move from collective categories to individual ones.[124] The following sections will build on this claim to first trace the original meaning and then offer an alternative explanation for the shift, namely that it is caused by the evolution of human rights obligations. Under such modern reading, protection in Article 1A(2) of the Convention refers to *rights protection in the country of nationality.*

2.3.3 *The Historic Understanding of 'Protection' in the International Refugee Regime*

This section will trace the evolution of the term 'protection' in international refugee instruments. It argues that the term did indeed originally refer to *protection* in the country of refuge, rather than in the country of nationality. It will do so by scrutinising, first, the drafting history of the Convention. Given the drafting history is inconclusive, it will scrutinise the ordinary meaning of the term at the time, as apparent in the instruments preceding the 1951 Convention and the UNHCR statute.

2.3.3.1 'Protection' and the 1951 Convention's Travaux Préparatoires

In 1949, the UN Economic and Social Council (ECOSOC) appointed a committee that would clarify whether a convention relating to the status of refugees was needed, after a recommendation to that effect by the UN Commission on

123 *Januzi v Secretary of State for the Home Department* [2006] 2 AC 426 para 66, with reference to Fortin, 'The Meaning of "Protection" in the Refugee Definition' (ibid).

124 Kneebone, 'Refugees as Objects of Surrogate Protection: Shifting Identities' (Ch 1 n 15) 100–103.

Human Rights.[125] The committee, named the Ad-hoc Committee on Statelessness and Related Problems, and later the Ad-hoc Committee on Refugees and Stateless Persons, in early 1950 discussed and commented on a draft convention prepared by the UN Secretary General. In July 1951, the Conference of Plenipotentiaries met in Geneva after the Ad Hoc Committee had submitted a revised draft convention to the General Assembly.

Both the Ad Hoc Committee, ECOSOC and delegates to the Conference of Plenipotentiaries used the term 'protection' in several ways. Protection was usually associated with legal matters; there was a clear distinction between 'protection' on the one hand and 'assistance' on the other.[126] 'Protection' went alongside the 'minimum rights granted [...] in the receiving countries'.[127] Similarly, the US representative referred to the problem of 'protection' of refugees as one of the status, the rights and the benefits they enjoyed in their states of refuge.[128]

However, delegates also used the term to allude to the activities of the host state, including to diplomatic protection in the state of refuge[129] and, more broadly, to the protective relationship between a foreigner and its country of citizenship. There was consensus that refugees were in a precarious situation because they did not enjoy the benefits of having a government intervening on their behalf in their host state. Therefore, 'international protection'[130] would step in. The Caritas Internationalis observer to the Conference of Plenipotentiaries put it succinctly when he stated that –

> even before legal relationships were established, the taking-in of a refugee by a State able to grant him its protection set up a bond of mutual

125 Commission on Human Rights, 'Report to ECOSOC on the 2nd Session of the Commission Held at Geneva from 2 to 17 December 1947', (1948) E/600, cited in: Weis, *The Refugees Convention, 1951: The Travaux Préparatoires Analysed* (Ch 2, n 83) 10.

126 UN Ad Hoc Committee on Refugees and Stateless Persons, 'UN Ad Hoc Committee on Refugees and Stateless Persons, First Session: Summary Record of the Third Meeting' UN Doc E/AC.32/SR.3 (1950).

127 See French representative at ibid.

128 Ibid para 55. 'The attitude of the United States Government was not due to financial considerations, as suggested by the French representative. The problem of the protection of refugees did not exist in his country, a fact of which he was proud. All the refugees who were received there enjoyed a status almost equivalent to that of its citizens.'

129 Conference of Plenipotentiaries on the Status of Refugees and Stateless Persons, 'Summary Record of the First Meeting', UN Doc A/CONF.2/SR.1 (1950), 5.

130 UN Conference of Plenipotentiaries on the Status of Refugees and Stateless Persons, 'Compte rendu analytique de la deuxième séance, tenue au Palais des Nations, à Genève' UN Doc A/CONF.2/SR.2 (1951).

> confidence between the person thus entrusting another country with the protection of his life and liberty and the State which was prepared to safeguard it by granting him asylum.[131]

In line with this statement, delegates discussed that the protection accorded by the Convention was closely tied to the absence of a bond between individual and state, notably in the context of a proposed amendment according to which refugees would have benefited from the provisions of the Convention, in particular welfare benefits, even after naturalisation. According to the UNHCR representative:

> Clearly, and in his view rightly, the authors of both texts had considered that refugee status, being abnormal, should not be granted for a day longer than was absolutely necessary, and should come to an end (or, possibly, should never even come into existence) if, in accordance with the terms of the Convention or the Statute, a person had the status of de facto citizenship, that was to say, if he really had the rights and obligations of a citizen of a given county [...][132]

Indeed, discussions on the draft convention's scope *ratione personae*[133] had first revolved around whether to draft an instrument that would be applicable both to refugees and to 'de jure stateless' persons. Delegates thought that 'lack

131 UN Conference of Plenipotentiaries on the Status of Refugees and Stateless Persons, 'Summary Record of the Fourteenth Meeting', A/CONF.2/SR.14 (1951), statement by Mr Haas (Caritas Internationalis), 'Even before legal relationships were established, the taking-in of a refugee by a State able to grant him its protection set up a bond of mutual confidence between the person thus entrusting another country with the protection of his life and liberty and the State which was prepared to safeguard it by granting him asylum. That meant that on both the spiritual and the human plane the right of asylum assumed an amplitude which admitted of no other limitations than those best fitted to safeguard it.'

132 UN Conference of Plenipotentiaries on the Status of Refugees and Stateless Persons, 'Summary Record of the Twenty-third Meeting', UN Doc A/CONF.2/SR.23 (1951).

133 The members of the Committee agreed that the Convention should encompass as refugees any person who (a) as a result of events in Europe after the outbreak of the Second World War and before 1 July 1950 has well-founded fears of being the victim of persecution for reasons of race, religion, nationality, political opinion, and (b) for such reasons has left or is outside the country of his nationality or, if he has no nationality, outside his country of former habitual residence, and (c) for such reason is unable or unwilling to avail himself of the protection of the Government of his country of nationality. See Ad Hoc Committee on Statelessness and Related Problems, 'Summary Record of the Seventh Meeting Held at Lake Success' UN Doc E/AC32/SR17 (1950).

of protection' was a shared feature of refugees and stateless persons, which was a natural consequence of nationality being the link between an individual and international law. However, the harm refugees feared in the home state set refugees apart from stateless persons who were not refugees. According to the delegate of the United Kingdom, 'since refugees were usually either de jure or de facto stateless persons, the difference between refugees and stateless persons was quantitative rather than qualitative' and therefore 'hardly any distinction could be drawn between the treatment to be applied to refugees and to stateless persons who were not refugees'.[134] The Ad Hoc Committee opted for an instrument applying to refugees, 'not by a desire to leave stateless persons who were not refugees without protection, but by the realisation that refugees were in much more urgent need of immediate protection'.[135] This urgent need lay in the need to ensure that refugees were not deported.[136]

Curiously, however, the delegates discussed neither the substance of the notion of 'protection' in Article 1A(2) and 1C of the draft Convention nor the provision governing cessation of refugee status, which uses the term with identical wording,[137] suggesting the meaning was so clear that it did not warrant discussion. The next section will discuss to what extent the term 'protection' in the refugee definition already at the time of adoption stemmed from relatively long-standing practice.

2.3.3.2 'Protection' and the Refugee Regime Prior to the 1951 Convention

Assistance to refugees by way of international efforts precedes the drafting of the 1951 Convention as the modern cornerstone of international refugee law; however, the lack of 'protection' has always been a core element of refugeehood. For the League of Nations' first refugee institution, the High Commissioner for (initially only Russian) Refugees,[138] *lacking protection* was a criterion

134 UN Ad Hoc Committee on Refugees and Stateless Persons, 'First Session: Summary Record of the Third Meeting Held at Lake Success' (Ch 2 n 126). See also 'Summary Record of the Hundred and Sixtieth Meeting of the Social Committee', UN Doc E/AC.7/SR.160, 7 (statement by Mr Henkin).

135 UN Ad Hoc Committe on Statelessness and Related Problems, 'Summary Record of the Fourth Meeting' E/AC.32/SR.4 (1950), para 11.

136 See the discussion in UN Ad Hoc Committee on Refugees and Stateless Persons, 'First Session: Summary Record of the Twenty-Third Meeting' UN Doc E/AC.32/SR.23 (1950).

137 Ibid.

138 The mandate was extended subsequent to the adoption of the 'Arrangement Relating to the Legal Status of Russian and Armenian Refugees' and the 'Arrangement Concerning the Extension to Other Categories of Refugees' and the 'Arrangement Concerning the Extension to Other Refugees of Certain Measures taken in Favour of Russian and Armenian Refugees'.

for establishing competence for coming to the assistance of refugees, to be remedied by the issue of identity documents to the displaced, known as *Nansen passports* after the first High Commissioner Fridtjof Nansen.[139] In addition, refugees were provided with relief and assistance for voluntary repatriation, emigration or integration (including employment),[140] primarily funded by private contributions.[141]

This early institution of refugee assistance followed the flight of Russians from the October Revolution[142] and, later, flights of Armenian, Assyrian, Assyro-Chaldean and Turkish refugees.[143] These early refugees had in common that they had suffered harm or were under a threat thereof in their state of nationality, were therefore displaced outside of that state, and were unable to return. As an upshot, they could not turn to their government for a passport or documentation of citizenship, and were thus left without a state advocating for their enjoyment of any legal entitlements (diplomatic protection). For international law at the time, individuals were relevant above all to the extent that they held a nationality; bilateral treaties, municipal law or merely the principle of reciprocity regulated the minimum standards to be accorded to aliens.[144] Refugees were regarded as having 'no regular nationality'.[145] Because

139 See 'Arrangement with regard to the issue of certificates of identity to Russian refugees' of 5 July 1922, 13 League of Nations Treaty Series 238 (1922).

140 Ivor C. Jackson, 'Dr. Fridtjof Nansen, a Pioneer in the International Protection of Refugees' (2003) 22 Refugee Survey Quarterly 7. The Arrangement Relating to the Legal Status of Russian and Armenian Refugees of 30 June 1928 went beyond the mere aspects of judicial status, encompassing non-refoulement and benefits in the country of refuge; Alessandra Roversi, 'The Evolution of the Refugee Regime and Institutional Responses: Legacies from the Nansen Period' (2003) 22 Refugee Survey Quarterly 21, 25.

141 Roversi, 'The Evolution of the Refugee Regime and Institutional Responses: Legacies from the Nansen Period' (ibid) 25. The institution succeeding the League of Nations High Commissioner for Refugees as of 1931, the Nansen International Office for Refugees, had broad tasks of collecting information, giving directions to existing or future relief institutions and national authorities, collecting funds of private organisations, facilitating arrangements with governments made for the benefit of refugees. Like the activities of its predecessor, those tasks were for a good part privately funded. Statutes of the Nansen International Office for Refugees as approved by the Council on 19 January 1931, 12 League of Nations Official Journal 308, 1931, Articles 3 and 14.

142 W C Huntington, *The Homesick Million: Russia-out-of-Russia* (Stratford 1933).

143 Paul Weis, 'The International Protection of Refugees' (1954) 48 American Journal of International Law 193, 208.

144 Gilbert Jaeger, 'Status and International Protection of Refugees', International Institute of Human Rights, Ninth Study Session, July 1978, on file with the author.

145 League of Nations Advisory Commission for Refugees, 'Report by the Secretary-General on the Future Organisation of Refugee Work', League of Nations Doc 1930.XIII.2, 3.

of the significance of legal protection by the state of nationality as a remedy for aliens, the denial thereof led to a 'malfunction in the international legal system'.[146]

The loss of protection in the country of refuge as a shared characteristic of refugees remained apparent in the 1938 Convention Concerning the Status of Refugees coming from Germany (1938 Convention). That Convention defined refugees as 'persons possessing or having possessed German nationality and not possessing any other nationality who are *proved not to enjoy, in law or in fact, the protection of the German government*'.[147] The lack of protection, 'in law or in fact', by the government was also the defining criterion for stateless persons.[148] However, lacking protection was still not a sufficient criterion for an individual to fall under the responsibility of the then newly-established body charged with negotiating asylum for German and Austrian Jews. The Intergovernmental Committee on Refugees was concerned only with people fleeing on account of political opinion, religious belief or racial origin.[149] Thus, while 'protection' in the 1938 Convention referred to protection within the state of refuge, and thus to the ability to have proof of nationality and a state acting on behalf of its national, the absence of such legal protection was also the expression of the defunct relationship between a government and a citizen, with the loss, in law or in fact, of the rights normally associated with citizenship. This is evident from the measures that the national socialist German *Reich* took against German Jews, which formed the background for the Convention Concerning the Status of Refugees Coming from Germany. In 1933, the German *Reich* adopted an act designed to denaturalise German citizens of Jewish descent or faith.[150] In 1935, the *Reich* adopted a package of laws that legally flanked the succeeding policy of deportation, ghettoisation, internment and ultimately murder of Jews. The *Reichsbürgergesetz* of 1935

146 James C Hathaway, 'The Evolution of Refugee Status in International Law: 1920–1950' (1984) 33 The International and Comparative Law Quarterly 348, 358, arguing that, 'The withdrawal of de jure protection by a State, whether via denaturalisation or the withholding of diplomatic facilities such as travel documents and consular representation, results in a malfunction in the international legal system.'

147 Article I(1)(a) Convention Concerning the Status of Refugees Coming from Germany (signed 10 February 1938) CXCII 4461 LNTS 59, emphasis added.

148 Ibid Article I(1)(b).

149 Resolution of the Committee, ICR Doc, 14 July 1938, cited in James C Hathaway, 'A Reconsideration of the Underlying Premise of Refugee Law' (1990) 31 Harvard International Law Journal 129, 139.

150 Gesetz über den Widerruf von Einbürgerungen und die Aberkennung der deutschen Staatsangehörigkeit, 14 July 1933, RGBL. I, 480 para 1–2.

explicitly created a system of dual citizenship, with only citizens of the *Reich* being entitled to 'the full political rights',[151] but made citizenship contingent on being of 'German or related blood' and willing 'to serve the German people and Reich loyally'.[152]

The first meaningful legal development in the understanding of asylum after World War II was the establishment of the International Refugee Organization (IRO).[153] The temporary organisation was put in place to react to the issues of displacement specific to the aftermath of World War II; its primary focus was the assistance, repatriation and resettlement of individuals displaced by the war.[154] The IRO Constitution defined refugees primarily with reference to their victimhood under the fascist regimes,[155] but also included a more general definition that influenced the 1951 Convention. Thereby, a person 'outside his country of nationality or former habitual residence, and who, as a result of events subsequent to the outbreak of the Second World War, *is unable or unwilling to avail himself of the protection* of the government of his country of nationality or former nationality' was a refugee.[156] Whether such refugees were then of concern for the organisation depended on whether they could be repatriated or whether they had 'valid objections' to being returned to their

151 Ibid para 2(3).

152 Reichsbürgergesetz, 15 September 1935, RGBL I, 1146 para 1–2. Similarly, the law relating to citizenship was amended with the effect of abolishing former entitlements to German citizenship and administrative discretion for granting it (*Gesetz zur Änderung des Reichs- und Staatsangehörigkeitsgesetzes vom 15. Mai 1935*, RGBl I, 593).

153 Constitution of the International Refugee Organization, as Annexed to UN General Assembly (signed 15 December 1946) 18 UNTS 3. Two institutions were created at the eve of and during World War II. The Intergovernmental Committee on Refugees was set up to facilitate resettlement of German Jews from Nazi Germany, without drawing on an abstract definition of protection, asylum or refugee. See also Tommie Sjoberg, *The Powers and the Persecuted: The Refugee Problem and the Intergovernmental Committee on Refugees, 1938–1947* (Lund University Press 1991). The United Nations Relief and Rehabilitation Administration offered aid to displaced citizens of the allies as well as to displaced Jews.

154 Article 2(a): '[The functions of the Organization] shall be exercised with a view: (*a*) To encouraging and assisting in every way possible the early return to their country of nationality, or former habitual residence, of those persons who are the concern of the Organization, having regard to the principles laid down in the resolution on refugees and displaced persons adopted by the General Assembly of the United Nations on 12 February 1946 (Annex III) and to the principles set forth in the Preamble, and to promoting this by all possible means, in particular by providing them with material assistance, adequate food for a period of three months from the time of their departure from their present places of residence [...].'

155 Constitution of the International Refugee Organization (Ch 2 n 153), Annex I, Section A3.

156 Ibid Section A(2), emphasis added.

countries. 'Persecution, or fear, based on [...] religion, nationality or political opinions' were among the valid objections.[157]

Thus, the lack of protection in the state of refuge was a defining criterion for refugees, while 'persecution' was the watershed for triggering the IRO's responsibility. As is evident from a statement by the IRO's Director General, this still followed the rationale that an individual lacking protection was abnormal from the international law perspective, because her treatment as alien depended on her citizenship or nationality,[158] and the risk of harm in the country of origin was taken as a given.

Meanwhile, refugee status was not accorded to everybody in need of assistance, but was designed to respond to the disadvantages that normally flowed from alienage.[159] Thus, there was a consensus that 'national refugees' from decolonisation, such as 'returning' Italians from former colonies such as Libya, Eritrea and the Dodecanese islands,[160] were not refugees for the purpose of the

---

157 Ibid C(1)(a)(i).

158 'Lacking the protection of the Government of his country of origin, the refugee does not enjoy a clearly defined status based upon the principle of reciprocity as enjoyed by nationals of those states which maintain normal diplomatic relations. The rights which are conferred on such nationals by virtue of their status, which is dependent upon their nationality, are generally unavailable to him. A refugee is an anomaly in international law [...]' Communication from the General Council of the International Refugee Organization, 11 July 1949, UN Doc. E/1392 para 5. It may also have served pragmatic considerations for identifying refugees; see Louise W Holborn, *The International Refugee Organization: A Specialized Agency of the United Nations, its History and Work 1946 – 1952* (Oxford University Press 1956). Besides, the definition was by no means free from ideology and political interest on the part of the dominant Western States. Hathaway, 'A Reconsideration of the Underlying Premise of Refugee Law' (Ch 2 n 149) 147.

159 Hathaway and Foster, *The Law of Refugee Status* (Ch 1 n 100), 22, stating that, 'The restriction of refugee status to persons who have left their own country is logical because it defines a class of persons to whom foreign states can, as a matter of practicality, undertake to provide an unconditional response of precisely the kind set by the Refugee Convention.' Besides, the exclusion of 'national refugees' made sure that States as well as the then responsible agencies could practically act on behalf of refugees, because they would not be compelled to exercise power on foreign territory; see ibid referring to the principle that States shall not exercise power in the territory of other States, *Lotus* [1927] PCIJ Rep 10, para 18/19.

160 Pamela Ballinger, 'Entangled or "Extruded" Histories? Displacement, National Refugees, and Repatriation after the Second World War' (2012) 25 Journal of Refugee Studies 366, 368–369. Cases mentioned are those of Dutch colonial returnees; Japanese repatriates forced by the Allied forces to return from Manchuria, Korea and Taiwan; and non-European refugees produced by the independence of India and Pakistan and by the creation of Israel. The question whether displacement of colonial repatriates indeed qualifies as 'forced' is disputed among scholars. It is, however, clear that there are incidents of

IRO.[161] Such individuals were excluded because they retained the legal protective bond of citizenship, despite being forcefully displaced and lacking social ties in the proper territory of the state of nationality.[162] While after World War II, refugee determination shifted to individual assessments,[163] 'the evaluation of individual narratives nonetheless proved part and parcel of the constitution of collective categories […]'.[164] The non-inclusion of the collective category of the 'national refugee' would later be codified in the 1951 Convention and would exclude large groups of individuals displaced by decolonisation.[165]

2.3.3.3 'Protection' and the UNHCR Statute

The parameters of the IRO's successor agency, the UNHCR, were heavily influenced by the legal setup and the practice of the preceding institutions in their responses to the plight of refugees. The defining feature of refugees was still the inability to return and the – related – lack of legal protection within the state of refuge.[166] In a report of the UN Secretary General that canvassed the design of a future refugee 'service', refugees were characterised as facing the dangers of expulsion, not enjoying those rights that depend on a residence permit, being

violence and intimidation against former colonialists in the case of former Italian colonies; see ibid 373.

161 Guy S Goodwin-Gil, 'Different Types of Forced Migration Movements as an International and National Problem' in Göran Rystad (ed), *The Uprooted: Forced Migration as an International Problem in the Post-War Era* (Chartwell-Bratt 1990) 28.

162 This is illustrated by the United Nations Relief and Rehabilitation Administration (UNRRA) rejecting any responsibility for repatriates who had retained Italian citizenship. The Italian Foreign Ministry had requested that the IRO take charge of colonists who had opted for Italian citizenship under the Peace Treaty with the former colonies' new administrations, but whose application for Italian citizenship had been rejected.

Ballinger instead suggests that the ignorance of such events for the conception of who merited international protection as a refugee was due to conceptual dilemmas regarding forced cross-border displacement, as well as open dislike of groups that were reminders of painful national histories. Ballinger, 'Entangled or "Extruded" Histories?' (Ch 2 n 160) 371.

163 Hathaway, *The Law of Refugee Status* (Ch 1 n 6) 5.

164 Ballinger, 'Entangled or "Extruded" Histories?' (Ch 2 n 160) 378.

165 The so-called '*pieds noirs*' in French Algeria, natives of the colony with ethnic roots in the French mainland, possessed the protective bond of French citizenship when forced to leave newly independent Algeria amidst fear of retaliation. The same holds true for repatriated Muslim Frenchmen from the colony. While in fact suffering serious discrimination as members of the disadvantageous administrative category of *Français musulmans rapatriés*, they were formally French citizens.

166 UN General Assembly, 'Refugees and Stateless Persons: Report of the Secretary-General, 26 October 1949', UN Doc A/C.3/527 para 20. 'The refugee's disabilities arise from the fact that he neither possesses the ultimate possibility of returning to his own country, nor enjoys the protection of that country while away from it.'

forced to enter a country clandestinely for lack of documentation, and for that matter being unable to document his legal capacity, family rights or rights of succession.[167] Accordingly, the report stated that, 'legal protection would consist in efforts to remove these and similar disabilities of refugees who do not enjoy the protection of their governments of nationality or former habitual residence'.[168] Such legal protection was primarily a 'duty' of the governments of the states of refuge. 'International protection' was, according to the report, a term used to differentiate the activities of the (future) institution of the UNHCR from that very duty by governments, and consisted 'essentially of efforts on the part of an international service to ensure that refugees who do not have the protection of the government of their countries of nationality or former habitual residence shall not be subject to legal and social disabilities arising from their peculiar status'.[169]

The proposed activities of the new UNHCR were of both a political and 'diplomatic' nature, in relation to groups as well as to individual interventions before state authorities on behalf of refugees, notably those interventions –

> related to deportation and expulsion, naturalization, restitution and indemnification, the exercise of certain trades and professions, applications for admission to educational institutions and many other proceeding [sic] which appeared to require international protection.[170]

In the test of the Statute eventually adopted, this proposal gave way to the wording that the UNHCR shall 'provide protection to refugees falling under [its] competence',[171] which comprised activities of advocacy and also supervision, assistance and coordination.[172]

---

167 Ibid para 12–16.

168 Ibid para 22.

169 Ibid 18–19.

170 Ibid para 37.

171 UNHCR Statute (Ch 2 n 71), Chapter II para 8 (emphasis added).

172 Ibid (a)–(i). The Office of the High Commissioner shall promote 'the conclusion and ratification of international conventions for the protection of refugees, supervising their application and proposing amendments thereto'. UNHCR shall promote the admission of refugees to States' territories and promote 'through special agreements with Governments the execution of any measures calculated to improve the situation of refugees'. It shall assist 'governmental and private efforts to promote voluntary repatriation or assimilation within new national communities' and endeavour 'to obtain permission for refugees to transfer their assets and especially those necessary for their resettlement'. Finally, the Statute names assistance of 'private' efforts in relation to the welfare of refugees and the establishment of contacts with private and governmental organisations concerned.

At the time of adoption, negotiations for a refugee convention were already under way, so that the Statute contained elements of the provisional refugee convention. The Statute first made explicit, in Paragraph 6(A)(ii), the refugee definition warranting a 'well-founded fear of being persecuted' as a criterion of refugeehood,[173] combined with an inability of the person to 'avail himself of the protection' of the country of nationality or, not having a nationality, being unable to return to it ('protection clause'). According to Atle Grahl-Madsen, protection in the clause means, above all, diplomatic protection:

> The stipulation in the various definitions that a denial of state protection constitutes a criterion of refugee status has given rise to the notion of "unprotected persons", persons without traditional or customary diplomatic and consular protection.[174]

However, protection in the clause also has more than the 'traditional textbook meaning' of diplomatic protection. This is because diplomatic protection in that traditional meaning is not explicitly requested, in contrast to what is as warranted by the wording of the Statute (and later on the 1951 Convention).

> In this context, protection cannot have the traditional textbook meaning in which it is neither explicitly requested nor denied. Protection, therefore, consists partly of the opportunity to apply to the diplomatic or consular authorities representing one's home country for a passport or a certificate of citizenship.[175]

Meanwhile, the introduction of the criterion of the well-founded fear of being persecuted contextualised the old criterion of denied diplomatic protection. Previously, the instruments had applied to groups in relation to which it was mostly clear why they had left their country of origin.[176] Because the new refugee definition was the first general definition, 'the notion of well-founded fear of persecution for certain enumerated reasons evolved and supplemented the time-honored notion of denial of protection'.[177] The criterion of denied

173 While the term 'persecution' was never the central defining criterion of refugee status before, it had been used in relation to refugees; see Jane McAdam, 'Rethinking the Origins of "Persecution" in Refugee Law' (2014) 25 International Journal of Refugee Law 667.

174 Grahl-Madsen, 'Protection of Refugees by Their Country of Origin' (1986) 11 Yale Journal of International Law 362, 374.

175 Ibid 363.

176 Ibid 374.

177 Ibid.

protection also 'incorporates the notion of persecution', because a refugee must be outside his country of origin precisely for the fear of being persecuted or be unwilling to avail himself of the protection of his country of nationality because of the fear of being persecuted.[178]

In sum, the early development of the international refugee regime suggests an understanding of the 1951 use of 'protection' in the protection clause of Article 1A(2) as protection in the country of refuge, including the documentation of citizenship and diplomatic protection by the country of citizenship. The 'protection clause' relates to the very essence of an early understanding of refugeehood. The denial of diplomatic protection is symptomatic of the denial of the protective relationship of citizenship, based on a well-founded fear of 'being persecuted', that is, the harm feared in the country of origin. According to Kimmenich and Grahl-Madsen:[179]

> [...] both early refugee groups and post-war refugees share the experience of the disruption or non-existence of the normal bond of trust and allegiance between citizen and government, leaving a relationship of fear and alienation. ... The denial of state protection is actually a symbol or a manner of speech to describe the broken bond. Denial of protection is, in fact, *a symptom rather than the disease itself.*[180]

Furthermore, the term protection was also used to refer to the status, rights and benefits granted by the host state or by the UNHCR. This use of the term was far broader than diplomatic protection. The 'protection' clause in Article 1A(2) thus provides a conceptual link *between the situation in the state of refuge and that in the state of nationality.*

2.3.4 *A Modern Reading of the Convention's Protection Clause in Article 1A(2)*

This section discusses how international law has evolved to change the ordinary meaning accorded to 'protection', and the implications for the interpretation of the 1951 Convention's protection clause.

As demonstrated in Section 2.3, the source of legal entitlements for foreigners were vastly different in 1951 than those of today. While entitlements at the

178 Ibid with reference to the refugee definition of the Statute and Convention.

179 Otto Kimminich, *Der Internationale Rechtsstatus des Flüchtlings* (Heymann 1962) 33–48 and Grahl-Madsen, 'Protection of Refugees by Their Country of Origin' (Ch 2 n 174) 375.

180 Grahl-Madsen, 'Protection of Refugees by Their Country of Origin' (Ch 2 n 174) 375 (emphasis added).

time stemmed from traditional aliens' law as well as general international law and were, chiefly, tied to citizenship, the evolution of human rights law has replaced traditional sources of entitlements. Indeed, given that human rights are bestowed on individuals for the sole fact of being human, citizenship has lost its original importance for the scope of entitlements enjoyed abroad.

The increased importance of human rights as a source of entitlements in the state of refuge is mirrored by its importance for defining harm relevant for the Convention's 'being persecuted' notion – a notion used well before the adoption of the 1951 Convention to describe a characteristic of refugeehood,[181] but defined neither before nor during the Convention's *travaux préparatoires*.[182] This is visible, first and foremost, in EU asylum law. According to Article 9 Qualification Directive:

1. Acts of persecution within the meaning of article 1 A of the Geneva Convention must:
   (a) be sufficiently serious by their nature or repetition *as to constitute a severe violation of basic human rights*, in particular the rights from which derogation cannot be made under Article 15(2) of the European Convention for the Protection of Human Rights and Fundamental Freedoms; or
   (b) be an accumulation of various measures, *including violations of human rights* which is sufficiently severe as to affect an individual in a similar manner as mentioned in (a).

The Directive thus adopts an approach revolving around a certain – undefined – subset of 'basic' human rights, the 'severe violation' of which must be 'sufficiently serious'. In practice, the CJEU has taken the ECHR in parallel with the CFR to examine whether there is, *prima facie*, an act of persecution. According to the court, it is the nature of the repression and its consequences rather than the substantive ambit of a right that forms the basis of identifying acts of persecution.[183] In other words, while the ambit of given human rights

181 McAdam, 'Rethinking the Origins of "Persecution" in Refugee Law' (Ch 2 n 173).

182 Storey, 'What Constitutes Persecution? Towards a Working Defintion' (Ch 1 n 95) 273. On the importance of human rights for the definition of the refugee definition, see, eg, Hathaway and Foster, *The Law of Refugee Status*, (Ch 1 n 100) 193–208; Nora Markard, 'Ein neues Schutzkonzept? Der Einfluss der Menschenrechte auf den internationalen Schutz' (2015) 11 Zeitschrift für Ausländerrecht und Ausländerpolitik 56.

183 Joined Cases C-71/11 and C-99/11 *Bundesrepublik Deutschland v Y and Z* [2012] digital reports para 65. 'It follows that acts which, on account of their intrinsic severity as well as the severity of their consequences for the person concerned, may be regarded as constituting persecution must be identified, not on the basis of the particular aspect of religious freedom that is being interfered with, but on the basis of the nature of the repression inflicted on the individual and its consequences […]'.

obligations makes out a *prima facie* case of 'being persecuted', the severity or seriousness of a measure restricting the exercise of the right provides the watershed. Thus the CJEU decided that sanctions such as ill-treatment or imprisonment imposed in the exercise of another right may give rise to an 'act of persecution' –

> for the purpose of determining whether interference with the right to freedom of religion which infringes Article 10(1) of the [...] [CFR] may constitute an 'act of persecution', the competent authorities must ascertain [...] whether that person, *as a result of exercising that freedom in his country of origin*, runs a genuine risk of, *inter alia*, being prosecuted or subject to inhuman or degrading treatment or punishment [...][184]

In addition to the definition of 'acts of persecution' in Article 9, the Qualification Directive also makes recourse to human rights in Article 15, the definition of 'serious harm'. According to Article 15(a)–(b) of the Qualification Directive, serious harm may consist of the death penalty or execution or of 'torture or inhuman or degrading treatment or punishment of an applicant in the country of origin'.[185] Both these types of harm correspond to human rights that are protected by the CFR and the ECHR.[186] In *Elgafaj*, the court stated that Article 15(b) 'corresponds, in essence, to Article 3 of the ECHR'.[187] Yet, Article 15(b) defines serious harm as torture or inhuman or degrading treatment or punishment *in the country of origin*, so that there is not a complete overlap between non-refoulement obligations under the ECHR and the inclusion criteria of subsidiary status.[188]

---

184 *Bundesrepublik Deutschland v Y and Z* (ibid) para 72 (emphasis added). Similarly, in the case of X, Y and Z, the CJEU ruled that while criminalisation of homosexual acts alone does not in itself constitute persecution, imprisonment sanctioning homosexual acts is a 'punishment which is disproportionate or discriminatory and thus constitutes an act of persecution'. *Minister voor Immigratie en Asiel v X* and *Y and Z v Minister voor Immigratie en Asiel* (Ch 1 n 55).

185 Emphasis added.

186 Articles 2 and 4 CFR and Articles 2 and 3 ECHR respectively.

187 *Meki Elgafaji and Noor Elgafaji v Staatsecretaris van Justitie* (Ch 1 n 67) para 27.

188 Case C-542/13 *Mohamed M'Bodj v Belgian State*, ECLI:EU:C:2014:2452 [2014] digital reports para 33: 'It is clear from that provision that it is applicable only to the inhuman or degrading treatment of an applicant in his country of origin. It follows that the EU legislature envisaged that subsidiary protection should be granted only in those cases in which such treatment occurred in the applicant's country of origin.' As Hailbronner points out, 'The drafting history of the Qualification Directive suggests that this phrase was introduced, in conjunction with Article 15(b) Qualification Directive, in order to limit the scope of the directive only to certain types of cases of non-return obligations under

What is more, the CJEU in *Moussa Abdida*, ruled that member states have non-refoulement obligations under the EU Returns Directive and the CFR that *exceed international protection*. In particular, member states must respect Article 19(2) of the CFR, interpreted in conjunction with Article 3, ECHR, when they apply Article 14(1) of the Returns Directive.[189]

The increased importance of human rights for defining harm relevant to the Convention's being persecuted notion is also apparent at the international level. While there are reasons to believe that the drafters intentionally left the term undefined in order to keep it open to evolution and because of the sheer breath of potentially persecutory treatments,[190] there have been multiple attempts to provide further guidance on the term, given its centrality for the refugee definition.[191] Because none of these attempts provide universal, abstract and evolutionary criteria that circumscribe persecution, the most popular approach has been to use human rights as interpretative guidance.

Article 3 of the ECHR, while excluding others, in particular cases of severe risk to health.' Hailbronner (ed), *EU Immigration and Asylum Law: Commentary of EU Regulations and Directives* (C.H.Beck 2010). For more recent case law specifying the overlap of Article 15, Qualification Directive and Article 3 in relation to state-inflicted health issues, see C-353/16 *MP v Secretary of State for the Home Department,* ECLI:EU:C:2018:276 [2018] digital reports. For a discussion of the differences between the serious harm and Article 3 ECHR, see also Jannis Broscheit; Andreas Gornik, 'Zur Abgrenzung von subsidiärem Schutz nach § 4 I 2 Nr. 2 AsylG und dem Abschiebungsverbot nach § 60 v AufenthG i. V. m. Art. 3 EMRK', (2018) 14 Zeitschrift für Ausländerrecht und Ausländerpolitik 302.

189 C-562/13 *Centre public d'action sociale d'Ottignies-Louvain-la-Neuve v Moussa Abdida,* ECLI:EU:C:2014:2453 [2014] digital reports. Indeed, the Qualification Directive is without prejudice to non-refoulement obligations arising from other legal sources, stating, in Article 21(1), that 'Member States shall respect the principle of non-refoulement in accordance with their international obligations.' The Directive is clear, however, that protection granted under any other obligations falls outside the scope of the Directive. Recital 15 of the Qualification Directive states that member states may, on humanitarian or compassionate grounds, take the decision not to return individuals to the state of origin, but that such individuals fall outside the scope of the Directive. Article 2(h) suggests that there is '*another kind of protection*' outside the scope of the Directive.

190 Atle Grahl-Madsen, *The Status of Refugees in International Law: Refugee Character* (Sijthoff 1966).

191 See Storey, 'What Constitutes Persecution? Towards a Working Defintion' (Ch 1 n 95) 274–276. Attempts for clarification include guidance by dictionary definitions of 'persecution', which require malign intent to restrict certain freedoms; guidance by Article 33 of the Convention, which prohibits the return of a refugee to a territory where their 'life or freedom' would be at risk; or guidance by the application of the term in jurisprudence. Some of these approaches have stressed the 'subjective' nature of the well-founded fear of being persecuted by attempting to capture the intensity for the person concerned and have often led to a narrow, physical understanding of relevant harm. See Hathaway and Foster, *The Law of Refugee Status* (Ch 1, n 100) 96.

The UNHCR Handbook was first in stating that a threat to life and freedom and 'serious violations of human rights' constitute persecution.[192] The Handbook further states that measures which on their own cannot amount to violations of human rights can reach an intensity that qualifies them as persecution.[193] Importantly, the human rights approach does not require a violation of human rights *as a matter of law* in order to identify relevant harm. The very requirement of a 'well-founded fear of being persecuted' – a real risk, that does not need to depend on the actual occurrence of harm in the past – precludes such a reading. Thus, the UNHCR in its Guideline on International Protection on Child Asylum Claims, argues that '[…] [in] determining the persecutory character of an act inflicted against a child, it is essential *to analyse the standards of the CRC and other relevant international human rights instruments* applicable to children'.[194]

The approach of using human rights law as interpretative guidance for the notion of 'being persecuted' has since then also been prominent in both civil law and common law countries, even outside the EU.[195] However, the approach is confronted by the challenge of identifying which human rights are relevant or of sufficient gravity, given that there is consensus that there is not a complete overlap between human rights norms and the notion of persecution. A first possibility is a hierarchy of human rights norms, in particular, differentiation between norms from which derogation can be made in case of public emergency, and norms that are non-derogable under the ICCPR. This is the universal equivalent to the approach of EU asylum law, which states that would-be violations of non-derogable rights under the ECHR are particular examples for 'acts of persecution' (an act that is 'sufficiently serious by its nature or repetition as to constitute a violation of a basic human right').[196] Related to

192 UN High Commissioner for Refugees, 'Handbook on Refugee Status Determination' (Ch 2 n 111) para 51. For a position similar to that of the UNHCR Handbook, see the 1995 Commentary by Weis, *The Refugees Convention, 1951: The Travaux Préparatoires Analysed* (Ch 2 n 83) 8 – according to which, 'At the very least, a connection exists between persecution and the failure on the part of states to observe certain human rights. The reference contained in the Preamble to the Convention concerning the principle that human beings shall enjoy fundamental rights and freedoms may provide a context for advancing the view that the violation of certain rights may either constitute persecution per se, or evidence thereof.'

193 UN High Commissioner for Refugees, 'Handbook on Refugee Status Determination' (Ch 2 n 223) para 53.

194 UN High Commissioner for Refugees, 'Guidelines on International Protection No 8: Child Asylum Claims under Articles 1(A)2 and 1(F) of the 1951 Convention and/or 1967 Protocol relating to the Status of Refugees' UN Doc HCR/GIP/09/08 (2009), para 13.

195 For a list of cases, see Hathaway and Foster, *The Law of Refugee Status* (Ch 1 n 100) 185, 196.

196 Article 9(1)(a).

this, another possibility is identification of the non-derogable 'core' of human rights obligations from which derogation cannot be made in the ICCPR[197] and the minimum core obligations in the ICESCR which are not subject to progressive realisation, such as non-discrimination in the allocation of available resources.[198] In common law jurisprudence, Hathaway's concept, which relied on certain 'levels' of rights, and defined persecution as a 'sustained or systemic violation of basic human rights demonstrative of a failure of state protection',[199] has been heavily influential. More recently, Hathaway and Foster have argued for a *hierarchy of duty* for human rights, according to which the nature of the duty attached to human rights norms defines whether a given harm is relevant. First, the 'interest at stake [has to be, A.N.] within the ambit of a human rights norm as defined by a widely ratified international human rights treaty'.[200] Second, a limitation clause in human rights law circumscribes the boundaries of protected action; infringements that fall under a lawful limitation clause are not relevant harm. Third, *de minimis* harm that satisfies the two first criteria is not relevant harm. Under this approach, an infringement of, for instance, the right to practice openly freedom of religion would as such be relevant harm, rather than only a particularly severe sanction imposed in the exercise of such right. The approach differs somewhat from the EU law approach, which gauges the severity of an infringement by reference to the sanction imposed for the exercise of a particular right.[201]

In sum, although there remain conceptual differences on the application of the human rights approach, that approach has become the most influential and is also undisputed in EU law, given the Qualification Directive's Definition of persecution and serious harm. What does this, together with the increased importance of human rights law for the entitlements in states of refuge, imply for the interpretation of the 1951 Convention's Protection clause?

A modern reading of the 1951 Convention that considers human rights law as part of the context referred to in the preamble and as relevant rules of international law applicable between parties[202] accords the clause two functions. First, the 'protection clause' embodies the notion of 'surrogacy', whereby

197 Human Rights Committee, 'General Comment No 29: States of Emergency (article 4)' (Ch 2 n 96).

198 Ibid 117.

199 Hathaway and Foster, *The Law of Refugee Status* (Ch 1 n 100).

200 Ibid.

201 *Bundesrepublik Deutschland v Y and Z* (Ch 1 n 183); *Minister voor Immigratie en Asiel v X and Y* and *Z v Minister voor Immigratie en Asiel* (Ch 1 n 55).

202 Articles 31(2) and 31(3)(c) VCLT respectively.

international protection only steps in once needed, in the case where there is no protection against relevant harm. Andreas Zimmermann and Claudia Mahler, in their 1951 Convention commentary, go as far as speaking of a 'basic principle of refugee law' that 'international protection only comes into play when national protection within the country of origin is not available'.[203] The same argument has been advanced in jurisprudence of the UK House of Lords case of *Horvath* –

> [...] the principle of surrogate protection finds its proper place in the second half of article 1A(2). If there is a failure of protection by the country of origin, the applicant will be unable to avail himself of that country's protection.[204]

Yet, to what extent is surrogacy actually a substantive 'principle' of refugee law? Jessica Schultz has succinctly distinguished between 'thin' and 'thick' perspectives on the surrogacy notion. While she suggests the former is a descriptive perspective on the characteristic of refugeehood, the latter is an interpretative principle in particular for the refugee definition and, thus, a condition for refugee status.[205] Schultz posits that the continued appeal of a 'thick' understanding is also created by the introduction of human rights concepts, in particular the principle of subsidiarity of remedies, according to which domestic remedies and rights protection take precedence over international

203 Zimmermann and Mahler, Article 1A(2), in Zimmermann; Dörschner; Machts (eds), *The 1951 Convention Relating to the Status of Refugees and its 1967 Protocol – A Commentary* (Ch 1 n 42), 448. A similar point is made by Chaloka Beyani in the introduction to the 1951 Convention commentary by Paul Weis. 'A remarkable feature of the Convention is the establishment of a system of international protection to persons who are in need of it. From the perspective of international law, the Convention accords the status of a refugee to a person who has lost the protection of their state of origin or nationality. It is essentially the loss, or failure, of state protection which makes international protection necessary for refugees.' Weis, *The Refugees Convention, 1951: The Travaux Préparatoires Analysed* (Ch 2 n 83) 4.

204 *Horvath v Secretary of State for the Home Department* (Ch 2 n 117); also *Canada v Ward* per Justice La Forest, '[t]he international community was meant to be a forum of second resort for the persecuted, a 'surrogate,' approachable upon failure of local protection. The rationale upon which international refugee law rests is not simply the need to give shelter to those persecuted by the state, but, more widely, to provide refuge to those whose home state cannot or does not afford them protection from persecution.' Also EXCOM No 80 (XLVII) – 1996, noting that 'internally displaced persons remain within the territorial jurisdiction of their own countries and that the primary responsibility for their welfare and protection lies with the State concerned'.

205 Schultz, *The Internal Protection Alternative in Refugee Law* (Ch 1 n 16) 121.

ones.[206] However, as shown in the previous analysis, this perspective on the role of human rights may also be questioned. While the protection clause in Article 1A(2) refers to protection in the country of nationality given the shift of meaning, the text also clearly links the clause to the well-founded fear of being persecuted. However, this implies that the clause *does not circumscribe a criterion for refugeehood in addition to the Convention's requirement of a well-founded fear of being persecuted.*[207]

Rather than containing an independent substantive condition for refugee status, the protection clause then points to the broken human rights protective relationship, and to the Convention's object and purpose of granting international protection in order to restore rights protection, earlier referred to as a bond between individual and state.[208] In a modern reading, this bond is (*surrogate*) *enfranchisement of refugees with human rights and rights under the 1951 Convention concurrently*.[209] Again, according to the UK House of Lords case of *Horvath:*

206 State recourse to a monitoring body with a complaint requires that the inter-state procedure has been resorted to at first instance and individual complaints also require the prior exhaustion of domestic remedies. In fact, under the respect, protect and fulfil framework, giving effect to human rights requires the creation of an effective domestic legal framework that includes avenues for redress. Thus, according to the HRC, '[...] [the] Covenant cannot be viewed as a substitute for domestic criminal law'. In the European context, the ECtHR has stated that the 'international machinery of collective enforcement established by the Convention' is of 'subsidiary nature' in relation to domestic enforcement. *See Case relating to certain aspects of the laws on the use of languages in education in Belgium v Belgium* (1968) Series A no 5. Also Article 41 ICCPR; Article 2 Optional Protocol to the ICCPR; Human Rights Committee, *General Comment No 31* (Ch 2 n 40) para 8.

207 This is reflected in the systematic of the Qualification Directive, which does not foresee the assessment of available protection as free-standing eligibility criterion for refugee or subsidiary protection status (Chapters III and V of the Directive), but as a consideration relevant in the assessment of either status. See Section 3.2.1., Zimmermann and Mahler, 'Article 1 A, para. 2' in Zimmermann; Dörschner; Machts, *The 1951 Convention Relating to the Status of Refugees and its 1967 Protocol* (Ch 1 n 42), 445 also appear to argue that the 'protection clause' is not an inclusion criterion independent from the well-founded fear of being persecuted notion, stating that 'it is only reasons which give rise to a well-founded fear of persecution [sic] that are also relevant reasons for not seeking protection in and by one's home State. Accordingly, the mere lack and inability of access to protection from other forms of human rights violations not amounting to persecution is not relevant for the purposes of Art 1 A, para 2 and thus cannot lead to an inability or a genuine unwillingness to seek protection of the respective country of origin'.

208 Earlier works spoke of broken bond Grahl-Madsen, *The Status of Refugees in International Law: Refugee Character* (Ch 2 n 190).

209 Stevens makes a similar point, stating that, 'From a historical perspective, it can be argued that a significant shift has taken place from interpreting the Convention as an instrument aimed at identifying individuals in need of protection from persecution by their own

> What [the 1951 Convention] seeks to achieve is the preservation of those rights and freedoms for individuals where they are denied them in their own state. Another state is to provide a surrogate protection where protection is not available in the home state. The convention assumes that every state has the obligation to protect its own nationals. But it recognises that circumstances may occur where that protection may be inadequate. The purpose of the convention is to secure that a refugee may in the surrogate state enjoy the rights and freedoms to which all are entitled without discrimination and which he cannot enjoy in his own state.[210]

The conceptualisation of international protection as a human rights-based surrogate protection has also been criticised in further academic literature, based on conceptual problems. One major argument is that human rights cannot provide the link between 'protection' in the state of nationality and in the state of refuge, because *everyone* is entitled to human rights, rather than only those that lose protection at home.[211] However, this criticism oversees that human rights are complementing the scope of entitlement under the Convention, as explored in Section 2.2.3. Even if the entitlements of the Convention does not make it distinct, the Convention does create a subset of persons who, by virtue of the prohibition of refoulement (and even though the Convention does not contain a duty to grant a residence permit), will typically remain in a country of refuge where the obligations of that state apply.

In sum, while surrogacy then is *no independent substantive criterion of refugeehood*, it does amount to a rule underlying the 1951 Convention's refugee definition.

2.4 Conclusion: Human Rights-Informed Surrogate 'International Protection'

This chapter has traced the origins of the notion of 'surrogacy' in EU asylum law – according to which a need for 'international protection' corresponds to lacking (domestic) protection. It contains three major observations. First, 'international protection' under the Qualification Directive is a concept

state to one that also sanctions "substitute protection of basic human rights"'. Stevens, 'What Do We Mean by Protection?' (Ch 1 n 104) 238.

210 *Horvath v Secretary of State for the Home Department* (Ch 2 n 117).

211 David J Cantor, 'Defining Refugees: Persecution, Surrogacy and the Human Rights Paradigm' (Ch 1 n 17) 367.

intertwining human rights law and the 1951 Convention. On the whole, the Convention and human rights norms complement each other in respect of the substantive rights granted to those individuals who qualify for international protection under the Qualification Directive.

Second, international protection is surrogate human rights enfranchisement, stepping in for a lack of domestic protection. That domestic protection refers to protection against harm relevant for the eligibility criteria of refugee status and subsidiary protection status. Which harm is relevant is increasingly influenced by human rights.

Third, the Qualification Directive's concept of human rights-informed surrogate international protection fits squarely with the 1951 Convention. It reflects the influence of human rights law on refugee entitlements as well as on the protection clause in the 1951 Convention's refugee definition. Given the structure of the law on aliens at the time, the term protection originally referred, among others, to diplomatic protection in the state of refuge, and was an expression of the lost bond between an individual and a state, at the origin of which was the harm feared in the state of nationality. The development of human rights law has gradually led to a shift in meaning, with human rights law defining the modern international law bond between individuals and states. This has ramifications on the protection clause, which no longer reflects a requirement of refugeehood additional to the well-founded fear of being persecuted but rather reflects the purpose of the Convention to entrust refugees with surrogate, rights-based international protection.

The notion that international protection is a 'surrogate' finds expression in concepts whereby an individual is not in need of international protection if they can find protection in their state of nationality (protection against harm by non-state actors, IPA), or in another country (safe third country and first country of asylum). The following three chapters will discuss the law and practice of these concepts.

CHAPTER 3

Protection against Harm

3.1 Introduction

EU asylum law (Article 6 on 'actors of persecution or serious harm' in conjunction with Article 7, Qualification Directive, on 'actors of protection') provides that individuals are not in need of international protection if they can find effective 'protection against persecution or serious harm'. In practice, this provision is primarily relevant in cases of harm inflicted by non-state actors. In principle, however, it could also be relevant in cases where 'rogue' state actors have inflicted harm but are sanctioned by superior authorities.

This chapter will discuss the analysis of available protection under the Qualification Directive, in conjunction with refugee and human rights law. In particular, how are such cases assessed under the 1951 Convention's refugee definition? When can it be said that such protection is effective and which actors can provide protection against harm? Should the Qualification Directive more strongly differentiate between actors of protection in the assessment of refugee status on the one hand, and in the assessment of subsidiary protection status on the other? Finally, does the Qualification Directive succeed in harmonising an international law-compliant actor of protection concept?

This chapter will argue, first, that non-return obligations under international human rights law and under refugee law have converged in respect of the means of assessing whether or not an individual can obtain effective protection against harm. Both systems require an individualised and factual assessment. In such assessment, the legal obligations of the state of nationality are only of evidentiary value in illustrating willingness and ability to protect against harm, but do not prove what is or not effective. Second, this chapter will argue that human rights law and refugee law have converged in respect of the actors that can, in principle, provide protection. Contrary to what academic criticism contends, both bodies of international law allow consideration of actors other than states as actors of protection, although there are serious doubts as to whether efforts to protect against harm by these actors will be effective in practice. In light of this commonality, the Qualification Directive rightly features a common 'actor of protection' article for both refugee status and subsidiary protection status. Third, the chapter will argue that a potential

 | DOI:10.1163/9789004430396_004

recast Qualification Directive should clarify to what extent states may consider as relevant evidence whether or not an applicant has already turned to the authorities of their state of nationality for protection, given divergent practice in the member states.

The analysis will begin with the interaction of relevant norms of EU secondary law. In order to test whether or not refugee and human rights law converge, it will then proceed to analyse separately the relevant standards of the 1951 Convention on the one hand, and of human rights law on the other hand.

3.2 Analysis of Available Protection in Status Determination: Anchoring Article 7(2) Qualification Directive in Refugee and Human Rights Law

3.2.1 *The Interplay of Article 7(2) Qualification Directive and the Directive's Eligibility Criteria*

The analysis of available protection is regulated by Article 7(2) of the Qualification Directive. The article features in the Directive's chapter containing rules for the assessment of refugee status and subsidiary protection status (Chapter II, providing for minimum standards on evidentiary assessment, *sur place* needs of international protection, actors of protection, actors of persecution and internal protection). Rather than an eligibility criterion for refugee or subsidiary protection status, the analysis of available protection is an overarching provision on relevant analysis in the assessment of status. Article 7 provides which actors can be assessed as providing protection under the rules for qualification as a refugee (Chapter III) or for subsidiary protection (Chapter V).

> Article 7 – Actors of protection
>
> [...][1]
>
> 2. Protection against persecution or serious harm must be effective and of a non-temporary nature. Such protection is generally provided when the actors mentioned under points (a) and (b) of paragraph 1 take reasonable steps to prevent the persecution or suffering of serious harm, inter alia, by operating an effective legal system for the detection, prosecution

1 Article 7(1) will be the focus of Section 3.5 below.

> and punishment of acts constituting persecution or serious harm, and when the applicant has access to such protection.

As is plain from the text, 'protection' means 'protection against persecution or serious harm', so that Article 7 links to the definition of a refugee (as having a 'well-founded fear of being persecuted') and to the definition of a beneficiary of subsidiary protection (facing a 'real risk of serious harm').[2] Article 9 and Article 15, Qualification Directive define such acts of persecution and serious harm,[3] while Article 6 provides for a specific subset of cases in which the assessment of available protection is relevant.

> Article 6 – Actors of persecution or serious harm
> Actors of persecution or serious harm include:
> (a) the State;
> (b) parties or organisations controlling the State or a substantial part of the territory of the State;
> (c) non-State actors, if it can be demonstrated that the actors mentioned in points (a) and (b), including international organisations, are unable or unwilling to provide protection against persecution or serious harm as defined in Article 7.

As apparent from the text of Article 6, the analysis of protection against harm is relevant primarily where there is harm inflicted by non-state actors.[4] However, the Qualification Directive does not exclude that available protection may have to be assessed in cases of harm inflicted by state actors, such as where a subset of state actors is inflicting relevant harm and central state institutions are sanctioning their behaviour.[5] Yet, the preamble of the Directive foresees a

---

2 Article 2d) and e) Qualification Directive.

3 On the interpretation of Articles 9 and 15 Qualification Directive, see above, Section 2.3.4.

4 Indeed, the Qualification Directive requires a state or non-state 'actor of persecution' in order for harm to fall into the definition of persecution or serious harm under Articles 10 and 15. Harm that is not inflicted by any actor, such as natural disasters or an epidemic, do not fulfil the actor requirement of Article 6. See Anna Lübbe, 'Zielgerichtetheit des Akteursverhaltens und Unterlassen im Flüchtlingsrecht' (2011) 5 Zeitschrift für Ausländerrecht und Ausländerpolitik 164.

5 For example, the Zimbabwean police has urged Zimbabwean women to report rapes cases committed by armed forces, in the context of raids against protests. See BBC, 'Zimbabwe Women Urged to Report Rape by Soldiers' (January 2019) <www.bbc.com/news/world-africa-47042101> accessed 1 July 2019.

presumption against available protection in other parts of the country when harm is inflicted by state actors.[6] *A fortiori*, this presumption would also apply for Article 6.

Other than relating Article 7 to the refugee definition, the Directive does not specify the interplay with the criteria of refugee and subsidiary status. In particular, at what stage of status determination is the assessment of available protection due? The question is relevant as this could affect outcomes of decisions.[7]

The text of the Directive is inconclusive. The EU Commission's Explanatory Memorandum for its proposal of the original 2004 Qualification Directive reasoned that protection analysis was to be grounded in the 'well-founded fear' limb of the refugee definition.[8] However, given that Article 7 is about 'protection against acts of persecution or serious harm', it appears to presuppose an applicant already has an established 'well-founded fear' or real risk of harm, suggesting that the analysis of available protection is linked to the assessment of acts of persecution under Article 9.

Furthermore, Article 9(3), Qualification Directive stipulates that in order to satisfy the criterion for a nexus between the persecution and a Convention ground, there must be a connection between those grounds and 'the acts of persecution as qualified in Paragraph 1 of this Article or the absence of protection against such acts'.[9] In other words, if actors of protection under Article 7 of the Directive do not provide effective protection on a Convention ground, such as race or religion, the harm is indeed 'for reasons of' such ground, as required by the refugee definition. Given that this requirement of a causal nexus succeeds the analysis of the well-founded fear, the text of the Directive suggests protection analysis is part of the being persecuted limb of the definition.

---

6 According to Recital 27, 'Internal protection against persecution or serious harm should be effectively available to the applicant in a part of the country of origin where he or she can safely and legally travel to, gain admittance to and can reasonably be expected to settle. Where the State or agents of the State are the actors of persecution or serious harm, there should be a presumption that effective protection is not available to the applicant.'

7 See Section 3.2.2.

8 Commission of the European Union, Qualification Directive Proposal 2009 (Ch 2 n 66) 44, 'available State protection means that the "fear of being persecuted" or otherwise suffering serious unjustified harm shall not be considered to be well founded, in which case Member States shall not recognize the need for protection.'

9 See also Recital 29, according to which, 'One of the conditions for qualification for refugee status within the meaning of Article 1(A) of the Geneva Convention is the existence of a causal link between the reasons for persecution, namely race, religion, nationality, political opinion or membership of a particular social group, and the acts of persecution or the absence of protection against such acts.'

The CJEU, in turn, appears to construe the analysis of available protection as a criterion anchored in the refugee definition's 'protection clause' and additional to the well-founded fear of being persecuted. In *Abdullah*, it stated that the circumstances existing in the country of origin –

> [...] form the reason why it is impossible for the person concerned, or why he justifiably refuses, to avail himself of the 'protection' of his country of origin within the meaning of Article 2(c) of the Directive, that is to say, in terms of that country's ability to prevent or punish acts of persecution.[10]

However, given the *Abdullah* judgment arose from a case on cessation and sits uneasy with the text of the Directive, the anchoring in the refugee definition is to be answered by looking at the 1951 Convention.

3.2.2 *The Analysis of Available Protection and the 1951 Convention's Refugee Definition*

Unlike other concepts that are taken verbatim from the 1951 Convention – such as the definition of refugee, the reasons for cessation or exclusion from refugee status – the material rules of Chapter II, Qualification Directive have no equivalent in the 1951 Convention. However, the analysis of available protection has long been relevant as a practical issue for the Convention. The UNHCR Handbook, as early as 1979, argued that:

> Where serious discriminatory or other offensive acts are committed by the local populace, they can be considered as persecution if they are knowingly tolerated by the authorities, or if the authorities refuse, or prove unable, to offer effective protection.[11]

Chiefly, there have in the past been discussed three approaches on how the analysis of protection against harm relates to the 1951 Convention's refugee definition. The approaches not only differ in respect of where they anchor the analysis of protection in the text, but they may also impact how the effectiveness of protection is gauged and whether or not a failure of protection can be linked to a Convention ground. Thus, scholars have cautioned that according to the analysis of available protection, a separate role in the definition

10 *Aydin Salahadin Abdulla, Kamil Hasan, Ahmed Adem, Hamrin Mosa Rashi and Dler Jamal v Bundesrepublik Deutschland* (Ch 1 n 54) para 59.

11 UN High Commissioner for Refugees, 'Handbook on Refugee Status Determination' (Ch 2 n 223) para 65.

would overstress its importance and make the burden upon a refugee more onerous,[12] or lead away from individualised assessments.[13] As the analysis of case law will show, a particularly problematic practice in this regard is to expect applicants to demonstrate they have first to local and then to higher level authorities when harm is inflicted by non-state actors,[14] so as to demonstrate they cannot avail themselves of protection.

First, and most obviously, given the occurrence of the term, the analysis of available protection in the country of nationality can be found in the 'protection clause' of Article 1A(2) of the 1951 Convention. However, this would effectively turn 'availing of protection' into a substantive inclusion criterion for refugee status, additional to the requirement of alienage and the well-founded fear of persecution for reasons of one of the five Convention grounds. As is apparent from Chapter 1, such a reading does not correspond to the modern meaning of the clause, as embodying the object and purpose of the Convention to provide surrogate international protection, and linked to the well-founded fear of being persecuted. Indeed, there is also no judicial practice on such an approach.

Second, the analysis of available protection in the country of nationality can be linked to whether or not a fear of being persecuted is *well-founded*. UNHCR, in a guidance note on the interpretation of Article 1, suggested that the analysis of available protection is part of the 'well-founded fear' enquiry, but in other statements it makes contradictory claims.[15] What is more, scholars critical of the attaching of relative weight to the analysis of protection in the country of nationality have stressed that the *well-foundedness* of fear of persecution is the only relevant text of the refugee definition for such analysis.[16]

---

12 Daniel Wilsher, 'Non-State Actors and the Definition of a Refugee in the United Kingdom: Protection, Accountability or Culpability?' (Ch 1 n 99); for a similar criticism, see Pia Zambelli, 'Problematic Trends in the Analysis of State Protection and Article 1F(a) Exclusion in Canadian Refugee Law' (2011) 23 International Journal of Refugee Law 252.

13 Goodwin-Gil and McAdam, *The Refugee in International Law* (Ch 1 n 15) 10.

14 See below, Section 3.5.3.

15 UN High Commissioner for Refugees, 'Interpreting Article 1 of the 1951 Convention Relating to the Status of Refugees' (2001), para 15 <https://www.refworld.org/docid/3b20a3914.html> accessed 1 July 2019. This stands in contrast to the UNHCR Handbook on Refugee Status Determination (Ch 2 n 111) para 65, suggesting that the analysis of protection is part of the enquiry on the being persecuted notion.

16 Antonio Fortin, 'The Meaning of "Protection" in the Refugee Definition' (Ch 2 n 122) 574, stating that protection is relevant only to the extent that it is 'an essential factor for assessing the well-foundedness of the person's fear of persecution by non-State agents'.

Third, and the most common approach in common law countries, the analysis of available protection can be conceived of as part of the Convention's notion of 'being persecuted'.[17] The approach stems from UK jurisprudence on the asylum application by a woman claiming a risk of domestic violence. In particular, it was argued that persecution consisted of two combined elements – the physical assaults and the unwillingness or inability of the authorities to protect against them – leading to the formula, 'Persecution = Serious Harm + The Failure of State Protection'.[18] Jurisprudence adopting this formula has linked the Convention's nexus clause to *either* the harm element or the failure of state protection, in particular in the UK,[19] Australia and New Zealand. Even in the case where a person feared serious harm unrelated to one of the Convention grounds, by a non-state actor, and there was a failure of protection against that harm for reason of a Convention ground, they would have a well-founded fear of being persecuted for reasons of a Convention ground.[20]

---

17 Hathaway and Foster, *The Law of Refugee Status* (Ch 1 n 100) 295 citing cases from New Zealand (eg, *Daniel Martin Butler v Attorney General and Refugee Status Appeals Authority* [1999] NZAR 205; *Refugee Appeal No 71427/99* [2000] NZAR 545; *AC (Egypt)*, [2011] NZIPT 800015); Canada (*Zalzali v Canada* [1991] 3 FC 605), *Minister of Employment and Immigration v Mayers* [1993] 1 FC 154); the UK (*Shah* (UKHL, 1999); *Horvath* (Ch 2 n 229)), Ireland (*Msengi v Minister for Justice, Equality and Law Reform* [2006] IEHC 241 and Australia (*Minister for Immigration and Multicultural Affairs v Khawar* [2002] HCA 14); *Rajaratnam v Minister for Immigration and Multicultural Affairs* [2000] FCA 1111; *Dranichnikov v Minister for Immigration and Multicultural Affairs* [2003] HCA 26; *NAGV and NAGW of 2002 v Minister for Immigration and Multicultural and Indigenous Affairs* [2005] HCA 6.

18 *Islam v Secretary of State for the Home Department Immigration Appeal Tribunal and Another, Ex Parte Shah* [1999] UKHL 20 (25 March 1999).

19 Ibid.

20 *Refugee Appeal No 71427/99* (Ch 2 n 17) para 112; *Minister of Multicultural Affairs v Khawar* (Ch 2 n 17) para 31 per Gleeson CJ, 'Where persecution consists of two elements, the criminal conduct of private citizens, and the toleration or condonation of such conduct by the state or agents of the state, resulting in the withholding of protection which the victims are entitled to expect, then the requirement that the persecution by reason of one of the Convention grounds may be satisfied by the motivation of either the criminals or the state.' See also UN High Commissioner for Refugees, 'Guidelines on International Protection No 2: 'Membership of a Particular Social Group' Within the Context of Article 1A(2) of the 1951 Convention and/or its 1967 Protocol Relating to the Status of Refugees', UN Doc HCR/GIP/02/02, para 22: 'There may also arise situations where a claimant may be unable to show that the harm inflicted or threatened by the non-State actor is related to one of the five grounds … Nonetheless, if the State is unwilling to extend protection based on one of the five grounds, then she may be able to establish a valid claim for refugee status: the harm visited upon her by her husband is based on the State's unwillingness to protect her for reasons of a Convention ground'.

The UNHCR has endorsed the establishment of a link between failure of state protection and the nexus ground in its *Guidelines on Gender-Related Persecution*.[21] Academic proponents of such an approach have therefore argued that 'failure to acknowledge the relevance of state protection as a part of the risk of "being persecuted" would result in an under-inclusive application of the Convention' where it is lack of protection, rather than the harm, that is linked to a Convention ground,[22] in particular in cases of gender-related violence.[23]

As stated in the previous section, the Qualification Directive in Article 9(3) does foresee that the causal nexus required by the refugee definition can also link to lacking protection. Article 9(3) should therefore harmonise divergent law and practice in member states, some of which link the failure of protection against harm to a Convention ground – race, religion, nationality, political opinion or membership of a particular social group – and some of which do not. Thus, in addition to the UK, judicial practice in Sweden has on several occasions made the link for gender-related harm, even before domestic law was amended to transpose the recast Qualification Directive. The Migration Court of Appeals stated that:

> State failure may be due to shortages in resources or due to inefficiencies which cannot be linked to any persecution ground. The victim is then not a refugee as defined by law. However, a person who risks being exposed to persecution by individuals on grounds of sex may in some cases be denied State protection as an apparent result of the current political, social, religious or cultural structures [...] In such cases, the person may be considered to be a refugee.[24]

21 UN High Commissioner for Refugees, 'Guidelines on International Protection No 1: Gender-Related Persecution within the context of Article 1A(2) of the 1951 Convention and/or its 1967 Protocol relating to the Status of Refugees', UN Doc HCR/GIP/02/01 (2002).

22 Matthew; Hathaway and Foster, 'The Role of State Protection in Refugee Analysis' (Ch 1 n 99) 447.

23 Roger Haines, 'Gender-related Persecution' in Erika Feller, Volker Türk and Frances Nicholson (eds), *Refugee Protection in International Law: UNHCR's Global Consultations on International Protection* (Cambridge University Press 2003).

24 Migrationsöverdomstolen, 21 April 2011, MIG 2011:8, UM7851-10 (author's translation), relying on a 2005 government proposition to grant people with a well-founded fear of persecution on grounds of gender or sexual orientation refugee status rather than subsidiary protection status, Sveriges Rikstag, 'Flyktingskap och förföljelse på grund av kön eller sexuell läggning: Regeringens proposition' 2005/06:6 <www.riksdagen.se/sv/dokument-lagar/dokument/proposition/flyktingskap-och-forfoljelse-pa-grund-av-kon_GT036> accessed 20 October 2016.

In two unreported decisions preceding the Migration Court of Appeals judgment, the Migration Division of the Göteborg County Court and the Stockholm Appeals Court applied a failure of state protection to a 1951 Convention ground for an Albanian victim of domestic violence.[25] The authorities had been reluctant to react to the claimant's request for protection, which the courts, based on the prevalent discrimination against women and the many cases of domestic violence, attributed to her sex. According to the County Court, 'Persecution in the private sphere can constitute grounds for refugee status if the person being stalked is refused protection in the home country as an apparent result of political, social, religious or cultural structures.'[26]

In contrast, Article 9(3) is expressly transposed into domestic law neither in Germany[27] nor in the Netherlands.[28] Nor is there judicial practice from these countries that links a failure of state protection to a Convention ground. In the Netherlands, the lack of protection from harm is traditionally conceived of as flowing from the protection clause, to the effect that it is the relevant harm, rather than the lack of protection, which must be attributed to one of the Convention grounds.[29] In France, where the national code on the right to asylum did transpose Article 9(3),[30] practice remains ambiguous.[31]

---

25 Länsrätten i Göteborg, Migrationsdomstolen, 2 December 2008; Kammarrätten i Stockholm, Migrationsöverdomstolen, 2 November 2008, both cited in Migrationsöverdomstolen, 21 November 2008, MIG 2008:39, UM1042-08.

26 Ibid (author's translation).

27 Paragraph 3b, Asylgesetz, 2 September 2008 (BGBl I, 1798), as amended by Article 6 of the Act of 31 July 2016 (BGBl I, 1939).

28 Article 3.37 Voorschrift Vreemdelingen 2000, as of 1 July 2016, BWBR0012002.

29 Raad van State, 20 January 2004, JV 2004/98, para 2.2.2, cited in Hemme Battjes, *European Asylum Law and International Law* (Ch 1 n 102) 259, also (implicitly) Rechtbank 's-Gravenhage, 16 November 2004, AWB 03/29538.

30 Code de l'entrée et du séjour des étrangers et du droit d'asile, consolidated version as of 3 July 2016, Légifrance.

31 There are several decisions that locate the analysis of protection into the Convention's protection clause, eg *Mme B.*, CNDA 5 December 2008, no 620881, which refer to protection by the authorities in the words of Article 1A(2) of the 1951 Convention, that a person is 'unwilling, or, owing to … [a well-founded fear of being persecuted] unable to avail himself of the protection' of the authorities. Similarly, the CNDA noted in a decision on a Bosnian applicant that '[…] no serious element permits us to assume that he would again be exposed to persecutions or serious threats, nor that he would not be able to avail himself effectively of the protection of the local authorities, in particular the police […]' *MH*, CNDA 9 April 2010, no 09013398 C+ (author's translation); also *MK*, CNDA 8 July 2010, no 09016217 C. There is some contradiction, however, as many decisions of the CNDA and CRR refer to availability or lack of protection as part of the risk analysis, eg *M et Mme M*, CNDA 6 February 2012, no 09002796 et no 09002797 C; *M*, CRR 25 May 2007, no 589662; *M.*, CNDA 24 July 2012, no 11017592 C; *Mme B*, CNDA 23 February 2011, no 10012782

Beyond the possibility to link the failure of protection to the nexus requirement, there are two additional reasons why relating the analysis of protection to the well-founded fear of being persecuted is indeed the correct legal approach. First, the object and purpose of the Convention that has been elaborated in Chapter 1 – to provide surrogate, rights-based international protection to those who have lost rights – suggests that the notion of 'being persecuted' is relevant to the analysis of available protection. The loss of 'protection' in the protection clause of the refugee definition is merely a synonym for the loss of protection as expressed in the 'being persecuted' notion. This was further developed in the House of Lords decision in *Horvath*. As per Lord Hope:

> It is an important reminder that there are indeed two tests that require to be satisfied. A person may satisfy the fear test because he has well-founded fear of being persecuted, but yet may not be a 'refugee' within the meaning of the article because he is unable to satisfy the protection test. But it seems to me that the two tests are nevertheless linked to each other by the concepts which are to be found by looking to the purposes of the Convention. The surrogacy principle which underlies the issue of state protection is at the root of the whole matter. *There is no inconsistency between the separation of the definition into two different tests and the fact that each test is founded upon the same principle.* I consider that it has a part to play in the application of both tests to the evidence. I would hold therefore that, in the context of an allegation of persecution by non-state agents, *the word 'persecution' implies a failure by the state to make*

C+; *M J*, CNDA, 28 October 2010, no 09015404 C+, C+; *M S*, CNDA, 30 November 2010, no 09001370, R; *Mlle A*, CNDA 18 December 2007, no 596205; *Mlle Y*, CRR 30 November 2006, no 535001; *Mlle R*, CRR 29 September 2006, no 533070. Meanwhile, the failure to establish a link between persecution and a Convention ground may also be caused by a restrictive interpretation of the nexus clause. See *Mlle V*, CNDA 6 September 2011, no 10023173 R; *Mme M*, CRR 19 July 2006, no 526541; *Mlle E*, CNDA 23 October 2009, no 642112/09000931; *M L*, CNDA 30 March 2011, no 10013804 R; *Mlle O*, CNDA 29 July 2011, no 10020534 C+; *Mlle O*, CNDA 3 April 2012, no 11020945 C, all granting subsidiary protection status rather than refugee status for women at risk of domestic violence, forced marriage or trafficking. This also seems to be the case in Denmark. Instead, a restrictive interpretation of the nexus clause has led the Board to grant subsidiary protection rather than refugee protection to applicants opposing the Taliban in Afghanistan, as well as to a woman who feared sexual violence by members of her family. Both of these claims could have been linked to a Convention ground, notably imputed political opinion and gender as a particular social group. See afgh/2012/18; afgh/2011/37; afgh/2011/52; afgh/2011/15; afgh/2011/52; afgh/2010/78; afgh/2010/46; Afg/2010/17; Se-Mo/2004/20.

> *protection available against the ill-treatment or violence which the person suffers at the hands of his persecutors.* In a case where the allegation is of persecution by the state or its own agents the problem does not, of course, arise.[32]

In contrast to the interpretation of the CJEU, this reading is also in line with a modern reading of the protection clause of the 1951 Convention, which does not stipulate a separate criterion of eligibility.

Finally, it is also the systematic element of interpretation[33] which suggests locating the analysis of available protection in the being-persecuted limb of the Convention. As Chapter 4 will show, the concept of the International Protection Alternative is to be construed as following the analysis of the well-founded fear, so that consistency precludes locating the analysis of protection in the well-founded fear limb.

3.2.3 *The Place of Analysis of Available Protection in Assessing Human Rights Law Non-return Obligations and Subsidiary Protection Status*

For human rights law obligations (which significantly overlaps with the eligibility criteria for 'subsidiary protection' status under EU law), the question of how to relate the analysis of protection to the text of the 1951 Convention does not of course arise – because the Convention applies to *refugees* only. Rather, the decisive question is whether, by returning an individual, state parties expose him or her to a risk of human rights harm, in particular the risk of ill-treatment. In the ECHR context, for instance, the relevant enquiry is whether substantial grounds have been shown for believing that the person concerned would be exposed to a risk of such harm (which is essentially the same standard as that of Article 2(f) of the Qualification Directive).[34] The analysis of available protection is framed as a matter of the analysis of risk, a risk that must be real, personal and foreseeable, and which goes beyond a mere possibility.[35] The Human Rights Committee, in a decision on the return of a Pakistani national who feared violent Islamic fundamentalists, considered that religious minorities continued to face relevant harm against which the Pakistani authorities were

---

32 *Horvath v Secretary of State for the Home Department* (Ch 2 n 117).

33 According to Article 31 VCLT, the text of an instrument provides part of its context. What is more, the systematic element appears in the interpretation principles formulated by Savigny (see Ch 1 n 109), so would be a relevant rule of interpretation of the Qualification Directive's refugee definition as based on Article 1A(2) of the 1951 Convention.

34 *Soering v United Kingdom* (1989) Series A no 161, para 91.

35 *Vilvarajah and Others v the United Kingdom* (1991) Series A no 215.

'unwilling or unable to protect'.[36] Similarly, as the ECtHR held in *H L R v France*, in cases involving harm by non-state actors, the analysis of risk must pertain to both the acts of the perpetrators and of the state. According to the court, 'it must be *shown that the risk is real and that the authorities of the receiving State are not able to obviate the risk by providing appropriate protection*'.[37]

The Qualification Directive, meanwhile, takes a somewhat autonomous position on how the analysis of available protection against harm relates to the assessment of subsidiary protection status. According to Article 2(f) of the Directive, a person eligible for subsidiary protection faces '[...] a real risk of suffering serious ham [...] *and* is unable, or owing to such risk, unwilling to avail himself of the protection of that country'.[38] Thus, the Directive has transferred the 1951 Convention's 'protection clause' in Article 1A(2) to the eligibility criteria for subsidiary protection, despite the clause coming from a refugee law context. As is clear from the discussion in Chapter 1, a modern reading of the clause, meanwhile, precludes its use as a substantive inclusion criterion in the refugee law context that is additional to the well-founded fear of being persecuted. *A fortiori*, the protection clause should not be so interpreted in respect of the eligibility criteria for subsidiary protection. Just as in respect of refugee status, the protection clause in Article 2(f) of the Directive should be understood as embodying the principle of surrogacy of international protection for those with loss of rights.

Given the overlap of non-return obligations under Article 3, ECHR and subsidiary protection under the Qualification Directive, the assessment of available protection in the context of subsidiary protection is best conceived of as a part of the requirement of a real risk in Article 2(f) Qualification Directive, as in the ECHR context. In contrast to the 'well-founded fear of being persecuted'

36 *Naveed Akram Choudhary v Canada Communication No 1898/2009*, 17 December 2013, CCPR/C/109/D/1898/2009 para 9.7. The CAT, it appears, has refrained from extending non-refoulement obligations under CAT to cases of non-state actor harm only because the UNCAT requires complicity by the authorities. See Article 1 UNCAT, which requires that 'such pain or suffering is inflicted by or at the instigation of or with the consent or acquiescence of a public official or other person acting in an official capacity'. In *G R B v Sweden* Communication no 83/1997, 15 May 1998, CAT/C/20/D/083/1997, para. 6.5, the Committee stated that 'the issue whether the State party has an obligation to refrain from expelling a person who might risk pain or suffering inflicted by a non-governmental entity, without the consent or acquiescence of the Government, falls outside the scope of article 3 of the Convention'.

37 *HLR v France* ECHR 1997-III 745. Also *Ahmed v Austria* ECHR 1996-VI 2206, para 44 in which a deportation would have been contrary to Article 3 because there was no indication that the authorities of the home country would protect the applicant.

38 Emphasis added.

notion of the refugee definition, the logical element of interpretation requires that the notion of 'serious harm' is not separated into two composite elements of 'harm' and 'protection against harm'.

In sum, the 1951 Convention suggests a reading of Article 7 whereby the analysis of available protection is not a separate enquiry following the analysis of harm, but is linked to the notion of a well-founded fear of being persecuted in relation to refugee status, whereas human rights law suggests the linking of the assessment of available protection to the analysis of a real risk when assessing eligibility for subsidiary protection.

What does this imply for the question as to when protection against harm is actually effective?

3.3 Assessing the Effectiveness of Protection against Harm – EU Law Requirements in Conjunction with the 1951 Convention and International Human Rights Law

3.3.1 *The Criterion of Effective Protection in the Qualification Directive*

Article 7 of the Qualification Directive defines which actors can be considered as 'actors of protection' and circumscribes the characteristics of protection against persecution or serious harm. First, protection must fulfil the criteria of being 'effective' and of a 'non-temporary nature'. According to Article 7(2) of the Directive,

> Protection against persecution or serious harm must be effective and of a non-temporary nature. Such protection is generally provided when the actors mentioned under points (a) and (b) of paragraph 1 take reasonable steps to prevent the persecution or suffering of serious harm, inter alia, by operating an effective legal system for the detection, prosecution and punishment of acts constituting persecution or serious harm, and when the applicant has access to such protection.

Second, actors of protection must be 'willing and able' to provide such effective and non-temporary protection (Article 7(1)). The wording of the Directive raises two principle questions on the two requirements of effectiveness and the 'non-temporary nature' of protection. First, how do the terms 'generally' and 'system' relate to the requirement of effectiveness and ability – must the analysis of available protection be an individualised one and does it imply particular evidentiary burdens for the applicant? Second, how does the requirement of *reasonable* steps relate to the *prevention* of harm?

3.3.1.1 Article 7(2), Qualification Directive and Evidentiary Assessment

Article 7(2) Qualification Directive states that protection is 'generally' provided when the authorities take reasonable steps to prevent harm. A comparison of the different language versions makes clear that the term generally is used in the sense of 'in most cases', or normally.[39] Article 7(2), s 2 then provides for indicative examples[40] of such reasonable steps ('inter alia by [...]'), including by the operation of an effective and accessible legal system. Therefore, Article 7(2), s 2 ('protection is generally provided [...]') does not provide a conclusive definition of the requirements of effectiveness and the 'non-temporary nature' of the protection. Rather, the actual effectiveness of protection remains the relevant enquiry.[41] The wording leaves open, however, whether Article 7(2), s 1 operates as a rebuttable *presumption of protection*.

According to Article 6, Qualification Directive, non-state actors are actors of persecution, '*if it can be demonstrated*' that the state is unwilling or unable to provide protection in accordance with Article 7. Articles 6 and 7 do not provide rules for evidentiary assessment, so that their application has to conform to the rules on evidentiary assessment in Article 4, Qualification Directive, which lays down the rules for assessing the facts and circumstances for both refugee and subsidiary protection status.[42] Applicants submit information, which is then assessed on its relevance by the adjudicator in cooperation with the applicant (Article 4(1)).[43] To substantiate an application for international protection, an applicant has to submit the '*reasons for applying* for international protection'.[44] It has been pointed out, albeit controversially, that the Article requires of the applicant to deliver enough information to initiate the procedure,

39 See, for instance, the Dutch- and the Danish-language versions of the Directive ('in het algemeen'; 'normalt').

40 To that effect, also *DM (Majority Clan Entities Can Protect) Somalia* [2005] UKAIT 00150.

41 See also European Council on Refugees and Exiles, 'The Impact of the EU Qualification Directive on International Protection' (2008) <http://www.refworld.org/docid/4908758d2.html> accessed 20 October 2016, recommending that member states should 'implement higher standards when applying article 7(2), and evaluate the actual availability of protection, rather than merely whether the state of protection "take[s] reasonable steps to" prevent persecution or serious harm.'

42 This is also apparent from the analogous Article 8(2) Qualification Directive, which provides that 'Member States shall at the time of taking the decision on the application have regard to the general circumstances prevailing in that part of the country and to the personal circumstances of the applicant in accordance with Article 4.'

43 Gregor Noll, 'Evidentiary Assessment in Refugee Status Determination and the EU Qualification Directive' (2006) 12 *European Public Law* 295.

44 Article 4(2), emphasis added.

making out a *prima facie* case, so that there is a 'burden of assertion' rather than a burden of proof on the applicant.[45] This would correspond to the shared duty of fact-finding under the 1951 Convention.[46] The subsequent assessment by the adjudicators is to be carried out on an individual basis. Country of origin information, statements and documents by the applicant, and their personal circumstances, are relevant factors to be taken into account (Article 4(3)). Despite some ambiguity in the German, Portuguese and Swedish text, this standard is also clear from most versions of Article 6(c), Qualification Directive, which makes it clear that no proof in the strict sense of the term is necessary to demonstrate a failure of protection. What is more, Article 4 only mentions *a presumption of risk,* in cases where the applicant has previously suffered relevant harm, and therefore does preclude a *presumption of protection*. Arguably, given the presumption of risk in Article 4(4), Qualification Directive, the fact that the authorities have in the past denied or failed to provide protection appears by analogy to be a serious indication of unwillingness or inability to provide effective protection in the future, unless there a good reason to consider the opposite.

Also by way of analogy, guidance on the assessment of evidence in the application of Article 7(2) can also be derived from Article 8(2), Qualification Directive. Although that Article circumscribes rules on the internal protection alternative, it is also relevant to the analysis of available protection in the home region of the applicant, given that the same principle of surrogacy underlies the assessment of the internal protection alternative and the assessment of protection in the home region.[47]

The CJEU has provided some guidance on the application of Article 7(2) in *Abdulla*.[48] Although the questions submitted to the court concerned the interpretation of Article 11 (cessation), that Article, in the interpretation of the CJEU,[49]

---

45 Gregor Noll, 'Evidentiary Assessment under the Refugee Convention: Risk, Pain and the Intersubjectivity of Fear' in Gregor Noll (ed), *Proof, Evidentiary Assessment and Credibility in Asylum Procedures* (Martinus Nijhoff 2005) 301. For a different opinion, see Hailbronner (ed), *EU Immigration and Asylum Law: Commentary of EU Regulations and Directives* (188) 1027, stating that member states may shift a burden of proof onto the applicant under Article 4(1).

46 Hathaway and Foster, *The Law of Refugee Status* (Ch 1 n 100) 118–120.

47 See Chapter 4 on the internal protection alternative.

48 *Aydin Salahadin Abdulla, Kamil Hasan, Ahmed Adem, Hamrin Mosa Rashi and Dler Jamal v Bundesrepublik Deutschland* (Ch 1 n 54).

49 For a different interpretation, see Hathaway and Foster, *The Law of Refugee Status* (Ch 1, n 100) 476; UN High Commissioner for Refugees, 'Guidelines on International Protection: Cessation of Refugee Status under Article 1C(5) and (6) of the 1951 Convention

mirrors the criteria for qualification for refugee status in Articles 9–10 in conjunction with Articles 6–7, Qualification Directive.

First, according to the court, the assessment of available protection is above all a question of fact –

> [...] [The] *circumstances* which demonstrate the country of origin's inability or, conversely, its ability to ensure protection against acts of persecution *constitute a crucial element* in the assessment which leads to the granting of, or, as the case may be, by means of the opposite conclusion, to the cessation of refugee status.[50]

Second, the court makes clear that the assessment of the circumstances must be an individualised one. The second sentence of Article 7(2), Qualification Directive ('reasonable steps to prevent') has to be related to the individual in question, even though it makes reference to systemic conditions:

> In order to arrive at the conclusion that the refugee's fear of being persecuted is no longer well founded, the competent authorities, by reference to Article 7(2) of the Directive, must verify, *having regard to the refugee's individual situation*, that the actor or actors of protection of the third country in question have taken reasonable steps to prevent the persecution, that they therefore operate, inter alia, an effective legal system for the detection, prosecution and punishment of acts constituting persecution and that the national concerned will have access to such protection [...][51]

This corresponds to the opinion of Advocate General Mazák, who stressed that '[...] the requirement of protection imposed pursuant to Articles 11(1)(e) and 7(2) of Directive 2004/83 *does not exist in the abstract but rather in concrete, tangible and objective terms*'.[52]

Third, in line with the individualised assessment, the court prescribes an assessment of the conditions of operation of both actors inflicting harm and of actors providing protection.

---

relating to the Status of Refugees (the 'Ceased Circumstances' Clauses)', UN Doc HCR/GIP/03/03 (2003).

50 Paragraph 59 (emphasis added).

51 Ibid paras 68–71.

52 Joined Cases C-175/08, C-176/08, C-178/08 and C-179/98 *Aydin Salahadin Abdulla, Kamil Hasan, Ahmed Adem, Hamrin Mosa Rashi and Dler Jamal v Bundesrepublik Deutschland* [2010] ECR I-01493, Opinion of AG Mazák, para 53.

> That verification means that the competent authorities *must* assess, in particular, the conditions of operation of, on the one hand, the institutions, authorities and security forces and, on the other, all groups or bodies of the third country which may, by their action or inaction, be responsible for acts of persecution against the recipient of refugee status if he returns to that country.[53]

Fourth, the court has ruled that that the wording of Article 11(2), whereby protection must be 'non-temporary', means that there are, on a permanent basis, no grounds for a 'well-founded fear of being persecuted'.[54] Given that the term 'non-temporary' in Article 11(2) is the same as that in Article 7, it is clear that 'non-temporary' requires permanence rather than transience.[55] Harald Dörig has pointed out how national case law on cessation can be used to specify that criterion in relation to individual cases, such as regime change or a 'liberalisation within a former persecutory system' – in particular, the German Federal Administrative Court has stated that 'the greater the risk of persecution, even if it remains below the threshold of a considerable probability [the evidentiary threshold used in German asylum law, AN], the more permanent […] the stability of change must be.'[56]

Finally, the CJEU provides, by way of example, further guidance as to how courts should individualise the evidentiary assessment of available protection. The CJEU not only refers to the application of laws and regulations, but also to compliance with basic human rights. Thus, the general human rights situation can be instructive in indicating whether actors of protection are *willing* to provide protection and whether they are able to do so, in particular whether protection against specific harm is effective. This is true even if the human rights thereby assessed do not form the basis for a claim of a well-founded fear of 'being persecuted' in the first place.

> In accordance with Article 4(3) of the Directive, relating to the assessment of facts and circumstances, […] [the competent authorities] *may* take into account, *inter alia*, the *laws and regulations of the country of origin and the manner in which they are applied,* and the *extent to which basic human rights are guaranteed* in that country.[57]

53 Ibid paras 68–71.

54 Ibid para 73.

55 On this point, see also Dörig, 'Asylum Qualification Directive 2011/95/EU', 1156 in Hailbronner and Thym (eds), *EU Immigration and Asylum Law – A Commentary* (Ch 1 n 7).

56 Ibid 1157.

57 Ibid paras 68–71.

The CJEU's guidance on the interpretation of facts and circumstances broadly echoes the Opinion of the EU Commission which had suggested a list of relevant factors in its 2001 proposal for a Qualification Directive. According to the Commission, member states should consider, when assessing the availability of protection against harm:

(a) General conditions in the country of origin
(b) The State's complicity with respect to the infliction of harm at stake
(c) The nature of State's [sic] policies with respect to the harm at stake, including whether there in [sic] force a criminal law which makes violent attacks by persecutors punishable by sentences commensurate with the gravity of their crimes
(d) The influence the alleged persecutors have with State officials
(e) Whether any official action taken is meaningful or merely perfunctory, including an evaluation of the willingness of law enforcement agencies to detect, prosecute and punish offenders
(f) Whether there is a pattern of State unresponsiveness
(g) A denial of State's services
(h) Whether any steps have been taken by the State to prevent infliction of harm

In the second part of this evaluation, relating to the determination whether the applicant has reasonable access to State protection, Member States should consider the following factors:

(i) Evidence by the applicant that the alleged persecutors are not subject to the State's control
(j) The qualitative nature of the access the applicant has to whatever protection is available, bearing in mind that applicants as a class must not be exempt from protection by the law
(k) Steps, if any, by the applicant to obtain protection from State officials and the State response to these attempts[58]

Although none of these criteria made their way into the adopted text of the Qualification Directive, they are illustrative, in conjunction with the *Abdualla* ruling, of the type of relevant considerations in the assessment of effective protection – in particular the acts of actors inflicting harm and of authorities seeking to protect from harm; and the conditions in which these actors operate, including past actions, records of responsiveness, influence and networks.[59]

58 Commission of the European Union, Qualification Directive Proposal 2001 (Ch 1 n 64).

59 For the application of these and similar considerations as relevant evidence, see Section 3.4 (p 115 and following) of this book.

Article 4 does not require the applicant to exhaust domestic remedies before applying for international protection or to turn to the authorities for protection against harm. However, given that the focus is on the effectiveness of protection, whether or not they did turn to the authorities, as well as the potential reaction of the authorities, appears a relevant element of evidence in the assessment of how effective protection is.[60]

In sum, the Qualification Directive requires an individualised assessment of whether or not an applicant can obtain effective and non-temporary protection against harm in the country of origin. However, objective and general considerations relating to the actions of actors inflicting harm or actors seeking to provide protection, the legal framework in the country of origin and its application, as well as general human rights compliance in that country, are relevant evidentiary considerations in that assessment.

3.3.1.2 Article 7(2), Qualification Directive and the Standard of Protection

Article 7(2) suggests a tension between the requirement that protection against harm must be 'effective' and the assumption that such protection is generally available when the authorities take '*reasonable steps* to prevent the persecution or suffering or serious harm'. While the wording makes clear that 'protection' is everything that reduces risk exposure to acts of persecution or serious harm,[61] there remains some ambiguity as to what the relevant standard of proof of Article 7 is. That ambiguity can be reduced, however, by considering the Directive's drafting history, and by interpreting the Qualification Directive consistently with the 1951 Convention.

First, the requirement of effectiveness of protection has been introduced in the recast Qualification Directive because of a lack of clarity on the standard of protection. Article 7(2) of the 2004 Qualification Directive had not explicitly required the 'effectiveness' or 'non-temporary nature' of protection. Neither had it explicitly required that actors of protection needed to be *willing and able* to provide such protection (Article 7(1) Qualification Directive). Rather, it

60 Hathaway and Foster, *The Law of Refugee Status* (Ch 1 n 100) 326, 'while it is clearly relevant to consider whether the applicant sought state protection prior to leaving his or her country of origin, caution must be exercised in importing into the protection-oriented refugee definition what amounts to a procedural rule intended to operate as a condition for invoking the responsibility of a state. In the context of refugee status determination, the only relevant question is whether there is evidence to establish that the state would be willing or able to provide protection in the future, with the applicant's past experience of seeking or obtaining such protection being merely "one factor in the assessment" of this element of the definition.'

61 Battjes, *European Asylum Law and International Law* (Ch 1 n 102) 247.

simply provided that protection was generally available when the authorities take reasonable steps to prevent persecution or serious harm. When presenting the proposal for a recast Directive, the European Commission stated that a new Directive ought to clarify that the actual availability of protection is decisive, given that Article 7(2) could be interpreted in a way that merely warrants the relevant actors to be willing to protect.

> The mere fact that an entity is able to provide protection is not sufficient; it should also be willing to protect the particular individual. Inversely, mere 'willingness to protect' is not sufficient in the absence of the 'ability to protect'. Moreover, even actors who are willing and able in principle to provide protection but who are not providing it in reality or who can provide protection only on a transitional or temporary basis are excluded from the scope of the concept.[62]

This is in line with previous attempts by the European Parliament to clarify the standard of protection in Article 7(2), in particular by amending the proposal to the effect that protection has to be 'effective' by the operation of an effective legal system, 'such that there is no significant risk of persecution or other serious harm being realised'.[63]

Second, Article 7(2) is intended to guide the application of the refugee definition of Article 1A(2) of the 1951 Convention. From the international law perspective, however, the only relevant standard for the assessment of available protection is that of the 'well-founded fear of being persecuted' in Article 1A(2) of the 1951 Convention. As pointed out in Chapter 1, and Sections 2.2.3–2.3.4, the protection clause of Article 1A(2) does not define a substantive inclusion

---

62 Commission of the European Communities, *Qualification Directive Proposal 2009* (Ch 2 n 66) stating that, 'The mere fact that an entity is able to provide protection is not sufficient; it should also be willing to protect the particular individual. Inversely, mere "willingness to protect" is not sufficient in the absence of the "ability to protect". Moreover, even actors who are willing and able in principle to provide protection but who are not providing it in reality or who can provide protection only on a transitional or temporary basis are excluded from the scope of the concept.'

63 See European Parliament, Committee on Citizens' Freedoms and Rights, Justice and Home Affairs, 'Report on the proposal for a Council directive on minimum standards for the qualification and status of third country nationals and stateless persons as refugees or as persons who otherwise need international protection', COM/2001/510. The parliament responded to the original wording of the proposal, whereby the provision required a 'system of domestic protection and machinery for the detection, prosecution and punishment of actions which constitute persecution or other serious and unjustified harm' (Commission of the European Union, 'Qualification Directive Proposal 2009').

criterion that is independent of or additional to the notion of a 'well-founded fear of being persecuted', and the assessment of available protection must therefore be conceived of as part of the well-founded fear of being persecuted. In consequence, the assessment of available protection must not introduce any standard of proof other than that of the Convention, with the Convention defining the standard as a *real chance* that a person would upon return be persecuted on one of the five Convention grounds, which is a lower standard than a balance of probabilities[64] but which does not require an absolute guarantee either.[65]

Crucially, the primacy of the Convention's 'real chance' standard is irrespective of whether, when separating the notion of 'well-founded fear of being persecuted' into multiple 'tests', the assessment of available protection is conceived of as part of the well-founded fear test, the harm test, or the protection test, because the real chance standard is the only one that Article 1A(2) knows.

The primacy of the Convention's real chance test has also been recognised by the UNHCR and legal commentators. In its comments on the 2004 Qualification Directive, the agency argued that '[...] [lack] of state protection should be assumed if the standard of proof for a well-founded fear of persecution is met'.[66] In a 2001 guidance paper on the interpretation of Article 1A(2), the UNHCR stated that the analysis of available protection is nothing but the assessment of the well-founded fear of being persecuted for cases involving harm by non-state actors.

64 Hathaway and Foster, *The Law of Refugee Status* (Ch 1 n 100) 170.

65 In the context of Article 7, it was undisputed that the Qualification Directive does not require total safety. For the Netherlands: Vreemdelingencirculaire 2000 (C) of 1 December 2017, Section 3.4. German Ministry of Interior Guidelines state that 'an absolute guarantee of protection' was not necessary. Instead, actors merely had to be, in principle, able and willing to provide the necessary protection. Bundeministerium des Innern, ‚Hinweise des Bundesministeriums des Innern zur Anwendung der Richtlinie 2004/83/EG des Rates vom 29. April 2004 über Mindestnormen für die Anerkennung und den Status von Drittstaatsangehörigen oder Staatenlosen als Flüchtlinge oder als Personen, die anderweitig internationalen Schutz benötigen, und über den Inhalt des zu gewährenden Schutzes in der Bundesrepublik Deutschland', Amtsblatt EU L 304, 30 September 2004.

66 UN High Commissioner for Refugees, 'UNHCR Annotated Comments on the EC Council Directive 2004/83/EC of 29 April 2004' (Ch 2 n 23). See also European Council on Refugees and Exiles, 'ECRE Information Note on the Council Directive 2004/83/EC of 29 April 2004 on Minimum Standards for the Qualification of Third Country Nationals and Others in Need of International Protection' (2004), 7 <www.ulb.ac.be/assoc/odysseus/CEAS/ECRE(%20OCT%202004).pdf> accessed 20 October 2016, arguing that if the steps taken to protect an individual from harm 'do not in fact reduce a risk of persecution below the well-founded fear threshold then there is no protection in reality.'

> Consideration of effective national protection is, in UNHCR's view, neither a separate nor a seminal issue, but rather one of a number of elements concomitant to determining refugee status in certain cases, particularly those involving a fear of persecution emanating from non-state agents. The question is whether the risk giving rise to the fear is *sufficiently mitigated by available and effective national protection from that feared harm.*
>
> Where such an assessment is necessary, it requires a judicious balancing of a number of factors both general and specific, including the general state of law, order and justice in the country, and its effectiveness, including the resources available and the ability and willingness to use them properly and effectively to protect residents.[67]

In its 2005 annotated comments, it stated that 'the assessment to be made is whether the applicant's fear of persecution continues to be well founded, regardless of the steps taken to prevent persecution or serious harm'.[68] In its *Guidelines on International Protection No 7*, on the application of Article 1A(2), 1951 Convention to victims of trafficking, the UNHCR pointed out that the effectiveness of protection is a question of fact, which includes the question of practical access,

> The mere existence of a law prohibiting trafficking in persons will not of itself be sufficient to exclude the possibility of persecution. If the law exists but is not effectively implemented, or if administrative mechanisms are in place to provide protection and assistance to victims, but the individual concerned is unable to gain access to such mechanisms, the State may be deemed unable to extend protection to the victim, or potential victim, of trafficking.[69]

---

67 UN High Commissioner for Refugees, 'Interpreting Article 1 of the 1951 Convention Relating to the Status of Refugees' (Ch 3 n 15) para 15. This resonates with the agency's 2003 Guideline on the Internal Protection Alternative. The UNHCR advised the assessment of the ability and willingness of the State to protect. 'Laws and mechanisms may reflect the State's willingness, but, unless they are given effect in practice, they are not of themselves indicative of the availability of protection.' UN High Commissioner for Refugees, 'Guidelines on International Protection No 4: 'Internal Flight or Relocation Alternative' Within the Context of Article 1A(2) of the 1951 Convention and/or 1967 Protocol Relating to the Status of Refugees', UN Doc HCR/GIP/03/04 (2003).

68 UN High Commissioner for Refugees, 'UNHCR Annotated Comments on the EC Council Directive 2004/83/EC of 29 April 2004' (Ch 2 n 136).

69 UN High Commissioner for Refugees, 'Guidelines on International Protection No 7: The Application of Article 1A(2) of the 1951 Convention and/or 1967 Protocol Relating to the Status of Refugees to Victims of Trafficking and Persons At Risk of Being Trafficked', UN Doc HCR/GIP/06/07 (2006), para 24.

Like UNHCR, academics have also pointed to the primacy of the Convention notion of a well-founded fear of being persecuted.[70] According to Hathaway and Foster,

> In applying the 'real chance' standard – the usual well-founded fear test – in relation to the failure of state protection limb, a decision-maker will inevitably consider what measures a home state has adopted or will embark upon to provide the infrastructure of protection required – such as legislation, police protection, and other enforcement measures – and the extent to which such measures are effective, meaningful, adequate, and accessible.[71]
>
> [...] The ultimate question is not, however, whether the home state has complied with any particular standard of conduct, but whether the result of even the best intentions and most diligent efforts is to 'reduce the risk of claimed harm below the well-founded fear threshold'.[72]

The primacy of the 1951 Convention's real chance standard also means that it must not be replaced with a standard of conduct intended to assess the *legal liability* of the state of nationality – in particular, in relation to the question as to whether or not the state of nationality acts with 'due diligence' to prevent harm under international human rights law.[73] This is also underlined when looking at past disputed cases concerning 'lacking protection' against harm, which the Qualification Directive has largely resolved.

3.3.2 *What Is Effective Protection? Revisiting Past Disputed Cases of Protection Failure*

3.3.2.1 The Qualification Directive Breaks with the 'Accountability View'

Prior to the adoption of the Qualification Directive, the standard of proof in assessing available protection was discussed as part of a debate on the relevance

---

70 Eg, Fortin, 'The Meaning of "Protection" in the Refugee Definition' (Ch 2 n 122); Goodwin-Gil and McAdam, *The Refugee in International Law* (Ch 1 n 15); Stevens, 'What Do We Mean by Protection?' (Ch 1, n 104); Haines, 'Gender-related Persecution' (Ch 3, n 23) 333, stating that, 'The level of protection provided by a State should be such as to reduce the risk to a refugee claimant to the point where the fear of persecution could be said to be no longer well-founded.'

71 Hathaway and Foster, *The Law of Refugee Status* (Ch 1, n 100) 318.

72 Ibid 319 with reference to US Department of Homeland Security, 'Asylum Officer Basic Training, *Female Asylum Applicants and Gender-Related Claims*' (12 March 2009), 25.

73 On this point, see also Döring, 1156 in Hailbronner and Thym (eds), *EU Immigration and Asylum Law – A Commentary* (Ch 1 n 7).

of harm inflicted by a non-state actor for the 1951 Convention.[74] At the heart of the debate was the question as to when the 1951 Convention accommodated cases of non-state actor-inflicted harm. While it was never disputed that such harm was relevant for the Convention's refugee definition, there was disagreement about cases in which authorities were simply unable, rather than unwilling, to provide protection against harm by non-state actors. Kälin, in a helpful taxonomy of harm inflicted by non-state actors, distinguished four types of cases, with debate revolving around types (c)–(d):

(a) Persecution is carried out by private parties, but is instigated, condoned or tolerated by the State.
(b) Non-state agents of persecution have gained such control over the whole or part of the country that they can be regarded as de facto authorities or 'quasi-state' organs.
(c) The State does not condone persecutory measures carried out by non-state agents but is unable to provide protection against them.
(d) Persecutory measures are carried out by non-state agents where the State has collapsed and where no State authorities exist that could protect the victims.[75]

In particular, Germany had restricted the notion of persecution to cases in which it considered that the persecutory action of third parties was attributable (*'zurechenbar'*) to the state of nationality and that this state was hence liable for harm.[76] Although this doctrine developed in the interpretation of

74 Eg, Kälin, 'Non-state Agents of Persecution and the Inability of the State to Protect' (Ch 1 n 99); Reinhard Marx, 'The Notion of Persecution by Non-State Agents in German Jurisprudence' (2001) 15 Georgetown Immigration Law Journal 448; Jennifer Moore, 'From Nation State to Failed State: International Protection from Human Rights Abuses by Non-State Agents' (1999) 31 Columbia Human Rights Law Review 81; Catherine Phuong, 'Persecution by Non-state Agents: Comparative Judicial Interpretations of the 1951 Refugee Convention' (2002) 4 European Journal Migration and Law 521; Ben Vermeulen and others, *Persecution by Third Parties* (commissioned by the Research and Documentation Centre of the Ministry of Justice of The Netherlands, 1998); Nykänen, *Fragmented State Power and Forced Migration – Study on Non-State Actors in Refugee Law* (Ch 2 n 122); Mathew, Hathaway and Foster, 'The Role of State Protection in Refugee Analysis' (Ch 1 n 99).

75 Kälin, 'Non-state Agents of Persecution and the Inability of the State to Protect' (Ch 1 n 99).

76 Marx, 'The Notion of Persecution by Non-State Agents in German Jurisprudence' (Ch 3 n 74). The European Council, in a Joint Position from 1996, took a similar position: 'Joint Position of 4 March 1996 defined by the Council on the basis of Article K.3 of the Treaty on European Union on the harmonized application of the definition of the term "refugee" in Article 1 of the Geneva Convention of 28 July 1951 relating to the status of refugees', [1996] OJ L63/2 para 5.1: 'Persecution by third parties will be considered to fall within the scope of the Geneva Convention where it is based on one of the grounds in Article 1A of

the constitutional right to asylum,[77] the German Constitutional Court also made reference to the 1951 Convention, in which 'international asylum' is subsidiary to 'national asylum'.[78] Above all, German jurisprudence explained its doctrine with reference to a link between protection and persecution, as well as with reference to the limits of legal obligations to protect own nationals. Under the German doctrine, the state was considered the sole legal guarantor of rights protection in the home state. Because its power to protect implied the power to harm, only states were considered able to inflict persecution.[79]

Under the German approach, conduct by non-state actors was not considered attributable where the state authorities were willing to protect, but were unable to do so in individual cases,[80] for no state is required to guarantee absolute protection.[81] If the state of nationality 'by and large' offered a person protection against harm, rather than systematically failing to do so, conduct was not considered attributable and the individual in question was not considered suffering relevant harm by the state.[82] What is more, past cases of protection failure were not in and of themselves sufficient to establish that the state was liable for the action of non-state actors.[83] In practice, courts seldom

that Convention, is individual in nature and is *encouraged or permitted by the authorities*. Where the official authorities fail to act, such persecution should give rise to individual examination of each application for refugee status, in accordance with national judicial practice, *in the light in particular of whether or not the failure to act was deliberate*. The persons concerned may be eligible in any event for appropriate forms of protection under national law.' (emphasis added).

77 For criticism on the conflation between the international legal framework and the domestic constitutional right to asylum, see Kälin, 'Non-state Agents of Persecution and the Inability of the State to Protect' (Ch 1 n 99) 423.

78 BVerfG, 19 July 1989, 2 BvR 502/86 – BVerfGE 80, 315, 5b).

79 BVerwG, 18 January 1994, 9 C 48.92 – BVerwGE 95, 42. According to the German Constitutional Court, the state's purpose was to protect individuals in an 'overarching order of peace'; the power to protect, meanwhile, included the power to persecute, BVerfGE 80, 315 (1989).

80 Marx, 'The Notion of Persecution by Non-State Agents in German Jurisprudence' (Ch 3 n 74).

81 BVerwG, 22 April 1986 BVerwG 9 C 31885 – 74 BVerwGE 160, 163.

82 BVerwG, 5 July 1994 BVerwG 9 C 194 – InfAuslR 1995, 24, 27.

83 Ibid VG Göttingen, 28 January 2002 – 3 A 3027/02. Some courts, however, interpreted the accountability view more liberally. Where protection against harm was not effective, other courts held, the State was accountable for it and refugee status thus warranted. For FGM cases see, VG Wiesbaden, 27 January 2000 – 5 E 31472/98.A (2), VG Freiburg, 5 February 2001 – A 2 K 10475/00; for a case of harm by religious groups, VG Darmstadt, 11 May 2000 – 3 E 30481/98. A.

questioned the willingness to 'protect' even where the means proved ineffective in practice. A German administrative court, for instance, ruled that information campaigns and consultations by state authorities were enough to demonstrate that the state was in principle willing to protect a girl against female genital mutilation.[84] In other decisions, courts held that the duty to protect a person from harm by non-state actors ended where the state had no more means at its disposal, irrespective of the type of means employed.[85] Only where the state refused to employ the means at its disposal, regardless of how effective they were in practice, could the conduct of non-state actors be attributed to the state.[86]

Although the German approach stressed the need for a systematic failure of protection rather than an individual failure of protection, the approach overlapped somewhat with the liability framework for positive obligations under international human rights law, which requires *due diligence to prevent, punish, investigate or redress the harm* caused by non-state actors.[87] Because the approach primarily focused on establishing the state's legal accountability for harm by non-state actors, legal academia called the doctrine the 'accountability view'.[88]

The German approach to non-state actor-inflicted harm has been rejected in other jurisdictions, most notably in the seminal United Kingdom House of Lords case of *Adan and Aitseguer,* in which the German interpretation of the 1951 Convention barred the return of an asylum seeker from the United Kingdom to Germany.[89] It was also rejected by academic commentators and UNHCR, on the ground that the 1951 Convention's definition of 'being persecuted' does not mention the role of the state, and that reading such a requirement into the Convention would amend the definition by the addition of an extra criterion.[90] Finally, the Qualification Directive responded to the divergence in

84 VG Trier, 27 April 1999 – 4 K 1157/98.TR.

85 VG Osnabrück, 21 March 2000 – 5 A 16/99.

86 VG Minden, 23 October 2000 – 3 K 2602/97.A; VG Göttingen, 28 January 2002 – 3 A 3027/02.

87 See Section 2.2.3 of this book.

88 Vermeulen and others, *Persecution by Third Parties* (Ch 3 n 74).

89 *Adan and Aitseguer v Secretary of State for the Home Department* [2000] UKHL 67.

90 Kälin, 'Non-state Agents of Persecution and the Inability of the State to Protect' (Ch 1 n 99) 419; Vermeulen and others, *Persecution by Third Parties* (Ch 3 n 74); UN High Commissioner for Refugees, 'Opinion of UNHCR regarding the question of non-State persecution, as discussed with the Committee on Human Rights and Humanitarian Aid of the German Parliament (Lower House) on 29 November 1999' (1999), <https://www.refworld.org/docid/3df755477.html> accessed 20 October 2016.

practice; Article 6 of the 2004 Qualification Directive clarified that non-state actors could be actors of persecution even where 'actors of protection' were *unable*, rather than simply *unwilling*, to provide protection in accordance with Article 7:

> Actors of persecution or serious harm include:
> (a) the State;
> (b) parties or organisations controlling the State or a substantial part of the territory of the State;
> (c) non-State actors, if it can be demonstrated that the actors mentioned in (a) and (b), including international organisations, are unable or unwilling to provide protection against persecution or serious harm as defined in Article 7.

If read in the context of its adoption, the Qualification Directive has rejected the approach whereby the *legal liability* of the state of nationality limits the relevance of non-state actor-inflicted harm for the refugee definition.[91] Meanwhile, in the application of the 1951 Convention, the only relevant standard when assessing the availability of protection remains the threshold of the well-founded fear of being persecuted. As Hathaway and Foster point out,

> The ultimate question is not [...] whether the home state has complied with any particular standard of conduct, but whether the result of even the best intentions and most diligent efforts is to 'reduce the risk of claimed harm below the well-founded fear threshold'.[92]

This is particularly true for the use of the human rights law standard of due diligence in the assessment of available protection. In light of these considerations, the reference to 'reasonable steps' in most language versions

---

91 See also Hathaway and Foster, *The Law of Refugee Status* (Ch 1 n 100) 306, stating that '[...] the question whether the risk relates to serious harm committed by the state, condoned by the state, tolerated by the state, or serious harm not condoned or tolerated by the state but nevertheless present because the state either refuses or is unable to offer protection, including where the state has completely failed, is not a threshold question determining qualification for status. It is rather only of evidentiary value in assessing the willingness and capacity of the state to protect.'

92 Ibid 319 with reference to US Department of Homeland Security, 'Asylum Officer Basic Training, *Female Asylum Applicants and Gender-Related Claims*' (12 March 2009), 25.

of the Qualification Directive is somewhat misleading. Indeed, the Czech-, German-, Hungarian-, Italian- and Slovakian-language versions of the Directive provide that steps must be 'adequate' rather than 'reasonable',[93] while France uses the wording 'appropriate' measures in domestic law,[94] a wording that better captures the primacy of the 1951 Convention's facts-oriented, well-founded fear standard in assessing whether or not protection is effective.

3.3.2.2 How Human Rights Coincide with the Assessment of Available Protection

Insisting on the primacy of the 1951 Convention's real chance standard is relevant because the human rights law due diligence standard fundamentally differs from the real chance standard. This is true even when interpreting due diligence in line with current jurisprudence on human rights obligations, in particular the rich jurisprudence on positive obligations under the ECHR. Positive obligations under the ECHR are obligations of process, not result, and depend on resources and the gravity of the harm involved. This contrasts with the enquiry under the 1951 Convention as to whether the authorities would provide protection so ineffective that the applicant has a real chance – a well-founded fear – of being persecuted. In an assessment as to whether the authorities of a contracting state had complied with their positive obligations, the ECtHR verified 'that the measures actually taken were appropriate and sufficient in the present case'.[95] However, all positive obligations under the ECHR have in common that they arise only '[...] insofar as the state is aware, or could have been aware, if sufficient caution had been exercised, of the violation or threat thereof and has the practical and legal means to prevent it'.[96] The scope of positive obligations under the ECHR must strike a fair balance 'between the general interest and the interests of the individual, the diversity of situations obtaining in Contracting States and the choices which must be made in terms of priorities and resources'.[97] In *Özgür Gündem v Turkey*, the court stated in relation to Article 10 (freedom of expression):

93 Czech: *přiměřené kroky*; German: *geeignete Mittel*; Hungarian: *megfelelő lépéseket*; Italian: *adeguate misure*; Slovakian: *primerané opatrenia*.

94 Article L713-2 Code de l'entrée et du séjour des étrangers et du droit d'asile, version consolidée au 3 juillet 2016, Legifrance.

95 *Ilașcu and Others v Moldova and Russia* ECHR 2004-VII 1 para 334.

96 Walter Kälin and Jörg Künzli, *The Law of International Human Rights Protection* (Oxford University Press 2009) 96 deriving from *Osman v United Kingdom* ECHR 1998-VIII 101; Harris and others, *Law of the European Convention on Human Rights* (Ch 2 n 50) 18.

97 *Ilașcu and Others v Moldova and Russia* (Ch 3 n 95) para 332.

> The scope of [...] [a positive obligation] will inevitably vary, having regard to the diversity of situations obtaining in Contracting States, the difficulties involved in policing modern societies and the choices which must be made in terms of priorities and resources. Nor must such an obligation be interpreted in such a way as to impose an impossible or disproportionate burden on the authorities.[98]

In *Osman v United Kingdom*, the ECtHR argued that for positive obligations to be practically workable, rather than imposing a disproportionate burden, not every claim of a risk to life required operational measures to prevent harm:

> [...] not every claimed risk to life can entail for the authorities a Convention requirement to take operational measures to prevent that risk from materialising. Another relevant consideration is the need to ensure that the police exercise their powers to control and prevent crime in a manner which fully respects the due process and other guarantees which legitimately place restraints on the scope of their action to investigate crime and bring offenders to justice.[99]

Rather, in the context of the right to life, the court has held that positive obligations, '[entail] above all a primary duty on the state to put in place a *legislative and administrative framework designed to provide effective deterrence* against threats to the right to life'.[100] In reiterating the relevant protective investigatory obligations in relation to the right to life in *Makaratzis v Greece*, the ECtHR stated that due diligence in respect of a criminal investigation into homicide 'is not an obligation of result, but of means. The authorities must have taken the *reasonable steps available to them* [...]'.[101] In the case of *Opuz v Turkey*, involving a female victim of domestic violence, the court noted that before assessing whether the state acted with due diligence to protect the applicant, the court 'must *bear in mind the gravity of the issue*'.[102]

98 *Özgür Gündem v Turkey* App no 23144/93 (ECHR, 16 March 2000) para 43.
99 *Osman v United Kingdom* (Ch 3 n 96).
100 *Öneryıldız v Turkey* ECHR 2004-XII 79.
101 *Makaratzis v Greece* ECHR 2004-X 195.
102 *Opuz v Turkey* ECHR 2009-III 107 para 132.

In addition to the differences between the 1951 Convention's real chance standard and the due diligence standard under human rights law, the scope of the latter standard will also not be sufficiently clear to serve as a benchmark for an assessment of available protection against harm in concrete cases. The jurisprudence of the ECtHR assesses positive obligations retrospectively, guided by the subsidiarity of the ECHR protection system *vis à vis* the domestic system, rather than in a forward-looking way, with a view to gauging the scope of risk and harm. That jurisprudence is not designed to provide detailed guidance on how to protect rights under the ECHR, but to establish liability, and for that reason limits itself to formulating abstract principles.[103]

Despite these clear differences in scope and purpose, there may in practice be an overlap between a finding on available protection and the positive obligations under human rights law. Although considerations of legal liability are irrelevant to the assessment of available protection, human rights obligations to which the authorities of the state of nationality are subject may be an important consideration of evidence.[104] Thus, UNHCR, in its *Guidelines on International Protection* on the application of Article 1A(2), 1951 Convention to victims of trafficking,[105] suggested that the protective obligations under human rights law can provide 'guidance' as to whether the authorities of the country of origin are 'able and willing to protect the victim or potential victim upon return'.[106]

103 See also Hathaway and Foster, *The Law of Refugee Status* (Ch 1 n 100). Hathaway and Foster also argue that the scope of due diligence is unclear in international, rather than European human rights, law, relying on James Crawford, *The International Law Commission's Articles on State Responsibility – Introduction, Text and Commentaries* (Cambridge University Press 2002) 82. Indeed, the HRC in its General Comment on the nature of obligations mentions positive obligations only in respect of some articles (Human Rights Committee, 'General Comment No 31' (Ch 2 n 40) para 8), and the provision-specific General Comments do not circumscribe in detail the positive obligations of all Covenant provisions.

104 Goodwin-Gil and McAdam, *The Refugee in International Law* (Ch 1 n 15) 100, arguing that 'the relation between human rights approaches based on State responsibility and the assessment of local protection is "coincidental [...], not normative" '.

105 UN High Commissioner for Refugees, 'Guidelines on International Protection No 7' (Ch 3 n 69) paras 21–22, referring in particular to obligations under the Trafficking Protocol to the UN Convention against Transnational Organized Crime Protocol to Prevent, Suppress and Punish Trafficking in Persons, Especially Women and Children, Supplementing the United Nations Convention Against Transnational Organized Crime (adopted 15 November 2000, entry into force 29 September 2003) 2237 UNTS 319, A/55/383.

106 UN High Commissioner for Refugees, 'Guidelines on International Protection No 7' (Ch 3 n 69) para 22: 'Whether the authorities in the country of origin are able to protect victims or potential victims of trafficking will depend on whether legislative and administrative mechanisms have been put in place to prevent and combat trafficking, as well as to protect and assist the victims and on whether these mechanisms are effectively implemented in

Meanwhile, the discussion on the due diligence standard in the assessment of available protection illustrates some of the complexities as well as the potential risks of an increasing role for human rights in the interpretation of the 1951 Convention. In particular, if human rights are used as interpretative guidance to identify the relevant harm for the notion of 'being persecuted', and that notion accommodates a test of the availability or lack of protection, then it is hard to see why human rights should not also play a greater role in the assessment of available protection.[107] This confusion is also apparent in some legal commentary,[108] in statements by UNHCR and in jurisprudence that influenced the drafting of the Qualification Directive. Thus, in its recent *Guidelines on International Protection* on the application of Article 1A(2), 1951 Convention to Lesbian, Gay, Bisexual, Transsexual and Intersex (LGBTI) people, the UNHCR alluded to a due diligence standard to measure effective protection:

> State protection would normally neither be considered available nor effective, for instance, where the police fail to respond to requests for protection or the authorities refuse to investigate, prosecute or punish (non-State) perpetrators of violence against LGBTI individuals with due diligence.[109]

---

practice. Part II of the Trafficking Protocol requires States to take certain steps with regard to the protection of victims of trafficking, *which can be of guidance* when assessing the adequacy of protection and assistance provided [...]. The protection measures set out in Part II of the Trafficking Protocol are not exhaustive and should be read in light of other relevant binding and non-binding human rights instruments and guidelines' (emphasis added).

107 A similar argument was made by Wilsher, 'Non-State Actors and the Definition of a Refugee in the United Kingdom: Protection, Accountability or Culpability?' (Ch 1 n 99) in respect of UK case law, pointing to the dogmatic inconsistencies between adopting a human rights approach to interpreting the harm relevant for the notion 'being persecuted' on the one hand, and rejecting the relevance of human rights for the standard of protection on the other.

108 Cecilia M Bailliet, 'Persecution in the Home: Applying the Due Diligence Standard to Harmful Traditional Practices within Human Rights and Refugee Law' (2012) 30 Nordic Journal of Human Rights 36, arguing that the 'due diligence obligation framework' under the Convention on the Elimination of Discrimination Against Women (CEDAW) and the Convention on the Rights of the Child (CRC) could prove helpful in assessing the ability and willingness of the authorities to protect.

109 UN High Commissioner for Refugees, 'Guidelines on International Protection No 9: Claims to Refugee Status based on Sexual Orientation and/or Gender Identity within the context of Article 1A(2) of the 1951 Convention and/or its 1967 Protocol relating to the Status of Refugees', UN Doc HCR/GIP/12/01 (2012).

In the United Kingdom House of Lords case of *Horvath*, the Law Lords argued that a standard of protection had to be practically workable and had to take account of the state's duties to its nationals, a position clearly influenced by the jurisprudence of the ECHR. According to Lord Hope,

> [...] the application of the surrogacy principle rests upon the assumption that, just as the substitute cannot achieve complete protection against isolated and random attacks, so also complete protection against such attacks is not to be expected of the home state. The standard to be applied is therefore not that which would eliminate all risk and would thus amount to a guarantee of protection in the home state. Rather it is a practical standard, *which takes proper account of the duty which the state owes to all its own nationals.*

Lord Clyde specified this rationale by stating that the state must install and have a '*reasonable willingness*' to operate 'a machinery for the detection, prosecution and punishment of actings [sic] contrary to the purposes which the Convention requires to have protected',[110] a wording that was reflected in the first draft of Article 7(2), Qualification Directive and was reminiscent of the human rights law due diligence standard.[111] What is more, the House of Lords in *Bagdanavicius*, albeit in an Article 3 case, explicitly stated that the failure of state protection provides the link explaining why non-state actors can be considered under the human rights approach, an argument prone to the old 'accountability view':

> Non-state agents do not subject people to torture or the other proscribed forms of ill-treatment, however violently they treat them: what, however, would transform such violent treatment into article 3 ill-treatment would be the state's failure to provide reasonable protection against it.[112]

110 *Horvath v Secretary of State for the Home Department* (Ch 2 n 117).

111 See also Wilsher, 'Non-State Actors and the Definition of a Refugee in the United Kingdom: Protection, Accountability or Culpability?' (Ch 1 n 99). However, subsequent jurisprudence in the UK applying the *Horvath* standard has clarified it does not mean that there is state protection 'every time the authorities are doing their best'; and assessed the reasonableness of protective efforts towards a single applicant, rather than a general system of 'protection'. What is more, the effectiveness of protection is determined by its capacity to deter or prevent, rather than merely ex-post criminal punishment. *Kacaj* [2001] UKIAT 0018; *Harakal* [2001] EWCA Civ 884; *Banomova* [2001] EWCA Civ 807; *McPherson* [2001] EWCA Civ 1955; *Kinuthia* [2002] INLR 133; *Banomova* [2001] EWCA Civ 807; *McPherson* [2001] EWCA Civ 1955; and *Kinuthia* [2001] EWCA Civ 2100.

112 *Bagdanavicius and another* [2004] 1 WLR 1207, para 24.

3.3.3 *The Differences between the Assessment of Protection against Serious Harm and Protection against Acts of Persecution*

Does the Qualification Directive warrant the same standard for the assessment of protection against serious harm than it does for the assessment of protection against acts of persecution? The text of Article 7(2), Qualification Directive requires that protection must be 'effective' and of 'a non-temporary nature' both in the assessment of harm relevant for refugee status (acts of persecution) and in the assessment of subsidiary status (serious harm). Article 7(2) requires an individualised assessment of protection against acts of persecution, in which the legal obligations of the authorities in the state of nationality are only of evidentiary value, rather than circumscribing what is or is not 'effective' in the individual case. Yet, there is some ambiguity as to whether Article 15b) differs. As previously discussed, the scope of serious harm under Article 15, Qualification Directive overlaps with, but is not congruent with the scope of relevant harm under human rights law obligations of non-return, given that the scope of Article 15(b), Qualification Directive is limited to torture, inhuman and degrading treatment or punishment *in the country of origin*. This wording makes clear that the relevant scope of serious harm is defined with reference to human rights law obligations to respect and protect the right to freedom from torture, inhuman or degrading treatment or punishment in the country of origin. The scope of these obligations is, however, determined by the due diligence standard of human rights law. Read in this way, Article 15(b) not only excludes medical cases, but also cases in which the authorities are unable to prevent relevant harm by non-state actors due to lack of resources, in contrast to Article 6(c).

Because Article 15 and Article 6 are interlinked, such reading does create a minor risk of reading a requirement of legal liability or due diligence into Article 6, thereby creating norm conflict with the Convention. This is apparent in the Opinion of Advocate General Bot in the case of *M'Bodj*, in which the ECtHR was requested to clarify the scope of Article 15(b) for medical cases:

> The EU legislature [...] expressly limits the scope of the harm referred to in Article 15 of that Directive to the harm caused by the State, by parties or organisations controlling the State or a substantial part of the territory of the State, or by non-State actors, if it can be demonstrated that the State or the parties or organisations controlling the State are unable or unwilling to provide protection against persecution or serious harm.
>
> [...] Therefore, in order for a person to be eligible for subsidiary protection, it is *not sufficient to prove that that person would face a risk of being subjected to inhuman or degrading treatment if he were returned to his*

> *country of origin*. It must *also* be demonstrated that the risk arises *from factors which are attributable, directly or indirectly, to the public authorities of that country*, either because the threats to the person concerned are being made or tolerated by the authorities in the country of which that person is a national, or because those threats are being made by independent groups against which the authorities of that country are unable to provide effective protection to their citizens.[113]

This reading clearly bridges a potential contradiction between the interlinked Article 15(b) in conjunction with Article 7(2).

However, any reading of a requirement of legal liability into Article 7 is not legally sound, for the 1951 Convention requires that available protection be assessed against the real chance standard of the Convention and in Article 7 is the relevant benchmark for both protection against acts of persecution and serious harm. The Convention's 'real chance' standard applies to both Articles 6 and 7, because these articles are common for both the assessment of refugee and subsidiary protection status. What is more, the restrictive wording of Article 15(b) has been eased by CJEU case law. Not only did the CJEU state in *Elgafaj* that the scope of Article 15(b) essentially corresponds to Article 3, ECHR, but what is more, it only excluded from the scope of Article 15b) cases in which harm does not 'take the form of conduct, such as general shortcomings in the health system'.[114] Indeed, the drafting history of the Qualification Directive shows that the wording of Article 15(b) was introduced with a view to excluding cases like the *Saint-Kitts* case,[115] rather than all cases of non-state actor harm in which the state attempts to provide protection with due diligence.[116]

3.3.4 *International Human Rights Law and the Assessment of Available Protection in Non-return Cases*

To the extent that the Qualification Directive overlaps with non-return obligations under human rights law, in particular Article 3 of the ECHR, that body of law provides additional guidance on the relevant standard of protection, but also shows the similarities between the analysis of protection against harm under the 1951 Convention and human rights law.

113 C-542/13 *Mohamed M'Bodj v Belgian State*, ECLI:EU:C:2014:2113 [2014] digital reports, Opinion of AG Bot, paras 57–58 (emphasis added).

114 *Mohamed M'Bodj v Belgian State* para 35.

115 *D v United Kingdom* ECHR 1997-III 792.

116 Council of the European Union, 'Note from the Presidency of the Council of the European Union to the Strategic Committee on Immigration, Frontiers and Asylum of 25 September 2002', COM 12148/02 (2002) 6.

To discuss the requirements for assessing 'protection', it is first helpful to reiterate the legal rationale of human rights law non-return obligations. The obligations arise *by virtue of the human rights obligations of the expelling/sending state*. In the European context, it is long-standing practice that the exposure of an individual to certain types of grave harm can give rise to an issue under Article 3, ECHR, but also under other Convention provisions.[117] The rationale is not that there is a breach, *as a matter of law*, of an article of the ECHR in a country where that Convention may not even apply. Rather, where the nature of the alleged suffering in the destination state falls within the material scope of a Convention article and is serious and irreparable,[118] the sending state incurs liability by reason of exposure to the harm under that very article. According to the ECtHR in the landmark case of *Soering*:

> [...] the decision by a Contracting State to extradite a fugitive may give rise to an issue under Article 3 (art. 3), and hence engage the responsibility of that State under the Convention, where substantial grounds have been shown for believing that the person concerned, if extradited, *faces a real risk of being subjected to torture or to inhuman or degrading treatment or punishment in the requesting country*. The establishment of such responsibility inevitably involves an assessment of conditions in the requesting country against the standards of Article 3 (art. 3) of the Convention. Nonetheless, *there is no question of adjudicating on or establishing the responsibility of the receiving country, whether under general international law, under the Convention or otherwise*. In so far as any liability under the Convention is or may be incurred, it is *liability incurred by the extraditing Contracting State by reason of its having taken action which has as a direct consequence the exposure of an individual to proscribed ill-treatment*.[119]

This rationale has also influenced the interpretation of obligations under other human rights law treaties,[120] and there are similar obligations under

117 In *F v United Kingdom*, the court stated that while 'on a purely pragmatic basis, it cannot be required that an expelling contracting state only return an alien to a country which is in full and effective enforcement of all the rights and freedoms set out in the Convention', there may be an issue arising under Article 6 ECHR in case of a flagrant denial of the right to a fair trial. This was first applied in *Abu Qatada 8139/09 ECHR 2012 817*. See also *Ahorugeze v Sweden* ECHR 2011 1829; *Al Nashiri v Poland* [2011] ECHR 1829.

118 *Soering v United Kingdom* (1989) Series A no 161 para 90.

119 *Ibid* para 91.

120 Indeed, the ECtHR appears to have impacted the practice of the Human Rights Committee and the Committee against Torture; see Helene Lambert, 'Consolidation and Development

the Convention against Torture,[121] and the Convention on the Rights of the Child.[122] For the ICCPR, the Human Rights Committee, which authoritatively interprets the Covenant, has clarified that contracting states may have non-return obligations under multiple articles of the Covenant,

> not to extradite, deport, expel or otherwise remove a person from their territory, where the necessary and foreseeable consequence of the deportation would be a real risk of irreparable harm, *such as* that contemplated by articles 6 and 7 of the Covenant, either in the country to which removal is to be effected or in any country to which the person may subsequently be removed.[123]

The fact that non-return obligations under human rights law, in particular Article 3, ECHR, revolve around liability of the sending state for exposing an individual to a real risk of harm, also has implications analysis of available protection. That analysis can only be conceived of as part of the test as to whether or not a risk is real. In consequence, 'effective' protection against harm is protection which negates a real risk of harm. This enquiry is not dependent on whether the actors of protection do everything that they are required to do by law or less; the sole relevant measure is the factual effectiveness of protection. As the ECtHR held in *Salah Sheekh v Netherlands*,

---

of the Asylum-Related Jurisprudence of the European Court of Human Rights – Key-Note Speech to the Second Colloquy on the European Convention on Human Rights and the Protection of Refugees, Asylum-Seekers and Displaced Persons' (2000) SSRN eLibrary. See also below, Section 1.4.1.

121 Article 3(1) CAT, 'No State Party shall expel, return ('refouler') or extradite a person to another State where there are substantial grounds for believing that he would be in danger of being subjected to torture.'

122 UN Committee on the Rights of the Child, *CRC General Comment No 6: Treatment of Unaccompanied and Separated Children Outside their Country of Origin*, CRC/GC/2005/6, para 27, 'in fulfilling obligations under the Convention, States shall not return a child to a country where there are substantial grounds for believing that there is a real risk of irreparable harm to the child, such as, but by no means limited to, those contemplated under articles 6 and 37 of the Convention, either in the country to which removal is to be effected or in any country to which the child may subsequently be removed.'

123 Human Rights Committee, 'General Comment No 31' (Ch 2 n 40) para 12 (emphasis added). See also Human Rights Committee, 'General Comment No 20 (Article 7)', Compilation of General Comments and General Recommendations Adopted by Human Rights Treaty Bodies, UN Doc HRI/GEN/1/Rev.1 (1994), para 9.

> [...] the existence of the obligation not to expel is not dependent on whether the risk of the treatment stems from factors which involve the responsibility, direct or indirect, of the authorities of the receiving country.[124]

A real risk under the jurisprudence of the ECtHR is a *foreseeable* and *personal* risk.[125] The burden is shared by both the individual claiming the risk and the authorities. While in *Saadi v United Kingdom,* the ECtHR held that '[it] is in principle for the applicant to adduce evidence capable of proving that there are substantial grounds for believing that [...] he would be exposed to a real risk of being subjected to treatment contrary to Article 3',[126] the court in *M. and Others v Bulgaria* clarified that the burden of proof cannot be on the applicant alone.[127]

Thus, in the ECtHR expulsion case of *HLR v France*,[128] the court asked whether the authorities of the receiving state were able to '*obviate the risk by providing appropriate protection*'.[129] This was despite the contention of the government that 'it was impossible to require total safety' because, 'despite the means deployed by developed countries, states were not always able to guarantee the security of, for instance, the most senior members of the judiciary'.[130] At the same time, however, the court noted that it was 'aware [...] of the difficulties the Colombian authorities face in containing the violence' and that 'the

124 *Salah Sheekh v the Netherlands* App no 1948/04 (ECtHR, 11 January 2007).

125 See above, 2.2.3.

126 *Saadi v United Kingdom* ECHR 2008-I 31, para 129.

127 *M. and Others v Bulgaria* App no 41416/08 (ECtHR, 26 July 2011). See also the concurring opinion of Judge Zupančič in *Saadi v United Kingdom* (ibid) stating that '... the role of the person being expelled in Rule 39 situations is to produce a shadow of a doubt, whereupon the burden of proof shifts to the country concerned. [...] In evidentiary doctrine this is called 'bursting the bubble', as for example in the case of presumption of sanity, where a minimum of doubt suffices to eliminate this presumption and shifts the burden to the prosecution. The reasons for that shift are, of course, completely different in the context of criminal trial, but are extenuated to the nth degree in an airport emergency situation in which the person is being expelled. In the context of human rights, the minimal empathy and the humanness of human rights dictate that a person threatened with expulsion should not bear an excessive burden of proof or risk of non- persuasion. The expelling State, in other words, is morally responsible for the mistaken assessment of risk, whereas the Court must in such situations favour the security of the person being expelled.'

128 *HLR v France* (Ch 3 n 37).

129 Ibid also *Ahmed v Austria* (Ch 3 n 37) para 44 in which a deportation would have been contrary to Article 3 because there was no indication that the authorities would protect the applicant.

130 *HLR v France* (Ch 3 n 37) para 32.

applicant has not shown that they are incapable of affording him appropriate protection'.[131]

More recently, in two cases of Iraqi citizens fearing honour crimes, *SA v Sweden*[132] and *DNM v Sweden*,[133] the analysis somewhat shifted to whether the applicant can be expected 'to avail himself of the protection' of the authorities, a wording clearly influenced by the 1951 Convention. However, this was not used as a threshold criterion for a violation under Article 3; the primary enquiry remained whether or not effective protection was available in practice, so that there was no real risk. Similar to the CJEU *Abdulla* ruling, the court will consider the actions of actors that inflict harm or seek to provide protection, the application of laws and policies, and the conditions in which those laws and policies operate:

> In the Court's view, there is a real risk that the woman's relatives would try to seek revenge in order to uphold their perception of honour, if the applicant were to be returned to his home town.
>
> [...] The question therefore arises whether the applicant can be expected to avail himself of the authorities' protection.
>
> [...] The Court does not find that the evidence supports the Government's point of view that it would be possible for the applicant to receive protection from the authorities in his home region. On the contrary, the above mentioned country information indicates that persons who are at risk of being subjected to honour-related crimes in Iraq might not receive effective protection from the authorities. For example, the Iraqi penal code allows for lenient punishments for "honour killings" and such crimes are reported frequently to be committed with impunity, given the high level of social acceptance of this type of crime, including among law enforcement officials.
>
> [...] Against this background, there is a real risk that the applicant would be unable to avail himself of the authorities' protection in his home town.[134]

In the case of *N v Sweden*, the ECtHR considered as relevant the country of origin information that –

131 Ibid, para 43.

132 *SA v Sweden* App no 66523/10 (ECtHR, 27 June 2013).

133 *DNM v Sweden* App no 28379/11 (ECtHR, 27 June 2013).

134 *SA v Sweden* paras 49–50.

> In the vast majority of cases women will not seek help because of their fears of police abuse or corruption, or their fears of retaliation by perpetrators of violence. Low social status and social stigmas deter women from going against their families to pursue justice, particularly in cases of domestic abuse. For a woman even to approach the police or courts requires her to overcome the public opprobrium affecting women who leave their houses without a male guardian, let alone women who seek protection from public authorities.[135]

While the potential legal liability of the authorities within the home state for actions of third parties is not decisive in gauging the availability and effectiveness of protection, it may in practice influence the understanding of relevant harm. Thus, the ECtHR has pointed out that Article 3 sets a particularly high threshold in cases which 'do not concern the direct responsibility of the Contracting State for the infliction of harm'.[136] What is more, the ECtHR has differentiated between harm directly inflicted by the authorities and that inflicted by non-state actors. First and foremost, this distinction is apparent in the medical non-return cases under Article 3 of the ECHR. In *N v United Kingdom*, the ECtHR ruled that the return of a HIV-positive Ugandan woman was permissible, despite the lack of accessible antiretroviral treatment in Uganda and evidence that she would face death after a few years.[137] As such, the judgment contrasts with the ruling in *D v United Kingdom* (also known as the '*Saint-Kitts* case') in which the applicant was 'close to death' and without support in her country of nationality, the case thus being 'very exceptional'.[138] The rationale for such a high threshold is, according to the court, the intentional act or omission by state or non-state actors:

> The Court does not exclude that there may be other very exceptional cases where the humanitarian considerations are equally compelling. However, it considers that it should maintain the high threshold set in *D v the United Kingdom* and applied in its subsequent case-law, which it regards as correct in principle, *given that in such cases the alleged future harm*

135 *N v Sweden* App no 23505/09 (ECtHR, 20 July 2010), para 57.

136 *AA and others v Sweden* App no 14499/09 (ECtHR, 28 June 2012) para 93, the court deplored the lack of 'substantial grounds', and stated that 'Article 3 of the Convention sets a high threshold particularly where the case, like the present one, does not concern the direct responsibility of the Contracting State for the infliction of harm.'

137 *N v United Kingdom* ECHR 2008-III 227.

138 Ibid para 42, referring to *D v United Kingdom* (Ch 3 n 115).

> *would emanate not from the intentional acts or omissions of public authorities or non-State bodies*, but instead from a naturally occurring illness and the lack of sufficient resources to deal with it in the receiving country.[139]

Accordingly, the court has contrasted the case of lack of available medical treatment with the dire humanitarian conditions in camps for internally displaced persons. In *Sufi and Elmi v United Kingdom*, the court stated that the parties to the conflict in Somalia had used indiscriminate violence and thereby caused 'widespread displacement and the breakdown of social, political and economic infrastructures', exacerbated, in the case of the *Al-Shabab* militia, by the refusal to let aid agencies operate. Given that the humanitarian conditions were a consequence of intentional acts or omissions of the parties to the conflict, the relevant considerations under Article 3 were whether the applicant was able to 'cater for his most basic needs, such as food, hygiene and shelter, his vulnerability to ill-treatment and the prospect of his situation improving within a reasonable time-frame'.[140]

In sum, similar to the assessment of refugee status under the 1951 Convention, assessing the effectiveness of protection against harm in the context of non-refoulement obligations, under Article 3, ECHR is a factual and individualised enquiry, in which available protection is measured against the real risk. While the intentional infliction of harm is relevant for the threshold of harm in Article 3, the risk is not assessed with reference to the scope of human rights law positive obligations of the receiving country, in particular the due diligence standard. This is also the relevant standard for the assessment of subsidiary protection status under the Qualification Directive.

3.3.5 *Jurisprudence of Selected Member States as Subsequent Practice: Evidentiary Considerations for the Effectiveness of Protection*

In addition to illustrating issues of compliance with the Qualification Directive, jurisprudence can also be considered in order to identify subsequent practice in the application of Article 7(2) Qualification Directive. This is particularly the case for the relevant evidentiary considerations for Article 7(2), which are not specified by the text of the Directive nor by domestic laws and for which guidance by the CJEU remains relatively scant.[141] Case law from the

139 Ibid para 43.

140 *Sufi and Elmi v United Kingdom* App nos 8319/07, 11449/07 (ECtHR, 28 November 2011) paras 281–283.

141 Indeed, there has been criticism that decision makers do not expound on their evidentiary considerations in assessing whether or not there is protection against harm.

member states, meanwhile, provides pertinent examples of factors impacting the ability to obtain effective protection against harm in 'typical' non-state actor cases, such as cases involving risk of domestic violence, trafficking, honour crime, physical harm and discrimination against religious or sexual minorities.

First, there is abundant legal practice on consideration of the legal framework in place in the country of nationality. The criminalisation of conduct protected by human rights law – such as freedom of religion, freedom from discrimination and the right to privacy, covering gender identity and sexual orientation[142] – may not amount as such to acts of persecution or serious harm under the Qualification Directive. Yet, if relevant groups such as religious minorities or LGBTI people fear relevant harm by non-state actors, such as physical assault, the criminalisation of conduct is evidence of the inability to provide effective protection.[143] What is more, a legal framework that is lenient on specific forms of crimes, such as gender-related crime, but severe on others, may indicate that a state is unwilling to provide protection,[144] as does

---

The UNHCR noted that 'in general, the decisions screened provided scant evidence of assessment of the adequacy and effectiveness of protection. Decisions tended, at best, to reflect the conclusion arrived at with regard to ability to protect, rather than provide evidence of the criteria employed or an assessment of the quality of the protection provided.' Specifically in respect of Sweden, the UNHCR noted that the Migration Board only in 'exceptional cases' expounded on state protection, for instance by referring to the lack of personnel, training and equipment, as well as to the misconduct, of the security forces; UN High Commissioner for Refugees, *Asylum in the European Union. A Study of the Implementation of the Qualification Directive,* UNHCR 2007, 51 < https://www.refworld.org/docid/473050632.html> accessed 1 July 2019.

142 James C Hathaway and Jason Pobjoy, 'Queer Cases Make Bad Law' (2012) 44 Journal of International Law and Politics 315.

143 VG Frankfurt a.M., 10 December 2014 – 8 K 4089/14.F.A; *a contrario* VG Hannover, 18 February 2015 – 1 A 109/13. Also UN High Commissioner for Refugees, *Guidelines on International Protection No 9: Claims to Refugee Status based on Sexual Orientation and/or Gender Identity within the context of Article 1A(2) of the 1951 Convention and/or its 1967 Protocol relating to the Status of Refugees*, HCR/GIP/12/09 (2009), para 36, stating that '[…] laws criminalizing same-sex relations are normally a sign that protection of LGB individuals is not available. Where the country of origin maintains such laws, it would be unreasonable to expect that the applicant first seek State protection against harm based on what is, in the view of the law, a criminal act. In such situations, it should be presumed, in the absence of evidence to the contrary, that the country concerned is unable or unwilling to protect the applicant.'

144 VG Wiesbaden, 14 March 2011 – 3 K 1465/09.WI.A. According to the court, while it was true that the perpetrators where private criminals, the protection of victims of trafficking was lower than the protection against other forms of crime. The prevalent discrimination, incidences of gender-based violence by the police and the stigmatisation of prostitutes meant that state protection was failing because the claimant was a victim of trafficking.

a legal framework that discriminates between men and women.[145] The French National Asylum Court (CNDA) took the restrictive laws against homosexuals as an indication of lack of state protection for a gay Senegalese applicant against harm by private actors.[146] In respect of gender-related harm and harm related to sexual orientation, French, Swedish and UK legal practice has also considered the wider political, social, religious or cultural structures in considering an applicant's prospects of obtaining effective protection. Where the traditional beliefs underlying ritual violence were also widespread among the authorities, the CNDA determined that there was no state protection.[147] Similarly, according to the Swedish High Court of Migration, 'the man's right to exercise power over women in some cultures is such a [...] fundamental part of the fabric of society that it is impossible for a woman to get state protection against violence and restrictions on their freedom or honor crimes [...]'.[148]

Second, courts have routinely considered general country conditions and their impact on the provision of effective protection. One such indication is the dissonance between law and the reality on the ground. Thus, the UK Immigration Appeals Tribunal argued that it is 'unlikely that the arm of the state operates with consistent force throughout the country [...] if the law provides for the criminalisation of a particular form of conduct and yet the incidence of the practice suggests in some areas it is almost universal [...]'.[149] Other factors taken into consideration were the available resources in general[150] or, specifically, the number of personnel in the police force and their equipment[151] or ethnic composition,[152] the general security situation,[153] and corruption.[154]

145 *MD (Women) Ivory Coast* CG [2010] UKUT 215 (IAC) in respect of law on adultery.

146 *D,* CRR 18 May 2007, no 589676; *M. B. N.,* CNDA 18 October 2012, no 12013647 C.

147 *Mlle D,* CRR, 2 November 2007, no 535997.

148 Migrationsöverdomstolen, 21 November 2008, MIG 2008:39, UM1042-08, author's translation. *MD (Women) Ivory Coast* CG [2010] UKUT 215, referring to the social inferiority of women.

149 Ibid 276; also Migrationsöverdomstolen, 3 September 2011, MIG 2011:6, UM3363-10 taking into account the rise in honour crimes and the small number of criminal convictions.

150 Rechtbank 's-Gravenhage, 09 October 2012, AWB 11/32480.

151 VG Minden, 18 August 2008 – 7 K 790/08.A; VG Karlsruhe, 3 March 2005 – A 4 K 10294/02; VG Stuttgart, 17 January 2005 – A 10 K 10587/04; VG Kassel, 6 May 2004 – 7 E 674/02.A.

152 *MH,* CNDA 9 April 2010, no 09013398 C+.

153 VG Ansbach, 24 July 2007 – AN 4 K 06.31070; VG Freiburg, 26 April 2007 – A 1 K 11083/04; VG Sigmaringen, 9 October 2010 – A 2 K 10792/05; VG Frankfurt a.M., 28 September 2006 – 2 E 1235/05.A (1); *S.,* CRR 28 June 2005, no 519680.

154 VG Wiesbaden, 14 March 2011 – 3 K 1465/09.WI.A; *RK (India)* [2012] CSOH 194 (19 December 2012), para 49; Rechtbank 's-Gravenhage, 25 November 2003, AWB 02/25468 and 02/25473; Rechtbank 's-Gravenhage, 8 October 2010, AWB 10/32872 and 10/32868; Rechtbank 's-Gravenhage, 09 October 2012, AWB 11/32480.

Third, there is widespread practice of consideration of subjective factors relating to the applicant, the perpetrators of harm and the authorities which could impact on the ability to obtain effective protection. In the case of *S A (political activist)*, the lower-instance decision was overturned because it did not consider elements of the family matrix that were relevant for the possibility of the provision of protection.[155] Likewise, Swedish case law considers the social relationship between applicant and actor of persecution or serious harm.[156] In addition to social relationships, courts have in particular considered the social and political position of the perpetrator,[157] the young age of applicants as a factor impacting on the effectiveness of protection,[158] and medical conditions.[159] In France, the social isolation of a family and their lack of education were considered relevant for assessing the ability to obtain protection against human trafficking from the authorities.[160]

Finally, there is practice which considers the severity of harm in the assessment of available protection. French courts have in several cases stated that the seriousness of past harm in itself meant that a person could not be expected to seek protection from the authorities.[161]

3.4 Past Jurisprudence of Selected Member States and International Law Compliance

It is the declared aim of the TFEU to create a uniform status of asylum as well as a uniform status of subsidiary protection in accordance with the 1951 Convention. The Qualification Directive is the major EU legal instrument for the achievement of this purpose, with binding minimum standards for all member

155 *SA* (political activist – internal relocation) Pakistan [2011] UKUT 30 (IAC).
156 Migrationsöverdomstolen, 3 September 2011, MIG 2011:6, UM3367-10.
157 VG Regensburg, 25 November 2004 – RN 8 K 04.30383; Rechtbank 's-Gravenhage, 25 March 2010, 09/11135; 09/14677; *Mlle G*, CNDA 23 December 2009, no 640410/08020867; *Mlle O*, CNDA 26 October 2009, no 08008209/627707; *Mlle R*, CNDA 29 September 2009, no 616251/07019306; *Mlle B*, CRR, 14 March 2006, no 558577.
158 Rechtbank 's Gravenhage, 25 November 2003, AWB 02/25468 and 02/25473.
159 Rechtbank 's-Gravenhage, 21 November 2003, AWB 01/69346.
160 *Mlle O*, CNDA 3 April 2012, no 11020945 C.
161 *M*, CRR 1 March 2007, no 566183; *Mlle S*, CRR 5 November 2007, no 557030; *T.*, CRR 14 April 2006, no 481175; *Mlle D*, CNDA 8 April 2011 no 10013535 C+. *A contrario*, in Denmark, where the fear of harm lacked intensity, this was an indicator for available protection by the authorities, Arme/2013/3.

states except those opting out. An interpretation of Article 7(2) conforming to international law requires a shared burden of fact finding. In relation to the authorities, there must be an individualised and fact-based enquiry into the willingness and ability to *provide* protection. In addition, there must be an enquiry as to the practical possibility for the individual to obtain protection that is, in the long-term, so effective that there is no well-founded fear of *being persecuted* or real risk of serious harm. Article 7 precludes presumptions of available protection as well as the placing of the burden of proof on the applicant alone to demonstrate the effectiveness of protection, and also precludes a requirement that the individual has actually turned to the authorities before seeking international protection. In past analysis of case law on the 2004 Qualification Directive,[162] there have been indications that the Directive did not always achieve harmonisation with such an international law-conforming interpretation of Article 7. In particular, there were criticisms in relation to the fact that some domestic laws did not transpose the example of an 'effective legal system' in Article 7(2) of the Directive;[163] that asylum decisions required the applicant to 'present facts or circumstances demonstrating that he or she addressed himself or herself to the authorities, to no avail';[164] and that the emphasis was on general protection, rather than protection for a specific

162 UN High Commissioner for Refugees, 'Asylum in the European Union. A Study of the Implementation of the Qualification Directive' (Ch 3 n 141); European Council on Refugees and Exiles, 'The Impact of the EU Qualification Directive on International Protection' (Ch 3 n 41); GHK, 'Impact assessment studies on the future development of measures on the qualification and status of third country nationals or stateless persons as persons in need of international protection and on the content of the protection granted, based on Council Directive 2004/83/EC and The future development of measures on procedures in MS for granting and withdrawing refugee status, based on Council Directive 2005/85/EC', Multiple framework service contract JLS/2006/A1/004 cited in Commission of the European Communities, Qualification Directive proposal 2009; Commission of the European Union, 'Report from the Commission to the European Parliament and the Council on the Application of Directive 2004/83/EC of 29 April 2004 on minimum standards for the qualification and status of third country nationals or stateless persons as refugees or as persons who otherwise need international protection and the content of the protection', COM/2010/0314 final (Qualification Directive Application Report 2010); European Council on Refugees and Exiles, 'Actors of Protection and the Application of the Internal Protection Alternative – European Comparative Report' (2014) <www.ecre.org/wp-content/uploads/2016/07/ECRE-Asylum-Aid-DCR-and-HHC_Actors-of-Protection-and-the-Application-of-the-Internal-Protection-Alternative_July-2014.pdf> accessed 20 October 2016.

163 Commission of the European Union, 'Qualification Directive Application Report' (Ch 3 n 162).

164 UN High Commissioner for Refugees, 'Asylum in the European Union' (Ch 3 n 141).

applicant.[165] These criticisms will be discussed in the following analysis of the jurisprudence with a view to illustrating *prima facie* conflict with the Qualification Directive rather than calling into question the outcome of particular decisions.

3.4.1 *Problem Area 1 – Individual Burden of Proof and 'Exhaustion of Remedies'*

Both the Convention's well-founded fear of being persecuted standard and the real risk standard of Article 3, ECHR (including the shared duty of fact-finding under those standards) preclude an interpretation of the Qualification Directive whereby it is for the applicant alone to prove the ineffectiveness of protection against harm, or for the applicant to be required to have turned to the authorities in order to prove such ineffectiveness. Yet, such practice remains apparent in some member states. A particular example of such an interpretation was the transposition and application of the Qualification Directive in the Netherlands. While the Qualification Directive takes precedence over domestic law under Article 93 of the Constitution and the Dutch Foreigners Act transposes Article 7 of the Qualification Directive verbatim,[166] the Foreigners Act required of the applicant to prove he or she has first turned to the authorities for protection. According to the application note, the burden is on the applicant to prove that no protection can be provided, unless there is objective information that protection in general is not possible or that a request for protection would be useless from the outset or even dangerous. The burden of proof in relation to the effectiveness of protection then shifts to the authorities.[167] This corresponds with Dutch judicial practice even before the 2004 Qualification Directive in the determination of both refugee status and subsidiary protection

165 European Council on Refugees and Exiles, 'The Impact of the EU Qualification Directive on International Protection' (Ch 3 n 41) 7. ECRE's 2008 note praised the emphasis put, in the jurisprudence of Austria, Belgium, France, Hungary, Ireland, Luxemburg, the Netherlands and the UK, on actual effectiveness of protection, but noted that, 'in Slovenia, as a rule, the refugee status determination authorities take into account the legal system as such and not the applicant's actual access to legal remedies.' Also, European Council on Refugees and Exiles, 'Actors of Protection and the Application of the Internal Protection Alternative – European Comparative Report' (Ch 3 n 162) 44, noting in respect of the assessment of facts and circumstances that 'in some countries, such as Hungary, the Netherlands and Spain, the availability of protection for the applicant is sometimes not demonstrated in practice, the decision maker being satisfied if the act of persecution is prohibited by the law of the country of origin.'

166 Article 3.37c; 3.37d Voorschrift Vreemdelingen 2000.

167 Vreemdelingencirculaire 2000 (C) of 1 December 2017, Section 3.4.

status.[168] In 2012, the State Council confirmed the jurisprudence in a subsidiary protection case by an applicant from Iraqi Kurdistan, holding that where general information shows that there 'generally' is protection, the burden is on the applicant to demonstrate that seeking protection from the authorities would have been meaningless for him.[169] In practice, the applicant's initial burden of proof and the requirement for deference to the protective abilities of the authorities have been relatively high. Thus, in a case of gender-based violence in Uganda, and a case of religious extremism in Serbia, the State Council argued that it was not enough to argue that the authorities in similar cases had failed to protect.[170] In a gender-based violence case from Turkey, the State Council held that there were no reasons to believe that there generally was no protection, despite the fact the applicant had appealed to the police three times. This was, inter alia, because of various general steps taken by the police, including the dissemination of a circular on domestic violence and improved police training.[171] A particularly striking feature of Dutch case analysis is that applicants were expected to appeal to a higher authority when they have turned to local authorities. This is evident in a 2010 domestic violence case taken by a Ugandan woman,[172] as well as in a lower-court decision on protection of a former Member of the Nepali Congress Party against a non-state armed group.[173]

The Dutch practice contrasts with practice in other countries, which either regard it as immaterial whether or not an applicant turned to the authorities,[174] or do consider whether they have done or could have done so, but do not separate

168 Raad van State, 19 July 2002 in Case No 200202206/1; 28 April 2003, 200300547/1; 27 February 2012, 201110164/1/V2. For example, courts held that not enough evidence had been produced to conclude that it would have been meaningless for the applicant to turn to the authorities for protection in a subsidiary protection case by individuals fearing violence by non-State armed groups; see Rechtbank 's-Gravenhage, 25 July 2003, AWB 03/37082 and 03/37080; Rechtbank 's-Gravenhage, 10 June 2003, AWB 01/50117 BEPTDN.

169 Raad van State, 27 February 2012, 201110164/1/V2. For more recent examples, also Rechtbank Den Haag, 7 August 2014, AWB 14/16874; Rechtbank Den Haag, 28 April 2015, AWB 15/7048 & 15/7047.

170 Raad van Staate, 9 March 2011, 201006822/1/V2; Rechtbank 's-Gravenhage, 15 January 2010, AWB 09/47171 and AWB 09/47169.

171 Raad van State, 29 July 2010, 201000726/1/V3.

172 Rechtbank 's-Gravenhage, 15 January 2010, AWB 09/47171 and AWB 09/47169.

173 Decision summarised in Rechtbank 's-Gravenhage, 9 October 2012, AWB 11/32480.

174 In *RK* (*India*), Lord Jones considered whether a failure to appeal to local authorities has any bearing on the question of sufficient protection. In the lower instance court, the claim of an Indian national had been rejected because he had not appealed to 'any higher authorities within the police force or any other government bodies in India.' Lord Jones, however, argued that the question whether a person sought help with the authorities had

this into different phases of evidentiary burdens.[175] However, there is also a milder equivalent to the Dutch practice whereby the burden to demonstrate a failure of protection is particularly onerous. In Germany, for instance, courts did not take past failure of authorities to protect against harm by non-state actors as indicative of the state's lacking the willingness or capacity to protect.[176]

3.4.2 *Problem Area 2 – Individualised, Factual Assessments*

Both the 1951 Convention's well-founded fear enquiry and human rights law non-return obligations preclude the assessment of the receiving state's legal liability as a benchmark for the assessment of availability of effective protection in the country of nationality under Article 7 of the Qualification Directive. While this is not the practice in any of the member states anymore,[177] there are individual decisions in some member states that include elements of the 'accountability view', irrespective of how their domestic law transposes the Qualification Directive.

Germany is a particularly illustrative case, given that the accountability view originated in German jurisprudence. Prior to the transposition deadline of the Qualification Directive, courts still regularly primarily assessed the authorities' willingness, rather than actual ability, to provide protection.[178] The

no bearing on the assessment of the sufficiency of protection. *R K (India)* [2012] CSOH 194 para 49.

175 Eg, Sweden, Migrationsöverdomstolen, 3 September 2011, MIG 2011:6, UM3363-10. According to the Refugee Board, the applicants had first to turn to the domestic authorities and there was nothing to suggest that turning to the authorities would be ineffective, an argument not taken up by the High Court of Migration. For Germany, eg, VG Hannover, 18 February 2015 – 1 A 109/13. In practice, courts will also consider whether or not an applicant has turned to the authorities as part of the assessment of credibility; see criticism by ECRE in European Council on Refugees and Exiles, 'Actors of Protection and the Application of the Internal Protection Alternative' (Ch 3 n 162).

176 For instance, an administrative Court argued that 'even if in individual cases the police did not grant effective protection it cannot be asserted that the Serbian State as a whole is not willing or able to protect Roma from assaults by third parties.' VG Ansbach, 13 August 2008 – AN 11 K 08.30252. The administrative court of Saarland stated that the authorities' call on an applicant to defend herself with a gun could not illustrate that the Kosovar authorities were not, 'on the whole', in a position to grant protection. *VG Saarland*, 13 May 2009 – 10 K 1067/08.

177 European Council on Refugees and Exiles, 'Actors of Protection and the Application of the Internal Protection Alternative' (Ch 3, n 162).

178 Eg VG Gera, 25 November 2004 – 4 K 20215/01.GE; VG Düsseldorf, 23 November 2005 – 7 K 3570/02.A;, VG Aachen, 20 April 2005 – 9 L 224/05; VG Aachen, 14 December 2004 – 9 K 3309/04.A; VG Ansbach, 25 January 2005 – AN 19 04.32135; VG Karlsruhe, 23 June 2005 – A 2 K 11324/04; VG Lüneburg, 10 May 2005 – 3 A 118/04 (Turkey); VG Aachen, 14 December

Qualification Directive was directly applicable as of October 2006 and was then partly[179] transposed into the Residence Act, including by a provision that the Directive was to be applied 'complementarily' in assessing whether or not there is persecution or serious harm.[180] Although courts only seldom continued to apply the 'accountability view',[181] some court decisions granted strong deference to the capacities of the state by pointing simply to the legal and institutional framework of a state to illustrate effective protection, rather than assessing the practical effectiveness of that framework.[182] In two cases on gender-based violence, for instance, the arguments put forward included the fact that the states had a functioning judiciary.[183] That practice has remained unchanged with the entry of force of the law transposing the recast Qualification Directive, which includes a verbatim equivalent of Article 7, Qualification Directive.[184]

The standard of protection is discussed extensively in UK jurisprudence, where some courts appear prone to deducing available effective protection from general factors only. This tendency has its roots in practice prior to the

2004 – 9 K 3309/04.A; VG Aachen, 15 October 2004 – 9 K 1480/03.A; OVG Saaraland, 11 May 2005 – 1 Q 16/05.

179 Whether or not the Qualification Directive exceeded the relevant German alien law at the time was the subject of controversial debate; see Kai Hailbronner, 'Die Qualifikationsrichtlinie und ihre Umsetzung im deutschen Ausländerrecht' (2008) 4 Zeitschrift für Ausländerrecht und Ausländerpolitik 209.

180 Gesetz zur Umsetzung aufenthalts- und asylrechtlicher Richtlinien der Europäischen Union, 19 August 2007, BGBl 2007-I Nr. 42, 1970.

181 In one case, a court argued that the legal framework in place against gender-based violence in Turkey, in particular as regards blood feuds, indicated that the Turkish state was not complicit in such acts of violence by private actors; VG Aachen, 23 October 2006 – 6 K 2348/05.A. More explicitly, in VG Aachen, 10 June 2005 – 9 K 4171/04.A, the court held 'it is to be pointed out that the limit of the duty to protect, as relevant for asylum law, is reached when the powers of the State in question are being surpassed. In other words, the responsibility, under asylum law, of a State ends beyond the means at its disposal. These principles also assume legal validity in those cases in which – as in the province of Kosovo – an international administration has taken the place of a State. In this respect it is unnecessary to further consider the argument that the establishment of State structures … cannot from the very beginning lead to the targeted proportionality [to protect, AN]' (author's translation).

182 For instance, in a Kosovar case, an administrative court referred to the Council of Europe's Framework Agreement on the Protection of National Minorities, the creation of a ministry for human rights and the existence of an ombudsperson, VG Berlin, 30 January 2009 – 37 X 193.05.

183 VG Arnsberg, 7 January 2010 – 6 K 197/09.A.

184 Germany: Gesetz zur Umsetzung der Richtlinie 2011/95/EU, 28 August 2013, BGBl I 2013, 3474.

adoption of the 2004 Qualification Directive and the regulation transposing the Directive. The 2005 case of *Hussein* is an example of the strict interpretation of the *Horvath* standard;[185] the Scottish Court of Session held that 'there must be evidence of *systemic or "institutionalised" unwillingness* to afford protection to the victims of persecution by non-state actors'.[186] According to the 2006 Refugee or Person in Need of International Protection (Qualification) Regulations, protection 'shall be regarded as generally provided when [...] [states or parties or organisations controlling the state or a substantial part of its territory] take reasonable steps to prevent the persecution or suffering of serious harm by operating an effective legal system for the detection, prosecution and punishment of acts constituting persecution or serious harm, and the person [...] has access to such protection' – thus leaving out the 'inter alia' section of Article 7(2) Qualification Directive. The section omitted makes clear that an effective legal system is illustrative of the required protection against persecution or serious harm.[187] Thus, in *M N*, the Scottish Court of Session reframed the standard of protection by upholding a decision in which it was stated that protection against harm by non-state actors had to be 'at such a low ebb as to amount to a systemic failure'.[188] What is more, the Asylum and Immigration Tribunal (AIT), and the Upper Tribunal (Immigration and Asylum Chamber) have frequently overturned lower-instance decisions which made findings on available state protection based only on general circumstances. For instance, in *A M and B M*, the AIT quashed a decision in which the first instance court had held that the authorities in Albania were making 'significant efforts' to protect women at risk of trafficking, including the prosecution and conviction of traffickers, but had not sufficiently taken into account the factors of the individual applicant.[189]

Similarly to the UK, failure to individualise assessments of available protection has also occurred in Swedish and Dutch jurisprudence. In particular, before the Swedish Aliens Act had been changed to transpose the requirement of effective and non-temporary protection included in Article 7 of the recast Qualification Directive,[190] the High Court of Migration overturned judgments

185 See above, Section 3.3.2.

186 *Hussein v SSHD* [2005] CSIH 45.

187 The Refugee or Person in Need of International Protection (Qualification) Regulations 2006.

188 *MN* [2012] ScotCS CSIH 63.

189 *AM and BM* (trafficked women) Albania CG [2010] UKUT 80.

190 Lag om ändring i utlänningslagen (2005:716), 1 January 2015, SFS 2014:1400 (Act amending the Aliens Act). Sweden initially transposed Article 7 of the 2004 Qualification Directive only in respect of refugee status, Lag om ändring i utlänningslagen (2005:716), 31 March

in which protection was assessed in general, rather than in respect of the particular circumstances of the individual applicant.[191] In the Netherlands, the Council of State held that the 'advice and assistance' that women fearing domestic violence could obtain from the Kosovar authorities were indicative of effective protection.[192]

3.5 Protection against Harm Provided by Non-state Actors

3.5.1 *The Reference to Non-state 'Actors of Protection' in the Qualification Directive*

To what extent can actors other than states or state authorities be considered in the analysis of available protection and do the Qualification Directive's rules on non-state actors of protection raise issues of compliance with international law? This is explored in the following sections.

Article 7(1) Qualification Directive foresees that 'parties or organisations, including international organisations', can be considered as relevant 'actors of protection' if they control the State or a substantial part of the territory of the State, and are 'willing and able to offer protection in accordance with' Article 7(2). As discussed above, the 'actors of protection' concept under the Qualification Directive serves to specify the refugee definition in Article 2(d), and the definition of persons eligible for subsidiary protection in Article 2(f). The provision circumscribes exhaustively[193] which actors can, in principle, be

2006, SFS 2005:1239, amending the Aliens Act to the effect that the refugee definition applies regardless of whether it is the national authorities who are responsible for acts of persecution or whether these authorities do not provide protection from harm inflicted by individuals; and Lag om ändring i utlänningslagen (2005:716), 31 March 2006, SFS 2005:1239.

191 Migrationsöverdomstolen, 3 September 2011, MIG 2011:6, UM3363-10, taking into account in particular the age of the applicants as well as the social and political position of the perpetrator.

192 Raad van Staate, 6 August 2013, 201205299/1/V1, 'The fact that the degree of effectiveness of protection is not clear from the outset … does not as such mean that the applicant cannot obtain protection. Unlike the applicant has argued, it follows from the official country report that it is possible, albeit on a limited scale, and independent from the "gender officers" [of the Kosovo police, AN], to receive advice and assistance.' (author's translation).

193 When the Commission tabled a proposal for a recast Qualification Directive in 2009, it proposed to amend Article 7(1)(b) to make it clearer that the list in Article 7(1)(a)–(b) was exhaustive. The Commission deplored the fact that the provision had in the past been applied to actors not mentioned in Article 7(1) (a)–(b) and without regard to the criteria

considered to provide protection, and what the quality of their actions must be to speak of available protection against harm. According to Article 7(1) of the Directive, protection can be provided not only by states, but also by parties or organisations, including international organisations, which control the state or a substantial part of its territory. Indeed, non-state actors such as clans or de facto authorities, and international organisations such as the United Nations Mission in Kosovo (UNMIK), may yield quasi-governmental functions such as providing safety and delivering services.[194] International organisations like the UNHCR are active in countries of asylum, assisting refugees or carrying out individual refugee status determinations, a function normally bestowed on states.[195]

Drafters of the Qualification Directive had in mind examples such as United Nations peace-keeping missions or military presences by NATO.[196] However, the wording of the Directive does not rule out consideration of other actors in control of substantial parts of the territory of a state, such as clans or militias. Although the recast Qualification Directive introduced a requirement of 'willingness' to provide protection, the form of that willingness is not specified; the 'legal system' of Article 7(2), s 2 is merely an example of the general requirement of effective protection of Article 7(2), s 1.[197] The Qualification Directive

of territorial control provided by Article 7(1)(b). This led to the introduction of the wording that protection can 'only' be provided by the type of actors named in Article 7(1). See Commission of the European Communities, 'Qualification Directive Proposal 2009' (Ch 2 n 66).

194 UNMIK for a long time assumed quasi-governmental responsibilities, including basic civilian administrative functions, establishment of police forces and maintenance of public order; S/RES/1244/99.

195 Commentators have thus referred to UNHCR as a 'surrogate state'; see Anne-Marie Slaughter and Jeff Crisp, 'A Surrogate State? The role of UNHCR in protracted refugee situations' in Gil Loescher et al (eds), *Protracted Refugee Situations* (United Nations University Press 2008) and Michael Kagan, '"We live in a Country of UNHCR": The UN Surrogate State and Refugee Policy in the Middle East' (2011) New Issues in Refugee Research No 201, <www.unhcr.org/4d5a8cde9.pdf> accessed 20 October 2016.

196 Commission of the European Union, 'Qualification Directive Proposal 2001' (Ch 1 n 64), 18.

197 This argument was discussed in *DM* (*Majority Clan Entities Can Protect*) *Somalia* [2005] UKAIT 00150, paras 28–29 but was rejected because the QD only sets out what is 'generally' required. For the opposing view, see eg, *Dyli* [2002] INLR 372, para 13, stating that 'A person who, for whatever reason, has protection in his own country has no basis for fear of persecution; and there is no basis for imposing international duties of surrogate protection in respect of a person who has adequate protection within his own country. Such protection is "the protection of the country". How it is achieved, whether directly by the authorities of the country, or by others, is irrelevant.'

does not aim to define a formal threshold that would render the actors specified in Article 7(1) into states bearing obligations under international law. The requirement of control may coincide with the standard generally advanced for recognition of de facto authorities or even de facto states as subjects of international law, bearing at least some of the rights and duties vested by the legal personality of states.[198] This is evident when considering the drafting of the Directive.

Importantly, drafters were of the opinion that protection by such non-state actors as international organisations was merely the corollary of considering non-state actors 'actors of persecution'. Not only did the original proposal by the European Commission name actors of persecution or serious harm, and actors of protection, in the same Article,[199] the Commission also explicitly argued that considering non-state actors as actors of protection 'continues from the logic' which considers these actors 'actors of persecution'.[200] At the heart of this is the factual enquiry that characterises the assessment of available protection: legal obligations on the actors of protection matter to the extent that they are evidence for the willingness and ability (effectiveness) of protection against harm. Yet, what ultimately matters is the result of these endeavours. This was also evident in the CJEU *Abdulla* ruling, which reiterated that the Qualification Directive does not rule out the provision of protection by international organisations, 'including protection ensured through the presence of a multinational force', but then provided guidance on the assessment of facts and circumstances to be considered in assessing protection.[201] Under such

198 In the *Reparations* case, Reparations for Injuries Suffered in the Service of the United Nations (Advisory Opinion) [1949] ICJ Rep 179, 178, the ICJ stated that, 'The subjects of law in any legal system are not necessarily identical in their nature or in the extent of their rights, and their nature depends upon the needs of the community.' For questions on legal personality, see Roland Portmann, *Legal Personality in International Law* (Cambridge University Press 2010).

199 Commission of the European Union, *Qualification Directive Proposal 2001* (Ch 1 n 64) Arts 9, 17.

200 Ibid.

201 *Kamil Hasan, Ahmed Adem, Hamrin Mosa Rashi and Dler Jamal v Bundesrepublik Deutschland*, opinion of Advocate General Mazák of 15 September 2009 (Ch 3 n 52) para 75. In the context of cessation of refugee status, the German Federal Administrative Court had also asked whether it was 'sufficient in that regard if protection can be assured only with the help of multinational troops' in order to clarify whether it would be possible to return people to territories in which no stable state authorities existed. The cjeu did not address that question because the referring German court had framed it as a secondary question arising only in case the primary question, on the criteria for cessation of refugee status, was to be answered in the negative. In particular, other than in the Advocate General's advisory opinion, the CJEU disregarded whether an actor of protection required

'factual approach' to assessing protection, the Qualification Directive's requirement that actors of protection need to control a substantial part of the territory of the state appears to ensure that these actors are vested with sufficient power to actually provide effective protection in practice.[202] This requirement precludes consideration of institutions such as shelters for women at risk of trafficking or domestic violence, unless these are part and parcel of the effective protection provided by authorities with control over the state or a substantial part of the territory of a state.

The extension of the Qualification Directive's 'actor of protection' concept to actors other than states has been criticised heavily by legal commentators and the UNHCR.[203] This criticism has been twofold. A first strand of criticism argued that only states were able to provide, in practice, effective protection. ECRE, for instance, argued that the endeavours of non-state actors to provide protection are usually limited in scope and time and may be volatile.[204] The UNHCR took the view that 'only in exceptional cases, where the party or organisation is comparable to a State can it be considered an actor of protection'.[205] A second strand of criticism has been directed not so much at the factual ability of international organisations or other 'parties' controlling state territory to provide effective protection in individual cases, but at whether or not considering such actors as 'actors of protection' complies in any way with the 1951 Convention.[206] Both criticisms will be addressed in the following sections.

---

an international mandate. The Advocate General had argued that 'to comply with the terms of Article 7' of the QD, 'a State may only rely on the assistance of multinational troops provided such troops operate under the mandate of the international community.' *Aydin Salahadin Abdulla, Kamil Hasan, Ahmed Adem, Hamrin Mosa Rashi and Dler Jamal v Bundesrepublik Deutschland* (Ch 1 n 54) para 58.

202 See Dörig 'Asylum Qualification Directive 2011/95/EU', 1153 in Hailbronner and Thym (eds), *EU Immigration and Asylum Law – A Commentary* (Ch 1 n 7), stating that 'from a protection point of view, it is essential how effective the protection against persecution is which an actor can afford as a matter of fact – be it a state or another authority'.

203 On the question of clans or other de facto authorities, see ibid 1154.

204 European Council on Refugees and Exiles, 'Comments from the European Council on Refugees and Exiles on the European Commission Proposal to recast the Qualification Directive' (May 2010) 8 <www.ecre.org/wp-content/uploads/2016/07/ECRE-Comments-on-the-Commission-Proposal-to-Recast-the-Qualification-Directive_March-2010.pdf> accessed 20 October 2016.

205 UN High Commissioner for Refugees, 'Asylum in the European Union. A Study of the Implementation of the Qualification Directive' (Ch 3 n 141) 50.

206 Hathaway and Foster, *The Law of Refugee Status* (Ch 1 n 100); O'Sullivan, 'Acting the Part: Can Non-State Entities Provide Protection under International Refugee Law?' (Ch 1 n 103).

3.5.2 *Can Non-state Actors Provide Effective Protection against Harm? an Analysis under the Factual Approach*

The assessment of effective protection against harm is an individualised one in which, among other things, different types of harm and of authorities, as well as different countries of origin, will invariably lead to different outcomes. However, there may be impediments to the willingness and ability to provide effective and non-temporary protection that are rooted in the typical conditions of operation of 'actors of protection' other than states.

First, in respect of militias, the concern for the protection needs of civilians varies considerably, depending on the type of conflict, the command structure, and the dependence on the local populace.[207] Even where militias or clans attempt to provide safety, the actual cases where militias managed to establish safety reveals the volatility of such endeavours. For example, in the Lebanese Civil War, the Christian militia Lebanese Forces had established a Christian enclave, in which they provided security and set up an economic infrastructure in exchange for tax collection.[208] Protection, however, was granted along the lines of ethnicity and the situation later went up in flames.[209] Many contemporary areas of militia or de facto authority control are equally volatile, yet lack of control over territory impacts the ability to shield from harm.[210] What is

207 Marie-Joëlle Zahar, 'Protégés, clients, cannon fodder: Civilians in the calculus of militias' (2000) 7 International Peacekeeping 107, 113–117.

208 Ibid 115.

209 Ihsan Hijazi I, 'Fighting Rages Between Lebanese Christian Forces' (New York Times, February 1990) <www.nytimes.com/1990/02/01/world/fighting-rages-between-lebanese-christian-forces.html> accessed 20 October 2016; Ihsan Hijazi, 'Lebanese Weigh Intervention in Christian Enclave' (New York Times, February 1990) <www.nytimes.com/1990/02/09/world/lebanese-weigh-intervention-in-christian-enclave.html> accessed 20 October 2016.

210 Indeed, confronted with the question whether it was duty-bound to assess the risks of persecution faced by witnesses who are applying for asylum, the International Criminal Court (ICC) in 2011 argued that respect for the principle of non-refoulement required control over territory. 'Admittedly, as an international organisation with a legal personality, the Court cannot disregard the customary rule of non-refoulement. However, since it does not possess any territory, it is unable to implement the principle within its ordinary meaning, and hence is unlikely to maintain long-term jurisdiction over persons who are at risk of persecution or torture if they return to their country of origin. In the Chamber's view, only a State which possesses territory is actually able to apply the non-refoulement rule. Furthermore, the Court cannot employ the cooperation mechanisms provided for by the Statute in order to compel a State Party to receive onto its territory an individual invoking this rule. Moreover, it cannot prejudge, in lieu of the Host State, obligations placed on the latter under the non-refoulement principle.' ICC Trial Chamber II, *Decision on an Amicus Curiae application and on the 'Requête tendant à obtenir présentations des témoins DRC-D02-P-03509, DRC-D02-P-0236, DRC-D02-P-0228 aux autorités néerlandaises*

more, clans and militias often build group coherence along ethnic or other demarcating lines, such as political opinion or religion.[211] Finally, there are issues of capacity, exacerbated by engagement in war effort or the reluctance of aid organisations to cooperate with politically disagreeable actors.[212] It is precisely for that reason that militias have attracted international attention for causing civilian suffering rather than shielding from harm.[213]

Doubts about the effectiveness and durability of protection given certain conditions of operation also arise in respect of peace-keeping missions, which have a track record of failing in relation to the protection of civilians.[214] By definition, peace-keeping operations are embedded in post-conflict settings or volatile security contexts, prone to relatively rapid changes in the security situation, as well as to particular challenges in respect of the required resources and the necessary prioritisation of larger-scale security issues. The UN Mission in Kosovo (UNMIK) and the Kosovo Force (KFOR), two explicit examples named in the drafting of the Qualification Directive, could not protect all ethnic Serbs from retaliation by Kosovar Albanians, despite deploying a relatively large police and military force immediately after the Kosovo war in 1999.[215] Five years post deployment, the international forces failed to foresee, prevent or restrain the sudden massive clashes between the two groups, which left 24 people dead, and hampered relations between KFOR and the Kosovar

aux fins d'asile' (articles 68 and 93(7) of the Statute), June 2011, ICC-01/04-01/07-3003-tENG, para 64.

211 Parties establishing control within a state territory have in the past often pursued the goal of installing Sharia, such as in the Pakistani Swat Valley or, in 2012, in Northern Mali.

212 UN Secretary General, 'Report of the UN Secretary-General on the Protection of Civilians in Armed Conflict', UN Doc S/2010/579 para 55; UN Secretary General, 'Report of the Secretary-General to the Security Council on the protection of civilians in armed conflict', UN Doc S/2002/1300 para 7.

213 According to the UN Secretary General, 'armed groups have often sought to overcome their military inferiority by employing strategies that flagrantly violate international law. These range from deliberate attacks against civilians, including sexual violence, to attacks on civilian objects such as schools, to abduction, forced recruitment and using civilians to shield military objectives. The risks for civilians are further increased as militarily superior parties, in fighting an enemy that is often difficult to identify, respond with means and methods of warfare that may violate the principles of distinction and proportionality, giving rise to further civilian casualties'. See UN Secretary General, 'Report of the UN Secretary-General on the Protection of Civilians in Armed Conflict' (ibid) para 8.

214 UN General Assembly, UN Security Council, 'Report of the Panel on United Nations Peace Operations', UN Doc A/55/305–S/2000/809.

215 OSCE Mission in Kosovo, 'As Seen, As Told, Part II. A Report on the Human Rights Findings of the OSCE Mission in Kosovo (June to October 1999)' <www.osce.org/odihr/17772?download=true> accessed 20 October 2016.

population, and thus the effectiveness of the police forces, for years.[216] *A fortiori*, such doubts pertain to situations of more open armed conflict. The United Nations Organization Stabilization Mission in the Democratic Republic of the Congo (MONUC/MONUSCO), despite being vested with a clear protection mandate, 'hard' military capabilities and high numbers of personnel, failed to prevent the advance of M23 rebels in late 2012.[217]

Despite these doubts, there is also evidence to the contrary, both in respect of clans and militias, and in respect of peace-keeping operations. The authorities of Somaliland, the de facto state at the horn of Africa, have assured security and relatively stable democratic governmental institutions, despite bordering the notoriously unstable and war-torn remaining territories of Somalia.[218] The UN, seeking to draw lessons from past failures in protecting civilians, has adopted the 'Rights up Front' Action Plan, designed to create clearer policies, procedures and mechanisms for the protection of civilians and for human rights protection throughout all UN operations.[219] In South Sudan, the Action Plan has led to the UN Mission in South Sudan (UNMIS) providing shelter from violence to 75,000 people – an unparalleled measure and important precedent.[220] While these examples do not provide evidence of control over territory combined with available protection for particular cases (indeed, UNMIS did *not* control territory so as to satisfy Article 7(1), Qualification Directive), they do however demonstrate that the spectrum of activities, failures and successes by 'parties and organizations', as provided in Article 7(1), is too broad for a general claim that these actors will never be, as a matter of principle, *willing and able* to provide effective protection against harm, or a legal presumption to that effect.[221]

---

216 Human Rights Watch, 'Failure to Protect: Anti-Minority Violence in Kosovo' (March 2004) <www.hrw.org/report/2004/07/25/failure-protect/anti-minority-violence-kosovo-march-2004> accessed 20 October 2016. UN Secretary General, *Report of the Secretary-General on the United Nations Interim Administration Mission in Kosovo*, UN Security Council, S/2004/348; Steffen Eckard, 'Managing Peacebuilding: Strategic Management, Organizational Performance and the Outcome of Post-Conflict Police Reform in Kosovo and Afghanistan' (PhD Dissertation, Universtät Konstanz 2013) 41.

217 Reuters, 'UN defends failed attempt to halt capture of Congo's Goma' (November 2012) <www.reuters.com/article/2012/11/21/congo-democratic-un-idUSL5E8MLH6J20121121> accessed 1 July 2019.

218 See eg, Michael Walls, 'The Emergence of a Somali State: Building Peace from Civil War in Somaliland' (2008) 108 *African Affairs* 371.

219 Andrew Gilmour, 'The Future of Human Rights: A View from the United Nations' (2014) 28 *Ethics and Interntional Affairs* 239.

220 Ibid.

221 Storey makes a similar point in respect of protection by non-state actors in the IPA, arguing against a presumption that such actors cannot provide effective protection: 'Even in

What is more, and as is apparent from the review of jurisprudence above, legal frameworks are a primary piece of evidence for the *willingness* to protect in practice, as may be human rights obligations.[222] This also appears to be the view of the Commission[223] as well as the European Parliament.[224] Yet, that willingness may, *in theory*, also be established by other pieces of evidence.

As previously stated, Article 7(1)–(2) takes account of these doubts with its high requirements of territorial control, ability and willingness to provide effective protection, and accessibility of protection. What is more, as will be

---

centralised States there may sometimes be no political will or apparatus for pursuing or detecting political opponents countrywide. This formulation prompts the question, that is to say, why presume something that may not be so in fact? Whilst it may be that such presumptions can be helpful tools, choice of such legal concepts is bound to raise difficulties for countries which prefer not to import into refugee law special rules governing the status of evidence.' Hugo Storey, ' "From Nowhere to Somewhere": An Evaluation of the UNHCR 2nd Track Global Consultations on International Protection: San Remo 8–10 September 2001 Experts Roundtable on the IPA/IRA/IFA Alternative' ('Stemming the Tide or Keeping the Balance – The Role of the Judiciary' – International Association of Refugee Law Judges Fifth World Conference, Wellington, New Zealand, 22 October 2002–25 October 2002).

222 UN High Commissioner for Refugees, 'UNHCR Annotated Comments on the EC Council Directive 2004/83/EC of 29 April 2004' (Ch 2 n 23) arguing that the different legal obligations meant that *in practice* their 'ability to enforce the rule of law is limited'. Also Madeleine Garlick, 'UNHCR and the Implementation of Council Directive 2004/83/EC on Minimum Standards for the Qualification and Status of Third Country Nations or Stateless Persons as Refugees or as Persons who Otherwise Need International Protection and the Content of the Protection Granted (The EC "Qualification Directive")' in Karin Zwaan (ed), 'The Qualification Directive: Central Themes, Problem Issues, and implementation in Selected Member States' (Wolf Legal Publishers 2007).

223 The original proposal only referred to non-State actors as potential 'actors of protection' when these were comparable to a state. According to the proposal, 'For the purpose of this Directive, "State" protection may also be provided by international organisations and stable quasi-State authorities who control a clearly defined territory of significant size and stability, and who are able and willing to give effect to rights and to protect an individual from harm *in a manner similar to an internationally recognised State*.'

224 The European Parliament voted to delete the provision on non-State actor protection, linking their factual capacity to protect with the legal obligation to do so. Non-state parties were not and could not be parties to international human rights treaties, making it impossible for people living 'under the jurisdiction' of non-state actors to 'hold them responsible at international level for ensuring that human rights standards are safeguarded'. See European Parliament, 'Report on the proposal for a Council directive on minimum standards for the qualification and status of third country nationals and stateless persons as refugees or as persons who otherwise need international protection' (Ch 3 n 63).

apparent from the analysis of jurisprudence below, many member states' courts are, rightly so, reluctant to apply Article 7(1)(b) on non-state actors in practice.

3.5.3 *Is the Concept of Non-state Actors of Protection in Compliance with the 1951 Convention?*

Several scholars have argued that non-state actor 'protection' is at odds with the terms of the 1951 Convention in light of its object and purpose. According to Hathaway and Foster, considering actors other than states capable of providing 'protection' would ignore the commitment of the Convention to reestablish a refugee in a national community. In consequence, a *formal* requirement should be introduced whereby only actors with clear obligations under international law should be considered capable of providing protection:

> Even if a clan or militia were able to prevent the immediate threat of harm, [...] the 'protection' afforded would be subject to little, if any, accountability at international law. The net result would thus be to deny refugee status on the basis of access to the efforts of some entity that, whatever its past record of *de facto* authority or power, bears no ongoing legal duty to protect anyone. This not only flies in the face of refugee law's forward-looking focus, but ignores completely the Refugee Convention's principled commitment to *restoring refugees to membership in a national community*, that is, in a political community that has clear protective duties under international law.[225]

225 Hathaway and Foster, *The Law of Refugee Status* (Ch 1 n 100) 291. This point was also made in the UK case of *Gardi* [2002] 1 WLR 2755, in relation to the authorities of the Kurdish Autonomous Region during the Saddam Hussein regime: 'The reference in Article 1A(2) is to an asylum seeker being unable or unwilling to avail himself "of the protection of that country", a reference to the earlier phrase "the country of nationality". That does seem to imply that the protection has to be that of an entity which is capable of granting nationality to a person in a form recognised internationally. [...] The KAR does not meet that criteria. I see force also in the point made by Hathaway and Foster in their paper at page 46, that protection can only be provided by an entity capable of being held responsible under international law. That decision in Vallaj is not inconsistent with that proposition since the UNMIK regime in Kosovo had the authority of the United Nations plus the consent of the Federal Republic of Yugoslavia. Yet no-one suggests that the KAR or any part of it is such an entity under international law.' However, the remarks were *obiter dictum* and the court was later found to have lacked jurisdiction in the case.

Others argued that the essence of refugeehood was 'the breaking of the bond between citizen and state', a bond that could only be repaired 'by the presence of a functioning government, able and willing to provide protection to its people, which operates with the consent of the governed'.[226] Principally, it was the *legitimacy and stability* of an authority that determined whether it could be an actor of protection. Actors that acted as 'stable, state-like authority', were present for a long time, and had an international mandate, could be considered in assessing available protection, otherwise they could not.[227]

Indeed, as the first chapter has demonstrated, the severed bond between an individual and a state is at the heart of refugeehood, and the object and purpose of the 1951 Convention is to reestablish that bond by enfranchising a refugee with human rights and rights under the 1951 Convention concurrently. This object and purpose is captured in the Convention's 'protection clause', which has lost most of its traditional meaning and does not contain a substantive criterion for eligibility to refugee status additional to those implied in the notion of the 'well-founded fear of being persecuted'.[228]

Yet, this does not in and of itself imply that the Convention prescribes consideration of states only when assessing whether there is effective protection against harm. First, the surrogate rights enfranchisement *for refugees* remains clearly distinct from the criteria for inclusion under Article 1A(2) of the 1951 Convention. Such rights enfranchisement is contingent on *refugee status*. Second, although the notion of surrogacy has impacted the inclusion criteria by pushing forward a human rights-informed understanding of relevant harm, it is clear that the Convention, like human rights law, requires a factual approach to the assessment of available protection. In such an approach, the legal obligations of the authorities of the state of nationality are only of evidentiary value for the willingness and ability to protect, measured against the Convention's real chance standard – the 'well-founded fear of being persecuted'. However, it is difficult to see how such a *factual* approach to the effectiveness of protection can at the same time be a *formal* approach when it comes to the permissible actors of protection, given that the enquiry is the same, namely, again, whether there is a well-founded fear of *being persecuted*.[229] Indeed, as discussed in

226 O'Sullivan, 'Acting the Part: Can Non-State Entities Provide Protection Under International Refugee Law?' (Ch 1 n 103) 102.

227 Ibid 103.

228 See above, Section 2.3.4.

229 In UK jurisprudence, the matter was discussed in *DM (Majority Clan Entities Can Protect) Somalia* [2005] UKAIT 00150 at para 22: 'All that is essential for Refugee Convention and Human Rights Convention purposes, therefore, is that as a matter of fact an entity within a country or state affords effective protection. Plainly, an entity which relies for its law and

Section 3.3.2, this conundrum explains the shift in practice on recognising non-state actors as relevant persecutory agents.[230]

Against this background, the (relatively) most compelling argument against non-state actor 'protection' under the 1951 Convention remains a literal reading of the 'protection clause' in Article 1A(2), in which 'country' means 'state'.[231] Under such literal reading, the Convention's surrogacy principle is surrogate *state* protection for lack of *state* protection against harm inflicted by any type of actor.[232] This state-focused reading is not derived from the rights enfranchisement achieved by refugee status, but from a simple remembering of the origins of the 1951 Convention, in which protection in the country of refuge was a symbol for a lack of protection by the state, evinced in the well-founded fear of being persecuted. Yet, as explored in Chapter 1, human rights law has diminished the practical importance of that clause, rendering such argument unconvincing. What is more, under non-return obligations of human rights law, the type of actor of protection is, in principle, irrelevant. As will be apparent in the following section, the Qualification Directive's common 'actor

order functions on drug barons or armed militias may be less able to provide effective protection than one which can rely on those functions being performed by properly trained, properly resourced and accountable police or army personnel whose standards of human conduct are exemplary. But variations of this type simply go to the factual question, "Is protection afforded?" not the legal question of "is there an entity or are there entities qualified to afford protection?"'

230 A similar argument has been made by Harald Dörig, 'Asylum Qualification Directive 2011/95/EU', 1153, in Hailbronner and Thym (eds), *EU Immigration and Asylum Law – A Commentary* (Ch 1 n 7), stating that 'To consider that protection can only be afforded by states that are signatories to international human rights treaties [...] risks inserting a state accountability requirement and confining ability to protect only to liberal democratic states.'

231 Battjes, *European Asylum Law and International Law* (Ch 1 n 102) 2. The argument, however, is not uncontested, see Storey, '"From Nowhere to Somewhere": An Evaluation of the UNHCR 2nd Track Global Consultations on International Protection: San Remo 8–10 September 2001 Experts Roundtable on the IPA/IRA/IFA Alternative'. Likewise, Chetail argues that non-state actor protection contravenes the 1951 Convention, pointing to the protection clause; Vincent Chetail, 'The Common European Asylum System: Bric-à-Brac or System?', 33 in Vincent Chetail, Philippe De Bruycker and Francesco Maiani (eds), *Reforming the Common European Asylum System: The New European Refugee Law* (Brill 2015).

232 Zimmermann and Mahler, 459 in Zimmermann; Dörschner; Machts (eds), *The 1951 Convention Relating to the Status of Refugees and its 1967 Protocol – A Commentary* (Ch 1 n 42) appear to follow this approach, by discussing the conditions of attribution from other entities to that of the state, but at the same time also adopt a factual approach, arguing that a well-founded fear of persecution [sic] 'might be considered to have ceased to exist once effective protection [...] is provided by such external actors'.

of protection' framework for refugee status and subsidiary status converges a human rights law approach to non-state actors of protection with a refugee law approach.

3.5.4 *Non-state Actors of Protection in the Assessment of Subsidiary Protection Status*

Under Article 7 of the Qualification Directive, the 'actor of protection framework' that includes 'parties or organizations' also applies to assessment of subsidiary protection. Given the overlap between Article 15(b) and the ECHR non-return obligations, the ECHR jurisprudence can again provide guidance as to interpretation of Article 7 in respect of subsidiary protection status. As discussed in Section 3.3, human rights law takes a purely *factual approach* to the question of available state protection and indeed has influenced the Convention in that regard. But what is more, given that human rights law non-return obligations are not based on refugee status, the protection clause of the Convention and its traditional emphasis on lack of *state protection* are irrelevant to these obligations. In consequence, there is nothing that would preclude, in principle, consideration of actors other than states in the assessment of available protection.

The court's readiness to consider non-state actors when assessing the risk of harm by a non-state actor is most evident in *Audad v Bulgaria,* in which the ECtHR assessed whether the expulsion of a stateless Palestinian from Lebanon would violate Article 3.[233] The applicant, a Member of Fatah and formerly in a salaried position for a Fatah commander, had fled from a refugee camp and feared being killed by a Palestinian Sunni Salafist Group. The court considered the UK's Operational Guidance Notes for Lebanon, according to which 'Palestinian groups operate autonomously in refugee camps and in the majority of cases would be able to offer the protection needed from within these camps'.[234] Although the court did not embrace that finding, it did consider protection by Fatah, taking note of the relationship between the group and the Lebanese state, internal and external power struggles and corruption:

> It is true that the situation in the country as a whole does not appear so serious that the return of the applicant there would constitute, in itself, a breach of Article 3 […] However, it cannot be overlooked that the applicant is a stateless Palestinian originating from a refugee camp in Lebanon

233 *Audad v Bulgaria* App no 46390/10 (ECtHR, 11 October 2011).

234 Ibid para 61.

> … The information available on the Palestinian refugee camps […] shows that they are not under the control of the Lebanese authorities, but of various Palestinian armed factions. They … have been described in reports as […] 'a safe haven for those who seek to escape the authority of the State'. They continue to be plagued by outbursts of violence and armed clashes between various factions. […] In addition, there appear to exist power struggles within the ranks of Fatah itself. They, together with corruption within the movement, have apparently contributed to various security breakdowns. […] *It is therefore not readily apparent that Fatah, despite its relative dominance in [the camp], would be able to provide the applicant with effective protection.*[235]

Most recently, the court did not appear to be interested in questions of the legal status of the Kurdish Autonomous Region in respect of Iraq when referring an applicant to an IPA (internal protection alternative) there.[236]

This is not to say that the actor of protection is irrelevant evidence in relation to the ability to provide protection. Thus, in *Ahmed v Austria*, the ECtHR had considered only whether there was any 'public authority' that would be able to protect the applicant against generalised violence, rather than naming clans as potential protectors.[237] In *Salah Sheekh v the Netherlands*, the court even went as far as to say that it was relevant whether applicants at risk of harm by non-state actors were able to 'seek redress'.[238] Although this was interpreted by some as a bar to considering actors other than states as actors of protection,[239] the court also pointed out that non-return obligations are independent from the (legal) responsibility of the receiving country and was also ready to consider the importance of clan affiliation for personal security in Somalia.[240]

235 Ibid para 103 (emphasis added).

236 *NMY and Others v Sweden* App no 72686/10 (ECtHR, 27 June 2013). For non-state actors of protection in the IPA, see below, Chapter 4, at 4.5.

237 *Ahmed v Austria* (Ch 3 n 37) para 44.

238 *Salah Sheekh v the Netherlands* (Ch 3 n 124) para 147.

239 European Commission, 'Actors of Protection and Internal Protection – The new legal framework: Articles 7 and 8 of Directive 2011/95/EU', presentation at the Contact Committee meeting 'Qualification Directive' (2011/95/EC) on 11 November 2014, on file with the author.

240 *Salah Sheekh v the Netherlands* (Ch 3 n 124) para 148, noting that 'It appears from the appellant's account that he and his family were targeted because they belonged to a minority *and for that reason it was known that they had had no means of protection*; they were easy prey, as were the other three Ashraf families living in the same village […]'.

3.5.5 *Non-state Actors of Protection in Jurisprudence of Selected Member States*

The Qualification Directive, in line with the 1951 Convention, allows actors other than states as 'actors of protection' under Article 7, but stipulates high requirements: in addition to being willing and able to provide effective protection that is accessible to the applicant, they have to possess control over substantial parts of territory. Case law serves to demonstrate the extent to which the Qualification Directive succeeds in harmonising these requirements in practice. In this regard, past studies have in particular pointed out that the actor of protection concept had been applied to actors other than parties or organisations controlling a substantial part of territory.[241] The European Commission 2010 report on the application of the Qualification Directive noted that some states had been 'ready to consider clans or tribes as capable of providing sufficient protection under certain conditions'.[242] These points of criticism will be discussed below. In addition, jurisprudence provides examples of the evidentiary considerations affecting the issue of non-state actors' ability and willingness to provide effective protection, on which guidance by Article 7, Qualification Directive and the CJEU is limited.

3.5.5.1 The Requirement of Control over Territory

Prior to the adoption of the recast Qualification Directive, which specified that Article 7(1) is an exhaustive list, courts in some member states indeed considered a broader variety of non-state actors as actors of protection, albeit that in practice these were seldom found to be willing and able to provide protection.[243] In Germany, for instance, a court considered whether a Lebanese woman at risk of honour killing could live, absent state protection, in a privately run shelter for battered women, but rejected this because of the many risks and uncertainties for the applicant.[244] In the case of an Afghan woman fearing ill-treatment by the Taliban, one court considered the possibility of protection by her family.[245] Finally, it was argued in one decision that an applicant fearing honour killing could obtain effective protection if she approached the authorities in an 'insistent and serious' manner, because of support she could expect

241 UN High Commissioner for Refugees, 'Asylum in the European Union' (Ch 3 n 141) 50.

242 Commission to the European Parliament and the Council, noting that in Belgium, Hungary and the United Kingdom, NGOs had been considered as actors of protection for women at risk of female genital mutilation and honour killings.

243 For a discussion of the transposition of the Qualification Directive, see above, section 2.4.3.

244 VG Stuttgart, 8 September 2008 – A 10 K 13/07.

245 VG Gießen, 9 June 2005 – 2 E 1383/04.A.

from a women's NGO.[246] With the transposition of the recast Qualification Directive, however, this practice has changed.

There is also evidence from the Netherlands that some courts are ready to consider actors other than those specified by Article 7(1), Qualification Directive, even after the adoption of the recast Qualification Directive and with relatively clear domestic guidance. The Dutch Circular on Foreigners specifies that NATO and the United Nations are relevant for the provision of protection.[247] The former version of the law still specified that protection is considered to be 'non-temporary' when there is 'no concrete evidence that effective protection will end in the foreseeable future'.[248] In a decision on Mauritanian women fearing slavery, the Dutch Secretary of State (*Staatssecretaris*) referred the applicants to protection by the gender officers of the church-run NGO Caritas.[249] The Dutch Council of State, upon reviewing the decision, concluded that it could not be said generally that there was protection because of doubts that the protection provided by anti-slavery NGOs was effective, but it did not object to the relevance of NGOs as a matter of principle.[250]

In contrast to such practice, other jurisdictions show a notable reluctance to consider any actors other than states as actors of protection. In particular, French domestic law had until mid-2015 considered only states and international and regional organisations as capable of offering protection against harm by non-state actors, rather than any other parties or organisations with control over territory.[251] Accordingly, French courts considered whether or not the UN Stabilization Mission in Haiti (MINUSTAH), the UN Stabilization Mission in Congo (MONUSCO) and UNMIK were in control of territory and able to provide effective protection, but found this not to be the case.[252] In the context

246 VG Aachen, 11 October 2006 – 6 K 4487/04.A.

247 *Vreemdelingencirculaire 2000* (C) of 1 December 2017, Section 3.4, consistent with previous text versions.

248 *Vreemdelingencirculaire 2000* (C) of 13 August 2015, Author's translation.

249 See Raad van Staate, 6 August 2013, 201205299/1/V1.

250 Rechtbank Den Haag, 11 November 2013, AWB 12/2596 en 12/2599 (author's translation).

251 This changed with the transposition of the recast Qualification Directive. Article L 713-2, Code de l'entrée et du séjour des étrangers et du droit d'asile (Ch 2 n 94), prior to the entry into force of Loi no 2015–925 du 29 juillet 2015 relative à la réforme du droit (1).

252 The CRR and CNDA denied in three cases on subsidiary status that the UN Stabilization Mission in Haiti (MINUSTAH) was capable of providing protection in practice; *S.*, CRR 28 June 2005, no 519680; CRR, 30 October 2006, 580781, v; *Mlle Y*, CNDA 4 September 2009, no 645353/09004158, D. In one subsidiary status case from DRC, the CRR stated that 'neither the authorities nor the special missions of the UN stationed in Iturie are capable of assuring a protection in this region.' *Mlle Y*, CRR 30 November 2006, no 535001. In the case of a Congolese national at risk of ethnic violence, the CRR found that 'neither the

of an asylum application by an Ivorian national, the CRR considered whether the authorities in the Northern Ivory Coast were to be considered capable of providing protection to a party militant of the *Rassemblement des Républicains,* a party close to the rebel forces, *Forces Nouvelles,* in the north. The court stated that the control requirement requires the establishment of civil structures, rather than military control alone.[253]

In the UK, courts have, wherever possible, considered actors other than states only jointly with state authorities.[254] In respect of Kosovo, the Tribunal considered UNMIK jointly with the Kosovar authorities in several cases involving Roma applicants and other ethnic minorities.[255] In *S I,* for instance, the Tribunal found that 'there is clear evidence of a sufficiency of protection within Kosovo *both from UNMIK and from the Kosovan authorities themselves*',[256] but the Tribunal exhibited a tendency to deduce the individual finding of available protection from general factors.[257] A notable exception to the rule is the frequent consideration of clans as actors of protection. However, in *D M,* the AIT made clear that it gave consideration to ruling clans because it considered them equivalent to the state:

MONUC nor the Congolese public authorities, which do not currently control the territory of Mahagi, were in a position to assure her a protection in this region [...]', *Mlle S,* CRR 15 mars 2007, no 585846 (author's translation). Finally, the CNDA granted subsidiary status to a female victim of domestic violence in relation to whom the court stated, 'by reason of the private character of the matter, ... cannot avail herself to the effective protection of the authorities that today hold the power in Kosovo by virtue of the United Nations mandate' *Mlle A,* CNDA 3 April 2008, no 584799.

253 *T,* CRR 16 February 2007, no 573815.

254 A notable exception being *S T (child asylum seekers) Sri Lanka* [2013] UKUT 00292(IAC) in which the AIT considered the availability of institutions for foster care, run by NGO s.

255 *FD (Kosovo – Roma) Serbia and Montenegro* CG [2004] UKIAT 00214, 'We have to bear in mind that the UNMIK police and the KPS together with the judicial system have been effective in reducing the level of attack upon ethnic minorities.' Also *ES* (Ashkaelians, mixed Ashkaelian ethnicity) Serbia and Montenegro (Kosovo) CG [2006] UKAIT 00071 and *S K (Roma in Kosovo – update) Serbia and Montenegro* [2005] UKIAT 0023, stating that, 'On the whole of the evidence which is before us (including the evidence referred to below), we affirm the view of the Tribunal in the *FD* case that the response of the UN and NATO forces was prompt, and clearly demonstrated the promptitude and effectiveness of the protecting response.'

256 *SI (mixed Serb/Roma parentage) Kosovo* CG [2009] UKAIT 00011 (16 March 2009).

257 Stating that, 'The Security Council report sets out details of the police and court system in Kosovo and, although it clearly has defects it cannot be said that it is not fully functioning. There is a fully operational Human Rights Advisory Panel [...] We note the US State Department Report which referred to police activities and to a number of trials.'

> […] there is no dispute that […] there are three major clans in Somalia who each control a substantial part of its territory […] Moreover, we see no logical difficulty with clan militiamen and other majority clan personnel performing quasi-governmental functions being considered as state actors (as opposed to non-state actors).[258]

Finally, in Sweden, the High Court of Migration has rejected outright the availability of effective protection where the authorities had no territorial control over the region in which there was a risk of harm.[259] Thus, in a decision on a woman fleeing honour killings in Iraqi Kurdistan, the court stated that it would not consider women's shelters run by private organisations.[260]

3.5.5.2 Evidentiary Considerations for Effective Protection

Evidentiary considerations relating to the willingness and ability of parties or organisations to provide effective protection against harm are, in principle, no different from those relating to the protective capacity and willingness of states.[261] Thus, objective factors such as the framework of policies and their implementation,[262] together with subjective factors relating to the applicant as well as the alleged perpetrator of harm, will be relevant.[263] There are, however, additional subjective factors unique to consideration of actors other than states. In particular, when considering the possibility of majority clan protection for a member of a minority clan, UK jurisprudence routinely considered whether the minority clan had been establishing 'clan protection relationships' with the majority clan, as well as potential differences in protection in rural

258 *DM (Majority Clan Entities Can Protect) Somalia* [2005] UKAIT 00150 para 31.

259 Migrationsöverdomstolen, 21 April 2011, MIG 2011:8, UM7851-10.

260 Migrationsöverdomstolen, UM3363-10, 2011-03-09 MIG 2011:6.

261 See above, 2.4.4.

262 For instance, a Dutch court considered whether the police in the autonomous region of Iraqi Kurdistan discriminates in practice against Arabs.

263 Eg Migrationsöverdomstolen, 3 September 2011, MIG 2011:6, UM3363-10, rejecting the option of shelters because of the age of the applicant; Germany – VG Göttingen, 01 April 2010, 4 A 43/09, considering that the criminal network inflicting the harm was well-connected and therefore capable of locating the applicant upon return. Even if there was international support for the buildup of a police and justice system and EULEX staff had executive functions, there were deficits in fighting organised crime and corruption – including a high number of illegal arms circulating, lack of criminal proceedings against holders of those arms, complicity of high government officials in organised crime, and the fact that the police and criminal justice system of Kosovo was still under construction.

and urban areas,[264] tribal clan history and the degree of assimilation through language and culture.[265]

3.6 Conclusion: Identifying Points of Convergence of Refugee Law and Human Rights Law in the Actor of Protection Concept

Under the EU Qualification Directive, particularly in cases where an applicant fears harm by non-state actors, it is relevant to assess whether or not 'actors of protection' provide effective protection against acts of persecution or serious harm, and whether the applicant has access to such protection. This chapter has discussed the analysis of available protection in conjunction with refugee and human rights law. In particular, the chapter has enquired as to how such analysis relates to the text of the 1951 Convention's refugee definition, how the effectiveness of protection against harm should be gauged, and whether the 1951 Convention standard is different from the requirements under human rights law non-return obligations. Finally, it has examined whether the Qualification Directive should or should not differentiate henceforward between actors of protection in the assessment of refugee status on the one hand and of subsidiary protection status on the other, and whether the Qualification Directive succeeds in harmonising an international law-compliant actor of protection concept.

Albeit both are grounded in the principle of the surrogacy of international protection, 'protection' against harm is a somewhat different concept in human rights law non-return obligations (and subsidiary protection) than it is in refugee status. In the 1951 Convention, the assessment of available protection is best conceived of as part of the Convention's *being persecuted* notion, whereas in non-return obligations under international human rights law it is part of the requirement of a *real risk*.

In accordance with the text of the Directive and CJEU guidance, the assessment of available protection has to be an individualised one with a shared duty of fact finding, and precludes presumptions of available protection or a formal requirement that the applicant first seek protection with the authorities in the state of nationality. Member states' jurisprudence provides further

264 *YS and HA* (Midgan, not generally at risk) Somalia CG [2005] UKIAT 00088.

265 *DJ* (Bantu, not generally at risk) Somalia CG [2005] UKIAT 00089. Regarding circumstances in which the actions of such actors are relevant, see also Hugo Storey, 'The Meaning of "Protection" Within the Refugee Definition' (2016) 35 Refugee Survey Quarterly 3, who also argues for a purely factual approach in the analysis of protection against harm.

guidance on the kind of evidentiary considerations that are relevant in assessing the willingness and ability to provide and the possibility of accessing effective protection. What is more, a reading of the Directive consistent with the 1951 Convention and the past contentious cases of non-state actor harm make clear that the Convention requires a *factual assessment* of whether or not the actions of actors of protection can quell a risk so that it falls below the real chance standard of the Convention's 'well-founded fear of being persecuted' notion. Likewise, non-return obligations under human rights law require a factual assessment of whether or not the actions of actors of protection quell a real risk of harm. In such a factual approach, the human rights *due diligence* obligations of the state of nationality are only of evidentiary value for the willingness to protect against harm, but do not provide the benchmark for what is or is not effective. Refugee law and human rights law hence converge in the factual approach that is evident in the Qualification Directive.

The factual approach is also key to the question of which actors can provide protection under the 1951 Convention. In contrast to the contention of some academic criticism, both the 1951 Convention and human rights law allow, in principle, for consideration of actors other than states, such as international organisations. However, there are serious doubts as to whether efforts to protect against harm by these actors will be effective in practice. These doubts are reflected in the Qualification Directive's stringent requirements for consideration of actors other than states, in particular in relation to control over the state or a substantial part of the territory of the state, the willingness and ability of such actors to provide effective protection, and the possibility of an applicant accessing such protection. Crucially, it is the prevalence of human rights law which is at the heart of a purely factual approach to the 'being persecuted' notion of the 1951 Convention. The protection clause in Article 1A(2) of the 1951 Convention refers to protection by states. Yet, the convergence of human rights law and refugee law in respect of rights granted to refugees has rendered the 'protection clause' irrelevant as a substantive criterion for refugee status that is additional to the 'well-founded fear of being persecuted'.

Against the background of the convergence of refugee law and human rights law in respect of protection against harm, the Qualification Directive rightly features a common actor of protection concept for both refugee and subsidiary protection status. However, even the recast Directive does not always succeed in harmonising an international law-compliant minimum standard in member state practice. In particular, there is a tendency to deduce individual findings on available protection merely from structural and general factors, to presume protection or to shift the burden of fact finding to the applicant alone. Hence, in a recast Qualification Directive, legislators may consider reformulating

Article 7 of the Directive with a view to clarifying the standard of protection and the link between Article 4 and Article 7. In particular, recast Qualification Directive may clarify that protection is only effective where it reduces the risk of harm below the level of a real chance. This would illustrate that state protection is no independent requirement limiting the 1951 Convention's refugee definition, but an implicit part of that definition.[266] Finally, the factors that courts considered relevant to finding effective protection available or lacking could feed into a separate paragraph of Article 7. This would not only provide more guidance to courts on how to assess available protection against harm, but would also clarify the weight that can be attributed to applicants' past attempts to obtain such protection.

266 Indeed, the recast Article 8 already refers to the relevance of Article 4 for the analysis of protection against harm, so that a reference to Article 4 in Article 7 would bring about greater consistency.

CHAPTER 4

The Internal Protection Alternative

4.1 Introduction

The previous chapter has scrutinised Article 7 of the Qualification Directive, circumscribing which actors can be considered as providing *protection against harm* and the quality of such protection. Article 7 is, first and foremost, relevant to harm feared within the home region of an applicant for international protection. This is apparent from Article 8 of the Directive, according to which a member state may determine that an individual is not in need of international protection if he or she can obtain internal protection *in a part of the country of origin*, that is, elsewhere in his or her country of origin. This concept will subsequently be referred to as the 'Internal Protection Alternative' (IPA).[1] This chapter will discuss the requirements of the IPA under the Qualification Directive in conjunction with refugee and human rights law. In particular, how does Article 8 of the Directive relate to the 1951 Convention and human rights law, and to what extent do the requirements under these bodies of law differ? How do they differ from Article 7, Qualification Directive? Should the Qualification Directive more strongly differentiate between IPA in the assessment of refugee status on the one hand, and in the assessment of subsidiary protection status on the other? Finally, does the Qualification Directive succeed in harmonising an international law-compliant actor of protection concept?

This chapter argues, first, that in respect of refugee status Article 8, Qualification Directive is rooted in the same principle of the 1951 Convention as Article 7 of the Directive. International protection is a surrogate for lack of protection in the state of nationality. However, Article 8 is also fundamentally different from Article 7, because individuals to whom the IPA concept is applied have established a well-founded fear of being persecuted in relation to their home region. Unlike protection against harm (Article 7), protection under the IPA should be assessed, therefore, with reference to rights available under the 1951 Convention *in conjunction* with human rights law. Again, in contrast to

1 The IPA is frequently referred to as the 'Internal Flight Alternative' or 'Internal Relocation Alternative'. Subsequent sections will address potential differences in the terminology. When speaking about refugee status, the preferred term will be the 'Internal Protection Alternative'.

 | DOI:10.1163/9789004430396_005

protection against harm in the home region, the IPA should be considered for state entities only. Second, the chapter argues that these safeguards under the 1951 Convention significantly exceed the IPA safeguards under human rights law obligations of non-return. However, in opting for a common IPA standard for both refugee status and subsidiary protection status, Article 8 risks being conflated with the lower standards derived from human rights law obligations of non-return. A recast Article 8 therefore may distinguish more clearly between the two standards or lift the IPA safeguards for both refugee and subsidiary protection status.

4.2 Analysis of Internal Protection in Status Determination: Anchoring Article 8 Qualification Directive in Refugee and Human Rights Law

4.2.1 *The Interplay of Article 8, Qualification Directive and the Directive's Eligibility Criteria*

The analysis of a potentially available IPA is regulated by Article 8 of the Qualification Directive:

> Internal protection
>
> 1. As part of the assessment of the application for international protection, Member States may determine that an applicant is not in need of international protection if in a part of the country of origin, he or she:
>   (a) has no well-founded fear of being persecuted or is not at real risk of suffering serious harm; or
>   (b) has access to protection against persecution or serious harm as defined in Article 7;
>
>   and he or she can safely and legally travel to and gain admittance to that part of the country and can reasonably be expected to settle there.
> 2. In examining whether an applicant has a well-founded fear of being persecuted or is at real risk of suffering serious harm, or has access to protection against persecution or serious harm in a part of the country of origin in accordance with paragraph 1, Member States shall at the time of taking the decision on the application have regard to the general circumstances prevailing in that part of the country and to the personal circumstances of the applicant in accordance with Article 4. To that end, Member States shall ensure that precise and up-to-date information is obtained from relevant sources, such as the United Nations High Commissioner for Refugees and the European Asylum Support Office.

Like Article 7, the provision features in the Directive's Chapter II containing rules for the assessment of refugee status and subsidiary protection status. Likewise, similar to Article 7, the Qualification Directive circumscribes it as an overarching provision on relevant analysis in the assessment of status rather than an independent eligibility criterion (which are contained in Chapter III and V, Qualification Directive). This is evident also from the fact that the analysis of the IPA is a discretionary provision; member states can chose whether they make it part of status determination.[2]

In the context of Chapter II, Article 8 is tied to Articles 6, 7, 10 and 15 of the Directive. Whether or not an applicant has a well-founded fear of being persecuted or faces a real risk of serious harm inflicted by an actor of persecution or an actor of serious harm, and cannot avail himself of the protection of his country of nationality, is assessed not just in relation to his or her home region, but also in relation to other parts of the country.

While the provision is, in principle, relevant for harm inflicted by either state or non-state actors in the home region, the Qualification Directive prescribes a presumption against available protection in another part of the country where state agents inflict the harm in the home region.[3] This presumption is also apparent from the drafting process.[4]

It is clear from the text that Article 8(1)–(2) foresees two alternative, but equivalent, criteria for the IPA, namely the absence of a real chance of relevant harm or the presence of effective protection against such harm. Both these alternatives, however, require additional safeguards, namely that an applicant can reach the area in law and fact and 'reasonably be expected to settle' in an IPA area.

Similar to Article 7, it may be relevant not only for the outcome of decisions but also for the interpretation of the Directive at what stage the analysis of the

2 See Article 8(1) according to which, 'As part of the assessment of the application for international protection, Member States *may* determine that an applicant is not in need of international protection if in a part of the country of origin [...]'.

3 According to Recital 27, 'Internal protection against persecution or serious harm should be effectively available to the applicant in a part of the country of origin where he or she can safely and legally travel to, gain admittance to and can reasonably be expected to settle. Where the State or agents of the State are the actors of persecution or serious harm, there should be a presumption that effective protection is not available to the applicant.'

4 Article 10(1) of the Commission of the European Union, *Proposal for a Council Directive on minimum standards for the qualification and status of third country nationals and stateless persons as refugees or as persons who otherwise need international protection*, stating that, 'In carrying out this examination there shall be a strong presumption against finding internal protection to be a viable alternative to international protection if the agent of persecution is, or is associated with the national government.'

IPA takes place in the assessment of refugee and subsidiary protection status. In particular, jurisprudential analysis has demonstrated that the IPA has in the past been used as a 'fall-back to an adverse credibility decision', thereby shifting the burden of proof to applicants.[5] Meanwhile, the Qualification Directive does not specify the interplay with the criteria of refugee and subsidiary status. In the 2001 proposal for the Directive as well as in earlier documents, the IPA was still conceived of as part of the well-founded fear of being persecuted.[6] Again like Article 7, the provision is one that does not find an express equivalent in the 1951 Convention. Nor is the IPA explicitly provided for by a human rights treaty featuring non-return obligations. Therefore, and given that the Qualification Directive has to be in line with both these bodies of law, the next section explores whether and how the IPA concept finds expression in the 1951 Convention and human rights law.

4.2.2 *Locating the IPA in the Refugee Definition of the 1951 Convention*

Is the assessment of internal protection – in principle and beyond the question of the IPA's substantive standards – in accordance with the 1951 Convention? The Convention is silent about harm being localised and does not expressly mention the possibility of internal protection.[7] Yet, there is

---

5 Christel Querton, *'Even if …' The Use of the Internal Protection Alternative in Asylum Decisions in the UK* (Asylum Aid 2014) <www.asylumaid.org.uk/wp-content/uploads/2014/07/Even-If…Asylum-Aid-2014.pdf> accessed 20 October 2016.

6 Article 10(1) of the Commission of the European Union, *Qualification Directive Proposal 2009* (Ch 2 n 66), stating that '[…] only if the applicant establishes a well-founded fear of being persecuted or otherwise suffering serious harm in a part of the country of origin shall an examination be made as to whether in another part of the country such fear would be unfounded.' Also 'Joint Position of 4 March 1996 defined by the Council on the basis of Article K.3 of the Treaty on European Union on the harmonized application of the definition of the term 'refugee' in Article 1 of the Geneva Convention of 28 July 1951 relating to the status of refugees', [1996] OJ L63/2, para 5.2, stating that, 'Where it appears that persecution is clearly confined to a specific part of a country's territory, it may be necessary, in order to check that the condition laid down in Article 1A of the Geneva Convention has been fulfilled, namely that the person concerned "is unable or, owing to such fear (of persecution), is unwilling to avail himself of the protection of that country", to ascertain whether the person concerned cannot find effective protection in another part of his own country, to which he may reasonably be expected to move.' ECRE criticised the fact that the eventual directive did not specify that the IPA concept is relevant only after an assessment of the well-founded fear of being persecuted in the home region; see European Council on Refugees and Exiles, 'ECRE Information Note on the Council Directive 2004/83/EC of 29 April 2004' (Ch 3 n 66).

7 In contrast to the 1951 Convention, according to Article 1A(2) of the 1969 OAU Convention, individuals facing generalised violence in the whole *or in a part of the territory* of their home state fall under the Convention.

widespread practice in relation to the concept since the early 1980s,[8] practice which has developed the IPA as an inherent part of the 1951 Convention's refugee definition.[9] How precisely the IPA concept relates to the refugee definition has been the subject of controversial debate, in which the arguments somewhat overlap with those discussed in respect of protection against harm (see Section 3.2.2).[10]

First, it may be argued that the IPA concept is inherent in the well-founded fear notion of the Convention, a view taken in some common law jurisdictions[11] but also by the UNHCR.[12] Yet, there is nothing in the text of the Convention

---

8 Among the earliest adopters of the IPA concept were courts in the Netherlands; the State Council applied the concept to Christians from Turkey as early as 1979, Raad van State, 18 August 1978, Ars Aequi Libri No 30; Raad van State, 21 June 1979, No 8. The use of the concept proliferated in the 1980s and 1990s in courts from both civil and common law jurisdictions; see G de Moffarts, 'Refugee Status and the "Internal Flight Alternative"' (Refugee and asylum law: assessing the scope for judicial protection: International Association of Refugee Law Judges, Second Conference, Nijmegen, 9–11 January 1997), n 13–21 citing decisions from Australia, Belgium, Canada, France, Germany, New Zealand, Switzerland, the United Kingdom and the United States. Also Hathaway and Foster, 'Internal Protection/Relocation/Flight Alternative as an Aspect of Refugee Status Determination' (Ch 1, n 101) 359. In the UK, for instance, the Immigration Appeal Tribunal first discussed in 1985 whether an applicant – a former trade unionist – could be expected to move to a remote village in order to avoid a risk of being persecuted by the State, *R v Immigration Appeal Tribunal, ex parte Jonah* [1985] Imm AR 7. In Germany, where the asylum law at the time was uniquely based on a constitutional right to asylum, but deemed to be in line with the 1951 Convention, the Federal Administrative Court applied the IFA concept to Syrian orthodox Christians from Turkey, purportedly not facing a risk of persecution in all parts of the country, BVerwG, 17 May 1983 – BVerwG 9 C 36.83, BVerwGE 67, 184.

9 Zimmermann and Mahler, 445 in Zimmermann; Dörschner; Machts (eds), *The 1951 Convention Relating to the Status of Refugees and its 1967 Protocol – A Commentary* (Ch 1 n 42) refer to the concept as an 'essential element of refugee status determination'.

10 For an extensive debate on the treaty basis of the IPA, see Schultz, *The Internal Protection Alternative in Refugee Law* (Ch 1 n 16) 80; 118–166.

11 In practice, these approaches appear to be not exactly clear cut. Rebecca Wallace, 'Internal Relocation Alternative in Refugee Status Determination: is the Risk/Protection Dichotomy Reality or Myth? A Gendered Analysis' in Satvinder Singh Juss and Collin Harvey (eds), *Contemporary Issues in Refugee Law* (Edward Elgar 2013) in respect of case law from outside the EU context.

12 UN High Commissioner for Refugees, 'UNHCR Position Paper on Relocating Internally as a Reasonable Alternative to Seeking Asylum (The So-Called 'Internal Flight Alternative' or 'Relocation Principle')', (1999) <www.refworld.org/docid/3ae6b336c.html> accessed 20 October 2016, para 9, stating that, 'The judgement to be made in cases where relocation is an issue is whether the risk of persecution that an individual experiences in one part of the country can be successfully avoided by living in another part of the country. If it can, and if such a relocation is both possible and reasonable for that individual, this has a direct bearing on decisions related to the well-foundedness of the fear. In the event that

that would suggest that the Convention requires that the well-founded fear extend to all parts of the territory of the state of nationality, or that requires multiple well-founded fears. Indeed, as noted by Hathaway, the Convention's real chance standard, together with the shared duty of fact-finding, would be unworkable if it were for the applicant and adjudicator to establish a well-founded fear in relation to all parts of the territory.[13] In addition, there has been debate as to whether such an approach makes the application of the concept prone to a variety of practical errors.[14]

Second, and consistent with the analysis of available protection in the home region, the IPA may be argued to be related to the being persecuted limb of the Convention, in particular as a composite definition of persecution as 'serious harm + failure of state protection', a formula coined by UK jurisprudence.[15] Such an approach faces, however, the same problem as the conceptualisation of the IPA as part of the well-founded fear enquiry; the Convention does not require a well-founded fear of *being persecuted* to extend to the entire territory. Indeed, such a requirement would mean that a finding of a well-founded fear of being persecuted for a Convention reason in one part of the territory would be negated by the absence of harm or protection against harm in another.[16] According to Hathaway,

---

there is a part of the country where it is both safe and reasonable for the asylum-seeker to live, the 'well-founded fear' criterion may not be fulfilled. The analysis about possible internal relocation can be a legitimate part of the holistic analysis of whether the asylum-seeker's fear of persecution is in fact well-founded.'

13 Hathaway criticises US case law in that respect, see Hathaway and Foster, 'Internal Protection/Relocation/Flight Alternative as an Aspect of Refugee Status Determination' (Ch 1 n 101) 368.

14 Ibid. Hathaway and Foster argued that approaching the matter as part of the refugee definition's well-founded fear limb could lead decision makers to short-cut analysis of that fear, jumping directly to the analysis of internal protection or showing insufficient care in establishing what the well-founded fear of being persecuted is in the home region. However, according to Hathaway, without clarity on the risk in the home region, there cannot be clarity on safety against that risk in the protection alternative. Second, a wrong conceptualisation of the internal protection alternative would wrongly place the burden of establishing the lack of an alternative on the applicant, and allow the application of analysis of internal protection in retrospect. Third, such approach also leads to wrong substantive safeguards in the application of the internal protection alternative, an issue that will be discussed further below.

15 *Islam v Secretary of State for the Home Department Immigration Appeal Tribunal and Another, Ex Parte Shah* [1999] UKHL 20 (25 March 1999), 653.

16 Indeed, UK case law makes clear that the assessment of the IPA is only relevant when there has been a finding on a well-founded fear within the home region; see *KD (Nigeria) v Refugee Appeals Tribunal & others* [2013] IEHC 481.

> Once [the well-founded fear of being persecuted] is established, it is neither logical nor realistic to find that the fact that the State can protect the person in some other region of the country (region 'B') means that she no longer has a well-founded fear of being persecuted in region A. The well-founded fear of being persecuted in region A has not been negated or removed by the provision of national protection in region B, just as the risk would not be removed or negated by the availability of protection in a country of second nationality or in an asylum State.[17]

What is more, if the IPA concept was rooted in the well-founded fear of the being persecuted limb of the Convention's Article 1A(2), it is unclear why there should be additional requirements for the IPA beyond the inclusion criteria for refugee status (the absence of a well-founded fear of being persecuted for a Convention reason). Yet, as will be apparent in the subsequent section, there is widespread agreement that the IPA has such additional requirements, as reflected in Article 8, Qualification Directive.[18]

The problems with reconciling such approach with the systematic of the 1951 Convention means that the IPA concept can, as is the practice in several common law jurisdictions, only be located in the 1951 Convention's protection clause in Article 1A(2),[19] according to which a refugee is unable or, owing to

17 Hathaway and Foster, 'Internal Protection/Relocation/Flight Alternative as an Aspect of Refugee Status Determination' (Ch 1 n 101) 368.

18 This was suggested as the correct approach in Ni Ghrainne B, 'The Internal Protection Alternative Inquiry and Human Rights Considerations – Irrelevant or Indispensable?' (2015) 27 International Journal of Refugee Law 29. In contrast, Zimmermann and Mahler, 448 in Zimmermann; Dörschner; Machts (eds), *The 1951 Convention Relating to the Status of Refugees and its 1967 Protocol – A Commentary* (Ch 1 n 42) take the view that the location of the IPA concept in the text of the Convention, while contentious, does not need to be solved: 'Ultimately, there is thus no need to to finally resolve the underlying question of whether the "internal flight" issue has to be considered from the angle of "well-founded fear of persecution [sic]" or rather from the angle of "protection", the two issues representing two sides of the same coin. [...] Since [...] the question of whether internal protection is available needs to be a concern under any of the two headings, both views prove to be able to provide appropriate results'.

19 Eg, Hathaway and Foster, *The Law of Refugee Status* (Ch 1 n 100) stating that, 'Despite the weight of authority, we believe that the correct and most logical approach is to anchor the internal protection concept squarely in the protection clause of the refugee definition', also *Thirunavukkarasu v Canada (Minister of Employment and Immigration)* [1994] 1 FC 589 (Canadian Court of Appeal) stating that, 'The idea of an IFA is "inherent" in the definition of a Convention refugee; it is not something separate. The definition of "Convention refugee" requires that claimants have a well-founded fear of persecution which renders them unable or unwilling to return to their home country. If claimants are able to seek safe refuge within their own country, there is no basis for finding that they

a well-founded fear of being persecuted, unable to avail him or herself of the protection his country of nationality. As is apparent from Chapter 1, a modern understanding of the clause precludes a reading whereby the clause is an additional requirement for refugeehood that is independent of, or additional to, the notion of a well-founded fear of being persecuted for one of the Convention grounds.[20] However, the clause does capture the rule that international protection is a surrogate for those who do not enjoy the protection of their state of nationality, as evinced by the well-founded fear of being persecuted. As such, the notion of surrogacy relates the IPA concept to the refugee definition.[21]

Importantly, then, the IPA concept is relevant only for those individuals that have a well-founded fear of being persecuted for a Convention ground (in the home region). Although based on the same notion of surrogacy, the IPA concept is fundamentally different from protection against harm by non-state actors, as discussed in Chapter 2. The IPA concept is not simply the analysis

are unable or unwilling to avail themselves of the protection of that country.' RSAA, 17 March 1995 Re RS 523/92, 'to pose any question postulated on an internal flight alternative is to ask the wrong question [...] The question is not one of flight but protection and is to be approached fairly and squarely in terms of the refugee definition which specifically emphasizes the protection issue: 'is unable or [...] is unwilling to avail himself of the protection of that country'. *Karanakaran* [2000] EWCA Civ, arguing that, 'Unfortunately both the special adjudicator and the tribunal failed to approach the Convention methodically. They treated the availability of internal flight as a reason for holding that the fear of persecution was not well-founded. [...] [A] clear limit is placed on this means of negating an asylum claim by the subsequent provision of the Article that the asylum-seeker must be, if not unable, then unwilling because of "such fear" – ex hypothesi his well-founded fear of persecution – to avail himself of his home state's protection. If the simple availability of protection in some part of the home state destroyed the foundation of the fear or its causative effect, this provision would never be reached. This is why in most cases, including the present one, it is in relation to the asylum-seeker's ability or willingness to avail himself of his home state's protection that the question of internal relocation arises.'

20 Zimmermann and Mahler, 449 in Zimmermann; Dörschner; Machts (eds), *The 1951 Convention Relating to the Status of Refugees and its 1967 Protocol – A Commentary* (Ch 1 n 42) even though they connect the protection clause in Article 1A(2) to the well-founded fear of being persecuted notion, appear to differ on this point, stating that the IPA would be an 'implied criterion', rather than a limitation or an exclusion clause.

21 See above, Section 2.3.4 on whether 'surrogacy' should be referred to as a principle. Reference to surrogacy as a 'principle' is common, for instance, in jurisprudence from Germany. Rather than referring to a specific textual home in the Convention, German courts traditionally refer to a principle of 'subsidiarity' of asylum law, according to which she who has protection at home is not in need of international protection. Thus, the Swedish Migration Court of Appeals stated that it was an 'internationally recognized principle' or a 'fundamental principle' of asylum law; Migrationsöverdomstolen, 21 November 2008, MIG 2008:3, UM1042-08.

of harm applied to another region of the state of nationality.[22] Rather, it has previously been argued by legal academics that the IPA concept is similar to an exclusion clause for individuals that are, *prima facie*, refugees.[23] This also appears to be the understanding in the 1979 UNHCR Handbook:

> The fear of being persecuted need not always extend to the whole territory of the refugee's country of nationality. Thus [...] persecution of a specific ethnic or national group may occur in only one part of the country. In such situations, *a person will not be excluded from refugee status merely because he could have sought refuge in another part of the same country*, if under all the circumstances it would not have been reasonable to expect him to do so.[24]

As will be discussed in Section 4.2. below, the conceptualisation of the IPA as similar to an exclusion clause has important ramifications for the application of the IPA concept under the 1951 Convention: it is *facultative*, rather than mandatory;[25] the burden of proof is no longer shared by an applicant for international protection; and it requires additional safeguards beyond the absence of a fear of being persecuted or real risk of serious harm. Before turning to those substantive requirements, the next section will enquire whether the analysis

22 This has been the interpretation in the early case law, for instance, in Germany, see BVerwG, 2 August 1983, BVerwG 9 C 600.81 – juris, para 11.

23 Hathaway and Foster, 'Internal Protection/Relocation/Flight Alternative as an Aspect of Refugee Status Determination' (Ch 1 n 101) 370. In recent academic writing, it was suggested that the IPA concept may also be conceived of as an 'implied limitation' to the right to refugee protection, similar to the limitation clauses of human rights law. This also construes the IPA concept as distinct from the refugee definition. Schultz and Einarsen, 'The Right to Refugee Status and the Internal Protection Alternative: What does the Law Say?' (Ch 1 n 101).

24 UN High Commissioner for Refugees, Handbook on Refugee Status Determination (Ch 2 n 111) para 91.

25 Indeed, there are member states that appear to be reluctant to deny the need for refugee or subsidiary protection status based on the ability of an IPA. In France, although the respective domestic codes do feature the IPA concept, there is very little practice on the application of those concepts. The French National Court of Asylum law has not rejected a single case on the standalone ground of an available IPA, instead taking the availability of an IPA only as a supplementary ground after applicants were found not to have a well-founded fear of being persecuted. In contrast, however, the Swedish Migration Court of Appeals appears to consider the IPA a mandatory requirement. Pointing to Sweden's international obligations, the court stated that it was impossible to conclude that there is a need for international protection without having considered the ability to settle elsewhere; Migrationsöverdomstolen, 11 February 2013, MIG 2013:2, UM2953-12.

of available protection is, in principle, in accordance with obligations under international human rights law.

4.2.3 *Locating the IPA in Human Rights Obligations of Non-return*

How is the analysis of internal protection anchored in non-return obligations of human rights law?[26] Similar to the 1951 Convention, there is no express text on the IPA in any of the relevant international human rights treaties, in particular on the prohibition of torture, inhuman and degrading treatment, such as enshrined by Article 3, CAT, Article 3, ECHR, or Article 7, ICCPR. However, the analysis of available internal protection has been the practice of both the authoritative and quasi-judicial Committee against Torture and the ECtHR. For example, the CAT considered in a 1997 decision whether there was a 'place of refuge within the country' for an applicant fearing torture if returned.[27] It is also the long-standing practice of the ECtHR to assess an applicant's risk of harm in relation to the whole of the territory when governments propose that an applicant can be returned to an alternative area. Already, the European Commission of Human Rights, a body preceding the ECtHR, as of the late 1980s expected that such risk needed to persist in the entire territory.[28] The European Court of Human Rights in *Chahal* reacted to the UK government's proposal to return the Punjabi applicant to an Indian airport of his choice by evaluating 'the risk of his being ill-treated with reference to *conditions throughout India, rather than in Punjab alone*'.[29] In a 2011 ruling, the court stated that it was 'a well-established principle that persons will generally not be in need of asylum or subsidiary protection if they could obtain protection by moving elsewhere in their own country'.[30]

In general, as laid out in Section 2.3.4, the rationale of non-return obligations under human rights law is the real risk that a contracting party exposes a person to certain, particularly serious or irreparable, harm.[31] This rationale is

---

26 On a more extensive discussion of this question, see Schultz, *The Internal Protection Alternative in Refugee Law* (Ch 1, n 16) 297.

27 *Orhan Ayas v Sweden* Communication no 97/1997, 12 November 1997, CAT/C/21/D/097/1997.

28 European Commission of Human Rights, 10 December 1986, no 12461/6 (Lebanon); European Commission of Human Rights, 13 October 1993, no 21250/90 (Togo); European Commission of Human Rights, 11 March 1994, no 23551/94 (Turkey).

29 *Chahal v United Kingdom* ECHR 1996-V, 54.

30 *Sufi and Elmi v United Kingdom* (Ch 3 n 140) para 35.

31 For example, *Soering v the Unitd Kingdom* (Ch 3 n 118) para 91, [...] the decision by a Contracting State to extradite a fugitive may give rise to an issue under Article 3 (art 3), and hence engage the responsibility of that State under the Convention, where substantial

the same for the assessment whether there is an alternative area of 'protection'. In *Salah Sheekh*, the court stated that the legality of return to an alternative area needs to be assessed against obligations under Article 3 ECHR, just like in cases of indirect removals to intermediary countries that are not the countries of origin (so-called 'chain-refoulement' or 'indirect refoulement').[32] According to the court,

> [...] the Court has previously held that the indirect removal of an alien to an intermediary country does not affect the responsibility of the expelling Contracting State to ensure that he or she is not, as a result of its decision to expel, exposed to treatment contrary to Article 3 of the Convention [...] It sees no reason to hold differently where the expulsion is, as in the present case, to take place not to an intermediary country but to a particular region of the country of origin.[33]

In particular, it must be assessed whether that risk is real, personal and foreseeable, and goes beyond a mere possibility.[34]

That the IPA concept under human rights law is part of the risk assessment distinguishes it from the IPA concept under the 1951 Convention, at least when the latter is conceived of as similar to an exclusion clause. What are the consequences of such differences for the substantive international law requirements and does the Qualification Directive fall short of these requirements? This will be discussed in the following sections.

4.3 The Qualification Directive's IPA Standard and Requirements of the 1951 Convention

4.3.1 *Evidentiary Assessment*

Unlike Article 7, Qualification Directive, Article 8 refers to Article 4 of the Directive, laying down rules for the assessment of facts and circumstances. Member states 'shall at the time of taking the decision on the application have regard to the general circumstances prevailing in that part of the country and to

grounds have been shown for believing that the person concerned, if extradited, faces a real risk of being subjected to torture or to inhuman or degrading treatment or punishment in the requesting country.

32 *Salah Sheekh v the Netherlands* (Ch 3 n 124) para 141.

33 Ibid.

34 *Vilvarajah and Others v the United Kingdom* (Ch 3 n 35).

the personal circumstances of the applicant in accordance with Article 4'. The requirement to have regard to both general and personal circumstances relates to Paragraph 1, so that it is relevant for (i) the assessment of a well-founded fear of being persecuted or of serious harm and the possibility for the applicant to travel, gain admittance and settle, and (ii) the assessment of protection against persecution or serious harm and the possibility to travel, gain admittance and settle.

As discussed in respect of Article 7, Article 4 arguably codifies only a burden of assertion; it is for the applicant to establish a *prima facie* case. Given that the IPA concept is relevant only when there is an established, well-founded fear of being persecuted or real risk of serious harm in the home region, it would appear that the applicant is relieved of his or her burden of assertion, so that the burden shifts to the authorities alone.[35] This would also take account of the fact that an applicant will not always be able to substantiate his or her claim in respect of an IPA. For instance, unlike protection against harm in the home region, applicants will not, for sheer practical reasons, furnish evidence on the potential reaction of the authorities to a risk of relevant harm.

Article 8 also makes clear that the assessment of facts and circumstances for an IPA is not retrospective, relating to the moment that an applicant left his or her country of nationality. Rather, the IPA is to be assessed against facts and circumstances prevailing *at the time of taking the decision*. This mirrors the character of the IPA as an alternative of internal protection, rather than *internal flight*, a term used in several EU jurisdictions.[36]

Finally, contrary to practice in some jurisdictions, for instance, France,[37] but as confirmed by practice from Germany[38] and the United

---

35 See also Reinhard Marx: Marx, 'Interner Schutz von Flüchtlingen nach Art. 1 A Nr. 2 GFK (Art. 2 Buchst. d) RL 2011/95/EU)' (2017) 13 Zeitschrift für Ausländerrecht und Ausländerpolitik 303, 309–311.

36 For criticism of the term 'internal flight alternative', see also Hathaway and Foster, 'Internal Protection/Relocation/Flight Alternative as an Aspect of Refugee Status Determination' (Ch 1 n 101).

37 French jurisprudence does compare the would-be situation of the applicant to the living conditions of the rest of the population in order to establish whether an IPA is 'reasonable', but does not specify whether that comparison can be unfavourable. *T*, CRR 16 February 2007, no 573815.

38 This is a notable shift from previous practice, for instance, in Germany. BVerwG, 29 August 2008, 10 C 11.07 – BVerwGE 131, 186, paras 30–32. In past case law from Germany, existential threats other than a well-founded fear of being persecuted (such as the possibility

Kingdom,[39] the IPA is not primarily a comparative exercise in which the conditions in a proposed IPA have to *compare unfavourably to the conditions in the home region*. Rather, the requirements of Article 8(1) must be assessed independently of the home region. This is based not only on the fact that the text of Article 8 explicitly mentions the relevant evidentiary considerations (the general circumstances in the country and the particular circumstances of the applicant) for the requirements of Article 8(1) (no well-founded fear of being persecuted, ability to travel, gain admittance and settle). It is also supported by substantive requirements of the IPA which will be discussed in the following.

to live a life above 'subsistence level') were relevant only if the conditions were worse than in the home region. Similarly, where infringements such as denial of access to basic services were directed against the entire population rather than against the applicant specifically or a group to which she belonged, they were not relevant, leading to the theoretic result that a blanket policy of rights violations – itself not sufficient for refugee status because of lack of a causal nexus with a Convention ground – might not preclude referring someone to an IPA. See Reinhard Marx, *Handbuch zur Qualifikationsrichtlinie: Flüchtlingsanerkennung und subsidiärer Schutzstatus* (Luchterhand 2009) with reference to OVG Nordrhein-Westfalen, 12 July 2005 – 11A 2307/03.A; OVG Schleswig-Holstein, 13 November 2005 – 1 LB 211/01 UA and Katrin Lehmann, 'Das Konzept der inländischen Fluchtalternative in der deutschen Rechtsprechung und deren Verhältnis zu Art. 8 der Qualifikationsrichtlinie (interner Schutz)' (2007) 5 Neue Zeitschrift für Verwaltungsrecht 507, Section 5.

39 Similar to Germany, there has been a shift of practice to the effect that a comparison is not decisive. In *AE and FE v SSHD*, the Court of Appeal still stated that the general conditions may only matter where they compare unfavourably to the home region; see *AE and FE* [2003] EWCA Civ 1032. This was repealed by *Januzi* [2006] UKHL 5. This is not to say, however, that comparisons are irrelevant in general. Conditions have to be compared with 'the general run of ordinary lives'; see *AH (Sudan)* [2007] UKHL 49, per Baroness Hale '[…] the Tribunal concluded that because the conditions faced by returning Darfuris, however appalling, would be no worse than those faced by other Sudanese IDPs it would not be not "unduly harsh" to expect them to return. The standard of comparison was, not with their lives in Darfur before their persecution, not with the general run of ordinary lives in Sudan, not even with the lives of poor people in Sudan, but with the lives of the poorest of the poor, internally displaced victims of the civil war in the south, living in camps or squatter slums, and "subject from time to time to relocations, sometimes involving force and human rights violations" (para 244). They too had been subsistence farmers, ill-equipped to survive in the city slums (para 239); they too had suffered the psychological horrors of civil war (para 238), if not of government-backed genocide; the Darfuris would be no worse off, unless particular individuals attracted the adverse interest of the authorities (para 242). With respect, this is not the individualised, holistic assessment which the question requires.'

4.3.2 *Safety – No Well-Founded Fear of Being Persecuted for a Convention Reason*

Article 8(1) stipulates that an IPA has to be safe for an applicant. The absence of safety means that the applicant has to have a well-founded fear of being persecuted in the relevant part of the country, including lacking protection against an act of persecution (Article 8(1)(a)–(b)). Typically, this requires first and foremost an assessment of whether all harm is localised, or whether there are factors contributing to a greater or lesser risk of harm in a particular part of the territory.[40] For instance, Dutch[41] and UK courts have in particular considered whether the actor of persecution is sufficiently powerful or influential to inflict harm on the applicant in an IPA – for example, in respect of a Kenyan woman at risk of Female Genital Mutilation (FGM),[42] or whether a clan had the necessary 'geographical and political reach' in order to trace an applicant in an IPA in Albania, for example, by maintaining relations with the government.[43] The Tribunal also cautioned that relocation to a rural area was no option for women with actual or perceived homosexual orientation, because newcomers to such areas were likely to be subject to questions about their lifestyle and thus identified as lesbians – placing them at risk of harm.[44] Relocation for somebody from a rural area to an urban area is not reasonable.[45]

Similarly, the Swedish Migration Court of Appeals considered whether a clan threatening an Afghan woman from outside Kabul was powerful enough

40 Eg, *Januzi*, para 21 (albeit in the context of whether there should be a presumption against available IPA): 'The decision-maker, taking account of all relevant circumstances pertaining to the claimant and his country of origin, must decide whether it is reasonable to expect the claimant to relocate or whether it would be unduly harsh to expect him to do so. The source of the persecution giving rise to the claimant's well-founded fear in his place of ordinary domicile may be agents of the state authorised or directed by the state to persecute; or they may be agents of the state whose persecution is connived at or tolerated by the state, or not restrained by the state; or the persecution may be by those who are not agents of the state, but whom the state does not or cannot control. These sources of persecution may, of course, overlap, and it may on the facts be hard to identify the source of the persecution complained of or feared [...] The more closely the persecution in question is linked to the state, and the greater the control of the state over those acting or purporting to act on its behalf, the more likely (other things being equal) that a victim of persecution in one place will be similarly vulnerable in another place within the state. The converse may also be true. All must depend on a fair assessment of the relevant facts.'

41 Rechtbank 's-Gravenhage, 19 April 2006, AWB 05/27593, rejecting the proposition that there is an IPA when the persecutor exercises influence on people in government.

42 *VM* (FGM risks Mungiki Kikuyu/Gikuyu) Kenya CG [2008] UKAIT 00049.

43 *AM and BM* [2010] UKUT 80 (IAC); *EH* (blood feuds) Albania CG [2012] UKUT 00348 (IAC).

44 *W* (lesbians – *HJ* and *HT* applied) Jamaica CG [2011] UKUT 251 (IAC).

45 *VM* [2008] UKAIT 00049; *Januzi* [2006] UKHL 5.

to pursue her in the capital, considering the lack of rule of law, corruption, nepotism, weak central administration and lack of training of the police forces.[46] In Germany, the extremely small size of a religious community was considered in gauging whether a perpetrator of domestic violence would find his former wife, who had moved elsewhere in the country.[47]

Since the adoption of the recast Qualification Directive, Article 8 explicitly refers to Article 7, making clear that in the case of potential harm by non-state actors in the home region, the assessment of whether or not there is protection against harm is the same as that for the home region. It is a factual and individualised enquiry as to the ability and willingness of 'actors of protection' to provide protection, that is, durably, so effective that it quells the Convention's real chance threshold, and as to the ability of the applicant to access such protection.

Relevant evidence in that enquiry includes, inter alia, laws and policies; the conditions of operation of law enforcement institutions as well as those of perpetrators of harm;[48] and the individual needs of the applicant. Thus, the preamble to the Qualification Directive specifies that protection analysis for unaccompanied minors should consider, 'When the applicant is an unaccompanied minor, the availability of appropriate care and custodial arrangements, which are in the best interest of the unaccompanied minor, should form part of the assessment as to whether that protection is effectively available.'[49]

Given that the analysis of protection presupposes that the authorities are more willing and able to provide protection in the IPA than in the home region, courts have in practice been reluctant to find that *protection against harm* is localised – as opposed to finding that the harm itself is localised – because of the geographic reach of the perpetrator.[50]

As such, the assessment of available protection it is not any different from the assessment of protection against harm in the home area.[51] First,

46 Migrationsöverdomstolen, 14 January 2009, MIG 2009:4, UM4118-07.

47 VG München, 22 April 2016 – M 16 K 14.30987.

48 See above, Sections 2.3–2.4.

49 Recital 27.

50 Eg, in the UK, courts have not considered the safety of an IPA in terms of the authorities' protection against harm. Thus, once courts have established a failure of protection in the home region and considered that the same harm could also materialise in a proposed IPA, they were not ready to make a finding on available protection against harm.

51 See also UN High Commissioner for Refugees, *Guidelines on International Protection No 4* (Ch 3 n 67) para 15, 'As with questions involving state protection generally, the latter involves an evaluation of the ability and willingness of the state to protect the claimant from the harm feared. A state may, for instance, have lost effective control over its territory and thus not be able to protect. Laws and mechanisms for the claimant to obtain

considerations of legal liability by the home state for a potential breach ('due diligence') do not have a place in the analysis of safety, given the Qualification Directive stipulates a purely factual approach requiring the effectiveness of protection in fact.[52] Second, it does not allow for a different standard of probability than that in relation to the assessment of harm in the home area, and the presumption of Article 4(4), whereby past harm is an indication of future harm, may also apply to the safety limb of Article 8, in cases where individuals comparable to the applicant are concerned. As recognised by the German Federal Administrative Court, this follows not only from the wording of Article 4(4), which like Article 8(1) speaks of a well-founded fear of being persecuted, but also from the purpose of the norm:

> [...] in view of the purpose of the norm, which is to ease the burden of proof, it is not comprehensible why there should be a stricter standard applied to the assessment of internal protection as an expression of the subsidiarity of refugee protection than to the assessment of the [...] [well-founded fear], which systematically is situated before [IPA analysis].[53]

What is more, there is no indication that Article 8 exceeds the requirements of Article 7 in respect of the durability of protection. Protection against harm has to be 'non-temporary', which, in the interpretation of the CJEU, requires permanence.[54] Finally, following the CJEU ruling in *X, Y and Z*, as well as in *Y and Z*, an applicant cannot be expected to suppress the open exercise of his or her religious belief or hide his or her sexual orientation in order to avoid a risk of harm.[55]

One relevant presumption is a presumption of risk in cases in which harm is inflicted by state actors, as introduced by the recast Directive in 2011. It is a rebuttable presumption, given that, as a matter of fact, the state's power may

protection from the State may reflect the State's willingness, but, unless they are given effect in practice, they are not of themselves indicative of the availability of protection.'

52 See above, Section 3.3.2. This stands in contrast to Döring, 'Asylum and Qualification Directive 2011/95/EU' 1161 in Hailbronner and Thym, *EU Immigration and Asylum Law – A Commentary* (Ch 1 n 7), who states, with reference to the UK case of *Horvath* (Ch 2 n 117), that the 'effectiveness of protection can be assessed by a due diligence test', contradicting an earlier emphasis on the factual effectiveness of protection required by Article 7 Qualification Directive (ibid at 1155).

53 BVerwG, 5 September 2009, 10 C 21.08, juris (author's translation).

54 See above, 3.3.1.

55 *Bundesrepublik Deutschland v Y and Z; Minister voor Immigratie en Asiel v X* and *Y and Z v Minister voor Immigratie en Asiel* (Ch 1 n 55).

not reach to all parts of the territory and may not be expected to do so in the future.[56]

The fact that the state is unwilling or unable to provide effective protection against relevant harm in the home area is a vital piece of evidence as regards the willingness and ability to provide such protection in the proposed IPA. In this regard UNHCR guidance goes as far as demanding a presumption against available protection. According to the *Guidelines on International Protection on the IPA*,

> Evidence of the state's inability or unwillingness to protect the claimant in the original persecution area will be relevant. *It can be presumed that if the state is unable or unwilling to protect the individual in one part of the country, it may also not be able or willing to extend protection in other areas.* This may apply in particular to cases of gender-related persecution.[57]

The requirement of safety in an IPA has been a core feature of the IPA concept since its early application[58] and its substance has proved uncontested. Although it is clear that the availability of an IPA requires more than an absence of a well-founded fear of being persecuted,[59] debate has rather revolved around the additional requirements beyond safety, which is also reflected in the Qualification Directive.

4.3.3 *Ability to Travel to the IPA and Gain Admittance*

According to Article 8(1), Qualification Directive, in addition to being safe, an applicant has to be able to 'safely and legally travel to and gain admittance to [...] [the] part of the country' considered for the IPA. The requirement of

---

56 The presumption against available protection in a proposed IPA, if harm is inflicted by state actors, mirrors guidance by the UNHCR (see UN High Commissioner for Refugees, *Guidelines on International Protection No 4* (Ch 3 n 67)) and flows from the same rationale as a presumption against available protection against harm in the home region, namely the territorial control of the state.

57 Paragraph 15, emphasis added.

58 For example, in the early application of the internal protection concept by German courts, there were already such safeguards. According to the Federal Constitutional court, an IFA has to be 'sufficiently safe against political persecution in the relevant areas' and has to be free of 'any disabilities or dangers which, by virtue of their intensity or seriousness are equivalent to political persecution, if such existential threat did not arise in the home location', BVerfG, 19 July 1989, 2 BvR 502/86, BVerfGE 80, 315 (author's translation).

59 This has been particularly debated in the UK, given that courts frequently limited themselves to the analysis of safety. *LT v The Minister for Justice & Ors* [2014] IEHC 290.

practical access and admittance had been practice in several member states[60] and is in notable contrast to the 2004 Qualification Directive, according to which member states may determine that there is an IPA 'notwithstanding technical obstacles to return to the country of origin'.[61] The failure to consider questions of access had set the Qualification Directive in direct contrast with UNHCR guidance, according to which an IPA is only practically relevant if it is safely and legally accessible,[62] and thus received ample criticism.[63] The ECtHR later adopted the UNHCR guidance on accessibility and admittance as regards the IPA in the case of *Salah Sheekh*; in consequence, the recast Qualification Directive deleted the former Article 8(3) and introduced the safeguards stipulated by the ECtHR.[64]

As noted earlier, the requirements of access and admittance were sometimes subsumed under an enquiry whether it would be 'reasonable' to expect of an applicant to return to an IPA.[65] The Qualification Directive makes clear that the reasonableness enquiry is to be assessed separately.

---

60 Many jurisdictions subsumed the practical access to the proposed site of the IPA to a test of reasonableness. Eg, Germany, BVerwG, 16 January 2001, 9 C 16.00 – BVerwGE 112, 345, enquiring whether it could reasonably be expected of an applicant to take the necessary steps in order to gain access and admittance. *R v Secretary of State for the Home Department, Immigration Appeals Tribunal, Ex parte Robinson* [1997] INLR 182 (Court of Appeal (England and Wales)).

61 Article 8(3) of the 2004 Qualification Directive.

62 UN High Commissioner for Refugees, *Guidelines on International Protection No 4* (Ch 3 n 67).

63 UN High Commissioner for Refugees, 'UNHCR Annotated Comments on the EC Council Directive 2004/83/EC of 29 April 2004' (Ch 2 n 23), 19. 'Subparagraph (3) [...] is problematic [...] and should not be implemented in national law or practice. The effect of this provision is to deny international protection to persons who have no accessible protection alternative. In UNHCR's view, this is not consistent with Article 1 of the 1951 Convention. An internal relocation or flight alternative must be safely and legally accessible for the individual concerned. If the proposed alternative is not accessible in a practical sense, an internal flight or relocation alternative does not exist and cannot be reasonable.' Similarly, ECRE criticised the fact that the paragraph failed to comply with Article 1 of the 1951 Convention. This was because of the protection clause of that Article, a person 'who cannot in reality be returned, must [...] logically be "unable" to "avail himself" of any protection, even if such protection was found to exist.' According to ECRE, where an IPA is not 'physically, safely and legally accessible', it does not exist. European Council on Refugees and Exiles, *'ECRE Information Note on the Council Directive 2004/83/EC of 29 April 2004'* (Ch 3 n 66).

64 The proposal of the EU Commission to delete that paragraph in order to align the provision with IPA case law by the ECtHR – Commission of the European Communities, 'Qualification Directive Proposal 2009' (Ch 2 n 66).

65 Eg, BVerwG, 16 January 2001, 9 C 16.00 – BVerwGE 112, 345. Thus, the Federal Administrative Court held that living in 'illegality' with constant exposure to police controls and sanctions

A contentious issue is whether modification of behaviour can be expected of an applicant travelling to an IPA in order to avert a risk existing on the way. Such expectation, it seems, would be legally flawed, given that it places false confidence in individual capacity to conform to a specific behaviour. Thus, in case law from the UK, it was suggested that individuals in a refugee claim had no obligation to 'play the game' – hiding their political or religious beliefs when travelling through Al-Shabab-controlled areas in order to reach an IPA.[66]

4.3.4 *Be Reasonably Expected to Settle*

A final requirement of Article 8 is that an applicant for international protection can 'reasonably be expected to settle' in the proposed part of the country in which he or she is deemed to have no well-founded fear of being persecuted or to face no real risk of serious harm, and is deemed to have access to protection against relevant harm by an actor of protection, in accordance with Article 7. Just as in respect of the requirements of accessibility and admittance, the drafting history shows that the word 'settle' was introduced to bring Article 8 in line with obligations under Article 3, ECHR, in particular per *Salah Sheekh*,[67] where the ECtHR held that '[...] as a precondition for relying on an internal flight alternative certain guarantees must be in place: the person to be expelled must be able to travel to the area concerned, gain admittance and *settle* there'.[68] The wording of the recast Directive thus merges the ECHR requirement with the language of Article 8(1) of the 2004 Qualification Directive, according to which an applicant must 'reasonably be expected to stay' in the area of the IPA.

The exact scope of the requirement to 'reasonably be expected to settle' is unclear from the text. In the following sections it is submitted that subsequent practice in the application of Article 8 does not clarify the requirement either, so that it risks being equated with non-return obligations under Article 3, ECHR, falling short of the wider exigencies of the 1951 Convention.

---

under criminal law would not be 'reasonable' for an applicant, BVerwG, 1 February 2007, 1 C 24.06 – NVwZ 2007, 590.

66 *AMM and others* (conflict; humanitarian crisis; returnees; FGM) Somalia CG [2011] UKUT 445 (IAC) para 213.

67 Commission of the European Communities, 'Qualification Directive Proposal 2009' (Ch 2 n 66).

68 *Salah Sheekh v the Netherlands* (Ch 3 n 124) para 141.

4.3.4.1 The Contested Scope of Reasonableness Prior to the Adoption of the Qualification Directive

While the ECHR requirement of being able to 'settle' in an IPA is relatively recent, the notion of 'reasonableness' has a history in the application of the IPA concept under the 1951 Convention. That history, however, is not sufficiently clear as to indicate a consensus on the term at the time of the adoption of the Qualification Directive.

UNHCR, in its 1979 Handbook on Procedures and Criteria for Determining Refugee Status, stated that an individual should not be excluded from refugee status for failure to have sought refuge in another part of the territory, 'if under all the circumstances *it would not have been reasonable to expect him to do so*'.[69] The requirement of reasonableness subsequently became an umbrella term for a variety of other factors considered in the jurisprudence.[70] Outside Europe, in *Thirunavukkarasu*, Linden JA, for the Federal Court of Canada, stated that an internal flight alternative, as the preferred term then was, had to be a 'realistic, attainable option'.[71] The relevant question was whether it would be 'unduly harsh to expect [...] [a] person, who is being persecuted in one part of his country, to move to another less hostile part of the country before seeking refugee status abroad'.[72] In the UK, the courts then subsumed the 'unduly harsh' test under the term 'reasonable'.[73] This was also the approach adopted by the UNHCR. In a 1999 position paper, the agency stated that relocation had to be 'both possible and reasonable'. Therefore, the proposed area must be physically accessible, applicants referred to the area must not have a well-founded fear of being persecuted, and the area must be durably stable. Finally, persons living in the area 'must not have to endure undue hardship or risk'.[74] The analysis of *reasonableness* then applied these factors to the particular circumstances of the applicant, including age, sex, health, family situation, ethnicity, political

69 UN High Commissioner for Refugees, Handbook on Refugee Status Determination (Ch 2 n 111) para 91.

70 UK jurisprudence explicitly used the term as of 1991 as a requirement for the IPA, *R v Secretary of State for the Home Department, ex parte Gunes* [1991] Imm AR 278. However, it did not specify the term for some time; see Hugo Storey, 'The Way Ahead – United Kingdom Case Law on the "Internal Flight Alternative"' (Refugee and asylum law: assessing the scope for judicial protection: International Association of Refugee Law Judges, Second Conference, Nijmegen, 9–11 January 1997).

71 *Thirunavukkarasu v Canada (Minister of Employment and Immigration)*.

72 Ibid.

73 *R v Secretary of State for the Home Department, Immigration Appeals Tribunal, Ex parte Robinson.*

74 UN High Commissioner for Refugees, 'UNHCR Position Paper on Relocating Internally as a Reasonable Alternative to Seeking Asylum' (Ch 4 n 12) para 9.

and social links and vulnerabilities, profession, and past persecution. According to UNHCR's 2003 *Guidelines on International Protection on Internal flight or Relocation*, it is relevant to enquire whether the applicant can, 'in the context of the country concerned, lead a *relatively normal life without facing undue hardship*',[75] exceeding mere subsistence and including the possibility to 'to earn a living', access accommodation, and obtain adequate medical care.[76] A failure to meet the latter test would make relocation unreasonable.[77]

Although most European states did apply some variation of a 'reasonableness' test, it was lower than that advocated by the UNHCR.[78] What is more, the scope of the test remained blurry and its application across member states heterogeneous, in particular in respect of requirements beyond safety and access. In UK case law, for instance, there were conflicting arguments about the relevance of social and economic rights,[79] and courts at times appeared to have confused reasonableness with protection against harm.[80] In Germany, only

75 UN High Commissioner for Refugees, 'Guidelines on International Protection No 4' (Ch 3 n 67) para 23 (emphasis added).

76 Paragraph 29.

77 Ibid.

78 Eg, in the UK, *G H* (Former Kaz, Country Conditions, Effect) Iraq CG [2004] UKIAT 00248 stating that 'general humanitarian concerns' such as those laid out in the UNHCR *Guidelines on the IPA*, 'have no place in the consideration of internal relocation under our own case law which imposes a significantly higher standard before relocation can be regarded as unreasonable because unduly harsh'.

79 Already in the 1990 UK case *Yunelki*, the applicant's separation from his family and the prospects for finding employment were considered in relation to the availability of internal protection, *R v secretary of State for the Home Department, ex parte Yunelki* [1990] Imm AR 278. Per *R v Secretary of State for the Home Department, ex parte Robinson* 18–19, appropriate factors to take into account in deciding what is reasonable include the questions of whether it is practically possible to access the area, whether travelling or staying there entails 'great physical danger' or 'undue hardship', and whether '*the quality of the internal protection fails to meet basic norms of civil, political and socio-economic human rights*.' Then in *AE and FE*, the England and Wales Court of Appeal denied that the enjoyment of basic norms of civil, political and socio-economic human rights is relevant in refugee cases, *AE and FE* [*2003*] *EWCA Civ 1032*.

80 In *RD* (Sufficiency of Protection), the UK Immigration Appeals Tribunal was of the opinion that a finding on a merely regional failure of protection meant that *prima facie* it would not be unreasonable to expect an applicant to relocate. Thus, it effectively reduced IPA analysis to the question of protection against harm. *RD* (Sufficiency of Protection, IFA Roma) Poland [2002] UKIAT 00983 paras 26–27 (emphasis added): 'Having found that there is "effective protection" in other parts of Poland, [...] then it is *prima facie* inconsistent to conclude that it would be "unduly harsh" to expect the claimants to relocate to other parts of Poland. As is spelt out clearly in the leading decisions of Horvath, and Shah and Islam, the central concept of the Refugee Convention is that of "surrogate protection". Thus where there is "effective protection" available concluded on objective evidence, it

'existential threats' comparable in intensity and seriousness to the original risk of persecution and to the otherwise adverse conditions in the home region were relevant.[81] Thus, threats other than a well-founded fear of being persecuted, for instance, threats that were economic in nature,[82] were relevant only to the extent that they compared unfavourably with the home region. Dutch courts did consider economic prospects in the IPA,[83] albeit that the relevant question under the reasonableness test was whether local conditions were not 'abnormal' in relation to the rest of the country.[84] In Sweden, the criteria of 'reasonableness' were not too clear.[85]

The inconsistent application of the 'reasonableness' criterion has led to criticism. A study by the European Legal Network on Asylum (ELENA) stated that the reasonableness criterion has a 'nebulous frame of reference'.[86] Academic commentators argued that the term is neither explicit nor inherent in the 1951 Convention, that the reasonableness test is 'amorphous', 'prone to arbitrariness', 'vague and open to vastly divergent subjective interpretation' and that it has led courts to focus on safety only.[87] A further criticism was that the analysis of reasonableness makes adjudicators prone to expect of applicants

---

is extremely difficult to see how it can then be argued, that applicants, such as these claimants, are placed in an unreasonable or unduly harsh position by expecting them to relocate. The subjective elements, clearly involved in tests of "unreasonableness" or it being "unduly harsh", would, in our view, need to be very strong and persuasive before the objective assessment of "effective protection" should be overridden. […] *This does not mean that unreasonableness or unduly harsh situations should not be considered but that these should be carried out against the backdrop of findings in relation to sufficiency or meaningful protection.*'

81 BVerfG, 19 July 1989, 2 BvR 502/86 – BVerfGE 80, 315. Note, however, that German courts did not frame this assessment as one of reasonableness.

82 Whereas some administrative courts already in the early case law did consider individual and economic factors, such considerations only gained traction in the mid-1990s, after clarification by the Constitutional Court; according to the court, harm equivalent to political persecution does not need to be of a political nature, but had to place the applicant in a 'precarious' situation. Therefore, factors such as the available social network and the possibility of living above the subsistence level are relevant for considering internal protection. BVerwG, 14 December 1993 C 45.92 – juris.

83 Rechtbank 's-Gravenhage, 13 September 1999, AWB 99/4335.

84 Rechtbank 's-Gravenhage, 9 December 2003, AWB 01/66695 and 01/66700; Rechtbank 's-Gravenhage, 11 October 2007, AWB 06/29887.

85 European Legal Network on Asylum, 'The Application of the Concept of Internal Protection Alternative' (2000) <www.refworld.org/docid/3ae6b3514.html> accessed 20 October 2016.

86 Ibid 69.

87 Hathaway and Foster, 'Internal Protection/Relocation/Flight Alternative as an Aspect of Refugee Status Determination' (Ch 1 n 101) 384–386.

a certain behavioural change for the purpose of avoiding harm, 'inconsistent with the very premise of the 1915 Convention'.[88] Even the UNHCR acknowledged that the reasonableness test has no basis in the 1951 Convention, but adhered to it because it had proved 'useful' and 'flexible'.[89] In comments on the EU Qualification Directive, thus, there were no demands to scrap reference to reasonableness altogether, but rather to specify the relevant consideration feeding into the test.[90]

4.3.4.2 Subsequent Practice Delineating the Scope of 'Reasonably Expected to Settle'

More recent legal practice on the IPA in the member states does provide additional indications on the contours of the requirement to be 'reasonably expected to settle'. Indeed, there is now a great level of overlap between practices in different member states on the scope of the requirement, but there also remain differences and inconsistencies in application.

In Germany, jurisprudence post-2004 neatly ties in with practice on the substantive level ('*Existenzminimum*'), focusing on the ability to survive economically, and does not in practice consider other human rights concerns. Whether or not a person will be able to live above the benchmark of the 'existential minimum' is a question of fact; legal entitlements to welfare benefits are not considered necessary.[91] However, courts frequently considered whether an applicant has family networks, or even networks of political parties, that would enable her to sustain herself.[92] In a 2006 decision by the Federal Administrative

88 Ibid 384–385.

89 UN High Commissioner for Refugees, *Guidelines on International Protection No 4* (Ch 3 n 67) para 23, 'The 'reasonableness test' is a useful legal tool which, while not specifically derived from the language of the 1951 Convention, has proved sufficiently flexible to address the issue of whether or not, in all the circumstances, the particular claimant could reasonably be expected to move to the proposed area to overcome his or her well-founded fear of being persecuted.'

90 UNHCR suggested that the 'reasonableness' shall be specified by explicitly mentioning that an applicant should not face 'undue hardship' in an IPA. ECRE stated that the QD should specify how 'reasonableness' plays out for particular groups, such as particularly vulnerable groups. See UN High Commissioner for Refugees, 'UNHCR Annotated Comments on the EC Council Directive 2004/83/EC of 29 April 2004' (Ch 2 n 136); European Council on Refugees and Exiles, 'ECRE Information Note on the Council Directive 2004/83/EC of 29 April 2004' (Ch 3 n 66).

91 BVerwG, 29 May 2008, 10 C 11.07 – BVerwGE 131, 186. See also Zimmermann and Mahler, 454 in Zimmermann; Dörschner; Machts (eds), *The 1951 Convention Relating to the Status of Refugees and its 1967 Protocol – A Commentary* (Ch 1 n 42).

92 OVG Saarland, 29 September 2006 – 3 R 6/06; VG Stuttgart, 21 May 2007 – 4 K 2563/07.

Court which affirmed the standard of the 'existential minimum', the court referred to the case law of the 1990s on whether employment for the applicant is considered reasonable – whether or not this is the case does not depend on the attractiveness of the work in question or the qualification of the applicant, but whether that work was 'reasonable in principle' and allowed the applicant to earn what is 'absolutely necessary' for subsistence.[93] Short-term employment and employment in the 'shadow economy' was no bar to the standard of assuring subsistence, but association with a criminal organisation for subsistence was not considered reasonable.[94] A 'very serious' economic situation is deemed acceptable.[95] This led one commentator to conclude that German judicial practice was focused on the 'extreme case of hardship, the pre-stage of death'.[96]

In some cases, the reasonableness test was also used to consider the applicant's level of education (mere rudimentary literacy was considered inhibiting of successful integration) and the question of psychological illness, for internal relocation required 'a high degree of personal stability'.[97] Besides, in 2008 the court noted that it remains open which economic and social standards had to be fulfilled beyond the subsistence level, stating there were 'many arguments in favor' of the view that the general circumstances that had to be considered under Article 8(2) to inform the reasonableness test went beyond the benchmark of the subsistence level.[98]

Since 2012, the German Asylum Procedures Act has transposed verbatim the requirements of Article 8, as the featured term 'internal flight alternative' had not previously been specified.[99] The standard of the subsistence level has remained the same, focusing on the immediate necessities to sustain oneself. In considering whether or not the immediate necessities would be available, courts in particular considered existing family relationships in the proposed IPA; whether or not an applicant had to sustain just himself or herself or a whole family;[100] their education and qualifications;[101] their state of health,[102]

93 Bundesverwaltungsgericht, 29 May 2008, BVerwG 10 C 11.07.

94 Ibid.

95 OVG Schleswig, 3 November 2005 – 1 LB 211/01.

96 Reinhard Marx, *Handbuch zum Flüchtlingsschutz – Erläuterungen zur Qualifikationsrichtlinie* (2nd edn, Luchterhand 2012).

97 VG Stuttgart, 29 January 2007 – A 4 K 1877/06.

98 BVerwG, 29 May 2008, 10 C 11.07 – BVerwGE 131, 186 para 35.

99 Gesetz zur Umsetzung der Richtlinie 2011/95/EU, 28 August 2013, BGBl I 2013, 3474.

100 VG Braunschweig, 12 August 2015 – 5 A 123/13; VG Köln, 15 September 2015 – 14 K 4683/14.A.

101 VG Bayreuth, 13 July 2015 – B 3 K 14.30344.

102 OVG Nordrhein-Westfalen, 20 July 2015 – 13 A 1531/15.A.

and in particular trauma;[103] the prospects for economic development;[104] and the capacity of local authorities to provide aid to the population.[105]

In the UK, the relevant test remained that of reasonableness/undue harshness. In applying the reasonableness test to the particular circumstances of applicants, courts have in particular paid attention to gender, sexual orientation, religion, professional occupation, health and age,[106] but also to marital status and social factors. The Upper Tribunal considered the difficulties for a single woman to 'reintegrate into a society where the family is the principal unit for welfare and mutual support as well as, it appears, the channel through which employment is most often obtained'.[107] For a woman fearing FGM in Somalia, relevant factors for reasonableness included 'the religious and cultural context'.[108] Meanwhile, it remains contested as to the extent to which the enjoyment of basic norms of human rights is relevant as regards the reasonableness/undue harshness test. Although the House of Lords in *Januzi* stated that the conditions in respect of the 'most basic of human rights that are universally recognized' – including the right to life and the right to freedom from torture, inhuman or degrading treatment or punishment – were relevant for the undue harshness test,[109] Lord Hope of Craighead also stated that the 'almost total absence of civil, political and socio-economic rights' was not sufficient in and of itself to make life in the camps unduly harsh. Instead, what is to be evaluated is 'the risk to his most basic human rights that being required to live there would expose him'.[110] In *AH*, a case revolving around the reasonableness of relocation to provisional urban squatter camps in Sudan, the House of Lords clarified that the threshold for the consideration of a risk to the most basic human rights could not be so high as to raise an issue under Article 3, ECHR by the host country, after stating that it was under 'the impression that the Tribunal may be equating "unduly harsh" with an article 3 risk', although these concepts have to be separated:[111]

103 VG Würzburg, 09 March 2015 – W 1 K 13.30030.
104 VG Dresden, 08 August 2016 – 7 K 915/16.A.
105 VG Hamburg, 19 February 2015 – 8 A 1470/13.
106 For the latter, see *KD (Nigeria) v Refugee Appeals Tribunal & others* [2013] IEHC 481.
107 *AM and BM* [2010] UKUT 80 (IAC). Similarly, *A T and Others* (Article 15c; risk categories) (CG) [2014] UKUT 318 (IAC).
108 *VM* [2008] UKAIT 00049.
109 *Januzi* [2006] UKHL 5, para 54, per Lord Hope of Craighead.
110 Paragraph 59.
111 Ibid 26.

> We are also all agreed that the test for internal relocation under the Refugee Convention is not to be equated either with a 'well-founded fear of persecution' under the Convention or with a 'real risk of ill-treatment' contrary to article 3 of the European Convention on Human Rights. By definition, if the claimant had a well-founded fear of persecution, not only in the place from which he has fled, but also in the place to which he might be returned, there can be no question of internal relocation [...]
>
> Further, although the test of reasonableness is a stringent one – whether it would be 'unduly harsh' to expect the claimant to return – it is not to be equated with a real risk that the claimant would be subjected to inhuman or degrading treatment or punishment so serious as to meet the high threshold set by article 3 of the European Convention on Human Rights. As Lord Bingham points out, 'this is not what was meant by the references to article 3 in *Januzi*, including what was said by my noble and learned friend, Lord Hope of Craighead, when he referred to "the most basic of human rights that are universally recognized" at para 54. Obviously, if there were a real risk of such ill-treatment, return would be precluded by article 3 itself as well as being unreasonable in Refugee Convention terms. But internal relocation is a different question'.[112]

Yet, neither *Januzi* nor *AH* have completely resolved the questions around the consideration of human rights as part of the reasonableness test, and there appears to be confusion in the case law.[113]

112 *AH* (*Sudan*) [2007] UKHL 49, para 25.

113 Thus, in *AB*, the UKAIT stated that undue hardship required a real risk of a violation of a non-derogable human right – in other words, a risk of harm that in refugee claims ought normally to be considered under the requirement of safety. 'As clarified by the House of Lords in *Januzi*, unreasonableness or undue hardship under the Refugee Convention as well as under Article 3 of the ECHR can only be shown if there is, in the particular circumstances of the individual's case, a real risk of a violation of a basic non-derogable human right'; *AB* (protection, criminal gangs, internal relocation) Jamaica CG [2007] UKAIT 00018. Somewhat in contrast, the Court of Appeal stated in *JK* (Serbia) that, 'Reasonableness is the test for assessing whether a relocation alternative is open to an asylum claimant and there is no rule that there must be satisfaction of the basic norms of civil, political and socio-economic human rights in the place of relocation nor that the minimum standard of human rights apply in the place of relocation,' *JK* (*Serbia*) [2007] EWCA Civ 1321. In contrast, in a more recent decision, the Upper Tribunal (Immigration and Asylum Chamber) discussed the human rights approach in relation to claims under Article 15(c) of the QD, noting that, 'it is difficult to conclude that the Law Lords in either *Januzi* or *AH* (*Sudan*) intended to reject all recourse to human rights norms', *AK* (Article 15(c)) Afghanistan CG [2012] UKUT 163 (IAC).

In France, where the respective applicable codes transposed the Qualification Directive verbatim,[114] the reasonableness standard has been interpreted to require that an applicant can live a 'normal life' in the IPA. Thus, in the case of a Nigerian woman fleeing forced marriage and female genital mutilation inflicted by her family, the National Court of Asylum Law stated that in Nigeria a particular importance was attached to the approval of the family to a marriage, which would not be given after she fled the clutches of her family, so that the applicant would not be able to marry in the future and therefore not be able to live a normal life elsewhere in Nigeria.[115]

In the Netherlands, where the Qualification Directive takes precedence over domestic law and the Foreigners Act transposes Article 8 verbatim,[116] the 2000 Circular on Foreigners specifies that under the Foreigners Acts an applicant has to be able to lead a relatively normal life (considered by local standards) and that human rights matter only to the extent that the applicant would be disadvantaged over the rest of the population.[117] The circular does not explicitly require that the applicant could self-reliantly assure her subsistence but provides that 'the general living conditions in the area should not be such that they would lead to a humanitarian emergency'.[118] Nevertheless, there seems to be a tendency to discard the reasonableness analysis.[119]

Finally, in Sweden the concept of the IPA is not transposed in written asylum law, but is firmly rooted in judicial practice[120] and courts have considered whether the IPA would be 'unreasonable from a humanitarian point of view'.[121] In other decisions, courts enquired whether the means of subsistence are assured in an IPA and whether the applicant can live a relatively normal live.[122] Auxiliary criteria were the presence of a social network and education,[123]

114 Article 2, Loi n° 52–893 du 25 juillet 1952 relative au droit d'asile; subsequently Article L713-3, Code de l'entrée et du séjour des étrangers et du droit d'asile (Ch 2 n 94).

115 CNDA, 2 April 2008, 574495, *Mlle N.*

116 Article 3.37d Voorschrift Vreemdelingen 2000.

117 Vreemdelingencirculaire 2000 (C) of 1 December 2017, Section 3.4, warranting a 'life under circumstances that can be considered normal by local standards', and not leading to a 'humanitarian emergency'. The applicant also 'may not be disadvantaged in the exercise of essential rights in relation to the other population' (author's translation).

118 Ibid para 6.1 (author's translation).

119 In the decision on a gay Indian applicant fearing harm because of his sexual orientation, the respective court affirmed the availability of an IPA after having discussed only the risk of harm, while not elaborating on the requirement of reasonableness, Rechtbank 's-Gravenhage, 11 November 2009, AWB 09/13455.

120 Migrationsöverdomstolen, 11 May 2010, MIG 2010:10, UM6397-09.

121 Ibid with reference also to ME 2008: 20 and *ME*, 2009: 4, author's translation.

122 Migrationsdostolen, 16 May 2011, UM 27323-10.

123 Migrationsdostolen, 21 November 2008, UM 1042-08.

as well as the assurance of family unity, comprising, with reference to the UNHCR Handbook on Procedures and Criteria for Determining Refugee Status, husband/wife and minor children.[124] The courts rejected the proposition that the Iraqi capital, Baghdad, was an IPA for a mixed Shiite/Sunnite couple, because both government and private organisations exercised pressure on such couples to divorce.[125] Application of the reasonableness standard appears partly conflicting, however. For example, the Migration Court of Appeals in a decision on an IPA in Kabul referred an applicant to an IPA because 'there are no reports of people starving to death in Kabul or any of the major cities'.[126] Case law also pointed out that the actual possibility of obtaining work was not decisive, rather, the right to work merely required access to the job market.[127]

In sum, there is considerable overlap between the member states in that the requirement to be 'reasonably expected to settle' includes an assessment in particular of the economic hardships within the IPA, dependent on general and individual factors. The Qualification Directive, however, does not succeed in harmonising case law. At times, the demarcation with non-return obligations under Article 3, ECHR are not entirely clear, given that the 'reasonably be expected to settle' requirement leaves considerable room for interpretation, and that some courts have interpreted the requirement restrictively.

Although it has been suggested that the IPA standard should be equated with the scope of non-return obligations under Article 3, ECHR in order to create greater consistency,[128] such equation, it is submitted, is legally flawed. Given that there is significant overlap between Article 15(b), Qualification Directive and non-return obligations under Article 3, ECHR, a risk of harm that would qualify as sufficiently severe to bar return under Article 3, ECHR would normally already be captured by the safety limb of Article 8(1)(a). Meanwhile, although the reasonableness criterion is not applied consistently, state practice on the application of the IPA has gone beyond the few cases that do not fall under Article 15(b) but under non-return obligations under Article 3 ECHR – in particular, medical cases. Not least, the equation of the IPA requirements with

124 According to the Migration Court of Appeals, family unity has to be assured in an IPA when applicants desire to unite with their families, even if the members of that family are currently not in Sweden. Migrationsöverdomstolen, 11 May 2010, MIG 2010:10, UM6397-09, with reference also to *ME* 2008: 20 and *ME*, 2009: 4.

125 Migrationsöverdomstolen 2 November 2011, MIG 2013:2, UM2953-12.

126 Migrationsöverdomstolen, 14 January 2009, MIG 2009:4, UM4118-07.

127 Ibid.

128 Ni Ghrainne, 'The Internal Protection Alternative Inquiry and Human Rights Considerations – Irrelevant or Indispensable?' (Ch 4 n 18).

non-return obligations under Article 3 ignores the 1951 Convention conceptualisation of the IPA as similar to an exclusion clause. This will be discussed in the following section.

4.3.4.3 Reconceiving the IPA Concept as an Exclusion Clause for Refugee Status

As previously discussed, under the 1951 Convention, the IPA concept is best conceived of as captured by the surrogacy principle, evident in the 'protection clause' of Article 1A(2). That clause, however, is not an additional criterion for refugee status (see Chapter 1), so that the IPA concept functions similarly to an exclusion clause – a person is, *prima facie*, a refugee, because he or she has a well-founded fear of being persecuted for a Convention reason, but may not be in need of international (surrogate) protection.

The conceptualisation of the IPA concept as an exclusion clause has significant bearing on the requirements of an IPA that go beyond safety (and set it apart from 'protection against harm' as explored in Chapter 3). In particular, requirements would exceed the narrow conceptualisation of reasonableness as mere economic subsistence. As argued by a group of legal academics in the 1999 Michigan Guidelines on the International Protection Alternative, conditions in the proposed IPA have to meet 'at least [...] the Refugee Convention's minimalist conceptualization of "protection", that is, the 1951 Convention's guarantees in Articles 2–33'. As discussed in Chapter 1, these include non-discrimination between citizens and other residents on the one hand, and refugees on the other hand, in respect of some civil, political and socio-economic rights,[129] including access to employment, public welfare and education ('Minimalist Commitment to Affirmative Protection').[130] According to the *Guidelines*, given that those individuals for whom an IPA is considered are, *prima facie*, refugees, they are 'presumptively entitled' to refugee status and the rights attached to it.[131] Importantly, the Michigan Guidelines do not argue that persons for whom an IPA is assessed are entitled to the rights under the

---

129 Hathaway and Foster, 'Internal protection/relocation/flight alternative as an aspect of refugee status determination' (Ch 1 n 101) 408.

130 University of Michigan Law School, 'International Refugee Law: The Michigan Guidelines on the Internal Protection Alternative' (April 1999) <http://www.refworld.org/docid/3dca73274.html> accessed 3 October 2016.

131 Ibid para 20. The Qualification Directive has already been criticised as failing to adopt the approach of the Michigan Guidelines, see Eaton, 'The Internal Protection Alternative under European Union Law: Examining the Recast Qualification Directive' (Ch 1 n 101).

Convention as a matter of law. Rather, Articles 2–33 should be considered as guidance for the relevant protected interests at stake.[132]

Although the approach of the Michigan Guidelines has been endorsed in one jurisdiction,[133] it has also attracted criticism and been explicitly rejected by other courts. First and foremost, criticism contended that the divide between the criteria for inclusion in refugee status on the one hand, and the rights attached to status following inclusion on the other hand, had to be strictly upheld.[134] Others have pointed out that the norms of the 1951 Convention were not designed to leverage the situation in the country of nationality, and were therefore not suitable for the analysis of the IPA.[135] In contrast, it was argued that human rights were designed also to address problems in the country of nationality and that, in contrast to the 1951 Convention, these rights are not just couched as non-discrimination standards and therefore provide for an objective international minimum standard.[136] Finally, there has been an argument that the distinction does not matter in practice, given both approaches may render similar results.[137]

The first criticism overlooks the fact that the IPA concept is not explicitly envisaged by the refugee definition of the 1951 Convention, but that the concept flows from a principle evident in a clause of the Convention (the protection clause' in Article 1A(2)) that is no longer a stand-alone inclusion criterion for refugee status. Although the 1951 Convention rights are about *international* rather than *domestic* protection, the fact that the IPA concept is anchored in the surrogacy principle points to the rights granted under Articles 2–34 – they are among the primary standards of surrogate international protection.

132 Hathaway and Foster, 'Internal Protection/Relocation/Flight Alternative as an Aspect of Refugee Status Determination' (Ch 1 n 101).

133 New Zealand Refugee Status Appeals Authority, 29 October 1999, No 71684/99 [2000] INLR 165.

134 *Januzi* [2006] UKHL 5.

135 Storey, ' "From Nowhere to Somewhere": An Evaluation of the UNHCR 2nd Track Global Consultations on International Protection: San Remo 8–10 September 2001 Experts Roundtable on the IPA/IRA/IFA Alternative' 378.

136 Ibid 377.

137 Zimmermann and Mahler, 457 in Zimmermann; Dörschner; Machts (eds), *The 1951 Convention Relating to the Status of Refugees and its 1967 Protocol – A Commentary* (Ch 1 n 42), stating that 'it may be left open whether the approach to be chosen ought to be based on the notion of protection or well-founded fear, ie reasonableness, since both approaches may be considered capable of generating the same results in the hands of experienced and thoughtful decision makers.' Obviously, the argument implies that less experienced and thoughtful decision makers would not come to equal results, raising the question whether the authors' indeterminacy is actually viable.

The second criticism, however, leads to the core characteristic of that surrogate international protection. The rights of refugees are no longer defined by the 1951 Convention alone, but by the rights of the 1951 Convention *in conjunction with* human rights law (see Chapter 1), so that fixation on either body of law does not capture the character of neither domestic nor international protection. Although human rights norms have proven more dynamic and there is now a significant overlap, the Convention still exceeds human rights law in some few but important respects, in particular as regards access to the labor market (Articles 17–18) and welfare (Article 23). Clinging to the Convention rights alone, however, does not capture such modern understanding of international protection. What is more, it ignores the fact that human rights are also used as interpretative guidance in other areas of status determination, in particular in circumscribing which harm is relevant for the 'being persecuted' notion of Article 1A(2) of the 1951 Convention. As succinctly explained by the UK Upper Tribunal in the case of *A K* (albeit in ruling on the scope of the 'reasonableness' test and *obiter dictum*),

> [...] what happens when an applicant for international protection cannot succeed under the 'safety' limb, so that his success turns on whether he can still succeed under the 'reasonableness' limb? As just highlighted, [...] in order to show reasonableness under Article 8(1), it is unnecessary to show these violations are in themselves at the Article 9(1) level. So the question is [...] what type of approach should continue to govern the less demanding 'reasonableness inquiry'. *For our part, it is difficult to see how the Article 8(1) inquiry, having begun (as it must) on a human rights basis under Article 8(1), can suddenly switch to a different type of approach having nothing to do with human rights. It would seem to make for more sense for the decision-maker to keep in mind the same human rights framework subject to recognising that even violations falling short of Article 9(1) levels may suffice to show unreasonableness.*[138]

Indeed, the proposal to consider human rights in the assessment of the IPA has been prominent in academic debate, although mostly as an alternative to the approach of the 1999 Michigan Guidelines on the IPA, and as interpretative guidance for the 'reasonableness' test.[139] The approach is not without

138 *AK* (Article 15(c)) Afghanistan CG [2012] UKUT 163 (IAC), emphasis added.

139 Eg, Ninette Kelley, 'Internal Flight/Relocation/Protection Alternative: Is it Reasonable?' (2002) 14 International Journal of Refugee Law 4; Storey, '"From Nowhere to Somewhere": An Evaluation of the UNHCR 2nd Track Global Consultations on International Protection: San Remo 8–10 September 2001 Experts Roundtable on the IPA/

flaws either, however. In particular, it is unclear how the economic considerations prevalent in case law could be reconciled with a human rights approach, given that human rights would only require formal, non-discriminatory access to the labour market, rather than the actual possibility of gaining a living. What is more, a human rights approach faces the struggle of determining which human rights are to be considered. Given that there is currently disagreement about the theoretic rationale by which human rights harm determines the notion of 'being persecuted',[140] *a fortiori* agreement is lacking over which human rights are relevant in assessing reasonableness in a proposed IPA. Some academic commentators, with reference to the Guiding Principles of Internal Displacement,[141] have suggested that all human rights harm is relevant.[142] Others have contended that such an approach would be regarded as 'too broad and over-inclusive'.[143] UNHCR guidance, meanwhile, remains unclear; the agency stated that violations of non-derogable rights would bar an IPA from being reasonable, and that other human rights would be relevant if they are 'fundamental to the individual'.[144]

The relevance of human rights for the character of surrogate international protection, but the apparent challenges in devising a practical, consistent approach, pose high hurdles for workable alternatives *de lege ferenda*. One

IRA/IFA Alternative'; UN High Commissioner for Refugees, 'An Overview of Protection Issues in Western Europe: Legislative Trends and Positions Taken by UNHCR' (1995) <www.unhcr.org/46e65e1e2.pdf> accessed 20 October 2016, para 38.

140 Julian M Lehmann, 'Persecution, Concealment and the Limits of a Human Rights Approach in (European) Asylum Law: The Case of *Germany v Y and Z* in the Court of Justice of the European Union' (2014) 26 International Journal of Refugee Law 1.

141 UN Economic and Social Council (ECOSOC), *Guiding Principles on Internal Displacement*, E/CN.4/1998/53/Add.2, Article 1, 'Internally displaced persons shall enjoy, in full equality, the same rights and freedoms under international and domestic law as do other persons in their country. They shall not be discriminated against in the enjoyment of any rights and freedoms on the ground that they are internally displaced.'

142 Mathew, 'The Shifting Boundaries and Content of Protection: The Internal Protection Alternative Revisited' (Ch 1 n 101) 191.

143 Hathaway and Foster, *The Law of Refugee Status* (Ch 1 n 100) 354.

144 UN High Commissioner for Refugees, 'Guidelines on International Protection No 4' (Ch 3 n 67) para 28, 'Where respect for basic human rights standards, including in particular non-derogable rights, is clearly problematic, the proposed area cannot be considered a reasonable alternative. This does not mean that the deprivation of any civil, political or socio-economic human right in the proposed area will disqualify it from being an internal flight or relocation alternative. Rather, it requires, from a practical perspective, an assessment of whether the rights that will not be respected or protected are fundamental to the individual, such that the deprivation of those rights would be sufficiently harmful to render the area an unreasonable alternative.'

alternative may be to combine regard for the protected interests under the 1951 Convention with consideration of respect for those rights that, if violated, would fall into the scope of the inclusion criteria, albeit with crucial differences to the assessment of harm in the home region: such human rights harm would not need to qualify as being persecuted for reasons of a Convention ground. Given that the combined scope of rights relevant for the being persecuted notion of the 1951 Convention and the protected interests under the Convention is wider than the scope of harm relevant for non-return obligations under human rights law, such an approach would not run the risk of being equated with human rights law non-return obligations. What is more, the approach would tie the IPA requirements to internationally recognised minimum standards, but would have inherent safeguards against being overly broad. Indeed, the approach would primarily exceed the safety requirement (no well-founded fear of being persecuted for a Convention ground) and the consideration of the protected interests under the 1951 Convention in the few cases where relevant human rights harm does not fall within a Convention ground but may affect an entire population. For instance, the denial of freedom to practise a religion in public and in private will typically fall under the safety limb of the IPA requirement, because such infringements typically affect one particular religion, or all religions. Similarly, most infringements of socio-economic rights will only be relevant if they are not subject to progressive realisation, as is the case with discrimination against particular groups. However, there are also cases of human rights infringements that cannot be said to be 'for reasons' of a Convention ground, such as deliberate and general retrogression on social and economic rights despite available resources, or the general absence of judicial remedies against harm by third parties.[145] Arguably, it is already in line with the wording of the Qualification Directive that no nexus to a Convention ground is required in the assessment of human rights harm. Article 8(1) requires the absence of a 'well-founded fear of being persecuted', omitting the requirement of a nexus to a Convention ground.

Under an approach combining the protected interests under the 1951 Convention's Articles 2–33 with those interests protected by human rights law, it would be relevant to consider physical integrity and security; freedom from arbitrary detention and penalisation of illegal entry; the documentation of

145 Committee on Economic Social and Cultural Rights, 'General Comment No 3' (Ch 2 n 43) para 9. There is significant debate about the content of such core obligations, however. See, for instance John Tobin, *The Right to Health in International Law* (Oxford University Press 2012); Katherine G Young, 'The Minimum Core of Economic and Social Rights: A Concept in Search of Content' (2008) 33 Yale Journal of International Law 113.

identity and status; freedom of thought, conscience and religion; access to the justice system; family unity and best interest considerations for children; internal movement; access to education, healthcare and the labour market; and property rights. However, it would be the objective standard of refugee law and human rights law that would determine *protection*, rather than reasonableness.

Crucially, a test based on objective standards precludes a mere comparison between the living conditions in the home area and the proposed IPA. In particular, conditions do not have to compare unfavourably with the home area. But the reverse is also true: the fact that the living conditions in the proposed alternative area of the country of origin are worse than those in the home area does not in and of itself mean that this area is not a *protection alternative*. A test based on objective criteria would not respond to widespread judicial concern that individuals for whom an IPA is considered may be privileged as compared to the rest of the population living in the IPA.[146] In the UK House of Lords, it was stated that the 'accident of persecution' should not serve to privilege a refugee *vis à vis* her fellow nationals.[147] However, comparative assessments with the rest of the population in the proposed area of the IPA will be relevant to assess whether there are rights infringements. For instance, a blanket denial of basic education that would circumvent the nature of obligations under the ICESCR would fail to satisfy the IPA requirements, but would not privilege a *prima facie* refugee in respect of the rest of the population.

While such approach based on objective standards would be dogmatically more stringent than the status quo, in particular in respect of integrating economic, social and cultural rights into IPA safeguards, it would also have flaws. This includes, first and foremost, the risk to conflate the additional IPA requirements with its safety requirements and to lose out on some of the considerations that are frequently applied in practice, such as the existence of a social network,[148] which *de lege ferenda* is best to become an explicit criterion based on past practice. Second, the approach would need to emphasise questions of

146 Marx, *Handbuch zum Flüchtlingsschutz – Erläuterungen zur Qualifikationsrichtlinie* (Ch 4 n 96) 137; Lehmann, 'Das Konzept der inländischen Fluchtalternative in der deutschen Rechtsprechung und deren Verhältnis zu Art. 8 der Qualifikationsrichtlinie (interner Schutz)' (Ch 4 n 38). OVG Nordrhein-Westfalen, 12 July 2005 – 11A 2307/03.A; OVG Schleswig-Holstein, 13 November 2005 – 1 LB 211/01 UA.

147 *Januzi* [2006] UKHL 5, para 19.

148 This point is considered in the UNHCR's 'Guidelines on International Protection No 4' (Ch 3 n 67), see also Schultz, *The Internal Protection Alternative in Refugee Law* (Ch 1 n 16) 217–219 and above, Section, 4.3.4 2.

de facto access to, and enjoyment of rights and basic services, so as to avert the risk that the IPA test is 'formalised'.

4.4 The Qualification Directive's IPA Standards and the Requirements of Human Rights Law

As discussed above, the Qualification Directive's Article 8 on the IPA is a common provision for refugee status and subsidiary protection status, implying the same substantive requirements for both statuses. Yet, are the international law requirements relating to evidentiary assessment (see 4.3.1) safety (see 4.3.2), ability to travel, gain admittance and be reasonably expected to settle (4.3.3–4) the same as those of the 1951 Convention? Given standards are most extensive from the jurisprudence of the ECtHR, reference will be made primarily to the ECHR.

4.4.1 *Evidentiary Assessment*

As previously discussed in Section 4.2.3, it is long-standing practice of the ECtHR to assess an applicant's risk of harm in relation to the whole of the territory when governments propose internal relocation. In the case of *Salah Sheekh,* the court explained that the legal rationale is the same as for all expulsion cases, whether applied to a particular country of transit or to a particular region of the country of origin – contracting states need to 'ensure that he or she is not, as a result of its decision to expel, exposed to treatment contrary to Article 3 of the Convention'.[149]

There has so far been no case law in which the distribution of the burden of proof was contested in the context of an expulsion case under Article 3. However, the standard of proof in return cases is comparable to the Convention's real chance standard. In *Soering v United Kingdom,* the Court has, for the first time, developed the burden of proof for such cases, according to which, 'substantial grounds have to be shown for believing that the person concerned, if deported, faces a real risk of being subjected to treatment contrary to Article 3'.[150] While there is no further definition of the standard of proof of the 'real risk', and the court has in several cases been extremely demanding on the probability required,[151] it is clear as per *Saadi v United Kingdom* that the likelihood

149 Ibid.

150 *Soering v United Kingdom* as per *Saadi v United Kingdom* (Ch 3 n 126) para 125.

151 Eg, *Garabayev v Russia*, 7 June 2007, para 76, requiring a standard of proof 'beyond reasonable doubt'.

can be below the standard of 'more likely than not'.[152] However, harm inflicted by an omission rather than an act does not normally raise above the threshold required.[153]

In *Salah Sheekh*, the court required that the substantive requirements for the analysis of internal flight, as it is more commonly called in the ECtHR context, need to be *guaranteed*.[154] The wording suggested that a high factual threshold is required with, as expressed by one judge of the court, 'likelihoods, chances or positive indications ... [not being] enough'.[155] Thus, in *Sufi and Elmi v United Kingdom*, the court considered country reports on Somalis 'beaten or flogged' by members of the jihadist militia 'Al-Shabab' for appearing 'westernized', as sufficient to deny that applicants could be required to travel through or settle in an Al-Shabab controlled area, despite these areas being generally safe.[156]

Beyond the ECHR, there is sparse practice from the Committee against Torture. Under the practice of the Committee, assessing whether a risk is only localised is a factual enquiry on a foreseeable, real and personal risk.[157] In the past, the Committee has in particular assessed the profile of an applicant,[158] and whether other parts of the territory have in the past proven safe.[159]

---

152 Ibid para 140.

153 *N v United Kingdom*, para 43.

154 *Salah Sheekh v The Netherlands* (Ch 3 n 124) para 141.

155 *MYH and Others v Sweden* App No 50859/10 (ECtHR, 27 June 2013). Dissenting opinion of Judge Power-Forde joined by Judge Zupanĉiĉ.

156 *Sufi and Elmi v United Kingdom* (Ch 3, n 140) paras 275–276. The evidentiary threshold was controversially debated in *M Y H and Others v Sweden*, in which the court affirmed the possibility of internal relocation in the Kurdistan Autonomous Region for the Iraqi Christian applicant. In a dissenting opinion, judges Power-Forde and Zupanĉiĉ criticised the fact that the court had failed to consider the criterion of safe transit at the level of a 'guarantee'. *MYH and Others v Sweden* (ibid).

157 UN Committee Against Torture, 'General Comment No 1: Implementation of Article 3 of the Convention in the Context of Article 22 (Refoulement and Communications)', UN Doc A/53/44, annex IX (1997) para 6; *Sathurusinghe Jagath Dewage v Australia Communication no 387/2009, 14 November 2013, CAT/C/51/D/387/2009*, para. 10.4.

158 Ibid. The Committee has noted that 'some of the available evidence suggests that high-profile persons may be at risk in other parts of India, but the complainant has not shown that he fits into this particular category.'

159 *Ismail Alan v Switzerland* Communication no 21/1995, 31 January 1995, CAT/C/16/D/21/1995, para 11.4, stating that, 'As regards the State party's argument that the author could find a safe area elsewhere in Turkey, the Committee notes that the author already had to leave his native area, that Izmir did not prove secure for him either, and that, since there are indications that the police are looking for him, it is not likely that a "safe" area for him exists in Turkey.'

4.4.2 *Safety – No Real Risk of Serious Harm*

According to Article 8(1)a), Qualification Directive, the IPA has to be free of a real risk of serious harm. As per the analysis in Section 3.3.2, in case of harm inflicted by non-state actors, the relevant test of protection against harm is a factual one, determined by the ability and willingness of actors of protection to act in way that quells a real risk of serious harm.

The requirement of safety is relatively well-reflected in the practice of international human rights law. Before international human rights law treaty bodies, few cases have arisen that concern the possibility of internal protection. From the practice of the CAT, it is clear that safety is the primary criterion. The CAT has, in several cases, refused to take up a state party's proposals on the possibility of internal relocation, instead referring only to whether a risk is real,[160] what is more, even when the CAT considered the conditions in an alternative area, the benchmark remained whether there is a risk of torture, or inhuman and degrading treatment or punishment in that area, not whether there is additional human rights harm. For example, in the 1997 decision, *Halil Haydin v Sweden*, the Committee, acknowledging that there was no 'place of refuge within the country', stated that the applicant was in danger of being subjected to torture if returned.[161] If this approach is applied to the ICCPR, the human rights requirement for internal relocation would be that states respect their obligation –

> not to extradite, deport, expel or otherwise remove a person from their territory, where the necessary and foreseeable consequence of the deportation would be a real risk of irreparable harm, such as that contemplated by articles 6 and 7 of the Covenant, either in the country to which removal is to be effected or in any country to which the person may subsequently be removed.[162]

The Committee has applied this principle to the Covenant several times under the individual complaint mechanism, but it remains, in practice, limited to

---

160 *Halil Haydin v Sweden* Communication no 101/1997, 16 December 1998, CAT/C/21/D/101/1997; *SSV v Canada* Communication no 49/1996, 15 May 1996, UN Doc. CAT/C/26/D/49/1996; *G R B v Sweden* Communication no 83/1997, 2 June 1997, CAT/C/20/D/83/1997; *SNAW et al v Switzerland* Communication no 231/2003, 25 November 2005, CAT/C/35/D/231/2003.

161 *Orhan Ayas v Sweden* CAT/C/21/D/097/1997 (Ch 4 n 27).

162 Human Rights Committee, *General Comment No 31* (Ch 2 n 40) para 12 (emphasis added).

the prohibition of torture or inhuman or degrading treatment and the right to life.[163]

Under the ECHR, the requirement of safety links to the Convention's non-return obligations primarily under Article 3, on torture and inhuman and degrading treatment.[164] The area in question has to be free of a real risk of irreparable harm that would bar return under Article 3 or, in very exceptional cases, under another article of the Convention.[165] However, in the practice of the court, this assessment does not differ from the assessment of safety in the home region or in cases in which the availability of an IPA is not in question. This is clear, for example, from the case of *Hilal v United Kingdom*, in which the court assesses the effectiveness of police action in comparative perspective between mainland Tanzania and Zanzibar.[166]

4.4.3 *Ability to Travel to the IPA and Gain Admittance*

Third, the IPA requires the possibility for the person to travel to the IPA and to gain admittance in that part of the territory.

In *Salah Sheekh*, the court argued that Article 3 does not as such preclude contracting parties from relying on an internal flight alternative when assessing the risk of ill-treatment.[167] Yet, there must be safeguards in place when applying the concept, in order to prevent a person being returned to a situation where she would face a violation of Article 3.

> The Court considers that as a precondition for relying on an internal flight alternative certain *guarantees* have to be in place: the person to be expelled must be able to *travel* to the area concerned, *gain admittance* and *settle* there, failing which an issue under Article 3 may arise, the more so if in the absence of such guarantees there is a possibility of the

163 Eg, *Mehrez Ben Abde Hamida v Canada* Communication no 1544/2007, 11 May 2010, CCPR/C/98/D/1544/2007; *ARJ v Australia* Communication no 692/1996, 28 July 1997, CCPR/C/60/D/692/1996; *X v Sweden* Communication no 1833/2008, 17 January 2012, CCPR/C/103/D/1833/2008. For the scope of non-refoulement obligations under the ICCPR, see eg, Cornelis Wolfram Wouters, *International Legal Standards for the Protection from Refoulement* (Intersentia 2009).

164 *Soering v the United Kingdom* (Ch 3 n 118).

165 Beyond Article 3, the court has recognised the relevance of other Articles in the context of harm arising in the receiving state, including Articles 5 and 6. See Section 3.3.4 and note 117.

166 Eg *Hilal v United Kingdom* ECHR 2001-II, 293.

167 *Salah Sheekh v The Netherlands* (Ch 3 n 124) para 141, emphasis added re internal relocation.

> expellee ending up in a part of the country of origin where he or she may be subjected to ill-treatment.[168]

The court has applied its safeguards from *Salah Sheekh* in posterior cases in respect of, among others, returns to Somalia. In particular, the court considered what ethnic relations were necessary to gain admittance to southern and central Somalia, or to Puntland and Somaliland.[169]

4.4.4 *Be Reasonably Expected to Settle*

Finally, Article 8 Qualification Directive requires that the applicant can 'reasonably be expected to settle' in the IPA, a requirement that, despite significant overlap in the practice of the member states, is not applied consistently. However, it is clear from the structure of Article 8, which sets out the 'reasonably be expected to settle' requirement in addition to the requirements of safety, access and admittance, that the requirement must be lower than the scope of serious harm under Article 15, Qualification Directive, just as in refugee status the requirements must be lower than the absence of a well-founded fear of being persecuted for a Convention reason. According to UK case law on that issue:

> It has also to be borne in mind that by analogy with the principles enunciated by the House of Lords in *Januzi* and *AG (Sudan)*, just as an applicant seeking to establish refugee protection eligibility by pointing to factors making it unreasonable for him to relocate does not need to show the difficulties in the place of relocation reach the level of persecution (or Article 3 ECHR ill-treatment), so an applicant seeking to establish subsidiary protection eligibility does not need to show that difficulties in the place of relocation cross the Article 15(c) threshold of serious harm.[170]

In contrast, it is questionable whether human rights law establishes additional criteria for an IPA beyond safety. As for the CAT, the CAT Committee acknowledged in a 2004 decision that the 'hardship' which internal relocation would bring about for the applicant, an Indian national residing in Canada, but made clear that the decisive standard was a risk of torture:

168 Ibid para 141.
169 *Sufi and Elmi v the United Kingdom* (Ch 3 n 140) para 267.
170 *AK* (Article 15(c)) Afghanistan CG [2012] UKUT 163 (IAC) para 232.

> The Committee considers that the complainant has failed to substantiate that he would be unable to *lead a life free of torture in another part of India.* Although resettlement outside Punjab would constitute a considerable hardship for the complainant, the mere fact that he may not be able to return to his family and his home village does not as such amount to torture within the meaning of article 3, read in conjunction with article 1, of the Convention.[171]

Thus, the relevant standard is whether an applicant would live a life free of torture in the entire territory, a wording reiterated by the Committee in later decisions.[172]

The ECtHR, too, appears to focus on the risks of safety. In *Salah Sheekh*, the court argued that Article 3 does not as such preclude contracting parties from relying on an internal flight alternative when assessing the risk of ill-treatment.[173] Yet, there must be safeguards in place when applying the concept, in order to prevent a person being returned to a situation where she would face a violation of Article 3. According to the court,

> [...] the Court has previously held that the indirect removal of an alien to an intermediary country does not affect the responsibility of the expelling Contracting State to ensure that he or she is not, as a result of its decision to expel, exposed to treatment contrary to Article 3 of the Convention [...] It sees no reason to hold differently where the expulsion is, as in the present case, to take place not to an intermediary country but to a particular region of the country of origin. The Court considers that as a precondition for relying on an internal flight alternative certain *guarantees* have to be in place: the person to be expelled must be able to *travel* to the area concerned, *gain admittance* and *settle* there, failing which an issue under Article 3 may arise, the more so if in the absence of such guarantees there is a possibility of the expellee ending up in a part of the country of origin where he or she may be subjected to ill-treatment.[174]

The ECtHR thus developed additional criteria for internal protection in analogy to its jurisprudence on indirect refoulement.[175] If is it not guaranteed that

171 *Mr BSS v Canada* Communication no 183/2001, CAT/C/32/D/183/2001 (2004), para 11.5.

172 *SSS v Canada* Communication no 245/2004, CAT/C/35/D/245/2004.

173 *Salah Sheekh v The Netherlands* (Ch 3 n 124) para 141, emphasis added re internal relocation.

174 Ibid para 141.

175 Ibid with reference to *TI v the United Kingdom* App no 43844/98 (ECHR, 7 March 2000).

the applicant can actually go to and remain within the proposed area of relocation, this would pose an issue under Article 3 because of a risk of harm exposure in the home region. In assessing the possibilities of access and settlement, the court has, in the past, considered, for instance, the clan structure of Somalia.[176] In *Salah Sheekh*, the court concluded that there was evidence that the authorities of the proposed site of relocation – Puntland and Somaliland – would not grant the applicant access, or would expel him. It was precisely this which meant that an issue under Article 3 arose.

The requirements of gaining admittance and *settling* in a proposed site of relocation raise the question as to what extent other human rights harm, socio-economic and humanitarian considerations are relevant for proposed internal protection alternatives. As per the court's case law, such considerations appear to be relevant only where conditions are so bad that they alone would make deportation a violation of Article 3, ECHR. Again in *Salah Sheekh*, the court has pointed out that socio-economic and humanitarian considerations, 'do not necessarily have a bearing, and certainly not a decisive one, on the question whether the persons concerned would face a real risk of ill-treatment within the meaning of Article 3 of the Convention'.[177] Although the court has in some few cases used the language of reasonableness in connection with internal relocation, it is clear that reasonableness does not amount to a requirement separate from the Article 3 threshold.[178]

176 *Sufi and Elmi v United Kingdom* (Ch 3 n 140) para 267.

177 *Salah Sheekh v the Netherlands* (Ch 3 n 124) para 141.

178 In *MYH and Others v Sweden* (Ch 4 n 155), the court stated that, 'Internal relocation inevitably involves certain hardship. Various sources have attested that people who relocate to the Kurdistan Region may face difficulties, for instance, in finding proper jobs and housing there, not the least if they do not speak Kurdish. Nevertheless, the evidence before the Court suggests that there are jobs available and that settlers have access to health care as well as financial and other support from the UNHCR and local authorities. In any event, there is no indication that the general living conditions in the KRI for a Christian settler would be unreasonable or in any way amount to treatment prohibited by Article 3.' See also *N M B v Sweden*, App no 68335/10, 27 June 2013. In *B K A v Sweden*, the court noted that the Iraqi applicant, although he would face a real risk of being subjected to treatment contrary to Article 3 if returned to his home region, 'may reasonably settle in, for instance, the Anbar governorate, where it has not been shown that he will face such a risk.' In *B N M v Sweden*, the court assessed the risk to the applicant in Iraqi Kurdistan, pointing out that, 'if the clan or tribe in question is not particularly influential, an internal flight alternative might be reasonable in many cases'. *B K A v Sweden*, App no 11161/11, 19 December 2013, *D N M v Sweden*. Similarly, *W H v Sweden*, App No 49341/10, 27 March 2014, in which the court stated that the events that the applicant – an Iraqi woman – had raised in proof of risk had occurred in Baghdad rather than in Kurdistan, where she would be returned.

Thus, the relevant threshold can be derived, inter alia, from the case law on expulsion in medical cases. As previously discussed,[179] the court has set a high threshold for all harm not deliberately inflicted by a human actor by act or by omission. In *N v the United Kingdom*, the court denied that the health of the applicant would bar his expulsion under Article 3, but stated that the fundamental importance of Article 3 meant that it was necessary to retain a certain degree of flexibility on the provision for the 'very exceptional cases'.[180] In *Budina v Russia*, the court did not exclude the possibility that a deporting state may violate Article 3, 'where an applicant, who was wholly dependent on state support, found herself faced with official indifference in a situation of serious deprivation or want incompatible with human dignity'.[181] The court applied this test in the case of *MSS v Belgium and Greece*,[182] holding that Greece violated Article 3, ECHR by exposing the applicant, an asylum seeker, and as such 'a member of a particularly underprivileged and vulnerable population group in need of special protection', to extreme poverty, the inability to cater for the most basic needs and the fear of being attacked, without the prospect of the situation improving.[183] Belgium for its part was found in breach of Article 3 for wanting to transfer the applicant to Greece while aware of the conditions. From the perspective of internal relocation, these rulings cumulated in *Sufi and Elmi v UK*,[184] in which the court applied the test of whether the applicant was able to cater for the most basic needs, such as food, hygiene and shelter, and the prospect of the situation improving, to the conditions in IDP camps in southern and central Somalia. In doing so, it considered in particular the means of warfare employed by the parties to the conflict, the absence of international aid agencies, and the fact that the dire situation resulted directly from the acts or omissions of the parties to the conflict. It was precisely the latter circumstances that required the court not to apply the *very exceptional cases* test it had developed in the case of *N v United Kingdom*.[185] Accordingly,

179 Section 3.3.4.

180 Paragraph 44.

181 *Budina v Russia* App no 45603/05 (ECtHR, 16 June 2009).

182 *MSS v Belgium and Greece* ECHR 2011-I 121.

183 Paragraph 254.

184 *Sufi and Elmi v United Kingdom* (Ch 3 n 140).

185 Ibid para 282, 'If the dire humanitarian conditions in Somalia were solely or even predominantly attributable to poverty or to the State's lack of resources to deal with a naturally occurring phenomenon, such as a drought, the test in *N v the United Kingdom* may well have been considered to be the appropriate one. However, it is clear that while drought has contributed to the humanitarian crisis, that crisis is predominantly due to the direct and indirect actions of the parties to the conflict.'

the court was not ready to compare the situation in Afghanistan for a male applicant from Afghanistan with a physical disability inflicted by a grenade with that of Somalia.[186] This was chiefly because humanitarian problems 'are [...] a result of the deliberate actions or omissions of the Afghan authorities rather than attributable to a lack of resources'.[187]

In sum, the ECtHR's jurisprudence on internal relocation revolves around whether or not there is a real risk of ill-treatment within the meaning of Article 3, which includes humanitarian considerations only in 'very exceptional cases'. This also means that the court may, in principle, consider whether an applicant can act discreetly so as to avoid being identified, for example, by political opponents when travelling to a proposed site of relocation.[188]

4.4.5 *Different Standards for the Eligibility Criteria on Subsidiary Status and on Refugee Status?*

The IPA concept provides an interesting insight into the relation between human rights law and refugee law in EU asylum law. The ECtHR influenced the the safeguards of Article 8, Qualification Directive, by requiring that an applicant must be expected to 'settle' in a proposed IPA, a criterion mirroring safeguards against indirect refoulement, but not primarily designed to ease the potential hardships of internal relocation beyond the requirements of Article 3, ECHR. But the Directive also features the 'reasonableness' wording, developed in member states' jurisprudence in their application of the 1951 Convention, and exceeding the non-return obligations under Article 3. Indeed, the 1951 Convention demands even more than the narrow readings of reasonableness, namely the consideration of human rights harm and of basic rights guaranteed by the Convention.

Given that this interpretation is based on the IPA being an exclusion clause *in relation to refugee status*, it would have to apply only to the assessment of refugee status rather than to the assessment of subsidiary protection status also. Yet, in light of the common provision in the Qualification Directive, it is submitted that the higher international law standard must apply for both groups.

By applying to both groups, the Directive clearly does raise the standard for subsidiary protection status above what international human rights law requires. In effect, EU law uses practice developed in the 1951 Convention context

186 *SHH v United Kingdom* App no 60367/10 (ECtHR, 29 January 2013).

187 Ibid para 91.

188 *Sufi and Elmi v United Kingdom* (Ch 3 n 140).

as a blueprint for people with wider protection needs. However, the case law also shows that the different standards are confused, or that the 'reasonableness' test as well as the German 'existential threat' jurisprudence on the IPA do in practice mean much the same as an Article 3 violation. In such instances, cross-fertilisation of EU asylum law and European refugee law risks being at the expense of the 1951 Convention.

4.5 The Legality of Non-state 'Actors of Protection' in the Application of the IPA

4.5.1 *The 1951 Convention Requirements on Non-state 'Actors of Protection'*

This section enquires whether it is accordance with the 1951 Convention and with international human rights law to consider non-state actors – international organisations and de facto authorities – as 'actors of protection' in the IPA. The question arises because of Article 8(1)(b), Qualification Directive, which specifies that protection against persecution or serious harm is to be understood in accordance with Article 7. As such, protection against persecution or serious harm can be provided by the actors specified in Article 7(1), namely the state or 'parties or organisations, including international organisations, controlling the state or a substantial part of the territory of the state'. Such actors of protection have to be willing and able to provide effective protection in a non-temporary manner (Article 7(2)).

To answer the question, it is helpful to distinguish between the different safeguards of the IPA under the Qualification Directive, namely that an applicant has to be (i) safe, (ii) able to travel to the proposed area and gain admittance, and can (iii) reasonably expected to settle.

The nature of the analysis of safety (i) as a purely factual enquiry on the ability to quell relevant harm beyond the real risk threshold has been discussed in detail in Chapter 3. As discussed in Section 3.5, international law does not in principle preclude consideration of actors other than states when analysing whether there is a well-founded fear of being persecuted or a real risk of harm relevant for human rights law non-refoulement obligations. However, there are important doubts whether actors other than states can provide protection against harm *in practice*. Meanwhile, whether or not an actor of protection is willing and able to provide effective protection is a question for case-by-case evaluation of the facts.[189] The capability to sign, or indeed the actual signing of, human rights treaties is relevant evidence of the ability to protect, but it is

189 Eg, *AM and AM* (armed conflict: risk categories) Somalia CG [2008] UKAIT 00091, para 190, '[...] we would emphasise the great importance of a case-by-case approach. That is

certainly no guarantee of the durable and effective protection of the provisions contained therein.[190] Protection against harm is, according to one commentator, a 'pragmatic and common sense analysis of just what range of protective functions are performed by particular de facto entities'.[191] Another commentator pointed out that consideration of states only as actors of protection would fail to take into account '… protection from long established authorities, whose proven track record suggests protection of a more durable kind, yet who may not be internationally recognized state authority'.[192] UNHCR, in its authoritative *Guidelines on International Protection on the IPA*, takes a similar position, emphasising the factual ability of actors of protection and its durability, stopping short of saying that only states can provide protection in an IPA.

> Not all sources of possible protection are tantamount to state protection. For example, if the area is under the control of an international organisation, refugee status should not be denied solely on the assumption that the threatened individual could be protected by that organisation. The facts of the individual case will be particularly important. The general rule is that it is inappropriate to equate the exercise of a certain administrative authority and control over territory by international organisations on a transitional or temporary basis with national protection provided by states. Under international law, international organisations do not have the attributes of a state.
>
> Similarly, it is inappropriate to find that the claimant will be protected by a local clan or militia in an area where they are not the recognised authority in that territory and/or where their control over the area may only be temporary. Protection must be *effective and of a durable nature: it must*

what is enjoined by the House of Lords in *Januzi* and *A H* (Sudan) and is also what is entailed by Article 8 of the Qualification Directive (see para 339O of the Immigration Rules), which refers to having "[…] regard to the general circumstances prevailing in that part of the country and to the personal circumstances of the applicant" '; *AT and Others* (Article 15c; risk categories) (CG) [2014] UKUT 318 (IAC). In *AM and AM*, the AIT also stated that in IPA analysis, the 'first issue is safety and that is all about risk'; hence, it will depend on a variety of circumstances whether those who end up in an IDP camp face a real risk of persecution or serious harm. For typical evidentiary considerations, see above, 3.3.

190 Storey, ' "From Nowhere to Somewhere": An Evaluation of the UNHCR 2nd Track Global Consultations on International Protection: San Remo 8–10 September 2001 Experts Roundtable on the IPA/IRA/IFA Alternative' 387.

191 Ibid.

192 Kelley, 'Internal Flight/Relocation/Protection Alternative: Is it Reasonable?' (Ch 4 n 139) 22.

> *be provided by an organised and stable authority exercising full control over the territory and population in question.*[193]

The consideration of non-state actors for the safety requirement of Article 8, Qualification Directive is also reflected in state practice. As observed by past commentators, courts have been ready to consider non-state actors of protection in relation to proposed IPAs, including, for instance, the de facto territories in Somalia and Iraq,[194] militias, or powerful individuals.[195] Whether or not these actors were found to provide protection against harm in an IPA then depended on both individual factors such as clan affiliation,[196] and objective factors such as a prognosis on the durability of the actor's power or control.[197] In Germany, non-state actors have been considered possible 'actors of protection' in an IPA since the 1990s,[198] and continue to be so considered, without a distinction being made in such assessments between refugee status and subsidiary status. In more recent case law, courts have referred to Nagorno-Karabakh, a de facto state within the territory of Azerbaijan, as a potential site of internal protection,[199] but also to Somaliland and

193 UN High Commissioner for Refugees, 'Guidelines on International Protection No 4' (Ch 3 n 67), paras 16–17.

194 European Legal Network on Asylum, 'The Application of the Concept of Internal Protection Alternative' (Ch 4 n 85).

195 Hugo Storey, 'The Internal Flight Alternative Test: The Jurisprudence Re-examined' (1998) 10 International Journal of Refugee Law 499, 520; Moffarts, 'Refugee Status and the "Internal Flight Alternative" '; Kelley, 'Internal Flight/Relocation/Protection Alternative: Is it Reasonable?' (Ch 4, n 139) 18.

196 Rechtbank 's-Gravenhage, 6 March 1997, AWB 96/7941.

197 VG Sigmaringen, 27 June 2000 – A 3 K 1209/98.

198 See also below for practice in the member states. Eg, Germany, BVerwG, 8 December 1998, 9 C 17.98 – BVerwGE 108, 84, para 14, ruling that that the de facto autonomous Kurdish provinces in Northern Iraq could be considered an IPA, although at the time they were partly under the control of the UN. A state or state-like order is not needed for an IPA. The only thing that is relevant is whether there is sufficient protection against risk of being persecuted or equivalent danger. On the other hand, the German Federal Administrative Court was of the opinion that where a state permanently loses control over a certain part of its country – for instance, by virtue of secession, annexation or permanent establishment of a de facto authority – that part could no longer be deemed an 'internal' flight alternative, but had to be considered a foreign country from the perspective of asylum law.

199 Eg, VG Frankfurt a.M., 21 January 2004 – 1 E 2518/03.A(1); OVG Mecklenburg-Vorpommern, 16 May 2007 – 3 L 54/03; OVG Thüringen, 28 February 2008 – 2 KO 899/03; VG Ansbach, 2 February 2005 – AN 15 K 04.31820; VG Meiningen, 2 March 2010 – 2 K 20133/08 Me and OVG Thüringen, 28 November 2013 – 2 KO 185/09 rejecting Nagorno-Karabach as IPA, in contrast OVG Schleswig-Holstein, 29 April 2009 – 1 LB 11/05.

Puntland.[200] These potential IPAs are also considered in Dutch case law.[201] In the UK, courts have referred primarily to clans as *de facto* authorities and as potential non-state actors of protection in an IPA.[202] In line with a strictly factual approach to the IPA enquiry, UK courts have also considered whether international organisations provide protection against harm, including assurance of a safe passage to an IPA.[203] Thus, UNISOM peace-keeping forces in Somalia were considered to provide safety as regards travel to an IPA.[204]

In Sweden, it is rare that the Migration Court of Appeals considers that non-state actors contribute to either safety or to the reasonableness of settlement within an IPA. However, the court did consider whether the support by ISAF for the Afghan National Police was so strong as to provide the applicant with protection against the threats of a clan were he to relocate to the capital.[205] More frequent are references to possible IPAs in areas under the control of non-state actors – notably Puntland or Somaliland – in Somalia. These cases do not analyse the protective capacity of the authorities to avert harm, but consider the degree to which harm is localised.[206]

However, that a non-state actor may *in* rare cases be able to quell a risk of relevant harm below the relevant threshold of probability does not mean that it is in accordance with international law to refer applicants to an IPA

---

200 Courts considered whether there was clan protection against risk of harm other than in the home area, but eventually denied that there was a relocation alternative, because of lack of access and the limited capacity of the area to absorb IDPs. Eg, VG Braunschweig, 24 June 2008 – 7 A 172/06; VG Magdeburg, 16 December 2011 – 5 A 59/11 MD.

201 Rechtbank 's-Gravenhage, 11 June 2012, 12/16751, 12/16750 and 12/16817; Rechtbank 's-Gravenhage, 10 July 2003, AWB 02/23734 and 01/68315; Rechtbank 's-Gravenhage, 30 December 2005, AWB 04/54263, 04/54264; Rechtbank 's-Gravenhage, 30 December 2005, AWB 04/54263 and 04/54264.

202 This practice clearly predating the 2004 Qualification Directive. For instance, *NM and Others* (lone women, Ashraf) Somalia CG [2005] UKIAT 00076, also *AJH* (minority group, Swahili speakers) Somalia CG [2003] UKIAT 00094; *S F* (Sufficiency of protection, KAA, Michigan Guidelines) Iraq CG [2002] UKIAT 07376.

203 *KX* (Mixed marriages, Roma, Albanian, *Januzi* applied) Serbia and Montenegro (Kosovo) CG [2006] UKIAT 00072.

204 *AM and AM* (Armed conflict, risk categories) Somalia CG [2008] UKAIT 00091.

205 Migrationsöverdomstolen, 14 January 2009, UM4118-07, MIG 2009:4.

206 Migrationsöverdomstolen, 24 February 2011, MIG 2011:4, UM10061-09. Thus, the court considered whether Puntland was an IPA for a woman hailing from Somaliland fleeing gender-based violence by her family. The applicant had claimed that the authorities would not be able to protect her from the male network on which she was dependent and from which she feared harm. However, because of the lack of a social connection to Puntland, the IPA was not considered relevant. Migrationsöverdomstolen, 21 April 2011, MIG 2011:8, UM7851-10.

controlled by non-state actors. This becomes clear when scrutinising the other requirements of the IPA, in particular that applicants must reasonably be expected to settle in the proposed area (iii). As discussed in Section 4.3.4, given that the IPA concept is comparable to an exclusion clause for those individuals who are, *prima facie*, refugees, it is not to be narrowly construed and requires more than saftey. While the IPA is not to be conflated with the enfranchisement of refugees with all rights under the Convention as a matter of law – international protection – the additional requirements mean the IPA needs to be faithful to the Convention's conception of international protection as surrogate rights enfranchisement. This would, however, mean that beyond the factual consideration of the IPA safeguards, the 1951 Convention does not allow referring applicants for international protection to an IPA controlled by any actor that is not bound by international law to provide them.[207]

International law has developed considerably in respect of both international law obligations of actors other than states (and in particular international organisations), as well as in respect of their responsibility for breaching such obligations.[208] The International Court of Justice recognised as

207 Hathaway and Foster in *The Law of Refugee Status* (Ch 1 n 100) 291 make a similar argument, albeit rejecting non-state actors of protection also for the home region. 'Only states can provide protection in the IPA because anything else would 'ignore [...] completely the Refugee Convention's principled commitment to restoring refugees to membership in a national community, that is, in a political community that has clear protective duties under international law.' The Commission's original proposal of the Qualification Directive did not foresee the possibility of non-State actor protection in the IPA. The draft directive did evoke the possibility of non-State actors protecting an applicant from a well-founded fear of being persecuted, but stopped there. Article 9 (on protection against harm) was not meant to apply to the IPA concept in Article 10 of the draft directive. In the drafting process, the European Parliament, in its legislative resolution on the directive, had voted, in line with ECRE's criticism, on an amendment such that 'protection must be afforded by a de jure and not just a de facto authority', 'European Parliament legislative resolution on the proposal for a Council directive on minimum standards for the qualification and status of third country nationals and stateless persons as refugees or as persons who otherwise need international protection', COM/2001/510, OJ [2003] C 300. For a discussion of the capability of actors other than states to bear obligations under international law, see Chapter 5 on protection in third countries.

208 On aspects of this evolution, see, eg, Rainer Hofmann and Nils Geissler (eds), *Non-State Actors as New Subjects of International Law. International Law: From the Traditional State Order Towards the Law of the Global Community* (Duncker & Humblot 1999); Maath Noortmann and Cedric Ryngaert (eds), *Non-State Actor Dynamics in International Law: From Law-Takers to Law-Makers* (Routledge 2010); Philip Alston (ed), *Non-State Actors and Human Rights* (Oxford University Press 2005).

early as 1951 that international organisations were subjects of international law and were bound as such by obligations under customary international law.[209] Since then, the UN have accepted that the principle of state responsibility applies to international organisations, including the potential delivery of compensation.[210] In 2011, the International Law Commission adopted its Draft Articles on Responsibility of International Organisations, which apply the principles of State responsibility to international organisations by analogy, in particular the elements of attribution, breach of obligation, and circumstances precluding wrongfulness.[211] Yet, despite this evolution, neither international organisations nor de facto authorities bear the same obligations that states would have and that are relevant for the additional IPA safeguards beyond safety. In respect of the 1951 Convention and human rights law, this is because it is questionable whether single provisions of the Convention have acquired the status of customary international law,[212] and because the scope of customary human rights obligations remains notoriously contested in light of divergent state practice.[213] What is more, for de facto authorities the scope of obligations would hinge on the actual and effective control over territory, a question often contested.[214] Yet, courts, for instance in Germany and the UK, have in the past, pointed to assistance of

209 Interpretation of the Agreement of 25 March 1951 between the WHO and Egypt (Advisory Opinion) [1980] ICJ Rep 73, 73.

210 A/51/389, p 4, para 6; Letter of 3 February 2004 by the United Nations Legal Counsel to the Director of the Codification Division, A/CN.4/545, sect. II.G.

211 International Law Commission, 'Draft articles on the responsibility of international organizations, with commentaries, Adopted by the International Law Commission at its sixty-third session' *(A/66/10)* (Yearbook of the International Law Commission, 2011, vol II, Part Two, 2011).

212 Customary international law as a source of law according to Article 38(1)b) of the ICJ Statute (Ch 4, n 86), requires consistent state practice accepted as law. For analysis on assessing these requirements in practice, see, eg, Jean-Marie Henckaerts and Louise Doswald-Beck, *Customary International Humanitarian Law, vol I: Rules* (Cambridge University Press 2005) xxxvii-li. The International Law Commission is currently engaged in the drafting of a guidance document on the identification of customary international law, see International Law Commission,' Identification of Customary International Law – Text of the draft conclusions as adopted by the Drafting Committee on second reading', 17 May 2018, UN Doc A/CN.4/L.908.

213 Hugh Thirlway, 'Human Rights in Customary Law: An Attempt to Define Some of the Issues' 28 Leiden Journal of International Law 495.

214 Julian M Lehmann, '"Outsourcing" Protection and the Transnational Relevance of Protection Elsewhere – The Case of UNHCR', in Thomas Gammeltoft-Hansen and Jens Vedsted-Hansen (eds), *Human Rights and the Dark Side of Globalisation* (Routledge 2016).

non-governmental NGO s,[215] churches,[216] and UN humanitarian agencies[217] to establish that applicants would live above subsistence level.

In sum, given non-state actors do not bear the relevant international law obligations on a par with states, in the assessment of refugee status the 1951 Convention precludes relying on such actors for the Qualification Directive requirement that an applicant can reasonably be expected to settle in the proposed IPA.

4.5.2 *International Human Rights Law Requirements and the Legality of 'Non-state Actors of Protection'*

Does international human rights law, too, preclude consideration of non-state actors as 'actors pf protection' when assessing the IPA? As discussed in Section 4.4., internal relocation follows a different logic in human rights law obligations of non-return than in the assessment of eligibility criteria for refugee status. In contrast to the IPA concept for refugee status determination, internal relocation in human rights law does not function as an exclusion clause for individuals who, absent an IPA, would be refugees. Rather, the risk of relevant harm is simply assessed in relation to different parts of a territory.[218] In consequence, human rights law obligations feature the same legal threshold for a home region as for a proposed relocation site, in particular the risk of torture, inhuman or degrading treatment. Indeed, the ECtHR has addressed questions of protection against harm in applicants' home areas from a purely factual perspective. The court did not stop at discussing protection against harm by de facto authorities, such as the ruling authorities in Somaliland or Puntland.[219] In *Collins and Akaziebie v Sweden*, the court also considered whether a family member could protect an applicant against the alleged risk of FGM in the home area or in an area of internal relocation.[220] Thus, under non-return

215 VGH Bayern, 31 August 2007 – 11 B 02.31724, referring to the assistance by international governmental and non-governmental organisations for Chechens in the Russian republic of Ingushetia.

216 VG Cottbus, 27 October 2006 – 5 K 718/02.A. *SR* (Iraqi Arab Christian, relocation to KRG) Iraq CG [2009] UKAIT 00038.

217 OVG Saarland, 29 September 2006 – 3 R 6/06.

218 See above, Section 4.2, with reference to *Salah Sheekh v The Netherlands* (Ch 3 n 124) para 141. '[…] the Court has previously held that the indirect removal of an alien to an intermediary country does not affect the responsibility of the expelling Contracting State to ensure that he or she is not, as a result of its decision to expel, exposed to treatment contrary to Article 3 of the Convention […]. It sees no reason to hold differently where the expulsion is, as in the present case, to take place […] to a particular region of the country of origin.'

219 *Salah Sheekh v The Netherlands.*

220 *Collins and Akaziebie v Sweden* App no 23944/05 (ECtHR, 8 March 2007).

obligations of human rights law, even actors falling short of the requirement in the Qualification Directive to *control the state or a substantial part of the territory of the state* would in principle appear to be able to provide protection against harm in an IPA. In light of its factual approach to internal relocation safeguards, there is also no indication that the court treats differently the additional requirements of gaining admittance and the ability to settle in the proposed area.

Given the Qualification Directive requires actors of protection to exercise control over territory, the Directive exceeds the requirements of international human rights law, while it falls short of the 1951 Convention requirements, precluding consideration of non-state actors for the IPA safeguards beyond safety.

Arguably, however, the Qualification Directive would already accommodate a state-only conceptualisation of the IPA as regards refugee status. This is because the text of Article 8(1)(b) makes clear that non-state 'actors of protection' are relevant only for *protection against harm*, as defined by Article 7, rather than for the additional requirements of Article 8 to be able to travel, gain admittance and be reasonably expected to settle in the IPA. Yet, there is no indication that this is the prevalent interpretation. Indeed, cross-country studies on the application of the IPA concept in EU member states[221] have pointed out that neither administrative decisions nor court decisions comprehensively analysed the requirements of a proposed IPA. Instead, according to UNHCR, applicants were referred to an IPA as 'an additional secondary argument to support the conclusion that the applicant is not in need of [...] international protection',[222] with analysis of the IPA perhaps 'mentioned only briefly as an additional option available to the applicant, without commensurate justification of the argument [...]'.[223] In the majority of cases, the analysis was 'superficial', 'biased', 'overgeneralized' and 'approached in a matter-of-fact manner rather than as a legal test which requires the observance of specific standards'.[224] Decisions often did not identify a specific geographic area and

221 UN High Commissioner for Refugees, 'The Internal Flight Alternative Practices. A UNHCR Research Study in Central European Countries' (2012) <https://www.refworld.org/docid/4ffaabdf2.html> accessed 1 July 2019; European Council on Refugees and Exiles, 'Actors of Protection and the Application of the Internal Protection Alternative' (Ch 3 n 162).

222 UN High Commissioner for Refugees, 'The Internal Flight Alternative Practices. A UNHCR Research Study in Central European Countries' (ibid).

223 Ibid. See also Querton, '"Even if ..." The use of the Internal Protection Alternative in asylum decisions in the UK' (Ch 4 n 5).

224 UN High Commissioner for Refugees, 'The Internal Flight Alternative Practices. A UNHCR Research Study in Central European Countries' (Ch 4 n 221).

were inattentive to the specific circumstances of the applicants.[225] A comparative study by ECRE also criticised the fact that member states in 'a significant proportion of IPA cases' raise the IPA to back up adverse findings on lacking a well-founded fear of being persecuted or lacking real risk of serious harm ('even if').[226] In respect of the safety requirement, the report observed that some countries do not adequately evaluate whether a proposed IPA is safe.[227]

4.6 Conclusion: the Risk of Tainting 1951 Convention Requirements by 'Non-refoulement Law' in Article 8 Qualification Directive

This chapter has discussed the requirements of the IPA under Article 8 of the Qualification Directive in conjunction with refugee and human rights law. In particular, it has discussed the concept's grounding in the 1951 Convention, the differences between the IPA requirements of Article 8 and Article 7, Qualification Directive, as well as the differences between the 1951 Convention requirements and those of human rights law.

This chapter has argued, consistent with parts of the academic literature on the issue, that Article 8, Qualification Directive is fundamentally different from Article 7. There is no express requirement in the 1951 Convention to consider a potential IPA, and the IPA is in practice considered only for individuals who do already have a well-founded fear of being persecuted for a Convention ground, typically in their home region. Therefore, under the 1951 Convention, the IPA concept should be conceived of as similar to an exclusion clause. In consequence, not only is the application of the concept optional rather than mandatory, but also the evidentiary burden lies solely on the authorities. Finally, the IPA's requirements go beyond *protection against harm* (safety). Respect for the protected interests under the 1951 Convention as well as respect for those human rights that are relevant for the notion of being persecuted ought to be considered in assessing the availability of internal protection for refugees – including civil and political, and economic, social and cultural rights. This implies that the IPA should only be considered for state actors, contrary to the purely factual approach on safety.

225 Ibid.

226 European Council on Refugees and Exiles, 'Actors of Protection and the Application of the Internal Protection Alternative' (Ch 3 n 162) 66.

227 Ibid 59.

In respect of international human rights law requirements, the chapter has argued that the safeguards for the IPA concept under the 1951 Convention exceed IPA safeguards under human rights law obligations of non-return. In the European context, these obligations are centered on Article 3, ECHR, which sets the same legal threshold for a home region as for any other region in the country of nationality. The ECtHR's language, which requires an applicant to be able to 'settle' in an IPA, does not extend to humanitarian considerations beyond the very exceptional ones under Article 3, ECHR. What is more, human rights law does not require actors of protection to control territory, as Article 7(1), Qualification Directive does.

The Qualification Directive features a common IPA standard for both refugee status and subsidiary protection status, and in that standard clearly has combined the inconsistent 'reasonableness' criterion from member states' jurisprudence with the ECHR requirements. As such, Article 8, Qualification Directive exceeds international law requirements for those who are not refugees. Meanwhile, its application in practice risks falling short of 1951 Convention requirements and being conflated with the lower standards derived from human rights law obligations of non-return – 'non-refoulement law'.[228]

Against this background, Article 8 is prone to divergent interpretations in member states. In particular, the United Kingdom, France, the Netherlands and Sweden all have a different test according to which the applicant must be able to lead a relatively normal life in the IPA.

The IPA concept illustrates some of the opportunities and risks of common rules for refugee status and subsidiary status, as well as the complexities in the relationship between human rights law and refugee law in the EU context. On the one hand, the common Article 8 for both statuses has benefited the EU's relatively generous subsidiary protection regime, which exceeds international law requirements. On the other hand, this has come at a price, given the Qualification Directive's actor of protection concept raises issues of compliance with the 1951 Convention when it comes to the IPA. It is questionable

228 The term is borrowed from Durieux, 'The Vanishing Refugee: how EU Asylum Law Blurs the Specificity of Refugee Protection' (Ch 1 n 95). James C Hathaway, 'EU Accountability to International Law: The Case of Aslyum' (2011) 33 Michigan Journal of International Law 1, 6 criticised the fact that 'the continuing effort to "shoe horn" respect for refugee law norms into the limited jurisdiction of the European Convention on Human Rights may actually be indirectly (if inadvertently) responsible for the pervasive belief in Europe that no more than minimal constraints (specifically, risk of refoulement or torture or cruel or inhuman treatment) restrict the authority of states to force refugees away.'

whether human rights law, as has been argued before,[229] provides an adequate framework for the IPA assessment. Contrary to what has been argued,[230] there remains a difference between the 1951 Convention criteria governing the use of the IPA concept from the criteria used in human rights jurisprudence. EU lawmakers should therefore consider lifting the requirements of Article 8 for both refugee status and subsidiary protection status to meet the 1951 Convention requirements, or else distinguishing more strongly between the two statuses.

229 European Legal Network on Asylum, 'The Application of the Concept of Internal Protection Alternative' (Ch 4 n 85) 69: 'However, with international and regional human rights bodies, such as the Committee against Torture in the *Alan* case and the European Court of Human Rights in the *Chahal* case, examining states' duties to respect and ensure the enjoyment of the civil, political and socio-economic human rights of asylum seekers, it is hoped that some framework of international precedent can be provided.'

230 Storey, '"From Nowhere to Somewhere": An Evaluation of the UNHCR 2nd Track Global Consultations on International Protection: San Remo 8–10 September 2001 Experts Roundtable on the IPA/IRA/IFA Alternative', 388, stating that, 'Arguably, from a public international law perspective, there should be no significant difference.'

CHAPTER 5

Protection in Third Countries

5.1 Introduction

The previous two chapters have revolved around the law behind different concepts of 'protection' *within the asylum seeker's country of nationality* – protection against harm and the internal protection alternative/IPA. Although these two concepts should not be conflated, they do share as a common thread their both being an expression of the principle of surrogacy, whereby international protection not needed when protection is available in the state of nationality. This chapter will focus on a practice that *goes beyond the surrogacy principle,* by extending a similar concept to third countries.[1] In particular, under the EU Procedures Directive, an application for international protection may be inadmissible or the standard of evidentiary assessment reduced if an applicant is deemed not in need of international protection, because he or she can obtain protection in another country *outside the EU.*[2] Similar rules and policies have in the past been referred to as 'protection

1 Zimmermann and Mahler, 460 in Zimmermann; Dörschner; Machts (eds), *The 1951 Convention Relating to the Status of Refugees and its 1967 Protocol – A Commentary* (Ch 1 n 42) also make the connection between the internal protection alternative and the protection in third states, referring to the latter as 'External Protection Alternatives', but argue that, strictly speaking, only the IPA is an expression of the surrogacy, given only the IPA refers to the home state of an asylum seeker: 'the principle does *prima facie* bear some resemblance with the internal flight alternative". While this is the case, a fundamental difference becomes apparent since only the latter concept of "International flight alternative" relies on the subsidiary nature of international refugee protection through refugee law as some form of surrogate protection.'

2 Similarly, under the Dublin Regulation, applications for international protection are normally deemed inadmissible if an applicant can obtain protection *within the EU.* However, this chapter will primarily focus on the Procedures Directive, because the Dublin Regulation raises specific issues on the EU's internal constitution as a legal entity *sui generis* in which members have a certain degree of mutual confidence in each other's level of fundamental rights protection. In contrast, the protection elsewhere rules of the Procedures Directive regulate the EU's legal minimum standards in respect of third states, which raises no such issues. Protection elsewhere is not to be conflated with the EU law concept of 'safe countries of origin', which establishes a rebuttable presumption that applicants normally do not have a *well-founded fear* of being persecuted for a Convention ground or face a real risk of serious harm. See Article 37 of the Procedures Directive.

 | DOI:10.1163/9789004430396_006

elsewhere',[3] a term that will in the following be used interchangeably with 'protection in third countries'.

Rules on protection elsewhere have gained new practical momentum with the adoption of the EU-Turkey statement, foreseeing, among others, the return of migrants who have arrived from Turkey on a Greek island and whose application is inadmissible in accordance with the Procedures Directive.[4] Most notably, this would pertain to cases in which available protection in Turkey is considered.

Contrary to the concepts of protection against harm and the IPA discussed in the two previous chapters, rules on 'protection elsewhere' revolve around the availability of *international protection* (rather than *'domestic'* protection). How do the legal safeguards relating to 'protection elsewhere' compare to those within the country of origin in particular, how is 'effective' protection circumscribed and who delivers such protection? Finally, what challenges does the 'protection elsewhere' enquiry pose to the relation between the 1951 Convention, EU law and human rights law?

This chapter argues, first, that *a fortiori* to the IPA concept, protection elsewhere should be conceived of as similar to an exclusion clause, which may be applied *before* the substantive, yet declaratory, assessment of status (procedurally) or *after* the substantive assessment of status. If applied before the assessment of status, as specified in the Procedures Directive, the substantive standards of protection elsewhere have to satisfy the requirements of the 1951 Convention, even if the persons for whom it is applied are not refugees. If it is applied after the assessment of status, it may distinguish between refugees and individuals with wider protection needs (that is, subsidiary status in the EU context).

Second, this chapter argues that, *de lege lata*, and again *a fortiori* to the IPA concept, the 1951 Convention features requirements for protection elsewhere that exceed the obligation not to return a refugee to a territory where his or her life or liberty may be in danger. These safeguards are higher than those under the IPA concept, because unlike for the IPA, protection elsewhere policies are applied to individuals who are refugees within the meaning of international law. Meanwhile, no such additional safeguards beyond physical integrity exist for individuals who are not refugees, so that EU law significantly exceeds obligations under human rights law. However, and finally, it is argued that some

3 This term has been used both in the 2016 New York Declaration on Refugees and Migrants (Ch 1 n 14) and in academic commentary, see above, Section 1.1.

4 See introduction, Section 1.2.

member states appear to neglect some of the Directive's requirements in their transposition and application of the Directive.

The chapter will begin by enquiring whether it is, in principle, in accordance with the 1951 Convention to consider whether an applicant for international protection has already found protection in another country. After answering this question in the affirmative, it will turn to examine the substantive legal standards of the two bodies in conjunction with the Procedures Directive.

5.2 Analysis of Protection in Third Countries: Anchoring Articles 35 and 38, Procedures Directive in Refugee and Human Rights Law

5.2.1 *The EU Procedures Directive's Rules on Protection in Third Countries – Overview and Relation to the Dublin Regulation*

This and the subsequent section depict the relation between the Procedures Directive's various rules on protection in third countries to the rules on allocating responsibility for deciding the merits of applications for international protection (the Dublin Regulation). They then enquire whether the very concept of protection in third countries is compliant with the 1951 Convention and international human rights law.

The EU Procedures Directive contains four principal concepts on protection elsewhere, which differ from one another by their application to EU countries vs third countries, and by the fact that an applicant for international protection has already found (and continues to enjoy) protection or could do so in the future:

(i) A provision for applicants who have already been granted international protection *by an EU member state* (Article 33(2)a);

(ii) A provision for applicants who have already been granted refugee status or another form of protection in a *non-EU country* to which they would be readmitted (first country of asylum, Article 35);

(iii) A provision for applicants who could in the future find protection in a European (EU or signatory of the ECHR) in the future (European safe third country, Article 39);

(iv) A provision for applicants who could in the future find protection (safe third country, Article 38).

In contrast to the material eligibility provisions under the Qualification Directive, these provisions are procedural rules. In the cases (i)-(ii) and (iv), the Procedures Directive allows member states to reject an application for international protection as inadmissible under Article 33, while the

European safe third country concept makes it permissible to lower the basic standards of evidentiary assessment laid out in Chapter II of the Directive. If member states have established on the facts that an applicant is seeking to enter or has entered their territory from a European safe third country, they may renounce from an individualised assessment of whether the applicant would be safe if returned.[5] In contrast, and as explored further below in a section on safeguards, the safe third country provision of Article 38 requires, as per the text of that article, a 'case-by-case consideration of the safety of the country for a particular applicant and/or national designation of countries considered to be generally safe.'

The Procedures Directive rules on protection elsewhere are closely related to the EU rules on allocating responsibility among member states for deciding on the merits applications for international protection, as codified in the Dublin Regulation.[6] Both the Dublin Regulation and the Procedures Directive allow to establish inadmissibility without requiring a member state to examine whether or not an applicant qualifies for international protection under the Qualification Directive.[7] Recourse to the safe third country and first country of asylum concepts can be made even after a state assumes responsibility for an application for international protection under the Dublin Regulation.[8] Meanwhile, the subsequent analysis will not look at the Dublin regime as distinct 'protection elsewhere' practice. Although the issues that arise in respect of compliance with the 1951 Convention are the same as for direct or intermediate transfers to third countries, the Dublin Regulation raises distinct questions on the principle of mutual confidence by EU member states into the compliance of other EU members.[9] The Regulation's Safeguards against transfers, which are discussed below for cases of intermediary returns to third

---

5 Article 39, Procedures Directive.

6 According to Article 3(3), Dublin Regulation, 'any Member State shall retain the right to send an applicant to a safe third country, subject to the rules and safeguards laid down in Directive 2013/32/EU'.

7 Article 33(1), Procedures Directive.

8 C-695/15 PPU *Shiraz Baig Mirza v Bevándorlási és Állampolgársági Hivatal* ECLI:EU:C:2016:188 [2016] digital reports.

9 Joined Cases C-411/10; C-411/10 *N S v Secretary of State for the Home Department and ME and Others v Refugee Applications Commissioner and Minister for Justice, Equality and Law Reform* [2011] ECR I-13905, para 83. 'At issue here is the raison d'être of the European Union and the creation of an area of freedom, security and justice and, in particular, the Common European Asylum System, based on mutual confidence and a presumption of compliance, by other Member States, with European Union law and, in particular, fundamental rights.'

countries, do not simply mirror return obligations of human rights law, given the creation of a common asylum system based on common, international law-compliant minimum standards and an assumption of compliance with those standards.[10]

In practice, the importance of the Dublin Regulation has outweighed the other protection elsewhere provisions that were little applied until 2016. However, with the 2015 spur in asylum applications, and the subsequent policy efforts to return migrants, the external dimension of 'protection elsewhere' has quickly gained momentum. This is evident, first, in the adoption of the EU-Tukey statement. The statement is applied automatically to Syrians and has served as a basis for numerous return decisions, based on the qualification of Turkey as a safe third country.[11] Second, the new momentum is evident in the negotiations of a recast Dublin Regulation. The 2016 Proposal of the Dublin Regulation mandatorily required member states to apply the first country of asylum and safe third country rules,[12] a requirement subsequently rejected by the Parliament[13] and one of the reasons for the deadlock in the legislative process.

Meanwhile, the new practice on the application of the Procedures Directive as part of the EU-Turkey Statement also creates a more direct relation between the Dublin Regulation and the Procedures Directive's rules on protection in third countries. In particular, the safeguards of the Dublin Regulation may be relevant to bar removal to a country that fails correctly to apply the Procedures Directive. Article 3(2) of the Directive circumscribes those safeguards,

10 Ibid. On this issues, see Anna Lübbe, "Systemic Flaws' and Dublin Transfers: Incompatible Tests before the CJEU and the ECHR?' (2015) 27 International Journal of Refugee Law 1. Dedicated commentary on the regulation (in German), Ulrich Koehler, *Praxiskommentar zum Europäischen Asylzuständigkeitssystem* (Berliner Wissenschaftsverlag 2018); Maria Bethke and Stephan Hocks, *Dublin III-Verordnung – Handkommentar* (Nomos 2019).

11 Yiota Masouridou and Evi Kyprioti, *The EU-Turkey Statement and the Greek Hotspots – A Failed European Pilot Project in Refugee policy, The Greens/European Free Alliance in the European Parliament* (June 2018) <www.greens-efa.eu/en/article/document/the-eu-turkey-statement-and-the-greek-hotspots/> accessed 20 August 2019.

12 Proposal for a Regulation of the European Parliament and Council establishing the criteria and mechanisms for determining the Member State responsible for examining an application for international protection lodged in one of the Member States by a third-country national or a stateless person (recast) COM/2016/270 final, Art 3(3).

13 European Parliament, 'Report on the proposal for a regulation of the European Parliament and of the Council establishing the criteria and mechanisms for determining the Member State responsible for examining an application for international protection lodged in one of the Member States by a third-country national or a stateless person (recast)', COM/2016/270 A8-0345/2017.

providing that member states do not examine the Regulation's responsibility criteria in relation to a country in which –

> there are substantial grounds for believing that there are systemic flaws in the asylum procedure and in the reception conditions for applicants in that Member State, resulting in a risk of inhuman or degrading treatment within the meaning of Article 4 of the Charter of Fundamental Rights of the European Union.

Given that the risk of inhuman and degrading treatment is linked not just to the conditions in the member state in question, but also to the asylum procedure,[14] it is clear that Article 3(2) is also relevant for indirect removals to a third country, irrespective of member states retaining, according to Article 3(3), the 'right to send an applicant to a safe third country, subject to the rules and safeguards laid down in Directive 2013/32/EU'.[15] While the interpretation of the notion of 'systemic flaws' has not been subject to further adjudication before the CJEU, member states' courts have applied it in specific cases to, among others, Hungary, Greece and Italy.[16]

The immediate question on Dublin transfers in the context of a member state's application of safe third country rules has so far been adjudicated only once, and only at administrative court level. In a 2019 decision, a German administrative court ruled that a transfer to Greece of a Syrian national was barred by Article 3(2) of the Dublin Regulation, given doubts on Greece's application on the required safeguards of Article 38, Procedures Directive in respect of Turkey.[17]

---

14 This has been settled case law since the decision in *NS v Secretary of State for the Home Department and ME and Others v Refugee Applications Commissioner and Minister for Justice, Equality and Law Reform* (Ch 5 n 9).

15 Indeed, Article 3(4) of the Regulation is not *lex specialis* to article 3(2), but provides for cases in which member states have accepted responsibility to decide an application for international protection. In such cases, they may still make use of the safe third country rules, as confirmed by *Shiraz Baig Mirza v Bevándorlási és Állampolgársági Hivatal* (Ch 5 n 8).

16 European Database of Asylum Law, 'France-Bordeaux Adminstrative Court of Appeal' (September 2016) <www.asylumlawdatabase.eu/en/case-law/france-%E2%80%93-bordeaux-administrative-court-appeal-27-september-2016-16bx00997#content> accessed 20 August 2019; European Database of Asylum Law, 'France Rennes Admistrative Tribunal' (January 2018) <www.asylumlawdatabase.eu/en/case-law/france-%E2%80%93-rennes-administrative-tribunal-5-january-2018-application-no-1705747#content> accessed 1 July 2019.

17 VG München, 17 July 2019 – M 11 S 19.50722, M 11 S 19.50759. See also below, 5.3.2 for the discussion of substantive safeguards.

5.2.2 *Locating Protection Elsewhere in the 1951 Convention and in Human Rights Law Obligations of Non-return*

How do protection elsewhere arrangements like those of the Procedures Directive relate to the text in its context and in light of its object and purpose?

The text of the Convention does not contain express provisions on 'protection elsewhere'. The Convention is silent on the allocation of responsibility for deciding asylum applications and infamously dissociates refugee status from asylum,[18] that is, from a permission to stay in the territory of the state of refuge. What is more, 'protection elsewhere' cannot be anchored in the refugee definition of Article 1A(2) of the Convention. As discussed in Chapter 1, the refugee definition, in particular the protection clause, embodies the principle that international protection is surrogate human rights enfranchisement for lacking domestic protection. In a modern understanding, the text of the protection clause refers to protection in the country of nationality, so that the clause cannot be interpreted to apply to another country without conflicting with the text. This means that 'protection elsewhere' cannot be anchored in the Convention's eligibility criteria. In other words, eligibility for refugee status has to be independent of any finding on available protection in a third country.

Although express provisions are absent, there are discreet textual hints to 'protection elsewhere' in the Convention. As noted by UNHCR and, subsequently, Kay Hailbronner, the fact that the 1951 Convention prohibits penalising refugees for legal entry only when these come, in the words of the Convention, 'directly from a territory where their life or freedom was threatened in the sense of article 1', means that there is some basis for such concepts in the Convention;[19] the provision can be interpreted to mean that the Convention does not include a 'free choice' of the asylum country.[20] This interpretation on the lack of an individual right to choose an asylum country is also supported by practice of Western European States.[21] Furthermore, the Schedule to the

---

18 Hathaway, 'A Reconsideration of the Underlying Premise of Refugee Law' (Ch 2 n 149) 166; Goodwin-Gil and McAdam, *The Refugee in International Law* (Ch 1 n 15) 355; Michelle Foster, 'Protection Elsewhere: The Legal Implications of Requiring Refugees to Seek Protection in another State' (2007) 28 Michigan Journal of International Law 223, 226.

19 UN High Commissioner for Refugees, 'Background Note on the Safe Country Concept and Refugee Status', EC/SCP/68, 26 July 1991, para 12, <https://www.unhcr.org/excom/scip/3ae68ccec/background-note-safe-country-concept-refugee-status.html> accessed 1 July 2019.

20 Kay Hailbronner, 'The Concept of "Safe Country" and Expeditious Asylum Procedures: A Western European Perspective' (1993) 5 International Journal of Refugee Law 1.

21 For a list of case law to that effect, see James C Hathaway and Michelle Foster, *The Law of Refugee Status* (Ch 1 n 100) Chapter 1, Section 1.2.

1951 Convention does foresee the possibility that refugees establish residence in other countries than their original asylum countries, and makes provision to ensure their travel documents are renewed.[22] Finally, as Michelle Foster points out, Article 1A(2) requires refugees who possess multiple nationalities to seek the protection from a second country of nationality before any other country, and the Convention ceases to apply when a refugee enjoys the protection of another country of nationality.[23]

Several of these textual hints, meanwhile, can also be (and indeed have been) challenged as too weak as a basis for protection elsewhere policies.[24] Ultimately, therefore, it appears to be rather the lack of Convention provisions that make it difficult to challenge their application as a matter of principle. If 'protection elsewhere' policies are not expressly forbidden by the Convention, in line with the ICJ's Lotus principle,[25] their illegality should not be presumed. Indeed, policies on 'protection elsewhere' are long established in state practice, and reflected, among others, in states concluding bilateral agreements on return to other countries of asylum.[26] More recent practice spans, beyond the EU's Dublin Regulation to a US-Canadian agreement and the Australian law and practice on safe third countries.[27]

State practice, however, has for a long time been very heterogeneous.[28] A frequent problem that occurred were the so-called 'refugees in orbit', referring to refugees for whom no country was ready to accept responsibility for deciding an asylum application or granting asylum.[29] The mismatch between the silence of the 1951 Convention and state practice on 'protection elsewhere' was attempted to be remedied with the 1974 Conference on Territorial Asylum, tasked to draft a draft convention.[30] Article 1(3) of the Draft Convention

22 Eg, paragraph 6(3) of the Schedule to the 1951 Convention.

23 Foster, 'Protection Elsewhere: The Legal Implications of Requiring Refugees to Seek Protection in another State' (Ch 5 n 18) 231.

24 Violetta Moreno-Lax, 'The Legality of the "Safe Third Country" Notion Contested: Insights from the Law of Treaties' (Ch 1 n 102) 687.

25 *Lotus* (Ch 2 n 159) para 18, according to which 'restrictions on the independence of States cannot [...] be presumed'.

26 Atle Grahl-Madsen, 'Refuges in Orbit – Some Constructive Proposals' in *Atle Grahl-Madsen, The Land Beyond: Collected Essays on Refugee Law and Policy* (Martinus Nijhoff 2001).

27 Moreno-Lax, 'The Legality of the "Safe Third Country" Notion Contested: Insights from the Law of Treaties' (Ch 1 n 102).

28 Ibid.

29 Ibid.

30 UN General Assembly, 'Note on International Protection Addendum 1: Draft Convention on Territorial Asylum (Submitted by the High Commissioner)', UN Doc A/AC.96/508/Add.1 (1974).

provided that, 'Asylum shall not be refused by a Contracting State solely on the ground that it could be sought from another State', a provision controversial among some of the involved states.[31] The Convention would have also featured an obligation by states to use their best endeavours to grant refugees permission to remain in the territory of a contracting state.[32] Yet, the negotiations ended in fiasco, and a Convention was never adopted. However, the UNHCR EXCOM did elaborate criteria on protection elsewhere that were informed by the drafting process and which are relevant because EXCOM conclusions are part of the context for the object and purpose of the 1951 Convention, in conjunction with Article 31(2) of the VCLT.[33] The EXCOM conclusion does not serve to specify the dogmatic legal foundation for protection elsewhere policies in the 1951 Convention, but does serve to identify a general principle on protection elsewhere. While states should not, according to the conclusion, reject asylum applications solely on the ground that that another state *could* grant asylum, they may call upon applicants who have an established connection to another state to request asylum from that state.[34] Where an applicant has already enjoyed protection in another country and has lost that protection, other states need to step in.[35]

In line with the EXCOM conclusion, the UNHCR has carefully endorsed protection elsewhere arrangements, possibly with a view to shaping specific standards when these arrangements are further developed,[36] and to embracing their potentially beneficial effects on responsibility sharing,[37] as well as the avoidance of refugees 'in orbit'. The UNHCR has thus never questioned that rules on protection elsewhere are, in principle, lawful under the 1951 Convention.[38]

---

31 Ibid. comments by the governments of Canada, Denmark and Liechtenstein.

32 Ibid, Article 1(1).

33 Hathaway proposes consideration of the following agreements as part of the context: The Final Act of the Conference of Plenipotentiaries, which negotiated the Convention; the conclusions of the UNHCR Executive Committee (EXCOM); and the 2001 Declaration of State Parties. Hathaway, *The Rights of Refugees under International Law* (Ch 1 n 113) 74.

34 EXCOM, Conclusion No 15 (XXX) – 1979 – Refugees without an Asylum Country, (iv).

35 Ibid (k), for a discussion of the substantive standard, see next section.

36 For the emergence of protection elsewhere arrangements, see Foster, 'Protection Elsewhere: The Legal Implications of Requiring Refugees to Seek Protection in another State' (Ch 5 n 18).

37 As stated by Hathaway and others, 'Michigan Guidelines on Protection Elsewhere (Ch 1 n 14), an authoritative document compiled by international law scholars in an expert seminar, rules on protection elsewhere can potentially contribute to the fairer allocation of responsibilities among states.

38 UN High Commissioner for Refugees, 'UNHCR Position on Readmission Agreements, 'Protection Elsewhere' and Asylum Policy,' (1994) 3 European Series 2, 465.

Although there is still no uniform practice on protection elsewhere policies, there have been efforts to regulate them beyond the bilateral *ad-hoc* or written agreement. The most advanced and early multilateral attempt was the Dublin Convention of the European Community, negotiated over ten years prior to any common eligibility or procedural standards as part of the CEAS.[39] The Convention, however, did not contain rules on asylum in third states, rather, it conceded that European Community member states, 'retain the right, pursuant to its national laws, to send an applicant for asylum to a third State, in compliance with the provisions of the Geneva Convention, as amended by the New York Protocol.'[40]

Beyond the 1951 Convention, there are also no other international or EU law obligations that prohibit 'protection elsewhere' policies. In particular, human rights do not enshrine an individual right to choose a particular country of asylum. Thus, Article 14 of the UDHR does not encompass a substantive right to be granted asylum, but a procedural right to the asylum process.[41] For that matter, it would also be a misconstruction to derive from the EU Charter of Fundamental Rights a bar to protection elsewhere. According to Article 18 of the Charter, 'the right to asylum shall be guaranteed with due respect for the rules of the [1951 Convention]'. While the right to asylum in the Charter may well go beyond the procedural right of asylum enshrined in the UDHR,[42] its particular European content would, in the absence of international law requirements, appear to be determined by member states' constitutional traditions.

39 Convention Determining the State Responsible for Examining Applications for Asylum Lodged in One of the Member States of the European Communities (signed 19 August 1997) 254 OJ 1 (Dublin Convention). For EC member states, the Dublin Convention, adopted by the Schengen states, first contained the principle that an application for international protection could be rejected if an applicant had already applied for international protection in one of the signatory states, because these states were all considered safe against refoulement under the 1951 Convention, leading to two consecutive 'Dublin' regulations. For the emergence of various forms of 'protection elsewhere' rules, see Cathryn Costello, 'The Asylum Procedures Directive and the Proliferation of Safe Country Practices: Deterrence, Deflection and the Dismantling of International Protection?' (2005) 7 European Journal of Migration and Law 35.

40 Article 3(5) Dublin Convention.

41 Thomas Gammeltoft-Hansen and Hans Gammeltoft-Hansen, 'The Right to Seek – Revisited. On the UN Human Rights Declaration Article 14 and Access to Asylum Procedures in the EU' (2008) 10 European Journal of Migration and Law 439.

42 See Maria-Teresa Gil-Bazo, 'The Charter of Fundamental Rights of the European Union and the Right to be Granted Asylum in the Union's Law' (2008) 27 Refugee Survey Quarterly 33.

Meanwhile, states enshrining a right to asylum in their constitutions also rely on protection elsewhere rules.[43]

In sum, while there is no express textual home of 'protection elsewhere' policies in the 1951 Convention, such policies are, in principle, in accordance with the Convention and reflected in state practice. A shared underlying rationale of such practice is an extension of the principle of surrogacy, applied this time not to international protection as a surrogate for lacking domestic protection, but to a need of international protection being contingent on lacking international protection. Yet, that 'protection elsewhere' policies are, in principle, in accordance with international law does not mean that international law does not restrict their application. This is explored in the next section, which scrutinises the safeguards of the EU Procedures Directive's first country of asylum and safe third country rules in light of international law obligations.

5.3 The Substantive Safeguards of the First Country of Asylum and Safe Third Country Rules

5.3.1 *First Country of Asylum*

The following sections scrutinises the Procedures Directive's substantive safeguards for the first country of asylum and safe third country concepts in light of international law requirements.

The Procedures Directive contains different safeguards for the first country of asylum and safe third country concepts. According to Article 35, a country can be considered a first country of asylum for an applicant if:

> (a) he or she has been recognised in that country as a refugee and he or she can still avail himself/herself of that protection; or
> (b) he or she otherwise enjoys sufficient protection in that country, including benefiting from the principle of non-refoulement,
>
> provided that he or she will be readmitted to that country.
>
> In applying the concept of first country of asylum to the particular circumstances of an applicant, Member States may take into account

43 In particular, Germany, which is featured by Gil-Bazo as an example of a country where there is a right to be granted, rather than merely to seek, asylum, has amended its constitutions so as to include arrangements for protection elsewhere (Article 16a Grundgesetz).

> Article 38(1). The applicant shall be allowed to challenge the application of the first country of asylum concept to his or her particular circumstances.

The first requirement of Article 35(a) appears to be relatively clear, warranting the formal recognition of refugee status ('recognised [...] as refugee'). The bigger question, however, is what the requirements of Article 35(a) are in respect of the continuous enjoyment of international protection as refugee ('avail himself/herself of that protection') by the applicant. The provision has been applied little in practice and has not been adjudicated by the CJEU. Given Article 35(b) is an alternative for (a) it comes with the enjoyment of rights, including non-refoulement, 'protection' in Article 35(a), sentence 2, has to refer to the actual enjoyment of rights of refugee status, rather than a mere recognition of status without the actual enjoyment of refugee rights. For that reason, it is submitted that Article 35(a) refers to international protection within the meaning of international law and as outlined in Chapter 1 – surrogate human rights enfranchisement with the 1951 Convention and human rights law circumscribing the content of international protection.[44] This interpretation is consistent with the text of Article 35, sentence 2, according to which member states may take into account the requirements of Article 38, Procedures Directive when applying the first country of asylum concept to the particular circumstances of an applicant. Article 38(1)e), meanwhile, requires the possibility 'to request refugee status and, if found to be a refugee, to receive protection in accordance with the Geneva Convention', a requirement that is additional to safety and non-refoulement (Article 38(1)).[45] However, the provision remains inconsistent in making the consideration of such safeguards optional, rather than mandatory.

The current reform proposal for the Procedures Directive would potentially add more clarity on the first country of asylum concept. The late 2018 Council and Parliament proposal includes a recital that specifies that the full ambit of Convention provisions is referred to, but that lawful limitations and derogations of the Convention provisions do not bar considering the respective country a first country of asylum. A notable exception is geographic

44 A similar view appear to be taken by Jens Vedsted-Hansen, 'Asylum Procedures Directive 2013/32/EU', 1357 in Hailbronner and Thym (eds), *EU Immigration and Asylum Law – A Commentary* (Ch 1 n 7), stating that 'protection in the non-Member State that has recognised the applicant as a refugee will therefore have to be afforded in compliance with the standards laid down in the Geneva Convention'.

45 For the safeguards of Article 38, see Section 5.3.2 below.

limitations such as Turkey's, which does not include in the refugee definition non-Europeans, and would mean that Turkey could not be regarded as a first country of asylum:

> In the context of the application of the concepts of first country of asylum and safe third country, protection in accordance with the Geneva Convention should be interpreted as meaning that the third country in question has ratified and respects the Geneva Convention within the limits of the derogations or limitations made by that third country, as permitted under the Convention. In case of geographical limitations made by the third country, protection in accordance with the Geneva Convention cannot be considered to be ensured for persons who fall outside of the scope of application of the Convention.[46]

More challenging than Article 35(a) is the interpretation of Article 35(b), given the Directive does not specify the notion of 'sufficient protection'.

The text, by using the term 'otherwise' draws a connection to Article 35(a), appearing to warrant a comparable form of international protection other than refugee status. What is more, the text makes an indicative mention of non-refoulement as one of the rights to be enjoyed under such comparable form of international protection. In the context of the EU's own subsidiary protection regime, of which the Directive is part, the notion of 'sufficient protection' may for that reason be understood to refer to protection *comparable to the EU's subsidiary protection regime*.[47] This is also supported when comparing the Directive's text to its evolution from its former version, which referred to asylum or 'other reasons justifying the granting of protection, and can still avail himself of protection in that country that is in accordance with the relevant standards laid down in international law.'[48] However, because the Directive does not

46 Article 44(1), Council of the European Union, 'Proposal for a Regulation of the European Parliament and of the Council establishing a common procedure for international protection in the Union and repealing Directive 2013/32/EU', 6238/18 <http://www.statewatch.org/news/2018/mar/eu-council-asylum-procedures-asylum-6238-18.pdf> accessed 1 July 2019 (Procedures Directive Proposal 2018).

47 Vedsted-Hansen, 1357 in Hailbronner and Thym (eds), *EU Immigration and Asylum Law – A Commentary* (Ch 1 n 7), takes no position on this issue, but argues that the standards need to go beyond Article 38(1)(a)–(d), given these merely reflect non-refoulement obligations.

48 Amended proposal for a Council Directive on minimum standards on procedures in Member States for granting and withdrawing refugee status, COM/2002/0326 final, OJ C 291E, 143–171.

refer to the scope of rights granted under its own subsidiary protection status, the scope of rights under the notion of 'sufficient protection' remains unclear. As UNHCR cautioned in its comment on the 2005 Procedures Directive (which used the identical wording to the recast), EU member states in practice had very different understandings of what protection in a first country of asylum had to entail, so that the notion was inapt to harmonise international law compliant practice.[49]

The late 2018 recast proposal of the Procedures Directive for the first time specifies the meaning of 'sufficient protection', stating that:

> Sufficient protection means:
> (a) protection in accordance with the Geneva Convention; or
> (b) protection that meets the following criteria:
> (i) a right to lawfully stay in the territory of the third country;
> (ii) access to means of subsistence sufficient to maintain an adequate standard of living;
> (iii) access to emergency healthcare and essential treatment of illnesses; and
> (iv) access to elementary education under the same conditions as for the nationals of the third country.[50]

Such understanding raises important issues, however. First, if the notion of sufficient protection does not refer to the EU subsidiary protection but to international protection comparable to refugee status, what would be the necessary scope of requirements for Article 35(b) from the international law perspective? It is submitted that the requirements for the first country of asylum notion should not fall below the 1951 Convention safeguards for other notions of 'protection elsewhere'. This is because these requirements are, through domestic law of member states, applied to individuals who have, typically after an assessment of risks of harm in the state of nationality, enjoyed refugee status or refuge as warranted by Article 35(b), and would otherwise be treated less favourably

49 UN High Commissioner for Refugees, 'UNHCR Provisional Comments on the Proposal for a Council Directive on Minimum Standards on Procedures in Member States for Granting and Withdrawing Refugee Status' (Council Document 14203/04, Asile 64, of 9 November 2004), 10 February 2005.

50 Article 44(1a) Council of the European Union, 'Procedures Directive Proposal 2018' (Ch 5 n 46). For a commentary on the reform proposal in light of international law requirements, see Anna Lübbe, 'GEAS-Reform: Standardsenkung bei den Drittstaatenkonzepten?' (2018) 14 Zeitschrift für Ausländerrecht und Ausländerpolitik 381.

than those for whom no assessment of their status has yet taken place. However, the definition of 'sufficient protection' omits important 1951 Convention obligations, such as access to public relief on the same conditions as nationals,[51] and its access provision on education falls short of Article 22(2) of the Convention.[52]

Second, the foreseen scope of 'sufficient protection' would also fall below the scope of human rights law obligations by the respective host country. For instance, the right to the highest attainable standard of health would at the very least require, in countries with limited resources, non-discrimination in access to available health care and access to essential primary healthcare.[53]

Nonetheless, are the Procedures Directive's requirements of the first country of asylum concept congruent with potential restrictions on the application of such concept by the 1951 Convention? This question will be discussed alongside the Convention's requirements for other 'protection elsewhere' concepts, in particular the safe third country notion, in the next section.

5.3.2 *Safe Third Country*

5.3.2.1 The Procedural and Substantive Requirements under the EU Procedures Directive

This section explores the substantive safeguards of the Procedures Directive's safe third country concept, in particular its accordance with international law.

Article 38(1), Procedures Directive requires that the authorities of a member state may only apply the safe third country concept if satisfied that the asylum seeker, will in the receiving states, 'be treated in accordance with the following principles':

> (a) life and liberty are not threatened on account of race, religion, nationality, membership of a particular social group or political opinion;
> (b) there is no risk of serious harm as defined in Directive 2011/95/EU;
> (c) the principle of non-refoulement in accordance with the Geneva Convention is respected;

---

51 Article 23 of the Convention. On the interpretation of that provision, see Hathaway, *The Rights of Refugees under International Law* (Ch 1 n 113) 800–813.

52 Stating that, 'The Contracting States shall accord to refugees treatment as favourable as possible, and, in any event, not less favourable than that accorded to aliens generally in the same circumstances, with respect to education other than elementary education and, in particular, as regards access to studies, the recognition of foreign school certificates, diplomas and degrees, the remission of fees and charges and the award of scholarships'.

53 See Committee on Economic Social and Cultural Rights, 'General Comment No 14, The right to the highest attainable standard of health' (Ch 2 n 44) and John Tobin, *The Right to Health in International Law* (Oxford University Press 2012).

(d) the prohibition of removal, in violation of the right to freedom from torture and cruel, inhuman or degrading treatment as laid down in international law, is respected; and
(e) the possibility exists to request refugee status and, if found to be a refugee, to receive protection in accordance with the Geneva Convention.

In addition, the Article 38(2) Directive obliges member states to adopt national laws with rules 'requiring a *connection* between the applicant and the third country concerned on the basis of which it would be *reasonable* for that person to go to that country' as well as rules that specify how the relevant authorities, 'satisfy themselves that the safe third country concept may be applied to a particular country or to a particular applicant' (Article 38(2)(b)–(c)).[54]

What do the requirements under Article 38 entail? So far, there has been no guidance by CJEU case law on the issue, after the Court denied it had jurisdiction to adjudicate the EU-Turkey statement, an agreement that is, according to the Court, one of the member states.[55]

First, the Directive does not further specify the required connection by Article 38(2)(b) between a country and an alleged safe third country. The requirement that this connection must make it 'reasonable' for the applicant to return to that country is not to be conflated with the widely-applied reasonableness test discussed in Chapter 3 in connection with the IPA, involving considerations of economic hardship. Rather, it appears to be a creating a flexible minimum standard on the required connection between the applicant and the country in question.[56] Thus, it would appear that mere passage through a country would not establish a connection that would make return reasonable.[57]

54 Emphasis added.

55 Case C-208/17 *NF v European Council* ECLI:EU:C:2018:705 [2017] digital reports. On this order, see, eg, Sergio Carrera, Leonhard den Hertog and Marco Stefan, 'It wasn't me! The Luxembourg Court Orders on the EU-Turkey Refugee Deal' (2017) <www.ceps.eu/system/files/EU-Turkey%20Deal.pdf> accessed 1 July 2019.

56 On the requirement of a connection, see Anna Lübbe, 'Migrationspartnerschaften: Verweisung auf Transitstaaten ohne Rücksicht auf die Familieneinheit?' (2017) 13 Zeitschrift für Ausländerrecht und Ausländerpolitik 15 and Anna Lübbe, 'GEAS-Reform: Standardsenkung bei den Drittstaatenkonzepten?' (2018) 14 Zeitschrift für Ausländerrecht und Ausländerpolitik 381.

57 UNHCR noted in its 2010 comments on the proposal for a recast Procedures Directive that transit would be insufficient to establish a meaningful connection between the applicant and another state; see UN High Commissioner for Refugees, 'UNHCR comments on the European Commission's proposal for a Directive of the European Parliament and of the Council on minimum standards on procedures in Member States for granting and withdrawing international protection', COM/2009/554 (2010), 34 <www.unhcr.org/4f35256c9.pdf> accessed 20 October 2016.

Few member states have created domestic legal rules on the required connection and methodology for the application of the first country of asylum and safe third country concepts. Dutch law is a notable exception. The Circular on Foreigners deems there to be three alternative criteria for establishing such connection, namely: whether or not the spouse or partner of the applicant has the nationality of that country; whether there is immediate family of the applicant residing in the country; or whether the alien has previously stayed in that country.[58] In contrast, German law, in respect of the required connection, merely provides that an applicant must have stayed in a particular country for three months,[59] while Swedish law does not feature any requirements dealing with the text of the Directive.[60] French law only provides that an application for international protection may be rejected as inadmissible if a non-EU country provides 'effective protection'.[61]

In respect of Article 38(2)c), the text does not provide further clarity what an acceptable methodology is by which the authorities may satisfy themselves as to whether or not the country in question is a safe third country; one obvious element would be the personal interview,[62] unless a state is deemed generally safe. The Directive does not require member states to consider the application of the first country of asylum concept on a case-by-case basis, but allows the 'national designation of countries considered to be generally safe'.[63] However, in both cases applicants need to be able to challenge the application of the safe third country requirements to their individual case.[64]

Article 39, meanwhile, specifies criteria for countries that are – politically speaking – European countries, as defined by membership in the Council of Europe:

58 Vreemdelingencirculaire 2000 (C) of 1 December 2017, section 6.3.

59 §27(3) Asylgesetz.

60 5 kap. 1 b § första stycket 3 Utlänningslagen.

61 Article L723-11, Code de l'entrée et du séjour des étrangers et du droit d'asile (Ch 2 n 94).

62 The Procedures Directive only specifies, in Article 14(2), the conditions under which a personal interview may be omitted in procedures 'on the substance' of an application for international protection, thus leaving a gap as to whether such interview may be omitted in the application of the safe third country and first country of asylum concepts. However, UNHCR deplored, in a 2010 comparative study on the application of the Procedures Directive, the fact that the domestic law of several member states allows the omission of a personal interview in such cases. UN High Commissioner for Refugees, UNHCR, 'Improving Asylum Procedures: Comparative Analysis and Recommendations for Law and Practice – Detailed Research on Key Asylum Procedures Directive Provisions' (2010) <http://www.refworld.org/pdfid/4c63e52d2.pdf> accessed 20 October 2016.

63 Article 38(2)b).

64 Article 38(2)c).

(a) it has ratified and observes the provisions of the Geneva Convention without any geographical limitations;
(b) it has in place an asylum procedure prescribed by law; and
(c) it has ratified the European Convention for the Protection of Human Rights and Fundamental Freedoms and observes its provisions, including the standards relating to effective remedies.

The requirements of Article 38(1) can helpfully be divided into two categories.

First, according to (Article 38(1)(a)–(d)), the relevant country must be safe in the individual circumstances of the applicant. It is clear not only from the text but also from the evolution of the safe third country concept[65] that this goes beyond the obligation of non-refoulement under Article 33 of the Convention',[66] but mirrors non-refoulement obligations under both Article 33 of the 1951 Convention and of human rights law. In contrast, Article 38 requires that the applicant must not have a well-founded fear of being persecuted for a Convention reason and be protected against return to any territory in respect of which he or she has such fear (a; c). He must also not face a risk harm relevant for the inclusion criteria of subsidiary status and for human rights non-refoulement obligations more widely, as well as be protected against return to any territory where he or she would face such risk (b; d).

65 Thus, previous arrangements on protection elsewhere only provided that a safe third country must provide 'effective protection [...] against refoulement, within the meaning of the Geneva Convention'. Council of the European Union, 'Council Resolution of 30 November 1992 on Manifestly Unfounded Applications for Asylum' ('London Resolution'), 30 November 1992. The 'London Resolutions' of the European Council first talked about 'host third countries' and influenced the drafting of the Regulation.

66 This requirement is a notable contrast with the Dublin Regulation. It was only in 2003 that the rules of the Dublin Convention became EU law – with the adoption of the Dublin Regulation. The Regulation did include a 'sovereignty clause' according to which any member state could, if it wanted to, accept responsibility for deciding an application for international protection. Yet, the regulation contained no provision on obligations of non-return to another signatory state, because those states were all considered 'safe' – in the sense of abiding by the principle of non-refoulement – and because they were all signatory states to instruments of the Common European Asylum System. According to Recital 2: 'The European Council [...] agreed to work towards establishing a Common European Asylum System, based on the full and inclusive application of the Geneva Convention relating to the Status of Refugees of 28 July 1951, as supplemented by the New York Protocol of 31 January 1967, thus ensuring that nobody is sent back to persecution, ie maintaining the principle of non-refoulement. In this respect, and without affecting the responsibility criteria laid down in this Regulation, Member States, all respecting the principle of non-refoulement, are considered as safe countries for third-country nationals.'

Second, however, it is clear that Article 38 exceeds a mere conceptualisation of protection as safety, given Article 38(1)(d) requires consideration of whether an applicant could *request refugee status* and obtain *'protection in accordance with the Geneva Convention'*. With reference to Chapter 2 and from an international law perspective, the meaning of 'protection' appears relatively clear: international protection is surrogate human rights enfranchisement with rights under the 1951 Convention and human rights law. However, the exact scope of 'protection in accordance with the Geneva Convention' is less clear from the internal systematic of the Directive, because Article 39 requires European Safe Third Countries to 'observe the provisions of' the 1951 Convention. Conversely, does this indicate Article 38 requires less? Given the declaratory nature of refugee status determination and because the declaration of a Safe Third Country is a general, rather than an individual, assessment, it is submitted that the standards should not differ from those of First Countries of Asylum. Indeed, this also appears to be the approach followed by the late 2018 proposal of the Recast Procedures Directive, which refers, in both the first country of asylum and safe third country concepts, to the notion of 'sufficient protection'. That notion, however, remains flawed for a number of reasons, as discussed in the previous section.

Yet, does international law require that the receiving country in question adheres to all Convention obligations under Articles 2–34, either in fact, or in fact *and* in law, by ratifying the 1951 Convention? To answer this question, the next section will first scrutinise the 1951 Convention obligations on safe third countries.

5.3.2.2 The Procedural and Substantive Requirements of Safe Third Country Rules under the 1951 Convention and Human Rights Law

Earliest commentary on the international law requirements for first countries of asylum and other protection elsewhere arrangements has in particularly come from the UNHCR and its EXCOM, relevant as context for the interpretation of the 1951 Convention. Both have focused on substantive rather than procedural safeguards. The EXCOM, in its Conclusion No 58 (XL), stated that individuals could be returned to a country of first asylum if –

> (i) they are protected there against refoulement and
> (ii) they are permitted to remain there and to be treated in accordance with recognized basic human standards until a durable solution is found for them. Where such return is envisaged, UNHCR may be requested to assist in arrangements for the re-admission and reception of the persons concerned;

> [...] It is recognised that there may be exceptional cases in which a refugee or asylum-seeker may justifiably claim that he has reason to fear persecution or that his physical safety or freedom are endangered in a country where he previously found protection. Such cases should be given favourable consideration by the authorities of the State where he requests asylum.[67]

In other words, the EXCOM first required *safety*, which includes the absence of a well-founded fear of being persecuted for a Convention reason, as relevant for the 1951 Convention's non-refoulement obligation (paragraph [g] of the above) and protection against non-refoulement to another country than the country of first asylum ([i] of the above). Second, the EXCOM also required the 'treatment in accordance with basic human standards', which are not further specified, but exceed the absence of harm and the protection against refoulement, given these are expressly mentioned ([ii] of the above). The requirement of 'durable solutions' – a UNHCR term to designate voluntary repatriation, local integration or resettlement – is potentially the most far reaching, because all three durable solutions are tied to further UNHCR and EXCOM guidance.[68]

The EXCOM conclusion is notable because it appears to exceed the 1951 Convention obligation of non-refoulement under Article 33. Article 33 typically is applicable in the context of first countries of asylum for two reasons. First, the Article merely necessitates a refugee to be within or subject to the jurisdiction of a contracting state, rather than physical presence, lawful presence, lawful stay or durable residence, like other Convention obligations.[69] The requirements for jurisdiction have evolved considerably in international law, spanning beyond the traditional territorial control to exercise of physical power or control over persons, even in extraterritorial settings.[70] In the context of migration control, jurisdiction has been established, for instance, in the

67 EXCOM Conclusion No 58 (XL) (1989).

68 In respect of local integration, see eg, EXCOM Conclusion No 104 (LVI) (2005); on resettlement, see UN High Commissioner for Refugees, UNHCR Resettlement Handbook (2011) <www.refworld.org.es/pdfid/4ecb973c2.pdf> accessed 1 July 2019; on return, see, eg, Executive Committee Conclusion No 101 (LV) – 2004, Conclusion on Legal Safety Issues in the Context of Voluntary Repatriation of Refugees, 8 October 2004.

69 For the required levels of attachment, see above, Section 2.2.2, with reference to Hathaway, *The Rights of Refugees under Internal Law*.

70 In the European context, see in particular *Al-Skeini and Others v United Kingdom* ECHR 2011-IV 99. For the evolution and requirements of the (extraterritorial) control criteria, see Milanovic, *Extraterritorial Application of Human Rights Treaties: Law, Principles, and Policy* (Ch 2 n 16).

context of interception and pushbacks,[71] so that the application of third country rules, by immigration officers of a contracting state, would appear to be unproblematic for triggering the Convention's jurisdiction requirement.

Second, Article 33 is applicable to first country of asylum contexts or, for that matter, other 'protection elsewhere' arrangements, because of the declaratory nature of refugee status, and independent of the legal status a country of first asylum has accorded to an individual. As argued by the UNHCR in its authoritative Handbook on Procedures and Criteria for Determining Refugee Status:

> A person is a refugee within the meaning of the 1951 Convention as soon as he fulfils the criteria contained in the definition. This would necessarily occur prior to the time at which his refugee status is formally determined. Recognition of his refugee status does not therefore make him a refugee but declares him to be one. He does not become a refugee because of recognition, but is recognized because he is a refugee.[72]

The declaratory nature of refugee status determination is also unmistakably recognised by the Qualification Directive.[73] It flows from that declaratory nature that 'protection elsewhere' concepts, which are usually procedural rules prior to a formal refugee status determination, may be applied to refugees, who are entitled to the rights of the 1951 Convention, including Article 33, by virtue of refugee status.

Article 33 provides that contracting parties –

> shall not expel or return ('refouler') a refugee in any manner whatsoever to the frontiers of territories where his life or freedom would be threatened on account of his race, religion, nationality, membership of a particular social group or political opinion.

The predominant interpretation of the scope of the Convention's non-refoulement obligations is that this obligation mirrors Article 1A(2) of the

71 *Hirsi Jamaa and Other v Italy* ECHR 2012 97 paras 125–126. On this question, see also Céline Trevisanut, 'The Principle of Non-Refoulement and the De-Territorialization of Border Control at Sea' (2014) 27 *Leiden Journal of International Law* 661.

72 UN High Commissioner for Refugees, 'Handbook on Refugee Status Determination' (Ch 2 n 111) para 28.

73 Recital 21, 'The recognition of refugee status is a declaratory act'.

Convention; it extends to all refugees, and the threat to 'life or freedom' are examples of the harm relevant to the notion of being persecuted, rather than exceeding that notion.[74] The Convention's non-refoulement duty applies both directly, in case of return to a country where such harm would occur, and indirectly, in case of return to a country that would in turn expel the individual to a source of harm. Thus, in the context of protection elsewhere rules, Article 33 would appear to prohibit return to a country in which it is not assured that authorities will assess refugee status in good faith[75] and permit the individual to reside in the territory if refugee status is assessed with a positive outcome. Article 33 would not, however, apply to risks of harm that do not reach the threshold of harm relevant for the notion of the well-founded fear of being persecuted. Returning to the EXCOM Conclusion No 58 (XL), this would mean that the requirement to only return individuals if they are treated 'in accordance with recognized basic human standards' is not directly derived from the Convention, but *exceeds* the Convention's non-refoulement obligation.

The EXCOM conclusion, according to which safeguards for the application of the 1951 Convention should exceed the 1951 Convention's non-refoulement obligation under Article 33, is also shared by other position papers of UNHCR.

---

74 See Hathaway, The Rights of Refugees under International Law (Ch 1 n 113) 305, with reference to the early commentary on the Convention by Grahl-Madsen, Atle Grahl-Madsen, *Commentary on the Refugee Convention 1951* (1997 Republished by the Division of International Protection of the United Nations High Commissioner for Refugees) 102.

As a notable exception, Lauterpacht and Bethlehem argued for an understanding of non-refoulement that exceeds the relevant harm in Article 1A(2) of the 1951 Convention, thus including 'a threat to life or freedom [that] may arise other than in consequence of persecution'. However, the argument has been questioned, because it is grounded in the expansion of UNHCR's mandate, and because it does not add anything to a modern understanding of relevant harm for the notion of 'being persecuted'. Elihu Lauterpacht and Daniel Bethlehem, 'The Scope and Content of the Principle of Non-Refoulement: Opinion' in Erika Feller, Volker Türk and Frances Nicholson (eds), *Refugee Protection in International Law: UNHCR's Global Consultations on International Protection* (Cambridge University Press 2003) and Hathaway, *The Rights of Refugees under International Law* (Ch 1 n 113) 305–306.

75 Foster notes that the sending state must ascertain that the receiving state has an accessible RSD procedure with an independent review process, and that it 'respects the "true and autonomous meaning" of the refugee definition in Article 1 of the Convention.' Michelle Foster, 'Responsibility Sharing or Shifting?' (2008) 25 *Refuge* 64, 71. A similar argument is made by Guild and Moreno-Lax, 'Current Challenges for International Refugee Law, With a Focus on EU Policies and EU Co-Operation with the UNHCR', Directorate-General for External Policies of Union, Briefing Paper, EXPO/B/DROI/2012/15 (2013) referring to 'countries without asylum laws' as a challenge.

In 1996, the UNHCR elaborated additional criteria and for the first time qualified the term 'protection'. In an expert seminar on planned EU 'safe third country' legislation, the UNHCR cautioned that states sending individuals to other countries when applying protection elsewhere policies need to consider whether the country in question grants fair refugee status determination procedures; and, after such procedures, grants '*effective and adequate* protection'.[76] In 2002, the UNHCR organised an expert roundtable to define criteria for 'effective protection'.[77] These criteria, known as the 'Lisbon Conclusions', necessitate that:

> there is no likelihood of persecution, of refoulement or of torture or other cruel and degrading treatment;
>
> there is no other real risk to the life of the person[s] concerned;
>
> there is a genuine prospect of an accessible durable solution in or from the asylum country, within a reasonable timeframe;
>
> pending a durable solution, stay is permitted under conditions which protect against arbitrary expulsion and deprivation of liberty and which provide for adequate and dignified means of subsistence;
>
> the unity and integrity of the family is ensured; and
>
> the specific protection needs of the affected persons, including those deriving from age and gender, are able to be identified and respected.[78]

The first two requirements capture the scope of the non-refoulement obligation of Article 33 of the 1951 Convention as well as non-refoulement obligations

76 UN High Commissioner for Refugees, 'Considerations on the 'Safe Third Country' Concept', presented at the EU Seminar on the Associated States as Safe Third Countries in Asylum Legislation (July 1996) <www.refworld.org/docid/3ae6b3268.html> accessed 20 October 2016. The list of considerations also includes 'ratification of and compliance with the international refugee instruments, in particular compliance with the principle of non-refoulement; ratification of and compliance with international and regional human rights instruments; readiness to permit asylum-seekers to remain while their claims are being examined on the merits; adherence to recognized basic human rights standards for the treatment of asylum-seekers and refugees; and, notably, the State's willingness and practice to accept returned asylum-seekers and refugees, consider their asylum claims in a fair manner and provide effective and adequate protection.

77 UN High Commissioner for Refugees, 'Summary Conclusions on the Concept of 'Effective Protection' in the Context of Secondary Movements of Refugees and Asylum-Seekers' (Lisbon Expert Roundtable, 9–10 December 2002), February 2003 (2003).

78 Feller E, 'Statement by Ms. Erika Feller, Director, Department of International Protection, at the Fifty-Fifth session of the Executive Committee of the High Commissioner's Programme, 7 October 2004' <www.unhcr.org/429d6f8e4.html> accessed 20 October 2016.

of human rights law. The remaining requirements, however, exceed non-refoulement obligations. It is notable that these standards are not modeled after obligations under Articles 2–34 of the Convention.

While both the UNHCR and its EXCOM share the legal opinion that the application of 'protection elsewhere' arrangement necessitates safeguards beyond non-refoulement under refugee and human rights law, it is not clear whether they are of the opinion that these are international law requirements and, if so, where they are anchored in the 1951 Convention or other relevant instruments. This question has also been posed by abundant past academic debate,[79] which also suggested somewhat different standards, albeit almost all beyond the scope of Article 33.[80]

First, the *Michigan Guidelines on Protection Elsewhere*, an expert paper compiled by international legal scholars, takes the view that states which apply protection elsewhere policies need to ensure that the transferred refugee, 'will in practice enjoy rights in line with the requirements of Arts. 2–34 of the Convention.'[81] Before relying on protection elsewhere policies, the *Guidelines* assert, there must be a 'good faith empirical assessment by the state which proposes to effect the transfer ("sending state") that refugees defined by Art. 1 will in practice enjoy the rights set by Arts. 2–34 of the Convention in the receiving state'.[82]

---

79 Eg, Legomsky, 'Secondary Refugee Movements and the Return of Asylum Seekers to Third Countries: The Meaning of Effective Protection' (Ch 1 n 102) and the literature cited therein.

80 The exception is Goodwil-Gil and McAdam, *The Refugee in International Law* (Ch 1 n 15) 393 who state that, 'From an International Law Perspective, the principal issue is the safety of State to which return of the asylum seeker is contemplated. Other relevant considerations include the procedural safeguards in place in the third State, and the connection between the receiving State and the asylum seeker.' The authors also list some basic requirements, in particular the enjoyment of 'fundamental human rights', due process, and that rights to a remedy are respected. These requirements, however, are not additional to the 1951 Convention but an indication of sufficient protection 'in order for states to observe their non-refoulement [...] obligations' [under the Convention and human rights law, AN].

81 Hathaway and others, 'The Michigan Guidelines on Protection Elsewhere' (Ch 1 n 14).

82 Also Hathaway, *The Rights of Refugees under International Law* (Ch 1 n 113) 332. This argument has also been made in court cases not on transfers to third countries, but on transfers from one EU country to another, as part of the Dublin Regulation. In particular, in *TI v UK*, the ECtHR stated that the sending state needs to ensure that the receiving cases would 'comply with its obligations under the [1951] Geneva Convention' – which evidently exceed Art 33. See also Walter Kälin; Martina Caroni; Lukas Heim, 'Article 33, para 1', 1382–1386 in Zimmermann; Dörschner; Machts (eds), *The 1951 Convention Relating to the Status of Refugees and its 1967 Protocol- A Commentary* (Ch 1 n 42).

Meanwhile, the approach to the substantive requirements faces several challenges. The first is of textual nature, *expressio unius est exclusio alterius*. Were every norm of the Convention to incur non-refoulement obligations, would the Convention not state so, rather than limiting the scope to risk of being persecuted, as made by the text of Article 33? A further problem with the approach of the *Michigan Guidelines* is the Convention's structure, which makes refugee rights contingent on the level of attachment in the asylum state, and knows different standards of treatment for different rights, with non-discrimination between refugees and nationals at the very end of the spectrum.[83] This makes it difficult to test, in practice, compliance of the Convention in relation to a first country of asylum. It also means that a refugee will not enjoy all Convention rights at the moment a protection elsewhere is applied but, depending on the circumstances of the case, only those that are subject to a state's jurisdiction or those that necessitate physical presence on the territory of a state party, including, among others, non-refoulement, physical safety, freedom from arbitrary detention and non-penalisation for irregular entry, freedom of religion and the Convention's provisions on the basic necessities of food, shelter and healthcare.

Foster, in an accompanying document to the *Michigan Guidelines*, suggests applying to the 1951 Convention the legal rationale of Article 3 cases before the ECtHR, which held that the Convention's object and purpose would preclude contracting states being resolved from their obligations, including from not exposing applicants to a real risk of inhuman and degrading treatment, by way of cooperating with other states.[84] Similarly, another academic commentator, Stephen Legomsky, argued in an extensive expert legal opinion for the UNHCR, that the substantive standard for safe third country concepts was determined by the international law principle that 'no state may knowingly assist another state to do what international law would forbid the first state from doing on its own'.[85] The principle is reflected in the ILC's Articles on

83 See above, 2.2.2. The Michigan Guidelines also make reference to this: 'The assessment of respect for refugee rights shall take account of the fact that most such rights are neither immediately owed nor absolute in character. In particular, the rights owed to a refugee increase as the level of attachment to the protecting state increases over time'. For the complicity principle see also Helmut Philipp Aust, *Complicity and the Law of State Responsibility* (Cambridge University Press 2011).

84 Foster, 'Protection Elsewhere: The Legal Implications of Requiring Refugees to Seek Protection in another State' (Ch 5 n 18) 268, with reference to *TI v the United Kingdom*.

85 Stephen H Legomsky, 'Secondary Refugee Movements and the Return of Asylum Seekers to Third Countries: The Meaning of Effective Protection' (Ch 1 n 102), 620.

State Responsibility, relevant because they may serve to indicate the *opinio iuris* element required for customary international law, or influence customary law as an authoritative judicial opinion within the meaning of Article 38d) of the ICJ Statute.[86] Article 16, according to which a state is internationally responsible for an internationally wrongful act by another state if it aids or assists that state in committing the wrongful act 'with knowledge of the circumstance of the internationally wrongful act', and if the act would be internationally wrongful if it had been committed by the complicit state itself.[87] Article 16 requires, according to the commentary of the ILC, that state organs, 'intended, by the aid or assistance given, to facilitate the occurrence of the wrongful conduct.'[88]

The rationale of applying this principle to the removal of an alien (the destination being a territory in which relevant rights are not protected) is that removal is *instrumental* to the international law violations occurring.[89] According to Legomsky, the complicity principle is underlying the prohibition of Article 33 of the 1951 Convention and reflected in non-return obligations of human rights law, but given the Convention's other obligations in Articles 2–34, the principle would also bar return in case of violation of another Convention provision.[90] Given the ILC's requirements of knowledge of a violation, Legomsky proposes that 'the degree of certainty required by the word "knowingly" should vary inversely with the importance of the individual right' of the 1951 Convention.[91] As some of the Convention obligations are contingent on a future prospect of lawful stay, the requirement of knowingly contributing to a violation could not be met for these obligations, so that they are exempt from barring return.[92]

While the argument is compelling, it also has important flaws. First, the ILC Articles on State Responsibility distinguish between the international

86 Statute of the International Court of Justice (signed 18 April 1946) 33, USTS 993. On the legal status of the Article, see James Crawford, Alain Pellet and Simon Olleson (eds), *The Law of International Responsibility* (Oxford University Press 2010) using the Articles as customary law rules.

87 International Law Commission, Report of the International Law Commission on the work of its fifty-third session, A/56/10 (2001), 66.

88 Ibid. ILC Commentary to Art 16, para 5.

89 Ibid. The ILC states that Article 16 does not require a particular intensity of contribution beyond the contribution having to be significant.

90 Legomsky, 'Secondary Refugee Movements and the Return of Asylum Seekers to Third Countries: The Meaning of Effective Protection' (Ch 1 n 102) 624.

91 Ibid 646.

92 Ibid.

wrongful act on the one hand, and the responsibility for it on the other hand.[93] It is therefore questionable whether the ILC Articles can be construed to define the scope of international law obligations in the first place.[94] What is more, the ILC articles could only be a source of law were they to reflect the *opinio iuris* and predominant practice of customary law. Yet, state practice does not support such wide scope of non-return obligations, even though many countries clearly warrant more than safety.[95]

Second, it is misconstrued to derive from the complicity principle in the ILC Articles the adequate scope of non-return obligation of human rights law. The difficulty lies, rather than in establishing knowledge of a future breach, in the fact that the complicity principle is triggered if the act would be internationally wrongful if committed by the (allegedly complicit) State. Were the complicity principle to circumscribe the scope of non-refoulement obligations, every act that would be a human rights violation by the receiving state would imply an obligation of non-refoulement. However, liability for return occurs under the *legal obligations of the sending state*, and may be a separate breach under a different legal obligation than the obligation breached by the receiving state. To illustrate this, it is helpful to again point to the ECtHR decision in *Soering*, discussed in the context of Chapter 2:

> [...] the decision by a Contracting State to extradite a fugitive may give rise to an issue under Article 3 (art. 3), and hence engage the responsibility of that State under the Convention, where substantial grounds have been shown for believing that the person concerned, if extradited, faces a real risk of being subjected to torture or to inhuman or degrading treatment or punishment in the requesting country. The establishment of such responsibility inevitably involves an assessment of conditions in the requesting country against the standards of Article 3 (art. 3) of the Convention. Nonetheless, there is no question of adjudicating on or establishing the responsibility of the receiving country, whether under

93 On this distinction, see Eric David, 'Primary and Secondary Rules' in Crawford et al (eds), *The Law of International Responsibility* (Ch 5 n 86).

94 The author credits Dominik Steiger for this point.

95 In addition to the Procedures Directive, there is also practice from other contexts where the required safeguards exceed non-refoulement obligations under Article 33. In particular, Australian legislation warrants compliance with relevant human rights standards in order that a country be considered a safe third country. In contrast, the US and Canada appear to be limiting the safe third country requirement to safety. See Goodwin Gil and McAdam, *The Refugee in International Law* (Ch 1 n 15) 405–406.

> general international law, under the Convention or otherwise. *In so far as any liability under the Convention is or may be incurred, it is liability incurred by the extraditing Contracting State by reason of its having taken action which has as a direct consequence the exposure of an individual to proscribed ill-treatment.*[96]

Indeed, it is the very distribution of legal responsibility incurred by the sending state that has led the ECtHR to read non-return obligations into Article 3 (and, theoretically, also in other Convention provisions) only in exceptional cases.[97] This is also visible in the court's case law on protection elsewhere, which will be explored in the subsequent paragraphs.

Obligations of non-return under the ECHR have evolved considerably to prescribe safeguards for protection elsewhere,[98] yet, they remain centered on Article 3 and therefore fall short of the full ambit of Articles 2–34 of the 1951 Convention. In *MSS v Belgium and Greece*, the court developed criteria for engaging responsibility under Article 3 of the Convention in situations of 'serious deprivation or want incompatible with human dignity'.[99] The applicant, an Afghan asylum seeker, had lived for several months in extreme poverty, unable to cater for basic needs such as housing, food and hygiene, and was under threat of attack and robbery. In addition to finding a violation by the receiving state, Greece, the court found the sending state, Belgium, to be in violation of Article 3, because it had knowingly exposed the applicant to such conditions.[100] In its finding, the court attached weight to the fact that asylum seekers were generally vulnerable and dependent on state support.[101] More recently, the court made clear that Article 3 can also be engaged in cases of inadequate accommodation (rather than a total lack of accommodation). In *Tarakhel v Switzerland*, the court found Switzerland in violation of Article 3 for returning a family to Italy despite the fact that a 'significant number of asylum seekers removed to that country may be left without accommodation or accommodated

96 *Soering v the United Kingdom* (Ch 3 n 118) para 91, emphasis added.

97 See above, Section 3.3.4 and note 117.

98 For a more detailed analysis, see Helen Lambert, '"Safe Third Country" in the European Union: An Evolving Concept in International Law and Implications for the UK' (2012) 26 *Journal of Immigration, Asylum and Nationality Law* 318.

99 *MSS v Belgium and Greece* (Ch 4 n 182) para 253.

100 Ibid para 367.

101 Paragraphs 252–253 with reference to *Budina v Russia* (Ch 4 n 181) and Council Directive 2003/9/EC of 27 January 2003 laying down minimum standards for the reception of asylum seekers [2003] OJ L31/18.

in overcrowded facilities without any privacy, or even in insalubrious or violent conditions'.[102]

In *Sufi and Elmi v United Kingdom,* the ECtHR applied its *MSS* decision to the conditions in a state not signatory to the ECHR, notably, to refugee camps in Kenya, although arguably invoking a higher threshold than for returns to other signatory states. Thus, the *extreme and exceptional nature* of the conditions in refugee camps, as well as the fact that the humanitarian crisis was largely brought about by the actions of the parties to the conflict, were decisive for a finding of a violation of Article 3 by the United Kingdom.[103] In the case of *Hirsi Jamaa and others v Italy,* the ECtHR again applied Article 3 of the Convention to an alleged safe third country outside the Council of Europe area.[104] The court held that the push-back of the applicants to Libya amounted to a violation of Article 3 of the ECHR because they faced detention in inhuman conditions, risk of torture, poor hygiene conditions, lack of appropriate medical care, 'particularly precarious living conditions' and risk of refoulement.[105]

Finally and more recently, the court in *Ilias and Ahmed v Hungary* tested the return of an applicant for international protection from Hungary to Serbia as a purportedly safe third country. The substantive standard by the Court was again Article 3, with the Court enquiring whether the applicant had been exposed to a risk of chain-refoulement by considering return to Serbia.[106]

In sum, as noted by another academic commentators, the ECtHR case law may help to construct a 'robust understanding of "effective protection"' in the ordinary scope of non-return obligations under Article 3.[107] Under the human rights law non-return obligations, it is risks against physical safety and integrity (including lacking medical care and insalubrious conditions) and detention that is relevant for third countries. Yet, the scope of Convention obligations is clearly narrower than the breadth of international protection obligations

102 *Tarakhel v Switzerland* ECHR 2014-VI, 195, para 120.

103 *Sufi and Elmi v United Kingdom* (Ch 3, n 140).

104 *Hirsi Jamaa and Other v Italy* (Ch 5, n 71).

105 Ibid paras 125–126. For an analysis of *Hirsi Jamaa and Other v Italy,* see also Cathryn Costello, 'Courting Access to Asylum in Europe: Recent Supranational Jurisprudence Explored' (2012) 12 Human Rights Law Review 287.

106 *Ilias and Ahmed v Hungary* App No 47287/15 (ECtHR, March 2017).

107 Costello, 'The Asylum Procedures Directive and the Proliferation of Safe Country Practices: Deterrence, Deflection and the Dismantling of International Protection?' (Ch 5, n 39) at 58, arguing that, 'It is possible to construct a robust understanding of "effective protection" by examining the ECHR non-refoulement case law, and the case law generally under Article 3 ECHR on human dignity.'

under Articles 2–34 of the 1951 Convention. For instance, under Article 3, access to employment, is not a relevant consideration, whilst it is for refugee rights, albeit with several restrictions.[108]

What else may explain the Procedures Directives standards, clearly anchored in the 1951 Convention refugee rights and exceeding Article 3? A powerful explanation relates to the Convention's effectiveness to achieve its object and purpose, as well as to the systematic relation to other concepts of 'protection' in the Convention.

First, as described in Chapter 2, the object and purpose of the 1951 Convention consists of contracting states to provide international protection, that is, surrogate rights enfranchisement, of refugees. Under the Convention structure, refugees enjoy a number of Convention rights immediately when physically present in a contracting state. Furthermore, the preamble of the Convention considers that states need to cooperate to find solutions for refugees.[109] Yet, would the Convention *not* provide any limits to the 'protection elsewhere' arrangements, this would mean that the sending state would be able to relieve itself from obligations at the expense of another country not because of that country's proven track record to safeguard Convention obligations,[110] but because of minimal compliance, a fact that would enable a 'downward' spiral of potential returns until the very bare minimum of physical safety, even below what Thomas Gammeltoft-Hansen has called 'protection lite':

> To the extent that protection responsibility is deflected or transferred to less developed States, or even to States with poor human rights records or underdeveloped asylum system [...] this may effectively erode the quality of protection afforded [...] The result is what could be termed 'protection lite', understood as the presence of formal protection, though with a lower certainty, scope and/or level of rights afforded.[111]

108 See Section 2.2.2.

109 See para 4 of the preamble, stating that, 'the grant of asylum may place unduly heavy burdens on certain countries, and that a satisfactory solution of a problem of which the United Nations has recognized the international scope and nature cannot therefore be achieved without international co-operation.'

110 In *NAGV and NAGW* [2005] HCA 6: Justice Kirby argued that, 'It would be an absurd result if the generosity of other States' refugee laws meant that Australia was thereby relieved of international obligations that it voluntarily accepted with other nations. Such a result should not be reached by implication' para 91.

111 Thomas Gammeltoft-Hansen, 'The Extraterritorialisation of Asylum and the Advent of "Protection Lite"' Danish Institute for International Studies Working Paper no 2007/2, <www.files.ethz.ch/isn/30673/2007-2.pdf> accessed 20 October 2016.

Yet, a downward spiral to 'protection lite' clearly runs counter to the realisation of the widest possible scope of refugee rights and of cooperation that states have committed to.

In the New York Declaration, a recent authoritative document on refugee protection by all UN member states, states recognise the importance of a 'full' application of the 1951 Convention and 1967 Protocol as well as 'the values they embody'.[112] What is more, states 'underline the centrality of international co-operation to the refugee protection regime' and 'commit to a more equitable sharing of the burden and responsibility for hosting and supporting the world's refugees, while taking account of the existing contributions and the differing capacities and resources among States.'[113]

Second, limiting safe third country safeguards to mere safety would also create inconsistencies with the application of Article 1A(2), in particular the IPA concept. In contrast to the IPA concept and given the declaratory nature of refugee status assessment, when 'protection elsewhere' rules are applied as part of procedural arrangements prior to the formal determination of status, they may well be applied to refugees, rather than individuals who are refugees *but for* the application of the IPA concept. For that reason, 'protection elsewhere' rules which are not higher than the IPA requirements would mean that refugees under the Convention are discriminated in respect of individuals with an IPA, an effect thwarting the Convention's object and purpose to achieve international protection *for refugees*. Although subsequent practice is not unequivocal about the IPA requirements, there is consensus in such practice that the IPA requires more than safety (protection against harm/non-refoulement under Article 33). Yet, the notion of 'effective protection' as conceived by UNHCR falls short even of the UNHCR's own IPA standard, which requires a 'reasonableness' assessment featuring more broad humanitarian concerns.[114] *A fortiori* this is true for emerging, more demanding IPA safeguards that have been discussed in Chapter 3, namely the consideration of the protected interests under the 1951 Convention in conjunction with basic human rights law.

The systematic coherence of 1951 Convention obligations also helps circumscribe the relevant substantive rights barring application of safe third country concepts. First, *de lege lata*, 'protection elsewhere' standards have to be higher

112 New York Declaration (Ch 1 n 14), para 65.

113 Ibid para 68.

114 UN High Commissioner for Refugees, *Guidelines on International Protection No 4* (Ch 3 n 67). Stevens argues that 'the UNHCR has attempted to persuade states of the need to employ a more generous attitude. But states have adopted their own unique view of "effective protection" '; Stevens, 'What Do We Mean by Protection?' (Ch 1 n 104) 260.

than the IPA safeguards as they are reflected in current law and practice in the Convention. This would appear to include not only the Convention rights granted once a refugee is lawfully present (freedom from detention and non-penalisation for irregular entry, freedom of religion, Convention provisions on the basic necessities of food, shelter and healthcare) but also considerations of economic hardship and family unity. Second, and *de lege ferenda* from the perspective of international law, safeguards should be based on 1951 Convention and human rights obligations in parallel, which form the basis of refugee law's modern conception of 'international protection'.[115] The EU Procedures Directive's Article 38 would seem already to reflect this higher level of safeguards, given it warrants that the use of the safe third country rules requires that a person, if found to be a refugee, would need to enjoy 'protection in accordance with' the 1951 Convention.

5.3.2.3 Does the Procedures Directive Requires Safe Third Countries to Ratify the 1951 Convention?

A particularly relevant sub-question[116] is whether the EU Procedures Directive allows for considering countries safe third countries when these have not ratified the 1951 Convention and 1967 Protocol. This was questioned by rights groups and academics, in respect of the EU-Turkey Statement,[117] given that Turkey has not signed the Protocol and thus continues to apply the geographic limitation of the 1951 Convention.[118]

115 For an alternative opinion, see not only the Michigan Guidelines, but also Moreno-Lax, 'The Legality of the "Safe Third Country" Notion Contested: Insights from the Law of Treaties' (Ch 1 n 102) 718.

116 Finally, there is a question as to whether Article 38 can be applied to a country that is a European country within the meaning of Article 39, by virtue of having ratified the ECHR. In particular, Article 39 may be considered a more specific provision than the general rule of Article 38. However, given that Article 39 reduces the level of scrutiny for an application of international protection ('no, or no full, examination of the application for international protection and of the safety of the applicant in his or her particular circumstances'), the provision is not strictly speaking an alternative, lex specialis provision to Article 38.

117 Eg, Mark Provera, 'The EU-Turkey Deal – Analysis and Considerations' Jesuit Refugee Service Europe Policy Discussion Paper' (2016) <https://jrseurope.org/assets/Publications/File/JRS_Europe_EU_Turkey_Deal_policy_analysis_2016-04-30.pdf> accessed 1 July 2019; Rainer Hoffmann; Adela Schmidt, 'Ist die Türkei für Asylantragsteller ein sicherer Drittstaat? – Das Urteil des Hellenischen Staatsrats vom 22.9.2017' (2018) 14 Zeitschrift für Ausländerrecht und Ausländerpolitik 1.

118 The position is also advanced by Vedsted-Hansen, 'Asylum Procedures Directive 2013/32/EU', 1363 in Hailbronner and Thym, *EU Immigration and Asylum Law – A Commentary* (Ch 1 n 7).

The wording of the Procedures Directive, which requires the opportunity to request refugee status and 'receive protection in accordance with' the 1951 Convention, is not conclusive. The other uses of these exact terms in the Directive, where they relate to other provisions, other instruments, or to general principles of law, indicates that the term regularly points to the result, or *practice*, of accordance, rather than to the means of achieving it.

This also appears to be the position of the European Commission, which stated, when tabling the text of the original Directive (the wording of which is unchanged in respect of Article 38):

> The original Annex did not take into account the situation in which a country has ratified the Geneva Convention but has not yet put appropriate rules in place. If such a country nonetheless consistently observes in practice the standards laid down in the Geneva Convention with respect to the rights of persons in need of international protection within the meaning of this Convention as evinced by the UNHCR, the country should be able to be qualified as a safe third country[119]

However, there are also important arguments that the wording of the Directive requires the third country in question to have ratified the Convention and the Protocol.[120] In particular, in conjunction with the use of the term 'protection in accordance with the Geneva Convention', Article 38 refers to 'refugee status', that is, to a term that has a clear international law meaning.[121] What is more, neither does EU asylum law know a concept of refugee status independent of

119 Commission of the European Communities, 'Amended proposal for a Council Directive on minimum standards on procedures in Member States for granting and withdrawing refugee status', COM/2002/326 final, OJ C 291 E/143.

120 For a legal opinion on the requirement of ratification, Reinhard Marx, 'Rechtsgutachten vom 29.2.2016 im Auftrag von PRO ASYL zur unionsrechtlichen Zulässigkeit des Plans der Staats- und Regierungschefs der EU, die Türkei als „sicheren Drittstaat" zu behandeln' <https://www.proasyl.de/wp-content/uploads/2016/03/160304_Gutachten_Marx_Tuerkei_als_sicherer_Drittstaat_korr.pdf> accessed 1 July 2019.

121 A different opinion was advanced by Daniel Thym, stating that, 'the terms "refugee" and "refugee status" employed in Articles 35 and 38 Directive 2013/32/EU do not necessarily require prior ratification of the Convention […], since they are technical terms which are defined explicitly in Article 2(j), (d) to refer, 'for the purposes of this Directive', to third-country nationals who are recognised as being persecuted for the reasons listed in the Convention. Of course, the state can afford this protection to someone without prior ratification.' Daniel Thym, 'Why the EU-Turkey Deal is Legal and a Step in the Right Direction' (March 2016) <https://verfassungsblog.de/why-the-eu-turkey-deal-is-legal-and-a-step-in-the-right-direction/> accessed 1 July 2019.

the 1951 Convention and *as amended by the protocol*.[122] For example, Finnish domestic law has transposed the Directive so as to require ratification of the Convention without the geographic limitation that the 1967 Protocol effectively repealed.[123]

Yet, the original proposal for the first Procedures Directive (2005/85/EC) did in a detailed manner specify when countries that did not ratify the Convention could be considered safe.[124] What is more, Article 39 of the Procedures Directive necessitates that a European Country can only be considered a safe third country if it, 'ratified and observes the provisions of the Geneva Convention without any geographical limitations', a wording that is clearly not chosen for Article 38.[125] In sum, Article 38, read on its own, does not appear to require a ratification of the 1951 Convention.

Meanwhile, it is a different question altogether whether this position raises issues of compliance with international law. In academic literature, it has been argued that international law requires that all countries taking part in third country arrangements ratify the Convention. Because such arrangements were subsequent agreements intended to facilitate shared responsibility, the sharing of responsibility required the same level of obligation by both cooperation partners, so that ratification is an insufficient but necessary condition[126] because it is the only way to obtain from a state a 'binding commitment' to respect the Convention.[127]

122 The requirement of formal ratification has stirred some controversy in connection with the agreement between the EU and Turkey to return migrants to Turkey; Council of the European Union, EU–Turkey statement, 18 March 2016, Press release 144/16. In particular, the Commission appeared to be of the view that protection factually comparable to the 1951 Convention was required, rather than full ratification. For the legal nature of that agreement, see Rainer Hofmann and Adela Schmidt, 'Die Erklärung EU–Türkei vom 18.3.2016 aus rechtlicher Perspektive' (2016) 11 *Neue Zeitschrift für Verwaltungsrecht* 743.

123 Laki ulkomaalaislain muuttamisesta, 194/2015, 6 March 2015 (Law of 6 March 2015 amending the Aliens Act), Finlex.

124 Commission of the European Communities, Proposal for a Council Directive on minimum standards on procedures in Member States for granting and withdrawing refugee status, COM/2000/0578 final OJ C 62E, 231–242.

125 Jessica Niehaus, 'Sichere Herkunfts- und Drittstaaten – Ergebnisse einer rechtsvergleichenden Analyse der europäischen Asylrichter', (2017) 13 Zeitschrift für Ausländerrecht und Ausländerpolitik 398, 393–394.

126 Moreno-Lax, 'The Legality of the "Safe Third Country" Notion Contested: Insights from the Law of Treaties' (Ch 1 n 102) 718.

127 Rosemary Byrne and Andrew Shacknove, 'The Safe Country Notion in European Asylum Law' (1996) 9 Harvard Human Rights Journal 185. Cited in ibid.

The requirement of a ratification of the Convention would, in theory, produce the result that a country that has not ratified the Convention but grants refugees all rights contained in the Convention, firmly enshrined in domestic law, could *not* be regarded as a safe country, while a country that has ratified the Convention with reservations and grants only a bare minimum of rights could be. While this appears to be more of an academic problem, it does illustrate an important point – the source of refugee rights. As submitted in the previous section, the 1951 Convention safeguards are grounded not only in the systematic coherence of the IPA and safe third country concepts, but primarily in the object and purpose of the Convention to enfranchise refugees with rights. Rights enfranchisement, meanwhile, presupposes a formal 'holding' of rights, not just as an indication for whether or not rights will be enjoyed in practice, but also as a matter of durability and reliability. Thus within the EU, multiple domestic legal frameworks exceed the minimum standard of the Procedures Directive and do require ratification of the 1951 Convention[128] and there is a strong case that reading the Procedures Directive in accordance with international law, does indeed require ratification of the Convention. It is notable in this regard that the late 2018 recast proposal of the Procedures Directive would explicitly allow non-ratification, as part of its definition of 'sufficient protection' as an alternative to full Convention rights[129] – a provision deeply problematic under international law.

Beyond this requirement, ratification can in any case be considered as an important element of evidentiary value for the respect and durability of Convention obligations *in practice*. In the EU context, this is similar to Article 38(1)(a)–(d) – the requirement of safety – the ratification of, and respect for, human rights treaties will be of evidentiary value, analogous to the assessment of the well-founded fear of being persecuted or the real risk of serious harm in relation to the substance of an application for international protection.[130]

128 European Comission, 'Ad-Hoc Query on Safe Countries of Origin and Safe Third Countries' (December 2014) <https://ec.europa.eu/home-affairs/sites/homeaffairs/files/what-we-do/networks/european_migration_network/reports/docs/ad-hocqueries/return/2014.615_emn_ahq_list_of_safe_countries_of_origin_%28wider_diss%29.pdf> accessed 1 July 2019.

129 Article 44(1) Proposal for a Regulation of the European Parliament and of the Council establishing a common procedure for international protection in the Union and repealing Directive 2013/32/EU (Ch 5 n 46).

130 For instance, Dutch law specifies that in determining whether or not a country is safe, the authorities must take the applicant's statements as a starting point and consider whether

5.3.2.4 The Legality of Applying the First Country of Asylum and Safe Third Country Concepts to Areas Controlled by Non-state Actors

Unlike for the 'actor of protection' concept in Article 7 of the Qualification Directive, the issue of which actors can provide protection has so far not been subject of debate in respect of the first country of asylum and safe third country concepts of EU law. Yet, in the negotiation process on the second recast of the Procedures Directive, still ongoing at the time of writing, the EU Council discussed whether to specify in the Directive that the safe third country concept can be applied to single zones within the third country in question.[131] This issue may well be practically relevant also in the future. In particular, rules on protection elsewhere could potentially be applied to territories under control by parties or organisations, including international organisations, or to situations in which the asylum system or a first response is not run by the state but by the UNHCR, or non-governmental humanitarian organisations,[132] or areas controlled by the presence of international forces. For example, the German Minister of Defence in 2019 suggested establishing in Syria an internationally mandated 'safe area'.[133]

The Procedures Directive leaves open whether 'protection in accordance with the 1951 Convention' could be assured by or with the assistance of actors other than states, and does not require the ratification of the 1951 Convention by a safe third country. However, it is clear that both Articles 35, 38 and 39 of the Procedures Directive all apply to countries, rather than to territories and 'actors of protection' as in the Qualification Directive. Likewise, the 1951 Convention would permit the application of 'protection elsewhere' rules only to states. As discussed in Chapter 3, the IPA concept should not be applied to territories under control of non-state actors, given that the IPA is applied to individuals who are, *prima facie*, refugees, and requires the consideration of protected interests under the 1951 Convention and basic human rights. *A fortiori*, this is true for protection elsewhere rules, given that these may be applied

---

that country complies with its obligations under international human rights treaties. Vreemdelingencirculaire 2000 (C) of 1 December 2017, section 6.3.

131 European Council of Refugees and Exiles, 'Debunking the Safe Third Country Myth: ECRE's Concerns about EU Proposals for Expanded Use of the Safe Third Country Concept' (2017) <www.ecre.org/wp-content/uploads/2017/11/Policy-Note-08.pdf accessed> 1 July 2019.

132 Generally, for the rise of private actors in migration control, see Gammeltoft-Hansen, *Access to Asylum* (Ch 1 n 16); Gammeltoft Hansen and Ninna Nyberg Sorensen (eds), *The Migration Industry and the Commercialization of International Migration* (Routledge 2012).

133 Deutsche Welle, 'Germany Defends Vision of International "Security Zone" in Syria' (December 2019) <www.dw.com/en/germany-defends-vision-of-international-security-zone-in-syria/a-50955092> accessed 1 July 2019.

to refugees. The Convention seeks to enfranchise refugees with surrogate international protection, as defined by the 1951 Convention in conjunction with human rights law. In contrast to protection against harm, the IPA and in particular 'protection elsewhere' are not just factual enquiries equating to safety. If international protection is rights enfranchisement, it has to be delivered by actors bearing obligations under international law.[134] Yet, as discussed in Section 4.5, while the position of non-state actors in the international legal system has evolved significantly, it is not on a par with states in law and practice, in particular given the contested notion of control over territory, and the unclear scope of customary obligations under refugee and human rights law. Beyond the question of whether and to what extent parties or organisations are bound by international law, another issue is that of legal accountability – whether or not victims could turn to domestic or international organisations in order to seek remedies against perpetrators of human rights violations.[135] In sum, given

134 A potential counter-argument is Article 1D of the 1951 Convention, which provides that the Convention, 'shall not apply to persons who are at present receiving from organs or agencies of the United Nations other than the United Nations High Commissioner for Refugees protection or assistance'. As argued by Hathaway and Foster, the drafting history shows that Article 1D is uniquely relevant to the United Nations Relief and Works Agency for Palestine Refugees in the Near East (UNRWA), which assists persons whose place of residence prior to the 1948 conflict was Palestine and who lost home and livelihood as a result of that and subsequent conflicts. Because Article 1 is the only place where the Convention mentions non-State actor 'protection', all other such cases must be excluded, under the rule *expressio unius est exclusio alterius*. Besides, the use of the term 'protection' in Article 1D does not circumscribe any substantial content of the term in other provisions of the 1951 Convention. The *travaux préparatoires* are relatively clear that the terms 'protection or assistance' in Article 1D were not intended to bear legal meaning, for other open terms as 'care' or 'aid' were also used. It is also apparent from the actual wording 'protection or assistance' (emphasis added), that a potentially wide range of activities may be included. Rather, it is UNRWA's activities that circumscribe the meaning of the term for the specific purposes of UNRWA. Mutaz M Qafisheh and Valentina Azarov, 'Article 1D', 558 in Zimmermann; Dörschner; Machts (eds), *The 1951 Convention Relating to the Status of Refugees and its 1967 Protocol – A Commentary* (Ch 1 n 42); also BVerwG 4 June 1991, 1C 42.88 – BVerwGE 88, 254 para cc), author's translation: 'The wording of Article 1D para 1 of the Geneva [Refugee, AN] Convention refers to persons that receive "protection" or "assistance" of an organ or agency of the United Nations. The concrete meaning of these two alternative forms of care is determined by the activities of UNRWA, as carried out in accordance with its mandate.'

135 See, in respect of refugee camps, Maja Janmyr, *Protecting Civilians in Refugee Camps – Unable and Unwilling States, UNHCR and International Responsibility* (Martinus Nijhoff Publishers 2014). Janmyr argues that where UNHCR fails to respect or protect customary law obligations, and the host state is willing but unable to give effect to its human rights obligations, responsibility for a violation of international human rights law was shared

the disparity between the legal obligations of states on the one hand and other subjects of international law on the other hand, the 1951 Convention's definition of international protection as rights enfranchisement would appear to be satisfied only by states.

Some jurisdictions in the EU have explicitly or implicitly recognised that prerequisite for protection elsewhere. Dutch law, for example, requires the observance of those treaties in a potential first country of asylum.[136] Indeed, the Dutch Council of State (*Raad van State*), when seized of the question whether the International Criminal Court (ICC) could be said to protect a person so as to render that person's claim for international protection inadmissible, argued that only states could be Safe Third Countries.[137] The Council discussed the basic premise of the 1951 Convention, stating that the Convention's purpose was to provide a back-up for the lack of protection in the home state, and that it includes rights that clearly exceed non-refoulement.[138] Protection can, according to the court, in principle be guaranteed only by states, because international refugee law requires more than a negative obligation not to expose refugees to a danger, namely a positive obligation to grant a certain quality of protection.[139] Finally, the UNHCR argued that its activities in a country of asylum amount to a *prima facie* indication of a lack of capability in the host state in relation to such operations:

> [...] the capacity of third state to provide effective protection in practice should be taken into consideration by Member States, particularly if the third state is already hosting large refugee populations. Countries where UNHCR is engaged in refugee status determination under its mandate should, in principle, not be considered first countries of asylum. UNHCR often undertakes such functions because the state has no capacity to conduct status determination or to provide effective protection. [...] The

between UNHCR and the state. This contrasts, she argues, with situations in which the host state of UNHCR operations was simply unwilling to uphold its human rights violations. In such cases, responsibility for violations fell on the state alone. However, there are open questions on how to determine the capacity and willingness of states to fulfil their human rights obligations. Finally, even if the rules on legal responsibility by international organisations have developed, immunity of the UN challenges the implementation of those rules. The Convention on the Privileges and Immunities of the UN exempts the UN from the jurisdiction of local courts.

136 Vreemdelingencirculaire 2000 (C) of 13 August 2017.

137 Raad van State, 12 November 2013, 201303197/2/V3 and 201303198/2/V3.

138 Ibid para 4.6.

139 Ibid para 1.12.

> return of persons in need of international protection to such countries should [...] not be envisaged.[140]

This is not to say that the Convention does not allow international organisations to support states in the realisation of some of their protective obligations under the 1951 Convention – notably not in relation to core legal tasks, but only in relation to promoting voluntary repatriation, welfare and maintaining contact.[141] Although the EXCOM of the UNHCR has often reiterated that 'refugee protection is primarily the responsibility of States',[142] it is also clear that the Convention prominently envisages the cooperation of states with international organisations. According to the preamble of the Convention, while the UNHCR is tasked with supervising the Convention and other instruments on refugee protection, '[...] the effective coordination of measures taken to deal with this problem will depend upon the co-operation of States with the High Commissioner'.[143] The Final Act of the Conference of Plenipotentiaries considered that '[...] in the moral, legal and material spheres, refugees need the help of suitable welfare services, *especially that of appropriate non-governmental organizations*'. The Final Act therefore recommended 'governments and inter-governmental bodies to facilitate, encourage and sustain the efforts of properly qualified organisations'. Finally, the EXCOM has endorsed and encouraged the cooperation of the UNHCR and of states with non-governmental organisations, for instance, in the fields of family reunification[144] and internal displacement,[145] in raising awareness about the plight of refugees,[146] or even in such core state functions as the personal security of refugees and asylum seekers.[147]

5.3.3 *Application of 'Protection Elsewhere' Rules by EU Member States*

In practice, the first country of asylum and safe third country concepts have so far been little applied in states outside Europe, in stark contrast with the EU's Dublin system.[148] Major reasons for this are of a practical nature. First, the

140 UNHCR Provisional Comments on the Proposal for an Asylum Procedures Directive 34–35.
141 Paragraph 8 of the UNHCR Statute (Ch 2 n 71).
142 Eg, No 85 (XLIX) – 1998.
143 See also Article 35 of the 1951 Convention (cooperation of the national authorities with the United Nations).
144 No 9 (XXVIII) – 1977.
145 No 75 (XLV) – 1994.
146 Eg, most recently No 93 (LIII) – 2002.
147 No 72 (XLIV) – 1993.
148 A notable exception is Denmark, which has, however, opted out from the Procedures Directive. The Danish Refugee Board considered whether Iraq, in particular the Kurdish

provisions of EU readmission agreements on the safe third country concept are only beginning to enter into force.[149] In addition, beyond the European Dactyloscopy (EURODAC) database, which is applied only in EU countries, there is no means of verifying that an applicant has been recognised as having refugee status elsewhere. Finally, not all states made use of the possibility to designate Council of Europe member states as European Safe Third Countries under Article 37 Procedures Directive.[150]

However, the use of the concepts has increased since 2015, not only given the declaration of Serbia as a safe third country by Hungary, but also given policy preference for concluding arrangements modelled on the agreement with Turkey of March 2016. Nonetheless, there is evidence that member states are not fully applying the requirements of Article 38, Procedures Directive.

First, some member states did not transpose the requirement that an applicant must, if found to be a refugee, be able to obtain 'protection in

Autonomous Region, could be deemed a 'first country of asylum' for an Iranian citizen. The Refugee Board required as an 'absolute minimum' for first countries of asylum the protection against refoulement, the possibility to enter and stay legally, as well as personal integrity and security. However, it also referred to the EXCOM Conclusion 58 (1989) in order to name additional criteria of basic socio-economic needs. The Board thus considered, in addition to non-refoulement and the legal conditions of stay, the socio-economic rights of the applicant, including rights granted under the 1951 Convention: access to housing, education, the possibility to move within Kurdistan, access to medical care, the right to work in the private and public sector, and the right to own property, Flygtningenævnet Iran/2012/20, marking a significant development from a contrary decision in Iran/2011/15.

149 On the interlinkage between protection elsewhere and readmission agreements, see Mariagiulia Giuffre, 'Readmission Agreements and Refugee Rights: From a Critique to a Proposal' (2013) 32 Refugee Survey Quarterly 79.

150 For a (somewhat dated) compilation of countries applying the concept, see European Commission, 'European Migration Network, Ad-Hoc Query on safe countries of origin and safe third countries' (2014) <www.emn.fi/files/1172/Compilation_BG_EMN_NCP_AHQ_list_of_safe_countries_of_origin_and_safe_third_countries_WIDER.pdf> accessed 20 October 2016. Eg, in 2011, the CNDA rejected the asylum application of refugees whose status had been recognised by Poland and who claimed to be at risk of ill-treatment in Poland. Thereby, it attached particular weight to the fact that Poland was an EU member, as well as a signatory state to the 1951 Convention and the ECHR, CNDA 17 October 2011, *MA et Mme K* Nos 10026678; 10026679 C. Similarly, the first country of asylum concept was applied by Denmark, which opted out from both the 2005 Procedures Directive and the recast Procedures Directive but seems to be applying similar rules. Thus, the Refugee Board rejected the asylum application of Syrian nations who had obtained refugee status in Italy and alleged being at risk of assaults by Italian criminals. According to the Refugee Board, they were 'likely to obtain protection against abuses by Italian criminals because Italy has an independent policy authority that the applicants could turn to, Flygtningenævnet Syri/2011/17.

accordance with the 1951 Convention' into domestic law. German law, for instance, merely requires that an applicant faces no well-founded fear of being persecuted, thus limiting the safeguards of the concept to safety.[151] French and Swedish law selectively transposed the Directive. Swedish law leaves out 'protection in accordance with the 1951 Convention' and requires simply the possibility of requesting refugee status.[152] French law only requires 'effective protection', which is reminiscent of the UNHCR opinion in the 'Lisbon Conclusions' (see Section 4.3.2), but is not language featuring in the Procedures Directive.

Second, in the practical application of the concept, the Procedures Directive requirement that a safe third country is to provide protection in accordance with the 1951 Convention does not appear to be assessed with the scrutiny it deserves under the Directive to ensure compliance with the 1951 Convention. Thus, the UNHCR raised concerns about the use of the safe third country concept by Hungary in respect of Serbia.[153] This is true in particular for the most important application of the safe third country concept to date, the implementation of the EU–Turkey agreement of March 2016. That agreement provides, inter alia, that migrants arriving on Greek islands from Turkey whose applications for asylum have been found inadmissible in accordance with the Procedures Directive will be returned to Turkey. The Greek Asylum Appeals Committees had initially ruled that the requirement to receive protection in accordance with the 1951 Convention required a set of 'core' obligations, including the individualised character of protection, integration with a view to life not just in safety but as a member of a community with a residence permit, and 'free movement and establishment and employment under conditions similar to those applicable to other non-nationals'.[154] These conditions were, according to the Appeals Committee, not satisfied in Turkey. In turn, the UNHCR cautioned that:

151 Paragraph 27 AsylG. Indeed, in connection with the EU–Turkey agreement of March 2016, the Federal Government was of the opinion that Turkey satisfied all requirements under Article 38 Procedures Directive, Bundesregierung der Bundesrepublik Deutschland, *Antwort der Bundesregierung auf die Kleine Anfrage der Abgeordneten Andrej Hunko, Sevim Dağdelen, Wolfgang Gehrcke, weiterer Abgeordneter und der Fraktion DIE LINKE, Drucksache 18/8205, 24 May 2015* (2016).

152 5 kap. 1 b § första stycket 3 utlänningslagen.

153 UN High Commissioner for Refugees, *Hungary as a country of asylum. Observations on restrictive legal measures and subsequent practice implemented between July 2015 and March 2016, May 2016* (2016).

154 *Decision 05/133782* 17 May 2016, on file with the author (Asylum Appeals Committees of Greece (Presidential Decree 114/2010)), translation by Minos Mouzourakis.

> Application of the concept requires an individual assessment of whether the previous state will readmit the person; grant the person access to a fair and efficient procedure for determination of his or her protection needs; permit the person to remain; and accord the person *standards of treatment commensurate with the 1951 Convention and international human rights standards*, including protection from refoulement.[155]

Academic analysis of the EU-Turkey Agreement has demonstrated that the Greek Appeal Committees initially squashed admissibility decisions on the grounds that Turkey is not a safe third country, in particular because refugee status could not be obtained given Turkey's geographic limitation to the 1951 Convention application.[156] However, the position changed after a change in the composition of the Appeals Committees, sparking concern about a correct interpretation of the law.[157]

5.4 Conclusion: the Distinctive Scope of Protection Elsewhere Safeguards

This chapter has focused on the EU Procedures Directive's rules on 'protection elsewhere', whereby an applicant is not in need of international protection and his or her application is therefore inadmissible where he or she could obtain protection outside the EU, in a first country of asylum or safe third country. The chapter has argued that such rules function as an exclusion clause in relation to refugee status. When applied procedurally before

155 UN High Commissioner for Refugees, 'Legal considerations on the return of asylum-seekers and refugees from Greece to Turkey as part of the EU–Turkey Cooperation in Tackling the Migration Crisis under the safe third country and first country of asylum concept', *23 March 2016* (2016). While UNHCR did not specify whether or not it thought these requirements to be satisfied in Turkey, NGOs criticised the fact that Turkey did not accord full Convention rights and maintains the geographic limitation to the Convention. See Danish Refugee Council and European Council on Refugees and Exiles, 'The DRC/ECRE Desk Research on Application of a Safe Third Country and First Country of Asylum Concepts to Turkey' (May 2016) <www.asylumlawdatabase.eu/sites/www.asylumlawdatabase.eu/files/aldfiles/turkeynote%20final%20edited%20DCR%20ECRE.pdf> accessed 20 October 2016.

156 Gkliati, Mariana, 'The Application of the EU-Turkey Deal. A Critical Analysis of the Decisions of the Greek Appeals Committees' (2017) 10 European Journal of Legal Studies 81.

157 Ibid.

an assessment of the substance of an application for international protection, the declaratory nature of refugee status means that the requirements of the 1951 Convention on protection elsewhere have to apply to all applicants for international protection, given that refugee status has not yet been assessed.

Meanwhile, under the 1951 Convention, rules on protection elsewhere are not to be conflated with the narrow concept of protection equaling *safety* (as inherent in the refugee definition's 'well-founded fear of being persecuted' notion). Although the 1951 Convention dissociates refugee status and asylum and thereby allows protection elsewhere rules, the Convention also requires that protection can be obtained in accordance with its catalogue of rights and obligations in conjunction with human rights law. *De lege lata*, these safeguards have to be higher than those applied to the IPA, meaning that questions of self-reliance/economic hardship, family unity and other human rights factors are relevant. What is more, international law, like EU law, allows for the application of protection elsewhere rules only to states.

De lege ferenda, international law should more clearly regulate the criteria for safe third country models, and tie them to 1951 Convention obligations, exceeding non-return obligations of human rights law. Arguably, the Procedures Directive does already reflect that higher level of safeguards, although in practice there is evidence that the Directive did not succeed in harmonising the requirement that protection in a safe third country has to be 'in accordance with the 1951 Convention'. Depending on the application of the current safe third country and first country of asylum concepts, 'protection' could in practice risk being reduced to safety (protection against harm, see Chapter 2), fall short of the safeguards applied in the IPA (see Chapter 3), or blur the scope of Convention rights for refugees with non-return obligations under human rights law. In the redrafting of the Directive, legislators should consider the enumeration of specific Convention and human rights as requirements for both the first country of asylum and safe third country concepts, such as access to the labour market, housing, health and education. This had been the approach of the original text of the Procedures Directive as proposed in 2000, before the text was changed to refer to 'protection' in the abstract.[158] Finally, in order to achieve a consistent application of the concept, it may be considered that the recast Procedures Directive

158 European Parliament, Legislative Observatory <https://oeil.secure.europarl.europa.eu/oeil/popups/ficheprocedure.do?lang=en&reference=2000/0238(CNS)> accessed on 1 July 2019.

will foresee competence by the EU Commission to designate safe third countries according to the criteria of the Directive,[159] and subsequently leave it to member states to apply the concept, which under international law should not be a mandatory consideration.

159 The author credits Dominik Steiger for this point.

CHAPTER 6

Conclusion: What Paradigm of Protection for EU Asylum Law?

6.1 Synthesis: Revisiting the Research Questions

This final chapter will proceed in two sections. First, it will revisit the book's research questions, which all cut across multiple chapters. In doing so, it will summarise the aims of the research before synthesising the findings across the different concepts of protection. Second, the chapter will provide a broader outlook on the legal trade-offs in the future development of EU asylum law as part of the international regime of refugee protection.

When can one say an asylum seeker receives, in another country, 'protection' strong enough so as to rejects his or her application for asylum? This is a controversial question that this book has explored in relation to multiple rules of EU asylum law – in respect of the *procedural law* of status determination in the EU Procedures Directive, and in *material law* of status determination.

In international law, the above question leads to the notion of 'surrogacy' (implying that the assessment and granting of refugee status is necessary only where there is no protection in the home country) and the meaning(s) of 'protection', a term that is at the core of the 1951 Convention. The book has used the 'surrogacy' notion as a bracket for different legal concepts of EU asylum law, demonstrating how they relate to each other and how international refugee law on the one hand, and international human rights law on the other hand, interplay and differ on these concepts. These overarching issues are captured in the research questions developed in Chapter 1, which will be revisited below. These questions are academic in nature, but the law ultimately has implications for real people in real life: For the victim of war in Syrian whom an asylum adjudicator tells to seek refuge in Turkey after having stayed there before. Or for the Afghan who is told he or she could live in Kabul instead of seeking refuge in Berlin.

Research Question 1: How does EU law, in line with international law, circumscribe protection in countries of origin, in EU countries of asylum and in countries of asylum outside the EU ('elsewhere')?

 | DOI:10.1163/9789004430396_007

1.1. (How) do human rights affect the scope of international protection in the EU Qualification Directive and the relevance of 'protection' in the 1951 Convention's refugee definition?

This question goes to the bottom of what is owed to refugees and other people fleeing human rights harm under EU and international law in their states of refuge – the meaning and scope of 'international protection'. Why is it relevant to understand that meaning and scope? In order to understand domestic protection, it is primordial to posit it against *international* protection and enquire whether there are any links or similarities between the two (see also next question).

What is international protection under EU law? First, it is *enfranchisement with rights* reflected in the 1951 Convention and human rights law in parallel. Although the minimum standards granted to refugees and beneficiaries of subsidiary protection under the Directive partly exceed those of international law, they are largely based on obligations under the 1951 Convention and international human rights law, which complement each other. An important point where EU law exceeds obligations under international law is in respect of beneficiaries of subsidiary protection, who are granted the same rights as refugees.

Second, the Qualification Directive puts a strong emphasis on international protection as 'surrogate' protection for lacking domestic protection. This understanding is mirrored by international law, and has been brought about by the influence of international human rights law: Not only does human rights law increasingly define the scope of rights granted to refugees in addition to those of the 1951 Convention, but human rights are also instrumental for the interpretation of the eligibility criteria for refugee status. Human rights have become a conceptual link between what is owed to an individual in his or her home state and in a state of asylum. From the perspective of international human rights law, an Eritrean draft dissenter fleeing his home country is entitled to rights on the same rationale in Calais, France, as back home.

Third, the influence of human rights law has resulted in a shift in the meaning of 'protection' in the 1951 Convention's refugee definition of Article 1A(2). The inability or unwillingness to avail of the protection of the country of nationality (the wording used in the part of the definition commonly referred to as the 'protection clause') traditionally alluded, among others, to diplomatic protection in the state of refuge, and was an expression of the lost bond between an individual and a state. With human rights law defining the bond between an individual and a state, this interpretation is outdated. Rather than reflecting a requirement for refugeehood that is additional to other elements of the refugee definition, the protection clause reflects the purpose of the Convention to entrust refugees with surrogate, rights-based international protection.

1.2. How do the legal requirements for the concepts of 'protection' in the country of origin (protection against harm, Internal Protection Alternative) compare legally to those in asylum countries (international protection; 'protection elsewhere') and do these requirements differ for refugee status and subsidiary protection status?

This question is about the difference between international protection and domestic protection and the corresponding standards of EU and international law. It cuts across all chapters. The surrogacy notion and the evolution of international human rights law suggest that these two concepts are linked, as international protection is a 'surrogate' for lacking domestic protection. Yet, the scope of international protection is and should be distinct from the meaning of 'protection' against harm feared by an applicant in the country of nationality. Under EU law, international protection is granted to individuals who have either refugee status or subsidiary protection status. In contrast, whether or not an asylum seeker is or is not protected in the country of origin is a question relevant for the *assessment of status*, as part of the enquiry whether an applicant has a well-founded fear of being persecuted or a real risk of serious harm, typically by non-state actors.

Why does this distinction matter? First, it matters because it precludes blurring the lines between safety on the one hand and 'protection' on the other hand. As noted in response to the research question 1.1., international protection is *rights enfranchisement*. The enquiry on the well-founded fear of being persecuted, meanwhile, is first and foremost a factual enquiry of *safety*. Second, the distinction matters because it precludes approaches that deny an applicant's risk by pointing to formal legal obligations or general commitment and willingness of those actors that can provide protection (Article 7 of the Qualification Directive). For instance, Police wanting to protect an Albanian woman against domestic violence is not good enough, protection needs to be effective *in practice*. In more legal terms, protection needs to be effective enough to quell a well-founded fear (real chance) of being persecuted (see also research question 2.1).

The legal requirements of the IPA (Article 8, Qualification Directive), meanwhile, exceed safety. While the lack of 'protection' in an applicant's home region is an inclusion criterion for refugee status, the IPA is not: For refugee status, the IPA is a facultative concept that is grounded in the surrogacy notion captured in Article 1A(2) of the 1951 Convention, and operates similarly to an exclusion clause after consideration of all required inclusion criteria. In other words: a Pakistani with a well-founded fear of being persecuted because of his religion, but with an available protection alternative in Lahore, meets all inclusion criteria of the Convention *but for* the IPA. The IPA is, therefore, a concept applied to individuals who are, *prima facie*, refugees and should for that reason be narrowly construed. While there is no consistent state practice on the additional requirements and the Qualification Directive remains inconclusive, it is submitted that additional requirements must be informed by protected interests under the 1951 Convention in conjunction with human rights law.

A fortiori, protection in third countries ('protection elsewhere' – first country of asylum and safe third country, Articles 35 and 38) should not be conflated with safety. First, 'protection elsewhere' is not a bar to inclusion into refugee status under the 1951 Convention. Second, the declaratory nature of refugee status also means that such rules may be applied procedurally to individuals who have refugee status. This is true, for example, for parts of the Syrians in Greece, in the context of the EU-Turkey agreement.

Because 'protection elsewhere' rules are procedural rules relevant before the (declaratory) assessment of status, 1951 Convention safeguards for such rules must apply to everyone, as is foreseen in the Procedures Directive. *De lege lata*, the international law safeguards have to be higher than those applied to the IPA, meaning that questions of self-reliance/economic hardship, family unity and other human rights factors are relevant. *De lege ferenda*, international law should more clearly regulate the criteria for safe, third country models, and tie them to 1951 Convention obligations, exceeding non-return obligations of human rights law. Arguably, the Procedures Directive does already reflect that higher level of safeguards, although in practice there is evidence that the Directive did not succeed in harmonising the requirement that protection in a safe third country has to be 'in accordance with the 1951 Convention' (see also research question 2.3.).

Research Question 2: In light of the interplay of human rights law and refugee law in these three contexts, does EU law succeed in harmonising international law compliant standards?

2.1. What role do human rights play in gauging the availability of 'protection' in the country of origin or elsewhere?

This question relates to one of the contentious issues on the interplay of human rights and refugee law – are human rights instrumental in gauging what is and what is not effective protection against harm (by non-state actors)? It is discussed in Chapters 3 and 5.

For both refugee status and subsidiary status assessment, the enquiry as to the availability of protection against harm (under Article 7, Qualification Directive) is a purely *factual enquiry* on the willingness and ability to quell relevant harm. The human rights obligations of an 'actor of protection' are only of evidentiary value in gauging that willingness and ability, rather than defining the scope of protective obligations by an actor of protection. Thus, while human rights law is used as interpretative guidance in determining which harm is relevant for the notion of being persecuted (Article 9, Qualification Directive) or serious harm (Article 15, Qualification Directive), the scope of human rights obligations, in particular the *due diligence* standard, does not guide the interpretation of effective protection under Article 7(2). For instance, laws, standard operating procedures and codes of conduct of law enforcement agencies are relevant indications of their willingness to protect against harm, but do not determine the actual effectiveness of protection.

2.2. Which actors are legally capable of providing protection in the country of origin or third countries?

This question is directly related to the preceding one and addresses another contentious issue: Is it lawful under international law to consider whether an international organisation controlling a substantive part of the territory or a state, or de-facto authorities, can provide protection as foreseen in Article 7(1)(c), Qualification Directive? Or does international law preclude such consideration as a matter of principle? In practical terms: is it a legitimate question to ask whether the de facto authorities in the autonomous region of Puntland (Somalia) can shield a woman applicant from gender-based violence? The question is addressed in Chapters 3, 4 and 5.

Article 7(1)(c), Qualification is a provision that is relevant both for the assessment of refugee status and of subsidiary protection status, and applies to both protection against harm in the home area (Article 7) and to the IPA (Article 8). This commonality is only partly mirrored in international law, however. First, neither the 1951 Convention nor human rights law preclude consideration of non-state actors as 'actors of protection' in assessing whether applicants have a well-founded fear of being persecuted or real risk of serious harm – for both bodies of law, the assessment of protection against harm is a factual test. Yet, there are important doubts as to the willingness and ability of non-state actors and even de facto authorities to provide effective protection against harm *in practice*.

Second, however, the 1951 Convention does preclude referring an applicant to an IPA where there is no duty bearer of legal obligation on par with a state. This is because the IPA concept is rooted in a surrogate principle of rights enfranchisement. Meanwhile, no such safeguard exist under non-return obligations of human rights law, so that even the lower EU standard exceeds the IPA requirements of international law in respect of people that are not refugees, but considered for subsidiary status.

The difference between 1951 Convention obligations and human rights law non-return obligations is prevalent, *a fortiori,* in the Procedures Directive's concepts of first country of asylum and safe third country, given that both concepts may be applied to individuals that have refugee status. Under the 1951 Convention, such concepts should only be applied to states, and indeed states that have ratified the 1951 Convention and the 1967 Protocol, so that the Procedures Directive raises issues of compliance under the Convention. Under international human rights law, however, protection in third countries is a purely factual enquiry, so that no issues of compliance arise.

2.3. Does the Qualification Directive succeed in harmonising international law-compliant 'actor of protection', IPA and 'protection elsewhere' concepts?

This question captures how the interplay of different bodies of law and compliance issues are playing out in the actual application of the Qualification and Procedures Directives. It cuts across Chapters 3, 4, and 5.

With the exception of the IPA concept, which falls short of 1951 Convention obligations (see answer to the next research question), the Qualification Directive can be interpreted consistently with the Convention. At the same time, the Qualification Directive does not succeed in harmonising such an international law-compliant interpretation. One apparent aspect is what counts as effective protection against harm (by non-state actors) under Article 7. In the application of that Article, courts have repeatedly pronounced individual findings on available protection on the basis of structural and general factors, and have presumed protection or shifted the burden of fact-finding to the applicant alone. Another aspect is the requirement of the IPA that the conditions must be such that an applicant must 'reasonably be expected to settle' there. This requirement has not achieved streamlining of practice on the IPA requirements beyond safety. Finally, when it comes to the first country of asylum concept, there has been a tendency in practice to dilute the requirement that applicants must be able to request refugee status and, if found to be refugees, receive protection in accordance with the 1951 Convention. Against this background, legislators may consider recasting Article 7 and 8 of the Qualification Directive to clarify evidentiary burdens, the standard of protection against harm, and the requirements of the IPA beyond safety. Legislators may also wish to consider Articles 38 and 39 of the Procedures Directive to clarify the substantive refugee law standards to be applied, such as access to the labour market, housing, health and education.

2.4. How do the common standards for refugees and beneficiaries of subsidiary protection in Article 7 and Article 8 of the Qualification Directive influence international law compliance?

While issues of compliance with international law have been raised throughout different research questions, this question aims at discerning the contribution of the Qualification Directive's common standards for assessing refugee status and subsidiary status, as stipulated by Articles 7–8, discussed in Chapters 3 and 4.

The Directive has not only approximated the substantive content of refugee status and subsidiary protection status, it also features common rules on the assessment of 'actors of protection' and the IPA. From an international law perspective, these common standards are unproblematic in respect of actors of protection, where refugee and human rights law have converged. Yet, for the IPA, the international refugee law obligations remain higher than the international human rights law requirements for individuals who are not refugees, but have other protection needs (precluding to consider an IPA when there is no duty bearer under international law on par with a state).

A common Article 8 for refugee status and subsidiary protection status implies that the Qualification Directive has to adapt IPA safeguards to the 1951 Convention level even for individuals who are not refugees. Yet, there is an inherent risk in letting the common standards of Article 8 be determined by human rights law obligations of non-return. This tension is evident not only in the wording of the Article, but is also apparent from practice in member states.

6.2 Outlook: What Paradigm of Protection for EU Asylum Law?

In 1989, Goodwin-Gil noted that 'protection' 'has become something of a term of art, obscuring the scope of an activity that ought to be fundamentally clear'.[1] In today's EU law context, the use of the term has hardly become less convoluted. EU asylum law uses the language of protection in many different contexts, yet the multiple use suggests greater commonalities between those contexts than indeed legally exist. In refugees' countries of origin, measures that shield an individual from relevant harm are referred to as 'protection'. Likewise, the possibility of seeking refuge internally in the country of nationality is referred to as 'protection', as is the rights enfranchisement that flows from refugee status. This book as attempted to analyse these concepts in conjunction with each other, to the extent that they are linked by a common thread – the notion

1 Goodwin-Gil, 'The Language of Protection' (Ch 1 n 29) 6.

of surrogacy, and the interplay of different bodies of law. What conclusions can be drawn for the future of EU asylum law as part of an international regime on refugee protection?

First, to what extent is the notion of surrogacy a helpful analytical concept, or a concept working against the inclusive application of the 1951 Convention?

Dallal Stevens argued that 'the interpretation of "refugee protection" as "surrogate protection" has a clear cost, it has encouraged states to find ways to limit their obligations to needy others'.[2] While true, this book has also demonstrated how the framing of refugee protection as a 'surrogate' helpfully describes an underlying rationale of the very international law obligations on which EU asylum law is built, and allows to distinguish between various concepts of protection. The problem, it seems, is not so much one of the surrogacy language, for the surrogacy notion cuts two ways. Yes, it has been used to restrict access to asylum. However, it can also serve to lay bare undue restrictions under international law, because of its underlying rights enfranchising purpose. Drawing the line between these two poles requires principled commitment to the 1951 Convention and to international cooperation. The real problem, then, lies in how the language gaps of the 1951 Convention are filled in a restrictive policy environment. Meanwhile, denying an asylum seeker international protection by referring him or her to protection in his home country or in a third state is just one of the many more and less subtle ways in which states all around the world have attempted to limit the number of refugees and others seeking protection on their territory, or limit the scope of their obligations.[3]

The challenge of compliance leads to a much broader context of supervision of the Convention, policy, and of reform that addresses multiple dimensions of responsibility sharing, not only of resources, but also of people.[4]

2 Stevens, 'What Do We Mean by Protection?' (Ch 1 n 104) 260.

3 See, eg, Gammeltoft-Hansen, *Access to Asylum – International Refugee Law and the Globalisation of Migration Control* (Ch 1 n 16); Thomas Gammeltoft-Hansen, Jens Vedsted-Hansen (eds), *Human Rights and the Dark Side of Globalisation Transnational Law Enforcement and Migration Control* (Routledge 2016).

4 On these different dimensions of responsibility sharing, see Gregor Noll, *Negotiating Asylum – The EU acquis, Extraterritorial Protection and the Common Market of Deflection* (Nijhoff 2000). There have been a number of policy-oriented and academic papers on responsibility sharing recently, eg Global Refugee Council, A Call to Action – Transforming the Global Refugee System, Centre for International Governance Innovation 2019; Susan F Martin et al, International Responsibility-Sharing for Refugees, KNOMAD Working Paper 32, 2018, KNOMAD 2018; James C Hathawy, 'The Global Cop-Out on Refugees' 30 (2018) International Journal of Refugee Law 4.

However, ambitious reform is not in sight, because of the ongoing contestation on refugee protection. Instead, a 'liberal consensus'[5] has emerged to promote greater collaboration, less aid dependence and more durable solutions within the existing parameters. That liberal consensus is also reflected in the Global Compact on Refugees, a UNHCR-facilitated policy framework on concerted international responses to forced displacement. The Compact states that, 'it is grounded in the international refugee protection regime, centred on the cardinal principle of non-refoulement, and at the core of which is the 1951 Convention and its 1967 Protocol.'[6] Yet, it is quite obvious that some elements of the Global Compact on Refugees framework are required *because* the Convention allows for ways to limit the scope of obligations.

This leads to a second theme of this concluding Chapter: to what extent is the Convention losing relevance, and to what extent may EU asylum law contribute to that trend in one or another way? If reform on the Convention is not going to happen in the short term, more than anything else, the 1951 Convention needs evolutionary interpretation in the global community of practice. Against the background of lacking legally binding international oversight of the Convention, the EU is a particularly important player in that community – not least because its top court produces binding interpretations on EU law[7] that adopts key concepts of the 1951 Convention.

It is against this background that this book has looked at the consequences of the influence of human rights law on the 1951 Convention. All things considered, and as argued elsewhere,[8] that influence has become a motor of evolution for the Convention, in particular in respect of the content of international protection, the interpretation of the 'being persecuted' notion and the factual approach to persecution by non-state actors. However, the EU context also lays bare some of the risks of that influence, fueled by common standards for both refugees and people with subsidiary status. The Qualification Directive's common standards in Chapter II (Articles 4–8), have not only raised safeguards for the latter category of people. The reliance of human rights law non-return obligations may drag down 1951 Convention safeguards on the IPA and could dilute the scope of 1951 Convention requirements on 'protection elsewhere', by confusing 'protection' with 'safety'.

5 This term has been borrowed from Thomas Alexander Aleinikoff and Leah Zamore, *The Arc of Protection – Reforming the International Refugee Regime* (Stanford University Press 2019) 108.

6 United Nations High Commissioner for Refugees, Global Compact on Refugees, para 5.

7 On this point, see Costello, 'Courting Access to Asylum in Europe: Recent Supranational Jurisprudence Explored' (Ch 5 n 105).

8 Storey, 'What Constitutes Persecution? Towards a Working Definition' (Ch 1 n 95).

It is worth noting that these risks are set against the specific logic of European integration, which exacerbate the influence of (regional) human rights law. As Jean-François Durieux has argued, the CEAS, '[...] can only be fully understood in relation to the broader European integration project in which it is embedded, and which imposes upon it a particular logic'.[9] This logic consists, argued the same commentator, of mutual trust amongst EU members in each other's fundamental rights guarantees, and reliance on obligations under the European Convention on Human Rights rather than under the 1951 Convention.[10] The Qualification Directive, meanwhile, created common rules for refugees and individuals with subsidiary protection needs not because international law requires it,[11] but inter alia to suppress onward movement of forced migrants.[12] This onward movement is possible due to the very core of the European project – a political union without internal border controls not just for goods, but also for people.

The interplay of the 1951 Convention and human rights law (and their convergence in some parts of EU asylum law) leaves the Convention in an ironic position. On the international level, the Convention has lost some of its original relevance when it comes to the rights granted to refugees, so that its specificity lies in its modality of operation as a status-based instrument, in the eligibility criteria for that status and the underlying rationale of status. As Durieux argues in respect of claims that the Convention should be applied to non-refugees:

> It is a different matter altogether, however, to argue [...] that the Convention dictates standards of treatment, not only for refugees, but indeed for all persons legally protected against refoulement, regardless of the source of such protection. Such argument obscures the specificity of refugee

9 Durieux, 'The Vanishing Refugee: how EU Asylum Law Blurs the Specificity of Refugee Protection' (Ch 1, n 95) 227.

10 Ibid.

11 For a different point of view, see Jane McAdam, 'The Refugee Convention as a Rights Blueprint for Protection for Persons in Need of International Protection' (2006) UNHCR New Issues in Refugee Research Working Paper no 125, <www.unhcr.org/research/RESEARCH/44b7b7162.pdf> accessed 20 October 2016.

12 See above, 2.2.3, with reference to para 13 of the Qualification Directive, stating that, 'The approximation of rules on the recognition and content of refugee and subsidiary protection status should help to limit the secondary movement of applicants for international protection between Member States, where such movement is purely caused by differences in legal frameworks.'

> protection which does not lie in a specific set of rights, *but in a specific rationale for granting such rights.*[13]

Paradoxically, the Convention's distinct value then lies in a status-based concept for surrogate enfranchisement with rights, of which many are rights that apply to everyone without distinction. So interwoven have human rights and refugee law become that, for the Convention to evolve and thrive, a 1951 Convention purism is not an option.

Neither, however, it seems that common rules for refugees and individuals with subsidiary protection, such as the Qualification Directive's status assessment criteria on available protection, are always helpful. It is in this conundrum that the EU contribution to the international regime of refugee protection needs to be observed. At the very extreme ends of the spectrum, EU asylum law can either contribute to an evolutionary interpretation of the 1951 Convention or become insular. In the parallel evolution and interplay of refugee law and human rights law in the EU, lawmakers' choices require tradeoffs: contribution to the international evolution of a global refugee regime versus a more autonomous European conception; separate refugee and 'subsidiary' regimes versus a more integrated conception influenced by human rights law obligations of non-return; and trading complexity for simplicity.

13 Durieux, 'The Vanishing Refugee: how EU Asylum Law Blurs the Specificity of Refugee Protection' (Ch 1 n 95) 251.

Bibliography

Academic Articles, Monographs, Edited Volumes, Conference Contributions

Aleinikoff TA and Zamore L, *The Arc of Protection – Reforming the International Refugee Regime* (Stanford University Press 2019).

Alston P (ed), *Non-State Actors and Human Rights* (Oxford University Press 2005).

Aust HP, *Complicity and the Law of State Responsibility* (Cambridge University Press 2011).

Aust HP and Nolte G (eds), *The Interpretation of International Law by Domestic Courts: Uniformity, Diversity, Convergence* (Oxford University Press 2016).

Aust HP, Rodiles A, and Staubauch P, 'Unity or Uniformity? Domestic Courts and Treaty Interpretation' (2014) 27 Leiden Journal of International Law 75.

Bailliet CM, 'Persecution in the Home: Applying the Due Diligence Standard to Harmful Traditional Practices within Human Rights and Refugee Law' (2012) 30 Nordic Journal of Human Rights 36.

Ballinger P, 'Entangled or "Extruded" Histories? Displacement, National Refugees, and Repatriation after the Second World War' (2012) 25 Journal of Refugee Studies 366.

Bank R, 'The Potential and Limitations of the Court of Justice of the European Union in Shaping International Refugee Law' (2015) 27 International Journal of Refugee Law 213.

Barnes AE, 'Realizing Protection Space for Iraqi Refugees: UNHCR in Syria, Jordan and Lebanon' (2009) UNHCR New Issues in Refugee Research Paper no 167 <www.unhcr.org/4981d3ab2.pdf> accessed 20 October 2016.

Battjes H, *European Asylum Law and International Law* (Brill Academic Publishing 2006).

Bethke M and Hocks S, *Dublin III-Verordnung – Handkommentar* (Nomos forthcoming 2019).

Boeles P and others, *European Migration Law* (Intersentia 2009).

Beck G, *The Legal Reasoning of the Court of Justice of the EU* (Hart Publishing 2012).

Bronckers M, 'The Relationship of the EC Courts with other International Tribunals: Non-Committal, Respectful or Submissive?' (2007) 44 Common Market Law Review 601.

Brunnée J and Toope S, *Legitimacy and Legality in International Law* (Cambridge University Press 2010).

Cantor DJ, 'Defining Refugees: Persecution, Surrogacy and the Human Rights Paradigm' in Cantor DJ (ed), *Human Rights and the Refugee Definition – Comparative Legal Practice and Theory* (Brill 2016).

Casolari F, 'Giving Indirect Effect to International Law Within the EU Legal Order: The Doctrine of Consistent Interpretation' in Cannizzaro E and others (eds), *International law as law of the European Union* (Martinus Nijhoff Publishers 2012).

Chetail V, 'Are Refugee Rights Human Rights? An Unorthodox Questioning of the Relations between Refugee Law and Human Rights Law' in Marin RR (ed), *Migration and Human Rights* (Migration and Human Rights, Oxford University Press 2011).

Chetail V, 'The Human Rights of Migrants in General International Law: From Minimum Standards to Fundamental Rights' (2014) 28 Georgetown Imigration Law Journal 225.

Chetail V, 'The Common European Asylum System: Bric-à-Brac or System?' in Chetail V and others (eds), *Reforming the Common European Asylum System: The New European Refugee Law* (Brill 2015).

Chynoweth P, 'Legal Research' in Knight A and Ruddock L (eds), *Advanced Research Methods in the Build Environment* (Wiley-Blackwell 2008).

Costello C, 'The Asylum Procedures Directive and the Proliferation of Safe Country Practices: Deterrence, Deflection and the Dismantling of International Protection?' (2005) 7 European Journal of Migration and Law 35.

Costello C, 'Courting Access to Asylum in Europe: Recent Supranational Jurisprudence Explored' (2012) 12 Human Rights Law Review 287.

Costello C, *Human Rights of Migrants and Refugees in European Law* (Oxford University Press 2016).

Crawford J, *The International Law Commission's Articles on State Responsibility – Introduction, Text and Commentaries* (Cambridge University Press 2002).

Crawford J, Pellet A, and Olleson S (eds), *The Law of International Responsibility* (Oxford University Press 2010).

Durieux J-F, 'The Vanishing Refugee: how EU Asylum Law Blurs the Specificity of Refugee Protection' in Lambert H and others (eds), *The Global Reach of European Refugee Law* (Cambridge University Press 2013).

Eaton J, 'The Internal Protection Alternative Under European Union Law: Examining the Recast Qualification Directive' (2012) 24 International Journal of Refugee Law 765.

Eckard S, 'Managing Peacebuilding: Strategic Management, Organizational Performance and the Outcome of Post-Conflict Police Reform in Kosovo and Afghanistan' (PhD Dissertation, Universtät Konstanz 2013).

Edwards A, 'Human Rights, Refugees, and The Right 'To Enjoy' Asylum' (2005) 17 International Journal of Refugee Law 293.

Fortin A, 'The Meaning of 'Protection' in the Refugee Definition' (2000) 12 International Journal of Refugee Law 548.

Foster M, 'Causation in Context: Interpreting the Nexus Clause in the Refugee Convention' (2002) 23 Michigan Journal of International Law 265.

Foster M, 'Protection Elsewhere: The Legal Implications of Requiring Refugees to Seek Protection in another State' (2007) 28 Michigan Journal of International Law 223.

Foster M, 'Responsibility Sharing or Shifting?' (2008) 25 Refuge 64.

Frank DJ, 'Making Sense of LGBTI Asylum Claims: Change and Variation in Institutional Contexts' (2012) 44 Journal of International Law and Politics 485.

Gammeltoft-Hansen T and Gammeltoft-Hansen H, 'The Right to Seek – Revisited. On the UN Human Rights Declaration Article 14 and Access to Asylum Procedures in the EU' (2008) 10 European Journal of Migration and Law 439.

Gammeltoft-Hansen T, *Access to Asylum – International Refugee Law and the Globalisation of Migration Control* (Cambridge University Press 2011).

Gammeltoft Hansen T and Nyberg Sorensen N (eds), *The Migration Industry and the Commercialization of International Migration* (Routledge 2012).

Gammeltoft-Hansen T and Vedsted-Hansen J (eds), *Human Rights and the Dark Side of Globalisation Transnational Law Enforcement and Migration Control* (Routledge 2016).

Gammeltoft-Hansen T, 'The Extraterritorialisation of Asylum and the Advent of "Protection Lite"' Danish Institute for International Studies Working Paper no 2007/2, <www.files.ethz.ch/isn/30673/2007-2.pdf> accessed 20 October 2016.

Garlick M, 'UNHCR and the Implementation of Council Directive 2004/83/EC on Minimum Standards for the Qualification and Status of Third Country Nations or Stateless Persons as Refugees or as Persons who Otherwise Need International Protection and the Content of the Protection Granted (the EC 'Qualification Directive')' in Zwaan K (ed), *The Qualification Directive: Central Themes, Problem Issues, and implementation in Selected Member States* (Wolf Legal Publishers 2007).

Geiß R, 'Armed violence in fragile states: Low-intensity conflicts, spillover conflicts, and sporadic law enforcement operations by third parties' (2009) 91 International Review of the Red Cross 127.

Gkliati, M, 'The Application of the EU-Turkey Deal. A Critical Analysis of the Decisions of the Greek Appeals Committees' (2017) 10 European Journal of Legal Studies 81.

Gil-Bazo M-T, 'The Practice of Mediterranean States in the context of the European Union's Justice and Home Affairs External Dimension. The Safe Third Country Concept Revisited' (2006) 18 International Journal of Refugee Law 571.

Gil-Bazo M-T, 'Refugee Status, Subsidiary Protection, and the Right to Be Granted Asylum Under EC Law' (2006) UNHCR, New Issues in Refugee, Research Paper no 136, 229.

Gil-Bazo M-T, 'The Charter of Fundamental Rights of the European Union and the Right to be Granted Asylum in the Union's Law' (2008) 27 Refugee Survey Quarterly 33.

Gilmour A, 'The Future of Human Rights: A View from the United Nations' (2014) 28 Ethics and Interntional Affairs 239.

Gilbert G, 'Rights, Legitimate Expectations, Needs and Responsibilities: UNHCR and the New World Order' (1998) 10 International Journal of Refugee Law 349.

Gilbert G, 'Is Europe Living Up to Its Obligations to Refugees?' (2004) 15 The European Journal of International Law 963.

Giuffre M, 'Readmission Agreements and Refugee Rights: From a Critique to a Proposal' (2013) 32 Refugee Survey Quarterly 79.

Godman R, 'The Incorporation of International Human Rights Standards into Sexual Orientation Asylum Claims: Cases of Involuntary "Medical" Intervention' (1995) 105 Yale Law Journal 255.

Godman R, 'Asylum and the Concealment of Sexual Orientation: Where Not to Draw the Line' (2012) 44 Journal of International Law and Politics 407.

Gorlick B, 'Human Rights and Refugees: Enhancing Protection through International Human Rights Law' (2000) 69 Nordic Journal of International Law 117.

Goodwin-Gil GS, 'The Language of Protection' (1989) 1 International Journal of Refugee Law 6.

Goodwin-Gil GS, 'Different Types of Forced Migration Movements as an International and National Problem' in Rystad G (ed), *The Uprooted: Forced Migration as an International Problem in the Post-War Era* (Chartwell-Bratt 1990).

Goodwin-Gil GS and McAdam J, *The Refugee in International Law* (Oxford University Press 2007).

Grahl-Madsen A, *The Status of Refugees in International Law: Refugee Character* (Sijthoff 1966).

Grahl-Madsen A, 'Protection of Refugees by Their Country of Origin' (1985) 11 Yale Journal of International Law 362.

Grahl-Madsen A, 'Refuges in Orbit – Some Constructive Proposals' in Atle Grahl-Madsen, *The Land Beyond: Collected Essays on Refugee Law and Policy* (Martinus Nijhoff 2001).

Greenman K, 'A Castle Built on Sand? Article 3 ECHR and the Source of Risk in Non-Refoulement Obligations in International Law' (2015) 27 International Journal of Refugee Law 264.

Guild E, 'The Europeanisation of Europe's Asylum Policy' (2006) 18 International Journal of Refugee Law 630.

Hailbronner K, 'Die Qualifikationsrichtlinie und ihre Umsetzung im deutschen Ausländerrecht' (2008) 4 Zeitschrift für Ausländerrecht und Ausländerpolitik 209.

Hailbronner K (ed), *EU Immigration and Asylum Law: Commentary of EU Regulations and Directives* (C.H. Beck 2010).

Hailbronner K and Thym D (eds), *EU Immigration and Asylum Law – A Commentary* (2nd edn, C.H.Beck 2016).

Haines R, 'Gender-related Persecution' in Feller E and others (eds), *Refugee Protection in International Law: UNHCR's Global Consultations on International Protection* (Cambridge University Press 2003).

Halberstam D, '"It's the Autonomy, Stupid!" A Modest Defense of Opinion 2/13 on EU Accession to the ECHR, and the Way Forward' (2015) 16 German Law Journal 105.

Harris DJ and others, *Law of the European Convention on Human Rights* (Oxford University Press 2009).

Hart N, 'Complementary Protection and Transjudicial Dialogue: Global Best Practice or Race to the Bottom?' (2016) 28 International Journal of Refugee Law 171.

Harvey CJ, 'Gender, Refugee Law and the Politics of Interpretation' (2000) 12 International Journal of Refugee Law 680.

Harvey C, 'Time for Reform? Refugees, Asylum-seekers, and Protection Under International Human Rights Law' 34 (2015) Refugee Survey Quarterly 1.

Hathaway JC, *The Law of Refugee Status* (Butterworths Canada 1991).

Hathaway JC, 'The Evolution of Refugee Status in International Law: 1920–1950' (1984) 33 The International and Comparative Law Quarterly 348.

Hathaway JC, 'A Reconsideration of the Underlying Premise of Refugee Law' (1990) 31 Harvard International Law Journal 129.

Hathaway JC, 'Reconceiving Refugee Law as Human Rights Protection' (1991) 4 Journal of Refugee Studies 113.

Hathaway JC, *The Rights of Refugees under International Law* (Cambridge University Press 2005).

Hathaway JC, 'Why Refugee Law Still Matters' (2007) 8 Melbourne Journal of International Law 89.

Hathaway JC, 'EU Accountability to International Law: The Case of Aslyum' (2011) 33 Michigan Journal of International Law 1.

Hathaway JC and others, 'The Michigan Guidelines on Protection Elsewhere: Adopted 3 January 2007' (2006) 28 *Michigan Journal of International Law* 207.

Hathaway JC and Foster M, 'Internal protection/relocation/flight alternative as an aspect of refugee status determination' in Feller E and others (eds), *Refugee Protection in International Law* (Cambridge University Press 2003).

Hathaway JC and Pobjoy J, 'Queer Cases Make Bad Law' (2012) 44 Journal of International Law and Politics 315.

Hathaway JC and Foster M, *The Law of Refugee Status* (2nd edn, Cambridge University Press 2014).

Heijer Md, 'Whose Rights and Which Rights? The Continuing Story of Non-Refoulement under the European Convention on Human Rights' (2008) 10 European Journal of Migration and Law 277.

Heyman MG, 'Domestic Violence and Asylum: Toward a Working Model of Affirmative State Obligations' (2005) 17 International Journal of Refugee Law 729.

Henckaerts J-M and Doswald-Beck L, *Customary International Humanitarian Law, vol 1: Rules* (Cambridge University Press 2005).

Hofmann R and Schmidt A, 'Die Erklärung EU-Türkei vom 18.3.2016 aus rechtlicher Perspektive' (2016) 11 Neue Zeitschrift für Verwaltungsrecht 743.

Hofmann R and Geissler N (eds), *Non-State Actors as New Subjects of International Law. International Law: From the Traditional State Order Towards the Law of the Global Community* (Duncker & Humblot 1999).

Holborn LW, *The International Refugee Organization: A Specialized Agency of the United Nations its History and Work 1946–1952* (Oxford University Press 1956).

Hunt M, 'The Safe Country of Origin Concept in European Asylum Law: Past, Present and Future' (2014) 26 International Journal of Refugee Law 500.

Huntington WC, *The Homesick Million: Russia-out-of-Russia* (Stratford 1933).

Jackson IC, 'Dr. Fridtjof Nansen a Pioneer in the International Protection of Refugees' (2003) 22 Refugee Survey Quarterly 7.

Jaeger G, *Status and International Protection of Refugees* (International Institute of Human Rights, Ninth Study Session July 1978).

Janmyr M, *Protecting Civilians in Refugee Camps – Unable and Unwilling States, UNHCR and International Responsibility* (Martinus Nijhoff Publishers 2014).

Jacquemet S, 'The Cross-Fertilization of International Humanitarian Law and International Refugee Law' (2001) 83 International Review of the Red Cross 651.

John-Hopkins M, 'The Emperor's New Safe Country Concepts: A UK Perspective on Sacrificing Fairness on the Altar of Efficiency' (2009) 21 International Journal of Refugee Law 218.

Juss SS, 'The Decline and Decay of European Refugee Policy' (2005) 25 Oxford Journal of Legal Studies 749.

Kagan M, 'The Beleaguered Gatekeeper: Protection Challenges Posed by UNHCR Refugee Status Determination' (2006) 18 International Journal of Refugee Law 1.

Kagan M, ' "We live in a country of UNHCR": The UN Surrogate State and Refugee Policy in the Middle East' (2011) New Issues in Refugee Research no 201, <www.unhcr.org/4d5a8cde9.pdf> accessed 20 October 2016.

Kälin W, 'Non-state Agents of Persecution and the Inability of the State to Protect' (2000) 15 Georgetown Imigration Law Journal 415.

Kälin W and Künzli J, *The Law of International Human Rights Protection* (Oxford University Press 2009).

Kaunert C and Léonard S, 'The European Union Asylum Policy after the Treaty of Lisbon and the Stockholm Programme: Towards Supranational Governance in a Common Area of Protection?' (2012) 31 Refugee Survey Quarterly 1.

Keith SK, 'The Difficulties of "Internal Flight" and "Internal Relocation" as Frameworks of Analysis' (2001) 15 Georgetown Immigration Law Journal 433.

Kelley N, 'The Convention Refugee Definition and Gender-Based Persecution: A Decade's Progress' (2001) 13 International Journal of Refugee Law 559.

Kelley N, 'Internal Flight/Relocation/Protection Alternative: Is it Reasonable?' (2002) 14 International Journal of Refugee Law 4.

Kesby A, *The Right to Have Rights: Citizenship, Humanity and International Law* (Oxford University Press 2012).

Kim S, 'Non-Refoulement and Extraterritorial Jurisdiction: State Sovereignty and Migration Controls at Sea in the European Context' (2007) 30 Leiden Journal of International Law 1.

Kneebone S, *Refugees as Objects of Surrogate Protection: Shifting Identities* in Kneebone S, Stevens D and Baldassar L (eds), *Conflicting Identities: Refugee Protection and the Role of Law* (Routledge 2014).

Kimminich O, *Der Internationale Rechtsstatus des Flüchtlings* (Heymann 1962).

Koehler U, *Praxiskommentar zum Europäischen Asylzuständigkeitssystem* (Berliner Wissenschaftsverlag 2018).

Koji T, 'Emerging Hierarchy in International Human Rights and Beyond: From the Perspective of Non-derogable Rights' (2001) 12 European Journal of International Law 917.

Lambert H, 'Consolidation and Development of the Asylum-Related Jurisprudence of the European Court of Human Rights – Keynote Speech to the Second Colloquy on the European Convention on Human Rights and the Protection of Refugees, Asylum-Seekers and Displaced Persons' (2000) SSRN eLibrary.

Lambert H, 'The Conceptualisation of 'Persecution' by the House of Lords: Horvath v Secretary of State for the Home Department' (2001) 13 International Journal of Refugee Law 16.

Lambert H, 'The European Convention on Human Rights and the Protection of Refugees: Limits and Opportunities' (2005) 24 Refugee Survey Quarterly 39.

Lambert H, 'The EU Asylum Qualification Directive, its Impact on the Jurisprudence of the United Kingdom and International Law' (2006) 55 International and Comparative Law Quarterly 161.

Lambert H, 'Transnational Judicial Dialogue, Harmonization And the Common European Asylum System' (2009) 58 International and Comparative Law Quarterly 519.

Lambert H, '"Safe Third Country" in the European Union: An Evolving Concept in International Law and Implications for the UK' (2012) 26 Journal of Immigration, Asylum and Nationality Law 318.

Lambert H, McAdam J and Fullerton M (eds), *The Global Reach of European Refugee Law* (Cambridge University Press 2013).

Lauterpacht E and Bethlehem D, 'The Scope and Content of the Principle of Non-Refoulement: Opinion' in Erika Feller and others (eds), *Refugee Protection in International Law: UNHCR's Global Consultations on International Protection* (Cambridge University Press 2003).

Lavrysen L, 'European Asylum Law and the ECHR: An Uneasy Coexistence' (2012) 4 Goettingen Journal of International Law 197.

Leboeuf L and Tsourdi EL, 'Towards a Re-defintion of Persecution? Assessing the Potential Impact of Y and Z' (2013) 13 Human Rights Law Review 402.

Legomsky SH, 'Secondary Refugee Movements and the Return of Asylum Seekers to Third Countries: The Meaning of Effective Protection' (2003) 15 International Journal of Refugee Law 567.

Lehmann JM, '"Outsourcing" Protection and the Transnational Relevance of Protection Elsewhere – The Case of UNHCR' in Thomas Gammeltoft-Hansen and Jens Vedsted-Hansen (eds), *Human Rights and the Dark Side of Globalisation* (Routledge 2016).

Lehmann JM, 'Persecution, Concealment and the Limits of a Human Rights Approach in (European) Asylum Law: The Case of Germany v Y and Z in the Court of Justice of the European Union' (2014) 26 International Journal of Refugee Law 1.

Lehmann K, 'Das Konzept der inländischen Fluchtalternative in der deutschen Rechtsprechung und deren Verhältnis zu Art. 8 der Qualifikationsrichtlinie (interner Schutz)' (2007) 5 Neue Zeitschrifft für Verwaltungsrecht 507.

Lübbe A, 'Zielgerichtetheit des Akteursverhaltens und Unterlassen im Flüchtlingsrecht' (2011) 5 Zeitschrift für Ausländerrecht und Ausländerpolitik 164.

Magner T, 'Does a Failed State Country of Origin Result in a Failure of International Protection – A Review of Policies toward Asylum-Seekers in Leading Asylum Nations' (2000) 15 Georgetown Imigration Law Journal 703.

Manfred N, *UN Covenant on Civil and Political Rights: CCPR Comentary* (2nd edn, Engel 2005).

Marx R, 'The Notion of Persecution by Non-State Agents in German Jurisprudence' (2001) 15 Georgetown Immigration Law Journal 448.

Marx R, 'The Criteria of Applying the "Internal Flight Alternative" Test in National Refugee Status Determination Procedures' (2002) 14 International Journal of Refugee Law 179.

Marx R, *Handbuch zur Qualifikationsrichtlinie: Flüchtlingsanerkennung und subsidiärer Schutzstatus* (Luchterhand 2009).

Marx R, *Handbuch zum Flüchtlingsschutz – Erläuterungen zur Qualifikationsrichtlinie* (2nd edn, Luchterhand 2012).

Mathew P, 'The Shifting Boundaries and Content of Protection: The Internal Protection Alternative Revisited' in Juss SS (ed), *The Ashgate Research Companion to Migration Law: Theory and Policy* (Ashgate 2013).

Mathew P, Hathaway JC, and Foster M, 'The Role of State Protection in Refugee Analysis' (2003) 15 International Journal of Refugee Law 444.

McAdam J, 'The European Union Qualification Directive: The Creation of a Subsidiary Protection Regime' (2005) 17 International Journal of Refugee Law 461.

McAdam J, 'The Refugee Convention as a Rights Blueprint for Protection for Persons in Need of International Protection' (2006) UNHCR New Issues in Refugee Research Paper no 125, <www.unhcr.org/research/RESEARCH/44b7b7162.pdf> accessed 20 October 2016.

McAdam J, *Complementary Protection in International Refugee Law* (Oxford University Press 2007).

McAdam J, 'Rethinking the Origins of "Persecution" in Refugee Law' (2014) 25 International Journal of Refugee Law 667.

McCrudden C, 'A Common Law of Human Rights?: Transnational Judicial Conversations on Constitutional Rights' (2000) 20 Oxford Journal of Legal Studies 499.

Milanovic M, *Extraterritorial Application of Human Rights Treaties: Law, Principles, and Policy* (Oxford University Press 2013).

Moffarts G, 'Refugee Status and the "Internal Flight Alternative"' (Refugee and asylum law: assessing the scope for judicial protection: International Association of Refugee Law Judges, Second Conference, Nijmegen, January 9–11, 1997).

Mooney ED, 'Presence, ergo protection? UNPROFOR, UNHCR and the ICRC in Croatia and Bosnia and Herzegovina' (1995) 7 International Journal of Refugee Law 407.

Moore J, 'From Nation State to Failed State: International Protection from Human Rights Abuses by Non-State Agents' (1999) 31 Columbia Human Rights Law Review 81.

Moore J, 'Whither the Accountability Theory: Second-Class Status for Third-Party Refugees as a Threat to International Refugee Protection' (2001) 13 International Journal of Refugee Law 32.

Moreno-Lax V, 'Of Autonomy, Autarky, Purposiveness and Fragmentation: The Relationship between EU Asylum Law and International Humanitarian Law' in Cantor DJ and Durieux J-F (eds), *Refuge from Inhumanity? War Refugees and International Humanitarian Law* (Brill 2014).

Moreno-Lax, V, 'The Legality of the "Safe Third Country" Notion Contested: Insights from the Law of Treaties' in Guy S Goodwin-Gill and Philippe Weckel (eds), *Migration & Refugee Protection in the 21st Century: Legal Aspects* (Martinus Nijhoff 2015).

Müller H, *Die Chancen der Kooperation: Regime in den internationalen Beziehungen* (Wissenschaftliche Buchgesellschaft 1993).

Nakasaka E, 'Too different to be relevant? Considering the Global Influence of EU Asylum Laws and Policy with Respect to Japan' in Wetzel J (ed), *The EU as a "Global Player" in Human Rights?* (Routledge 2011).

Ni Ghrainne B, 'The Internal Protection Alternative Inquiry and Human Rights Considerations – Irrelevant or Indispensable?' (2015) 27 International Journal of Refugee Law 29.

Noll G, *Negotiating Asylum – The EU acquis, Extraterritorial Protection and the Common Market of Deflection* (Nijhoff 2000).

Noll G, 'Evidentiary Assessment under the Refugee Convention: Risk, Pain and the Intersubjectivity of Fear' in Noll G (ed), *Proof, Evidentiary Assessment and Credibility in Asylum Procedures* (Martinus Nijhoff 2005).

Noll G, 'Evidentiary Assessment in Refugee Status Determination and the EU Qualification Directive' (2006) 12 European Public Law 295.

Noortmann M and Ryngaert C (eds), *Non-State Actor Dynamics in International Law: From Law-Takers to Law-Makers* (Routledge 2010).

Nykänen E, *Fragmented State Power and Forced Migration – Study on Non-State Actors in Refugee Law* (University of Turku 2012).

O'Sullivan M, 'Acting the Part: Can Non-State Entities Provide Protection Under International Refugee Law?' (2012) 24 International Journal of Refugee Law 85.

O'Sullivan M, 'Territorial Protection: Cessation of Refugee Status and Internal Flight Alternative Compared' in Juss SS (ed), *Ashgate Research Companion to Migration Law, Theory and Policy* (Ashgate 2013).

Obolensky-Ossinky VV, 'Emigration from and Immigration into Russia' in Wilcox WF (ed), *International Migrations*, (vol 2. Bur. Econ Res. 1931).

Peers S, *The EU Charter of Fundamental Rights: A Commentary* (Hart Publishing 2013).

Phuong C, 'Persecution by Non-state Agents: Comparative Judicial Interpretations of the 1951 Refugee Convention' (2002) 4 European Journal Migration and Law 521.

Portmann R, *Legal Personality in International Law* (Cambridge University Press 2010).

Querton C, *''Even if ...' The Use of the Internal Protection Alternative in Asylum Decisions in the UK'* (Asylum Aid 2014) <https://web.archive.org/web/20171229230548/https://www.asylumaid.org.uk/wp-content/uploads/2014/07/Even-If...Asylum-Aid-2014.pdf> accessed 20 October 2016.

Reneman M, *EU Asylum Procedures and the Right to an Effective Remedy* (Hart Publishing 2014).

Rösler H, 'Interpretation of EU Law' in Basedow J, Hopt K, Zimmermann R (eds), *The Max Planck Encyclopedia of European Private Law* (Oxford University Press 2012).

Roversi A, 'The Evolution of the Refugee Regime and Institutional Responses: Legacies from the Nansen Period' (2003) 22 Refugee Survey Quarterly 21.

Rüegger S and Bohnet H, 'The Ethnicity of Refugees (ER): A New Dataset for Understanding Flight Patterns' (2018) 35 Conflict Management and Peace Science 1.

Savigny, FC von, *System des heutigen Römischen Rechts* (vol 1, Berlin 1840).

Schabas WA, *The European Convention on Human Rights – A Commentary* (Oxford University Press 2015).

Schønberg S and Frick K, 'Finishing, refining, polishing: On the Use of Travaux Préparatoires as an Aid to the Interpretation of Community legislation' (2003) 7 European Law Review 149.

Schultz, J, *The Internal Protection Alternative in Refugee Law – Treaty Basis and Scope of Application under the 1951 Convention Relating to the Status of Refugees and Its 1967 Protocol* (Brill 2018).

Schultz J and Einarsen T, 'The Right to Refugee Status and the Internal Protection Alternative: What does the Law Say?' in Cantor DJ (ed), *Human Rights and the Refugee Definition – Comparative Legal Practice and Theory* (Brill 2016).

Simeon JC, 'Introduction: the Research Workshop on Critical Issues in International Refugee Law and Strategies towards Interpretative Harmony' in Simeon JC (ed), *Critical Issues in International Refugee Law – Strategies Towards Interpretative Harmony* (Cambridge University Press 2010).

Sjoberg T, *The Powers and the Persecuted: The Refugee Problem and the Intergovernmental Committee on Refugees, 1938–1947* (Lund University Press 1991).

Slaughter A-M, 'A Typology of Transjudicial Communication' (1994) 29 University of Richmond Law Review 99.

Slaughter A-M, *A New World Order* (Princeton University Press 2004).

Slaughter A-M and Crisp J, 'A Surrogate State? The role of UNHCR in protracted refugee situations' in Loescher G et al (ed), *Protracted Refugee Situations* (United Nations University Press 2008).

Stevens D, 'What Do We Mean by Protection?' (2013) 20 International Journal on Minority and Group Rights 233.

Storey H, 'The Way Ahead – United Kingdom Case Law on the "Internal Flight Alternative"' (Refugee and asylum law: assessing the scope for judicial protection: International Association of Refugee Law Judges, Second Conference, Nijmegen, January 9–11, 1997).

Storey H, 'The Internal Flight Alternative Test: The Furisprudence Re-examined' (1998) 10 International Journal of Refugee Law 499.

Storey H, '"From Nowhere to Somewhere": An Evaluation of the UNHCR 2nd Track Global Consultations on International Protection: San Remo 8–10 September 2001 Experts Roundtable on the IPA/IRA/IFA Alternative' ('Stemming the Tide or Keeping the Balance – The Role of the Judiciary' – International Association of Refugee Law Judges Fifth World Conference, Wellington, New Zealand, 22 October 2002–25 October 2002).

Storey H, 'EU Refugee Qualification Directive: a Brave New World?' (2008) 20 International Journal of Refugee Law 1.

Storey H, 'What Constitutes Persecution? towards a Working Defintion' (2014) 26 International Journal of Refugee Law 272.

Storey H, 'The Meaning of "Protection" Within the Refugee Definition' (2016) 35 Refugee Survey Quarterly 3.

Storgaard LH, 'EU Law Autonomy Versus European Fundamental Rights Protection – On Opinion 2/13 on EU Accession to the ECHR' (2015) 15 Human Rights Law Review 485.

Tams CJ, *Enforcing Obligations Erga Omnes in International Law* (Cambridge University Press 2010).

Thirlway H, 'Human Rights in Customary Law: An Attempt to Define Some of the Issues' 28 Leiden Journal of International Law 495.

Thym D, 'Respect for Private and Family Life under Article 8 ECHR in Immigration Cases: A Human Right to Regularize Illegal Stay?' (2008) 57 The International and Comparative Law Quarterly 87.

Tobin J, *The Right to Health in International Law* (Oxford University Press 2012).

Trevisanut C, 'The Principle of Non-Refoulement And the De-Territorialization of Border Control at Sea' (2014) 27 Leiden Journal of International Law 661.

University of Michigan Law School, 'International Refugee Law: The Michigan Guidelines on the Internal Protection Alternative' (April 1999) <www.refworld.org/docid/3dca73274.html> accessed 20 October 2016.

Ventzke I, *How Interpretation Makes International Law* (Oxford Universtiy Press 2012).

Vermeer A, 'Diplomatic Protection as a Source of Human Rights Law' in Shelton D (ed), *The Oxford Handbook of International Human Rights Law* (Oxford University Press 2013).

Vermeulen B and others, *Persecution by Third Parties* (Commissioned by the Research and Documentation Centre of the Ministry of Justice of The Netherlands, 1998), <http://cmr.jur.ru.nl/cmr/docs/thirdparties.pdf> accessed 20 October 2016.

Wallace R, 'Internal relocation alternative in refugee status determination: is the risk/protection dichotomy reality or myth? A gendered analysis' in Juss SS and Harvey C (eds), *Contemporary Issues in Refugee Law* (Edward Elgar 2013).

Walls M, 'The Emergence of a Somali State: Building Peace from Civil War in Somaliland' (2008) 108 African Affairs 371.

Weis P, 'The International Protection of Refugees' (1954) American Journal of International Law 193.

Weis P, *The Refugees Convention, 1951: The Travaux Préparatoires Analysed with a Commentary by Dr. Paul Weis* (Cambridge University Press 1995) <www.unhcr.org/4ca34be29.html>.

Wendel M, 'Der EMRK-Beitritt als Unionsrechtsverstoß: Zur völkerrechtlichen Öffnung der EU und ihren Grenzen' (2015) Neue Juristische Wochenschrift 921.

Wilsher D, 'Non-State Actors and the Definition of a Refugee in the United Kingdom: Protection, Accountability or Culpability?' (2003) 15 International Journal of Refugee Law 68.

Wouters CW, *International Legal Standards for the Protection from Refoulement* (Intersentia 2009).

Young KG, 'The Minimum Core of Economic and Social Rights: A Concept in Search of Content' (2008) 33 Yale Journal of International Law 113.

Zahar M-J, 'Protégés, clients, cannon fodder: Civilians in the calculus of militias' (2000) 7 International Peacekeeping 107.

Zambelli P, 'Problematic Trends in the Analysis of State Protection and Article 1F(a) Exclusion in Canadian Refugee Law' (2011) 23 International Journal of Refugee Law 252.

Zimmermann A (ed), *The 1951 Convention Relating to the Status of Refugees and its 1967 Protocol: A Commentary* (Oxford University Press 2011).

European Union Documents

Commission of the European Comunities, 'Proposal for a Council Directve on minimum standards for the qualification and status of third country nationals and stateless persons as refugees or as persons who otherwise need international protection', COM/2001/510 final.

Commission of the European Communities, 'Amended proposal for a Council Directive on minimum standards on procedures in Member States for granting and withdrawing refugee status', COM/2002/326 final, OJ C 291 E/143.

Commission of the European Communities, Proposal for a Directive of the European Parliament and of the Council on minimum standards for the qualification and status of third country nationals or stateless persons as beneficiaries of international protection and the content of the protection granted, COM/2009/0551 final.

Commission of the European Communities, 'Report from the Commission to the European Parliament and the Council on the Application of Directive 2004/83/EC of 29 April 2004 on minimum standards for the qualification and status of third country nationals or stateless persons as refugees or as persons who otherwise need international protection and the content of the protection', COM/2010/0314 final.

Commission of the European Communities, 'European Migration Network, Ad-Hoc Query on safe countries of origin and safe third countries', (2014) <www.emn.fi/files/1172/Compilation_BG_EMN_NCP_AHQ_list_of_safe_countries_of_origin_and_safe_third_countries_WIDER.pdf> accessed 20 October 2016.

Commission of the European Communities, 'A European Agenda on Migration', May 2015 <https://ec.europa.eu/anti-trafficking/sites/antitrafficking/files/communication_on_the_european_agenda_on_migration_en.pdf> accessed 3 January 2019.

Commission of the European Communities, 'Proposal for a Regulation of the European Parliament and of the Council establishing a common procedure for international protection in the Union and repealing Directive 2013/32/EU', COM/2016/467 final.

Commission of the European Communities, 'Proposal for a Regulation of the European Parliament and of the Council, establishing the criteria and mechanisms for determining the Member State responsible for examining an application for international protection lodged in one of the Member States by a third-country national or a stateless person (recast)', COM/2016/270 final/2.

Council of the European Union, 'Council Resolution of 30 November 1992 on Manifestly Unfounded Applications for Asylum ('London Resolution')', 30 November 1992, <http://www.refworld.org/docid/3f86bbcc4.html> accessed 20 October 2016.

Council of the European Union, Presidency Conclusions, Tampere European Council, 15–16 October 1999 (1999), <http://www.refworld.org/docid/3ef2d2264.html> accessed 20 October 2016.

Council of the European Union, 'Note from the Presidency of the Council of the European Union to the Strategic Committee on Immigration, Frontiers and Asylum of 25 September 2002', 12148/02 (2002), <https://zoek.officielebekendmakingen.nl/kst-30925-E-b7.pdf> accessed 20 October 2016.

Council of the European Union, 'Proposal for a Regulation of the European Parliament and of the Council stablishing a common procedure for international protection in the Union and repealing Directive 2013/32/EU (First reading)', 14098/17 (2017).

Council of the European Union, 'Proposal for a Regulation of the European Parliament and of the Council establishing a common procedure for international protection in the Union and repealing Directive 2013/32/EU', 6238/18 (2018) <http://www.statewatch.org/news/2018/mar/eu-council-asylum-procedures-asylum-6238-18.pdf> accessed 1 July 2019.

Council of the European Union, EU-Turkey statement, 18 March 2016, Press release 144/16 (2016), <http://www.consilium.europa.eu/en/press/press-releases/2016/03/18-eu-turkey-statement/> accessed 20 October 2016.

Council of the European Union, 'Joint Position of 4 March 1996 defined by the Council on the basis of Article K.3 of the Treaty on European Union on the harmonized application of the definition of the term ' refugee ' in Article 1 of the Geneva Convention of 28 July 1951 relating to the status of refugees' [1996] OJ L63/2.

Council of the European Union, The Hague Programme – Strenghening Freedom, Security and Justice in the European Union, [2005] OJ C 53/01.

European Parliament, 'Report on the proposal for a regulation of the European Parliament and of the Council establishing the criteria and mechanisms for determining the Member State responsible for examining an application for international protection lodged in one of the Member States by a third-country national or a stateless person (recast)', COM/2016/0270 final.

European Parliament, Committee on Citizens' Freedoms and Rights, Justice and Home Affairs, 'Report on the proposal for a Council directive on minimum standards for the qualification and status of third country nationals and stateless persons as refugees or as persons who otherwise need international protection', COM/2001/510.

European Parliament legislative resolution on the proposal for a Council Directive on minimum standards for the qualification and status of third-country nationals and stateless persons as refugees or as persons who otherwise need international protection, COM/2001/510, [2003] OJ C 300.

United Nations Documents and International Law Commission

Ad Hoc Committee on Refugees and Stateless Persons, 'Status of Refugees and Stateless Persons – Memorandum by the Secretary-General', 3 January 1950, UN Doc E/AC.32/2.

Ad Hoc Committee on Refugees and Stateless Persons, 'First Session: Summary Record of the Third Meeting, 17 January 1950', UN Doc E/AC.32/SR.3.

Ad Hoc Committe on Statelessness and Related Problems, 'First Session: Summary Record of the Fourth Meeting, 10 January 1950', UN Doc E/AC.32/SR.4.

Ad Hoc Committee on Refugees and Stateless Persons, 'First Session: Summary Record of the Fifth Meeting, 18 January 1950', UN Doc E/AC.32/SR.5.

Ad Hoc Committee on Statelessness and Related Problems, 'Summary Record of the Seventh Meeting, 31 January 1950', UN Doc E/AC32/SR17.

Ad Hoc Committee on Refugees and Stateless Persons, 'First Session: Summary Record of the Tenth Meeting, 24 January 1950', UN Doc E/AC.32/SR.10.

Ad Hoc Committee on Refugees and Stateless Persons, 'First Session: Summary Record of the Twenty-Third Meeting, 3 February 1950', UN Doc E/AC.32/SR.23.

Ad Hoc Committee on Refugees and Stateless Persons, 'First Session: Summary Record of the Twenty-Fourth Meeting Held at Lake Success, 3 February 1950', UN Doc E/AC.32/SR.24.

Conference of Plenipotentiaries on the Status of Refugees and Stateless Persons, 'Summary Record of the First Meeting', UN Doc A/CONF.2/SR.1 (1951).

Conference of Plenipotentiaries on the Status of Refugees and Stateless Persons, 'Compte rendu analytique de la deuxième séance, 2 juillet 1951', UN Doc A/CONF.2/SR.2.

Conference of Plenipotentiaries on the Status of Refugees and Stateless Persons, 'Conférence de plénipotentiaires sur le statut des réfugiés et des apatrides: Compte rendu analytique de la sixième séance, 4 juillet 1951', UN Doc A/CONF.2/SR.6.

Conference of Plenipotentiaries on the Status of Refugees and Stateless Persons, 'Conference of Plenipotentiaries on the Status of Refugees and Stateless Persons: Summary Record of the Nineteenth Meeting', UN Doc A/CONF.2/SR.19 (1951).

Conference of Plenipotentiaries on the Status of Refugees and Stateless Persons, 'Summary Record of the Fourteenth Meeting, 22 November 1951', UN Doc A/CONF.2/SR.14.

Conference of Plenipotentiaries on the Status of Refugees and Stateless Persons, Summary Record of the Thirtieth Meeting, 28 November 1951, Un Doc A/CONF.2/SR.30.

Conference of Plenipotentiaries on the Status of Refugees and Stateless Persons, 'Conférence de plénipotentiaires sur le statut des réfugiés et des apatrides: Compte rendu analytique de la vingtième séance, 13 juillet 1951', UN Doc A/CONF.2/SR.20.

Conference of Plenipotentiaries on the Status of Refugees and Stateless Persons, Summary Record of the Twenty-third Meeting, 26 November 1951', UN Doc A/CONF.2/SR.23.

Executive Committee of the UNHCR (EXCOM), Conclusions No 9 (XXVIII) – 1977; No 15 (XXX) – 1979; No 25 (XXXIII) – 1982; No 72 (XLIV) – 1993; No 75 (XLV) – 1994; No 80 (XLVII) – 1996; No 85 (XLIX) – 1998; No 93 (LIII) – 2002; No 95 (LIV) – 2003; No 100 (LV) – 2004 in Thematic Compilation of Executive Committee Conclusions, June 2014, Seventh edition, <www.refworld.org/docid/5538cfa34.html> accessed 20 October 2017.

League of Nations Advisory Commission for Refugees, 'Report by the Secretary-General on the Future Organisation of Refugee Work', Leage of Nations Doc. 1930.XIII.2.

Economic and Social Council, 'Summary Record of the Hundred and Sixtieth Meeting of the Social Committee', ECOSOC Official Records, 11th Session (1950) UN Doc E/AC.7/SR.160.

Economic and Social Council (ECOSOC), 'Guiding Principles on Internal Displacement', 22 July 1998, UN Doc E/CN.4/1998/53/Add.2.

General Council of the International Refugee Organization, 'Communication of 11 July 1949', Doc E/1392.

Commission on Human Rights, 'Report to ECOSOC on the 2nd Session of the Commission Held at Geneva from 2 to 17 December 1947', Doc E/600 (1948).

Committee Against Torture, 'General Comment No 1: Implementation of Article 3 of the Convention in: the Context of Article 22 (Refoulement and Communications)', UN Doc A/53/44, annex IX.

Commitee on Economic Scocial, and Cultural Rights, 'General Comment No 13 (Twenty-first session, 1999): The right to education (article 13 of the Covenant)', UN Doc E/C.12/1999/10.

Committee on Economic Social and Cultural Rights, 'General Comment No 3: The nature of States parties obligations (Art 2, para 1)', UN Doc E/1991/23.

Committee on Economic Social and Cultural Rights, 'General Comment No 14: The right to the highest attainable standard of health (article 12 of the International Covenant on Economic, Social and Cultural Rights)', UN Doc E/C.12/2000/4.

Committee on Economic Social and Cultural Rights, 'General Comment No 20 – Non-discrimination in economic, social and cultural rights (art. 2, para 2, of the International Covenant on Economic, Social and Cultural Rights)', UN Doc E/C.12/GC/20 (2009).

Committee on the Elimination of Discrimination against Women, 'General recommendation on women's access to justice', UN Doc CEDAW/C/GC/33 (2015).

Committee on the Rights of the Child, 'General Comment No 6: Treatment of Unaccompanied and Separated Children Outside their Country of Origin', UN Doc CRC/GC/2005/6.

General Assembly, Refugees and Stateless Persons: 'Report of the Secretary-General', 26 October 1949, A/C.3/527.

General Assembly, 'Note on International Protection Addendum 1: Draft Convention on Territorial Asylum (Submitted by the High Commissioner)', UN Doc A/AC.96/508/Add.1 (1974).

General Assembly, Resolution 32/120, 16 December 1977, UN Doc A/RES/32/120.

General Assembly, UN Security Council, 'Report of the Panel on United Nations Peace Operations', 21 August 2000, UN Doc A/55/305–S/2000/809.

General Assembly, Resolution 63/148, 27 January 2009, UN Doc A/RES/63/148.

General Assembly, Resolution 64/127, 27 January 2010, UN Doc A/RES/64/127.

General Assembly, Resolution 65/194, 28 February 2011, UN Doc A/RES/65/194.

General Assembly, New York Declaration for Refugees and Migrants, 2 October 2016, UN Doc A/RES/71/1.

UN High Commissioner for Refugees, 'Background Note on the Safe Country Concept and Refugee Status', EC/SCP/68, 26 July 1991, para 12, <https://www.unhcr.org/excom/scip/3ae68ccec/background-note-safe-country-concept-refugee-status.html> accessed 1 July 2019.

High Commissioner for Refugees, "Protection Elsewhere' and Asylum Policy'(August 1994, 3 European Series 2) 465, <www.refworld.org/docid/3ae6b31cb8.html> accessed 20 October 2016.

High Commissioner for Refugees, 'Considerations on the "Safe Third Country" Concept, Presented at the EU Seminar on the Associated States as Safe Third Countries in Asylum Legislation' (1996) <www.refworld.org/docid/3ae6b3268.html> accessed 20 October 2016.

High Commissioner for Refugees, 'Opinion of UNHCR regarding the question of non-State persecution, as discussed with the Committee on Human Rights and Humanitarian Aid of the German Parliament (Lower House) on 29 November 1999', (1999) <www.refworld.org/pdfid/3df755477.pdf> accessed 20 October 2016.

High Commissioner for Refugees, 'UNHCR Position Paper on Relocating Internally as a Reasonable Alternative to Seeking Asylum (The So-Called "Internal Flight Alternative" or "Relocation Principle")', (1999) <www.refworld.org/docid/3ae6b336c.html> accessed 20 October 2016.

High Commissioner for Refugees, 'Interpreting Article 1 of the 1951 Convention Relating to the Status of Refugees (2001)' <www.refworld.org/docid/3b20a3914.html> accessed 20 October 2016.

High Commissioner for Refugees, 'UNHCR's Observations on the European Commission's Proposal for a Council Directive on Minimum Standards for the Qualification and Status of Third Country Nationals and Stateless Persons as Refugees or as Persons Who Otherwise Need International Protection (COM(2001) 510 final)', (2001) <www.refworld.org/docid/3c6a69254.html> accessed 20 October 2016.

High Commissioner for Refugees, 'Guidelines on International Protection No 1: Gender-Related Persecution within the context of Article 1A(2) of the 1951Convention and/or its 1967 Protocol relating to the Status of Refugees', UN Doc HCR/GIP/2002/01.

High Commissioner for Refugees, 'Declaration of States Parties to the 1951 Convention and or Its 1967 Protocol relating to the Status of Refugees', UN Doc HCR/MMSP/2001/09.

High Commissioner for Refugees, 'Summary Conclusions on the Concept of "Effective Protection" in the Context of Secondary Movements of Refugees and Asylum-Seekers (Lisbon Expert Roundtable, 9-10 December 2002' (2003) <https://www.refworld.org/docid/3fe9981e4.html> accessed 20 October 2016.

High Commissioner for Refugees, 'Guidelines on International Protection No 4: "Internal Flight or Relocation Alternative" Within the Context of Article 1A(2) of the 1951 Convention and/or 1967 Protocol Relating to the Status of Refugees, (2003), UN Doc HCR/GIP/2003/04.

High Commissioner for Refugees, 'Guidelines on International Protection: Cessation of Refugee Status under Article 1C(5) and (6) of the 1951 Convention relating to the Status of Refugees (the 'Ceased Circumstances' Clauses), UN Doc HCR/GIP/2003/03.

High Commissioner for Refugees, 'UNHCR Provisional Comments on the Proposal for a Council.

Directive on Minimum Standards on Procedures in Member States for Granting and Withdrawing Refugee Status (COM 14203/04, of 9 November 2004)', (2005) <https://www.refworld.org/docid/42492b302.html> accessed 1 July 2019.

High Commissioner for Refugees, 'UNHCR Annotated Comments on the EC Council Directive 2004/83/EC of 29 April 2004 on Minimum Standards for the Qualification and Status of Third Country Nationals or Stateless Persons as Refugees or as Persons Who Otherwise Need International Protection and the Content of the Protection Granted (OJ L 304/12 of 30 September 2004)', (2005) <www.refworld.org/docid/4200d8354.html> accessed 20 October 2016.

High Commissioner for Refugees, 'Guidelines on International Protection No 7: The Application of Article 1A(2) of the 1951 Convention and/or 1967 Protocol Relating to the Status of Refugees to Victims of Trafficking and Persons At Risk of Being Trafficked', UN Doc HCR/GIP/2006/07.

High Commissioner for Refugees, 'Asylum in the European Union. A Study of the Implementation of the Qualification Directive', (2007) <www.refworld.org/docid/473050632.html> accessed 20 October 2016.

High Commissioner for Refugees, 'UNHCR's Role in Supervising Protectionn Standards', Keynote Address by Volker Türk, 20 May 2010 at the International Conference on Forced Displacement, Protection Standards, Supervision of the 1951 Convention and the 1967 Protocol and Other International Instruments, York University, Toronto, Canada (2010), <www.refworld.org/docid/4bfb8c962.html> accessed 20 October 2016.

High Commissioner for Refugees, 'UNHCR comments on the European Commission's proposal for a Directive of the European Parliament and of the Council on minimum standards on procedures in Member States for granting and withdrawing international protection (COM/2009/554, 21 October 2009)', (2010) <www.unhcr.org/4f35256c9.pdf> accessed 20 October 2016.

High Commissioner for Refugees, 'Improving Asylum Procedures: Comparative Analysis and Recommendations for Law and Practice – Detailed Research on Key Asylum Procedures Directive Provisions', (2010) <http://www.refworld.org/pdfid/4c63e52d2.pdf> accessed 20 October 2016.

High Commissioner for Refugees, 'Guidelines on International Protection No 2: 'Membership of a Particular Social Group' Within the Context of Article 1A(2) of the 1951 Convention and/or its 1967 Protocol Relating to the Status of Refugees', UN Doc HCR/GIP/2002/02.

High Commissioner for Refugees, 'Guidelines on International Protection No 8: Child Asylum Claims under Articles 1(A)2 and 1(F) of the 1951 Convention and/or 1967 Protocol relating to the Status of Refugees', UN Doc HCR/GIP/2009/08.

High Commissioner for Refugees, 'Guidelines on International Protection No 9: Claims to Refugee Status based on Sexual Orientation and/or Gender Identity within the context of Article 1A(2) of the 1951 Convention and/or its 1967 Protocol relating to the Status of Refugees', UN Doc HCR/GIP/2012/01.

High Commissioner for Refugees, 'The Internal Flight Alternative Practices. A UNHCR Research Study in Central European Countries', (2012) <www.refworld.org/pdfid/4ffaabdf2.pdf> accessed 20 October 2016.

High Commissioner for Refugees, 'Legal considerations on the return of asylum-seekers and refugees from Greece to Turkey as part of the EU-Turkey Cooperation in Tackling the Migration Crisis under the safe third country and first country of asylum concept', (2016) <www.refworld.org/pdfid/56f3ee3f4.pdf> accessed 20 October 2016.

High Commissioner for Refugees, 'Hungary as a country of asylum. Observations on restrictive legal measures and subsequent practice implemented between July 2015 and March 2016', (2016) <www.refworld.org/pdfid/57319d514.pdf> acessed 20 October 2016.

High Commissioner for Refugees, 'Handbook on Procedures and Criteria for Determining Refugee Status under the 1951 Convention and the 1967 Protocol relating to the Status of Refugees (reissued 2011) <www.unhcr.org/3d58e13b4.pdf> acessed 20 October 2016.

High Commissioner for Refugees, 'An Overview of Protection Issues in Western Europe: Legislative Trends and Positions Taken by UNHCR', (1995) <www.unhcr.org/46e65e1e2.pdf> accessed 20 Ocotber 2016.

High Commissioner for Refugees, 'Resettlement Handbook', (2011) <https://www.refworld.org.es/pdfid/4ecb973c2.pdf> accessed 1 July 2019.

High Commissioner for Refugees, 'Global Trends – Forced Migration in 2018', (2019) <www.unhcr.org/5d08d7ee7.pdf> accessed 20 June 2019.

High Commissioner for Refugees, 'Report of the UNHCR Part 2, Global Compact on Refugees', UN Doc A/73/12 (2018).

High Commissioner for Refugees, 'Global Trends – forced Migration in 2017', (2018) <www.unhcr.org/5b27be547.pdf> accessed 20 June 2019.

Human Rights Committee, 'General Comment No 19: The Family (Article 23)', Compilation of General Comments and General Recommendations Adopted by Human Rights Treaty Bodies, HRI/GEN/1/Rev.1 (1990).

Human Rights Committee, 'General Comment No 15: The Position of Aliens Under the Covenant', UN Doc HRI/GEN/1/Rev.1 (1994).

Human Rights Committee, 'General Comment No 20 (Article 7)', Compilation of General Comments and General Recommendations Adopted by Human Rights Treaty Bodies, UN Doc HRI/GEN/1/Rev.1 (1994).

Human Rights Committee, 'General Comment No 24: Issues relating to reservations made upon ratification or accession to the Covenant or the Optional Protocols thereto, or in relation to declarations under article 41 of the Covenant', UN Doc CCPR/C/21/Rev.1/Add.6 (1994).

Human Rights Committee, 'General Comment No 29: States of Emergency (Article 4)', UN Doc CCPR/C/21/Rev.1/Add.11 (2001).

Human Rights Committee, 'General Comment No 31: The Nature of the General Legal Obligation Imposed on State Parties to the Covenant', UN Doc CCPR/Rev.1/Add. 13 (2004).

International Law Commission, 'Draft Articles on the Law of Treaties with commentaries', (1966) II Yearbook of the International Law Commission.

International Law Commission, 'Report of the International Law Commission on the work of its fifty-third session', A/56/10 (2001).

International Law Commission, 'Draft Articles on Diplomatic Protection with commentaries', Fifty-eighth session, A/61/10, (2006) II Yearbook of the International Law Commission, Part Two.

International Law Commission, 'Annex A to the Report by the ILC, Sixtieth Session', Supplement No 10, A/63/10, (2008) II Yearbook of the International Law Commission, Part Two.

International Law Commission, 'Draft articles on the responsibility of international organisations, with commentaries', Sixty-third session, A/66/10, (2011) II Yearbook of the International Law Commission, Part Two.

International Law Commission, 'Subsequent agreements and subsequent practice in relation to the interpretation of treaties – Text of the draft conclusions provisionally adopted by the Drafting Committee on first reading, 6 June 2016', A/CN.4/L.874.

International Law Commission, 'Identification of Customary International Law – Text of the draft conclusions as adopted by the Drafting Committee on second reading', A/CN.4/L.908 (2018).

UN Secretary General, 'Report of the Secretary-General on the United Nations Interim Administration Mission in Kosovo', UN Doc S/2004/348.

UN Secretary General, 'Report of the UN Secretary-General on the Protection of Civilians in Armed Conflict', UN Doc S/2010/579.

UN Secretary General, 'Report of the Secretary-General to the Security Council on the protection of civilians in armed conflict', UN Doc S/2002/1300.

UN Security Council, Resolution 1244, 10 June 1999, S/RES/1244.

Government Official Documents

Austrian Federal Ministry of Interior, Danish Ministry of Immigration and Integration, 'Vision for a Better Protection System in a Globalized World' (2018) <http://uim.dk/filer/nyheder-2018/vision-for-a-better-protection-system-in-a-globalized-world.pdf> accessed 3 January 2019.

Bundeministerium des Innern, 'Hinweise des Bundesministeriums des Innern zur Anwendung der Richtlinie 2004/83/EG des Rates vom 29. April 2004 über Mindestnormen für die Anerkennung und den Status von Drittstaatsangehörigen oder Staatenlosen als Flüchtlinge oder als Personen, die anderweitig internationaln Schutz benötigen, und über den Inhalt des zu gewährenden Schutzes in der Bundesrepublik Deutschland (Amtsblatt EU L 304, 30 September 2004)'.

Bundesregierung der Bundesrepublik Deutschland, 'Antwort der Bundesregierung auf die Kleine Anfrage der Abgeordneten Andrej Hunko, Sevim Dağdelen, Wolfgang Gehrcke, weiterer Abgeordneter und der Fraktion DIE LINKE', Drucksache 18/8205 (2015).

Sveriges Rikstag, 'Flyktingskap och förföljelse på grund av kön eller sexuell läggning: Regeringens proposition 2005/06:6' <www.riksdagen.se/sv/dokument-lagar/dokument/proposition/flyktingskap-och-forfoljelse-pa-grund-av-kon_GT036> accessed 20 October 2016.

US Department of Homeland Security, 'Asylum Officer Basic Training, Female Asylum Applicants and Gender-Related Claims' (12 March 2009), <www.uscis.gov/sites/default/files/USCIS/Humanitarian/Refugees%20%26%20Asylum/Asylum/AOBTC%20Lesson%20Plans/Female-Asylum-Applicants-Gender-Related-Claims-31aug10.pdf> accessed on 1 July 2019.

Other Secondary Sources

BBC, 'Zimbabwe Women Urged to Report Rape by Soldiers' (January 2019) <www.bbc.com/news/world-africa-47042101> accessed 1 July 2019.

Carrera S; den Hertog L; Stefan M, 'It wasn't me! The Luxembourg Court Orders on the EU-Turkey Refugee Deal' <www.ceps.eu/system/files/EU-Turkey%20Deal.pdf> accessed 1 July 2019.

Commission of the European Communities, 'Actors of Protection and Internal Protection – The new legal framework: Articles 7 and 8 of Directive 2011/95/EU', presentation at the Contact Committee meeting 'Qualification Directive' (2011/95/EC) on 11 November 2014, on file with the author.

Danish Refugee Council and European Council on Refugees and Exiles, 'The DRC/ECRE Desk Research on Application of a Safe Third Country and First Country of

Asylum Concepts to Turkey' (May 2016) <www.asylumlawdatabase.eu/sites/www.asylumlawdatabase.eu/files/aldfiles/turkeynote%20final%20edited%20DCR%20ECRE.pdf> accessed 20 October 2016.

European Commission, 'European Agenda on Migration – Factsheets' <https://ec.europa.eu/home-affairs/what-we-do/policies/european-agenda-migration/background-information_en> accessed 3 January 2019.

European Council on Refugees and Exiles, 'Debunking the Safe Third Country Myth – ECRE's Concerns about EU Proposals for Expanded Use of the Safe Third Country Concept' (2017) <www.ecre.org/wp-content/uploads/2017/11/Policy-Note-08.pdf> accessed 3 January 2019.

European Council on Refugees and Exiles, 'ECRE Information Note on the Council Directive 2004/83/EC of 29 April 2004 on Minimum Standards for the Qualification of Third Country Nationals and Others in Need of International Protection', <www.ulb.ac.be/assoc/odysseus/CEAS/ECRE(%20OCT%202004).pdf> accessed 20 October 2016.

European Council on Refugees and Exiles, 'The Impact of the EU Qualification Directive on International Protection' (2008) <http://www.refworld.org/docid/4908758d2.html> accessed 20 October 2016.

European Council on Refugees and Exiles, 'Comments from the European Council on Refugees and Exiles on the European Commission Proposal to recast the Qualification Directive' (May 2010) <www.ecre.org/wp-content/uploads/2016/07/ECRE-Comments-on-the-Commission-Proposal-to-Recast-the-Qualification-Directive_March-2010.pdf> accessed 20 October 2016.

European Council on Refugees and Exiles, 'Actors of Protection and the Application of the Internal Protection Alternative – European Comparative Report', (2014) <www.ecre.org/wp-content/uploads/2016/07/ECRE-Asylum-Aid-DCR-and-HHC_Actors-of-Protection-and-the-Application-of-the-Internal-Protection-Alternative_July-2014.pdf> accessed 20 October 2016.

European Legal Network on Asylum, 'The Application of the Concept of Internal Protection Alternative', (2000) <www.refworld.org/docid/3ae6b3514.html> accessed 20 October 2016.

Eurostat, Asylum and First Time Asylum Applicants – data (rounded), <https://ec.europa.eu/eurostat/databrowser/view/tps00189/default/table?lang=en> accessed 3 January 2019.

Feller E, 'Statement by Ms Erika Feller, Director, Department of International Protection, at the Fifty-Fifth session of the Executive Committee of the High Commissioner's Programme, 7 October 2004' <www.unhcr.org/429d6f8e4.html> accessed 20 October 2016.

GHK, 'Impact assessment studies on the future development of measures on the qualification and status of third country nationals or stateless persons as persons in need of international protection and on the content of the protection granted, based on Council Directive 2004/83/EC and the future development of measures on procedures in MS for granting and withdrawing refugee status, based on Council Directive 2005/85/EC', Multiple framework service contract JLS/2006/A1/004.

Guild E and Moreno-Lax V, 'Current Challenges for International Refugee Law: With a Focus on EU Policies and EU Co-Operation with the UNHCR', Directorate-General for External Policies of Union, Briefing Paper, EXPO/B/DROI/2012/15 (2013), <www.europarl.europa.eu/RegData/etudes/note/join/2013/433711/EXPO-DROI_NT(2013)433711_EN.pdf> accessed 20 October 2016.

Hijazi I, 'Fighting Rages Between Lebanese Christian Forces' (New York Times, February 1990) <www.nytimes.com/1990/02/01/world/fighting-rages-between-lebanese-christian-forces.html> accessed 20 October 2016.

Hijazi I, 'Lebanese Weigh Intervention in Christian Enclave' (New York Times, February 1990) <www.nytimes.com/1990/02/09/world/lebanese-weigh-intervention-in-christian-enclave.html> accessed 20 October 2016.

Human Rights Watch, 'Failure to Protect: Anti-Minority Violence in Kosovo' (March 2004) <www.hrw.org/report/2004/07/25/failure-protect/anti-minority-violence-kosovo-march-2004> accessed 20 October 2016.

Human Rights Watch, 'World Report 2018' (2018) <www.hrw.org/sites/default/files/world_report_download/201801world_report_web.pdf> accessed 3 January 2019.

Inter-Agency Standing Committee, 'Handbook for the Protection of Internally Displaced Persons', (2010) <http://www.unhcr.org/4c2355229.pdf> accessed 20 October 2016.

International Committee of the Red Cross, 'Workshop on Protection for Human Rights and Humanitarian Organizations: Doing Something About It and Doing It Well, Report of the workshop held at the International Committee of the Red Cross, Geneva, 18-20 January', (1999).

International Crisis Group, 'Herders against Farmers: Nigeria's Expanding Deadly Conflict, Africa Report No 252' (2017) <www.crisisgroup.org/africa/west-africa/nigeria/252-herders-against-farmers-nigerias-expanding-deadly-conflict> accessed 1 July 2019.

IRIN, 'Boko Haram: Nigeria winning the battle but losing the war?' (May 2017) <www.refworld.org/docid/591316d94.html> accessed 3 January 2019.

Masouridou Y and Kyprioti E, 'The EU-Turkey Statement and the Greek Hotspots – A Failed European Pilot Project in Refugee policy', The Greens/European Free Alliance in the European Parliament (June 2018) <www.greens-efa.eu/en/article/document/the-eu-turkey-statement-and-the-greek-hotspots/> accessed 1 July 2019.

NN, France-Germany Note, 'A Crisis-Resistant Common European Asylum System (CEAS)' (February 2017) <www.statewatch.org/news/2017/feb/eu-refugees-france-germany-note-feb-17.pdf> accessed 3 January 2019.

OSCE Mission in Kosovo, 'As Seen, As Told, Part II. A Report on the Human Rights Findings of the OSCE Mission in Kosovo (June to October 1999)' (1999) <www.osce.org/odihr/17772?download=true> accessed 20 October 2016.

Provera M, 'The EU-Turkey Deal – Analysis and Considerations, Jesuit Refugee Service Europe Policy Discussion Paper', (2016, <https://jrseurope.org/assets/Publications/File/JRS_Europe_EU_Turkey_Deal_policy_analysis_2016-04-30.pdf> accessed 1 July 2019.

Reuters, 'UN defends failed attempt to halt capture of Congo's Goma' (November 2012) <www.reuters.com/article/2012/11/21/congo-democratic-un-idUSL5E8MLH6J20121121> accessed 1 July 2019.

Reuters, 'Merkel: We need migrant deals with African states like EU-Turkey pact' (September 2016) <www.reuters.com/article/us-europe-migrants-germany/merkel-we-need-migrant-deals-with-egypt-tunisia-like-eu-turkey-pact-idUSKCN11W1FR> accessed 3 January 2019.

Thym D, 'Why the EU-Turkey Deal is Legal and a Step in the Right Direction' (March 2016) <https://verfassungsblog.de/why-the-eu-turkey-deal-is-legal-and-a-step-in-the-right-direction/> accessed 1 July 2019.

Index